Whose Trees?

Rural Studies Series

†Available in hardcover and paperback.

Whose Trees?

Proprietary Dimensions
of Forestry

edited by Louise Fortmann
and John W. Bruce

Westview Press / Boulder and London

Rural Studies Series, Sponsored by the Rural Sociological Society

This Westview softcover edition is printed on acid-free paper and bound in softcovers that carry the highest rating of the National Association of State Textbook Administrators, in consultation with the Association of American Publishers and the Book Manufacturers' Institute.

Published in 1988 in the United States of America by Westview Press, Inc.; Frederick A. Praeger, Publisher; 5500 Central Avenue, Boulder, Colorado 80301

Library of Congress Cataloging-in-Publication Data
Whose trees?: proprietary dimensions of forestry/edited by Louise
Fortmann and John W. Bruce.
     p.   cm.—(Rural studies series)
   ISBN 0-8133-7601-7
   1. Forest landowners—Case studies.   2. Forest policy—Case
studies.   3. Land tenure—Case studies.   4. Forest conservation
—Case studies.   I. Fortmann, Louise.   II. Bruce, John W.
III. Series: Rural studies series of the Rural Sociological Society.
HD9750.5.W48   1988
333.33′5—dc19   88-4976
                                                                                                                    CIP

Printed and bound in the United States of America

The paper used in this publication meets the requirements of the American National Standard for Permanence of Paper for Printed Library Materials Z39.48-1984.

6   5   4   3   2

Table of Contents

Preface

This book had its genesis in a 1984 effort by the Land Tenure Center and the International Council for Research in Agroforestry to review and annotate the literature on rights in trees and land with trees, and the impact of those rights on the planting and conservation of trees (Fortmann and Riddell, 1985). We found that there were a number of good case studies, many published some years ago, often in far-away places and rare publications, and now quite difficult to obtain. We were struck that no attempt had been made to develop a conceptual framework for these studies and to draw out their lessons for developing countries who are now seeking, urgently and often unsuccessfully, to stem the destruction of their forests and initiate reforestation.

In undertaking this book, our objectives have been to give readers access to these studies and to provide such a framework. The process of selection involved discarding many items, some interesting but anecdotal, others overly brief observations made in the course of inquiries that had little directly to do with tenure. Those that remained were the more substantial items from which only small excerpts could be included. We have edited freely to obtain a greater density. Finally, we seized the opportunity to publish for the first time several items (Menzies, Moench, and Turner) written as we were assembling this volume.

Our first four chapters explain the relevance of tenure to the planting and husbandry of tree resources in a variety of situations. The first chapter is an essay which introduces the concept of "tenure" and how such "bundles of rights" affect human behavior involving trees. The second chapter, on tree tenure, emphasizes at the outset a point commonly neglected—that rights in trees often exist independent of rights in land—and explores some of the implications of this fact. The third chapter examines how land tenure affects tree planting and conservation, and how tree planting and clearing affect the evolution of land tenure systems. The fourth chapter considers how local communities manage forest resources.

The remaining four chapters concern categories that most foresters and forestry project planners should readily recognize. These chapters have a more distinctly applied, development "project" slant. Chapter 5 deals with tree/tenure interactions in deforestation, Chapter 6 with tenure impacts upon afforestation efforts. Chapter 7 examines how women stand in special and often disadvantageous tenurial relationships to trees. Chapter 8 looks at the State as the conservator of trees and forests, a role sometimes inadequately conceived and/or poorly performed, and some alternative approaches to the preservation of forests. Chapter 9 is a concluding essay.

Each chapter (other than the first and last) consists of several cases, with an introductory note by the editors. In those notes we attempt to place our cases in a framework with reference to other relevant publications. In the introductory notes, those items which are provided in the body of the chapter appear in italics.

We would like to issue here a caution which will be reiterated throughout the text. Many of the selections are written in the ethnographic present. Others make rather sweeping generalizations about countries or ethnic groups. The wary reader will remember that systems of tenure often differ within very small distances even within the same ethnic group and that tenure, like all forms of social organization, changes over time. Thus, the selections here are not a handbook to existing systems of tenure but windows into the vast array of once and present tenures.

Louise Fortmann and John W. Bruce

Acknowledgements

Many people have had a hand in the making of this book. First, we owe a thanks to Chuck Geisler for suggesting that we undertake this volume. We are particularly indebted to Paul Starrs. Not only did he come up with Homer Aschmann's wonderful piece on childhood fruit stealing, but he proofread and formatted the final version for printing. Both we and the reader have reason to be extraordinarily grateful for Paul's painstaking attention to detail, readability and quality. Thomas G. Barnes, University of California at Berkeley, explained the mysteries of English medieval law. Professor A. Alim graciously consented to review the section on Betagi village. Patty Grubb, Nick Menzies, Greg Myers, and Pauline Wynter tidied up numerous loose ends, and Carol Dickerman read and commented on the chapter introductions. Word processing was done by Jane Dennis-Collins, Kathleen Leslie, Fe Barcena and Linda Joslin. Kathleen Leslie, who worked weekends to help us meet deadlines, did the final manuscript preparation and laser printing. Lynn Arts of Westview Press answered all our questions (some of them more than once) graciously.

In these days of high tech, a new recipient of thanks has appeared—the computer expert. When disks converted from one system to another appeared to require days of tedious cleaning, Al Stangenberger assured us that the problem could be fixed and Walter Meerschaert figured out how to fix it.

The support of the Department of Forestry and Resource Management, University of California at Berkeley; Land Tenure Center, University of Wisconsin; and the University of California Survey Research Center facilitated our endeavors.

Finally, we are grateful for the continuing encouragement and understanding of our families.

This manuscript was processed on an Apple Macintosh™ SE. Final copy was produced using Microsoft® Word 3.01. Camera ready copy was produced on an Apple Laserwriter™ Plus, in Palatino and Narrow Helvetica type.

L.F. and J.W.B.

1

Why Land Tenure and Tree Tenure Matter: Some Fuel for Thought

John W. Bruce and Louise Fortmann

An ecologist from a state department of natural resources once visited a peri-urban wetland with the local mayor. As they drove around the area, the ecologist exclaimed again and again over the uniqueness of the wetlands and the need to preserve this natural resource. The mayor, irritated, finally snapped: "That's no natural resource, that's folks' property." In spite of recent calls for multi-purpose land information systems, we continue to have a remarkable amount of difficulty integrating our technical information about natural resources with another very relevant body of data that concerns the rights in those resources. This is unfortunate because there are important causal relationships between rights in natural resources and the patterns of their use and abuse.

The forests and other tree resources of industrialized and developing countries, the subject of this book, are also "folks' property." Groups and individuals have distinctly proprietary attitudes about these resources, attitudes that may or may not receive formal legal recognition but which certainly affect behavior. Trees may be "owned" directly, distinct from rights in land, or as a part of a landholding. People and communities assert rights in trees and the land that sustains trees, and these rights—the "tenure" in which the trees and land are held—affect incentives and so are one determinant of how these resources are utilized.

In Henry Maine's (1920:174) concept, a "tenure" is simply a "bundle of rights," in our case, rights to use land, trees, and their products in certain ways and sometimes to exclude others from use. We have names such as "leasehold" or "freehold" for the standard bundles of rights in our society, while other societies have different tenures. These tenures

1

can be held by individuals, communities or the state, and it is not at all unusual for a village to have a certain tenure over a piece of land, while an individual or family has another tenure over part of the same land, and the state asserts a residual title in the same land.

This book has been driven primarily by the demands of applied social science and development, only very secondarily by theory. But since the purpose of the book is, in part, to interpret these cases, theory cannot be ignored. There are two bodies of theory in particular which can help us to understand many if not all of the cases that follow. The first is theory of individual tenure and investment developed in the eighteenth century; the second is common property theory, developed more recently to provide a framework for the analysis of the management of natural resources by communities. Depending upon where trees are planted, on the individual or household holding or in commons areas variously defined, one or the other of these bodies of theory usually provides our assumptions and hypotheses.

The notion that tenure affects agricultural production is relatively recent. Classical redistributive reforms aimed frankly at equity and a new political equilibrium. The eighteenth century philosophers, however, saw France's pre-revolutionary tenure patterns as stifling agricultural improvement. In 1776 Adam Smith argued in *The Wealth of Nations* that large-scale landowning and servile tenures discouraged progress, and John Stewart Mill urged productivity as well as equity considerations when he established the Land Tenure Reform Association in 1870. A variety of development-oriented arguments for land reform have since been articulated, but the one of particular interest to us here has less to do with distribution than with tenure itself. It is the argument that a landholder's incentive to invest in agriculture and especially in a landholding increases with the exclusivity and security of tenure. The investments that concern us are the planting and conservation of trees, which investment sometimes includes the opportunity costs of slow-maturing perennials. Tenure rules may also provide incentives for tree cutting, as when a tenure regime which confers tenure on those who clear land encourages deforestation driven by land hunger.

Common property theory entered popular parlance with Garrett Hardin's notorious tragedy of the commons thesis. Hardin (1968) contended that resources held in common were inevitably overexploited and degraded. Since Hardin arguably misused the term "commons," we shall begin this discussion with a definition. Common pool resources (more popularly called common property) can be distinguished from private and public goods in two ways. First, excluding others from the use of common pool resources is difficult and/or costly. Second, such resources can be utilized by more than one person either simultaneously or sequentially. Most forests and trees outside the boundaries of homesteads fall within this definition.

Theories of common property management have their intellectual roots in Mancur Olson's treatise on collective action. Olson (1965) argued that except in small face-to-face groups most people will "free ride" rather than participate in collective action to produce public goods unless they are coerced or provided with special individual incentives. However, since there is ample empirical evidence of effective common property management of natural resources (Gilles and Jamtgaard, 1981; Panel on Common Property Resource Management, 1986), the theoretical questions of current interest are how do user groups that manage common property resources arise, under what conditions do they persist, and what makes them effective. Prevailing thought would suggest that groups arise when the user population lives close to the resource and is relatively small, supply is moderately scarce compared to demand and is subject to multiple uses requiring management and coordination (Ostrum, 1986). Groups seem to survive if they have clear-cut rules that are enforced by both users and officials, internally adaptive institutional arrangements, the ability to nest into external organizations for dealing with the external environment, and different decision rules for different purposes. And their chances are better if they are subject to slow exogenous change (Ostrum,1986). This last criterion seems particularly problematic for forest management since many forest areas are subject to rapid multiple changes— settlement by outsiders, rapidly increasing population growth, large-scale logging by local or multinational firms, the establishment of ecological reserves and parks by local and international environmental interests, and changing forestry legislation and enforcement. Under such conditions, the kinds of community management described in Chapter 4 may well be endangered.

At the policy and programatic level, this book addresses the concerns of those who are searching for the institutions, organizations and tenurial strategies to facilitate the protection of existing trees and forests and the planting of new ones. From this standpoint, four areas deserve special attention. First, the tenure of land and trees affects the surrounding ecosystem. Second, access to land and forest resources under different tenure schemes affects the standard of living of people who depend on those resources. Third, rules of tenure affect the preservation, protection, and planting of trees. Finally, the prevailing system of tenure determines the beneficiaries and victims of forest policies and forestry projects, and sets the framework for conflict over benefits.

ECOLOGICAL EFFECTS

Much of the present interest in forestry and agroforestry stems from ecological concerns—protecting the "lungs of the earth," preserving genetic diversity and preventing immediate natural hazards such as floods, erosion and landslides. Different tenure regimes vary in their ecological effects.

The best known theory positing a connection between tenure and the condition of the ecosystem is Hardin's tragedy of the commons thesis. Hardin wrote of tenure as if it could be isolated from the realities of the associated system of land use and the encompassing social system. While degraded commons do exist, their degradation has not been a simple and direct result of common ownership. Preservation and protection also occur under common management. Common management of forests has been practiced with considerable success to accomplish such ecological ends as avalanche control or watershed management (Hosmer, this volume).

The link between tenure and the state of the ecosystem must be examined in the light of the mediating effect of technology and the economic use of the land. As the latter mediating factors change, tenure typically changes with them (Millon, this volume; Berry, 1975; introduction to chapter 3 of this volume). Large numbers of trees may be planted on communal land for household or communal subsistence use, but once those trees take on a commercial value, private rights in that land tend to develop.

The links between production system, tenure, and ecological change have been spelled out in numerous studies. Cronon (1983) links environmental changes in the forests of the northeastern United States with the shift from American Indian communal tenure, in hunter-gathering and shifting agriculture systems, to the private land tenure of Europeans. Others have shown that the practices of the California Miwok Indians slowed vegetational succession in the Yosemite Valley and that subsequent white settlement resulted in significant vegetational changes (Gibbens and Heady, 1964). In the Arun Valley of Nepal studied by Cronin (1979), subtle but significant changes in the forest ecosystem took place in a community-managed forest. Certain species of insects and birds characteristic of virgin forest were gone. On the other hand, less strict tenure arrangements would have resulted in the devastated forest that Cronin's team found further downslope. The tenure regime can affect behavior that in turn has ecological effects. Dube (1958) noted that proposed land consolidation in India led people to postpone planting trees. And in many places ecological niches and biological diversity have been preserved in sacred groves where rules of tree tenure linked to religious practices have prohibited cutting and other forms of use (Edwardes, 1922; Elias, 1962; Gadgil and Vartak, 1976; Malhotra, n.d.; Mann, 1981; Meiggs, 1982)

STANDARDS OF LIVING

Access to forest and tree products for domestic use or for sale affects household standards of living in general and the workload of women in particular. The tree tenure component of forest policy governs access for people living in or near forests; in non-forest areas still other land and tree tenure systems prevail.

John Briscoe (1979) has shown that the amount and kind of fuel used in Bangladesh is a function of class. In Kenya, the privatization and registration of land, combined with rapid population growth, has reduced the availability of fuelwood and changed it into a commercial product (Brokensha and Njeru, 1977; Brokensha and Riley, 1978; Brokensha and Riley, 1977; Fisher, 1953)

Access to food in the form of windfalls (fruit or nuts that have fallen or been blown to the ground, which customarily were available for the taking) helped feed more than one American family through the Great Depression. Fuelwood gathered on U.S. national forestland has kept thousands of families warm through the winter. And the customary right to hunt wild animals (defined in statutory law as the illegal act of poaching) from the forests has increased the protein content of many a poor person's diet (Ives, 1988).

PRESERVING, PROTECTING AND PLANTING TREES AND FORESTS

Most forestry and agroforestry initiatives are based either on the premise that rural people will plant trees or that they will preserve and protect trees planted by someone else including the government. However, people will not preserve, protect or plant trees nor allow others to, if doing so is costly to them personally. The rules of land and tree tenure can make these activities very costly indeed. For example, tree species that belong to the national government are unlikely to have a high survival rate on private or community land (Brain, 1980; Thomson *et al.*, 1986). Tree planting that transfers land to others is rarely permitted. In Burkina Faso, for example, farmers are not usually permitted to plant trees on borrowed land (Swanson, 1979). Nor are farmers likely to plant trees if adverse effects are perceived as likely to follow. In some Indian villages farmers were reluctant to plant trees on their own land for fear that the forestry department would assume control of the land (Sarin, 1980; Sitaraman, 1980). (See also, Sellers, this volume). Further, the rules of land and tree tenure may provide positive incentives for destroying extant trees. For example, if title to land is established by clearing, trees may fall victim to land hunger. (See Chapter 5).   Another strategy is harvesting tree produce on another's land. Where tenure rules hold that only the owner of the land may harvest tree produce irrespective of what others may be doing with the land, this action serves to make a claim of ownership to that land (Berry, 1975:114).

In sum, planting, protecting, and preserving trees often has social significance equal to or greater than the trees' strictly utilitarian value. & cutting (clearing)

BENEFICIARIES AND CONFLICTS

Land and tree tenure are pivotal in determining whether the benefits of forestry and agroforestry programs, projects and policies reach their intended beneficiaries.

Cernea (this volume) describes how failure to delineate property rights carefully led to a project that benefited the rich instead of the poor. Such projects are not as rare as they should be. Thus, having rights in a tree or controlling the land on which it is planted is often crucial to obtaining afforestation benefits. Those not permitted to plant trees (e.g., women), those not present at the right time (pastoralists, seasonal migrants) or those without the resources that would enable them to plant trees (the landless and the poor) are likely to be permanently disadvantaged. Benefits tend to accrue to the people with permanent residence, who have the right to plant trees with the disposable income or resources at their command.

The effects of uneven land distribution may be mitigated by compensatory tree tenure mechanisms—for example, in Korea there was a strong tradition of communal use of both public and private forests (Ahn, 1978; Gregerson, this volume).

Finally, an understanding of land and tree tenure can help predict the lines of conflict that are likely to arise from changes in the status quo. A sizable source of such conflict is the clash between customary and statutory law. An unexpected example of such a clash occurs on the national forests of the United States. A sort of customary law has grown up around the use of national forest land in which proximity gives rights. Local residents consider the national forest "theirs". This sometimes unarticulated customary practice stands at odds in a number of ways with national statutory law that assigns rights to the forest to all citizens. Perceived usufructuary rights to fuelwood is one example.

Local residents become exercised when outsiders arrive at "their" forest to collect firewood, or when the government imposes a collection fee. Other restrictions on forest use such as closing roads or regulating hunting and fishing in the forest are also sources of conflict.

Such conflicts between customary and statutory law over forest use have occurred around the world for centuries (Fernandes and Kulkarni, 1983; Guha, 1987; Guha and Gadgil, 1987; Holdsworth, 1922: 94-108; Pongsapich, 1982; Regan, 1981). In places where these conflicts have become armed struggles or where forested areas are caught up in the path of rebellion, deforestation and/or the manipulation of tenure may become military strategies with forest-dwelling citizens as victims. Similarly, struggles over tenure are often only one piece of a series of struggles for rights by minority groups. Conflict over tenure thus must be understood not just in terms of property rights but also in terms of human rights.

Finally, an exhortation. "Tree tenure" takes diverse forms in different societies and often develops a wonderous complexity. This volume should serve as an introduction to tree tenure, and we hope, as provocation. Scholars and travelers, over the years, have observed tree tenure but generally dealt with it only glancingly. Ideally, this book will encourage continued observation while adding reflection and theoretical analysis.

REFERENCES

Ahn, Bong Won. 1978. "Village Forestry in Korea." in *Proceedings, VII World Forestry Congress.* Jakarta: IUFRO.

Berry, Sara S. 1975. *Cocoa, Custom, and Socio-economic Change in Rural Western Nigeria.* Oxford: Clarendon Press.

Brain, James. 1980. "The Uluguru Land Usage Scheme: Success and Failure." *Journal of Developing Areas* (January): 175-190.

Briscoe, John. 1979. "The Political Economy of Energy Use in Rural Bangladesh." Unpublished Manuscript.

Brokensha, David and E.H.N. Njeru. 1977. "Some Consequences of Land Adjudication in Mbere Division". Working Paper, No. 320. Nairobi: University of Nairobi.

Brokensha, David and Bernard Riley. 1978. "Vegetation Changes in Mbere Division, Embu." Working Paper, No. 319. Nairobi: University of Nairobi.

Brokensha, David and Bernard Riley. 1978. "Forest, Foraging, Fences and Fuel in a Marginal Area of Kenya." In USAID Africa Bureau Workshop. Washington, D.C.: USAID.

Cronin, Edward W. 1979. *The Arun: A Natural History of the World's Deepest Valley.* Boston: Houghton MIfflin Company.

Cronon, William. 1983. *Changes in the Land.* New York : Hill and Wang.

Dube, S.C. 1958. *India's Changing Villages.* London: Routledge and Kegan Paul, Ltd.

Edwardes, S.M. 1922. "Tree-Worship in India." *Empire Forestry* 1(1): 78-86.

Elias, T.O. 1962. *The Nature of African Customary Law.* Manchester: Manchester University Press.

Fernandes, Walter and Sharad Kulkarni (eds.). 1983. *Towards a New Forest Policy: People's Rights and Environmental Needs.* New Delhi: Indian Social Institute.

Fisher, Jeanne. 1953. "The Anatomy of Kikuyu Domesticity and Husbandry." Department of Technical Cooperation.

Gadgil, Madhav and V.D. Vartak. 1976. "The Sacred Groves of Western Ghats in India" *Economic Botany* 30 (1): 152-160.

Gibbens, Robert P. and Harold F. Heady. 1964. "The Influence of Modern Man on the Vegetation of Yosemite Valley." California Agricultural Experiment Station Extension Service Manual 36.

Gilles, Jere L. and Keith Jamtgaard. 1981. "Overgrazing in Pastoral Areas: The Commons Reconsidered." *Sociologia Ruralis* 21: 129-141.

Gregerson, H.M. 1982. Village Forestry Development in the Republic of Korea. (Document (FAO) GCP/INT/347/SWE.) Rome: Food and Agriculture Organization.

Guha, Ramachandra. 1987. "Chipko: A Grassroots Perspective on the Environmental Debate" Mimeo. Helsinki: World Institute of Development Economics Research.

Guha, Ramachandra and Madhav Gadgil. 1987. "Forestry and Social Conflict in British India: A Study in the Ecological Bases of Agrarian Protest" Mimeo. Bangalore, India: Centre for Ecological Sciences, Indian Institute of Science.

Hardin, Garrett. 1968. "The Tragedy of the Commons" *Science* 162: 1243-1248.

Holdsworth, W.S. 1922. *A History of English Law. Volume I* Third Edition. Boston: Little, Brown and Company.

Ives, Edward D. 1988. *George Magoon and the Down-East Game War: A Study in History, Folklore and the Law.* Urbana: University of Illinois Press.

Maine, Henry. 1920. *Ancient Law.* (10th edition)

Malhotra, S.P. n.d. "Socioeconomic Structure of Population in Arid Rajasthan." Jodhpur: Central Arid Zone Research Institute.

Mann, H.S. 1981. "Afforestation at the Village Level" *Arid Lands Newsletter* 13 (March):11-15.

Meiggs, Russell. 1982. *Trees and Timber in the Ancient Mediterranean World*. Oxford: Clarendon Press.

Millon, Rene F. 1957. "Trade, Tree Cultivation, and the Development of Private Property in Land" *American Anthropologist* 57: 698-712.

Olson, Mancur. 1965. *The Logic of Collective Action : Public Goods and the Theory of Groups*. Cambridge: Harvard University Press.

Ostrum, Elinor. 1986. "Issues of Definition and Theory: Some Conclusions and Hypotheses" in Panel on Common Property Resource Management. Board on Science and Technology for International Development. Office of International Affairs, National Research Council. 1986. *Proceedings of the Conference on Common Property Resource Management. April 21-26, 1985.* Washington, D.C.: National Academy Press: 599-615.

Panel on Common Property Resource Management. Board on Science and Technology for International Development. Office of International Affairs, National Research Council. 1986. *Proceedings of the Conference on Common Property Resource Management. April 21-26, 1985.* Washington, D.C.: National Academy Press.

Sarin, S. 1980. "Experiences in Community Forestry: Madhya Pradesh" In R.N. Tewari and O.A. Mascarenhas (eds.) *Community Forestry Management for Rural Development*. Dehra Dun: Natraj Publishers: 62-90.

Sellars, S. 1977. "The Relationship between Land Tenure and Agricultural Production in Tucurrique, Costa Rica. Turrialba: Centro Agronomico Tropical de Investigacion y Enseñanza.

Sitaraman, S. and S. Sarin. 1980. "Experiences in Community Forestry: Uttar Pradesh" in R.N. Tewari and O.A. Mascarenhas (eds.) *Community Forestry Management for Rural Development*. Dehra Dun: Natraj Publishers: 91-112.

Swanson, Richard Alan. 1979. Gourmantche Agriculture: Part I, Land Tenure and Field Cultivation. United States Agency for International Development. Integrated Rural Development Project, Eastern ORD, BAEP, Upper Volta Contract AID-686-049-78.

Thomson, James T., David H. Feeny and Ronald J. Oakerson. 1986. "Institutional Dynamics: The Evolution and Dissolution of Common Property Resource Management" in Panel on Common Property Resource Management. Board on Science and Technology for International Development. Office of International Affairs, National Research Council. 1986. *Proceedings of the Conference on Common Property Resource Management. April 21-26, 1985.* Washington, D.C.: National Academy Press: 391-424.

2

Tree Tenure

People who have been exposed only to the more familiar forms of western property law often assume that trees are part and parcel of the land on which they grow. But, like minerals and water, trees can be a form of property separable from the land on which they are located, a concept intuitively obvious to anyone who has witnessed the Japanese transplanting a twenty foot tree carefully wrapped in rice straw or the wholesale movement of twenty-five foot palm trees from a nursery to a California subdivision. Special rules for trees have been known since antiquity. The Visigoths, for example, had rules protecting the olive tree (Stanislawski, 1963:177).

Failure to recognize the relationships between property in trees and property in land has led to bad policy, failed projects and projects with unanticipated consequences such as the one described by Cernea (Chapter Four, this volume). A number of observers have comented that the nationalization of trees by various governments has led to especially thorough destruction of young volunteer trees by farmers who don't want the government's property on their land. Trouble can also arise when the government exercises its statutory claim to land that is also claimed under local custom. Hoskins (1980) describes a West African case in which project personnel, under the impression that it was "worthless bush" and belonged to no one, bulldozed the community forest for a plantation site. The local villagers returned the favor by burning the project plantation of fast-growing exotics to the ground. The distribution of rights within a community or within a household is also important as shown in the discussion by Chavangi et al. (Chapter Seven, this volume) of how gender differences in tenure can affect a project.

Good policy and successful projects depend on understanding who can do what, when, and where. They depend on analyzing how changes

11

will affect individuals, communities and ecosystems. Toward this end, *Fortmann* provides a conceptual framework for analyzing the bundle of rights that comprise tree tenure and discusses the implications of tree tenure for agroforestry projects. Specific constellations of rights discussed in her article are illustrated in the other selections.

Duncan and *Obi* illustrate tenure systems that distinguish between planted trees and wild trees. This distinction was also found in the Ethiopian Amhara village studied by Hoben (1973:52), where wood in mountainside thorn forest was an open-access good[1] for residents of the parish where the forest was located, while trees and bamboo planted on cleared land were the property of individual households.

Obi and *Cory* demonstrate that tree tenure rules may differ with varying land tenure. That is, rights to what one has planted may depend on the type of land tenure system. Denman (1969:1) quotes an old English epigram, "Oaks scorn to grow except on free land." Before the abolition of copyhold[2] tenure, he notes, oaks belonged not to the copyholder, but to

> the lord who held the manor in fee. Copyholders would not plant oaks to enhance a bounty which was not their own. Freeholders in contrast owned what grew on their land.

The factors involved in the allocation of rights to tree produce require careful examination. Under the English Charter of the Forest (1217), for example, a freeman was entitled to honey found in his own woods, while honey found in royal forests belonged to the Crown (Cox, 1905:39-40). A similar split distribution of rights between the people and the government in the United States occured among the Klamath Indians of northern California who, in the 1870s, could sell trees that had been cut in the process of clearing land, although trees cut for sale as timber were legally the property of the United States government and could only be sold through various devious stratagems (Stern, 1965:62). Lakshmi-Narayana (1942:138) notes an Indian law in which one of the criteria for ownership was whether or not the tree had been planted before 1908.

Leach describes a particularly complex system of allocation of rights to the produce of date palms in Sudan was linked to providing the tree, land, labor and water. Leach's example raises the interesting question of whether the women who cook for the work parties that plant trees in the Majjia Valley of Burkina Faso (Williams, 1985) should be entitled to a share of the produce. In the same region, Ahmed (1974) found that those involved in tapping gum arabic got shares for their work, including an equal share for the camel used for transport. Stanislawski's (1963: 21, 204) description of tree tenure in parts of Portugal is remarkably similar to Leach's. The division of the fig and olive crops between the farmer and the land owner depended on the division of labor and costs. In addition, the valuable prunings were the property of whoever paid for the work. And fragmentation of property led to fig trees with five owners. Elwin (1953:55) describes a similar system of heirs sharing the produce of sago palms in the Bondo highlands of India.

Commonly property rights are thought of in terms of commercial or economic influences. But religion also sometimes influences property rights. The persistence of holy trees and sacred groves is the best known manifestation of this influence. For example, in 1847 a royal order stated that the plants and trees around the Pashupatinah temple in Nepal were "actually hermits and sages... not a single twig shall be cut from these" (Regmi, 1968:49). *Bennett* illustrates the opposite effect with a Nepali case in which religion turned fruit into an open-access good and thereby influenced willingness to undertake horticultural production.

Obi discusses how rights to land are related to rights to the trees on that land. Many of the principles found in Obi can also be found in Hutton's (1921:68) study of the Naga tribe in India. Bamboos were the property of the planter irrespective of the ownership of the land. Unless a landowner had forbidden the planting in advance, s/he could not uproot the new plants on land near the village and was responsible for clearing a fireline around them to protect them when burning the land for shifting cultivation. However, if the land were far from the village, the landowner could uproot and discard the bamboos.

Some uses or products may be considered more acceptable than others or incompatability of activities may restrict the uses to which a tree may be put. Desai (1948:43) reported that some famers in the Indian state of Gujarat were allowed to collect honey from the forest but nothing else.

Not only may property rights in trees differ from property rights in land, but rights to forested land or wildland as it is often called may be distinguished from rights to agricultural land. *Menzies* details such distinctions for historical China including the by now familiar distinction between rights to land and rights to trees.

Finally, certain users may allocate to themselves special rights. *Aschmann* describes tree tenure in a southern California "child culture". While Aschmann's article has in it a certain amount of whimsy, in Kenya and Sri Lanka (and probably other cultures as well) children have special rights to the fruits of certain trees (personal communication, Dianne Rocheleau and Yvonne Everett). In other places such as England, stealing fruit is one of the perquisites of childhood regardless of the law (personal communication, Michael Thompson). In addition, the ethical distinction noted by Aschmann between taking fruit with and without economic value parallels the differences found in many systems between the right to take tree produce for personal and commercial use (Brokensha and Riley, 1977; Mukwaya, 1953).

A common theme is repeatedly sounded in these selections. Tree tenure is a system of property rights every bit as variable as land tenure, mineral rights or riparian rights. Property rights in trees are by no means attached to the land on which they grow nor even to any single individual. Rights can be established to trees or their produce through planting, through provision of the labor, capital, or other resources needed to make them productive, through inheritance, through various temporary arrangements including leasing, through religious custom, or through ownership of the land on which they grow. The existence and diversity of tree tenure is not some bizarre phenomenon found in out of the way places. Rather, tree tenure is a constantly evolving part of every day life providing a common social organizational link in places as far apart as California, England, Sudan, and Portugal.

Notes

1. An open-access good is one from which no potential user is excluded as distinguished from a common property good to which only a defined group of users have access.

2. Copyhold tenure was held at the will of the lord of the manor according to the custom of the manor (Barnes, n.d.). That is, a tenant under copyhold tenure enjoyed no protection of law, rather the continuation and terms of his/her tenure were subject to the will of the lord of the manor. However, over time, the lord of the manor increasingly was understood to be able to exercise his own will only in accord with the custom which had grown up among the copyhold tenants of the manor. Thus, although copyhold tenure was in theory a tenure at will, it gradually became constrained by customary law.

References

Ahmed, Abd-al, Ghaffar Muhammad. 1974. *Shlaykhs and Followers.* Khartoum: University of Khartoum Press.

Barnes, Thomas G. n.d. "Notes on Tenures and Estates." Typescript.

Brokensha, David and Bernard Riley. 1977. "Vegetation Changes in Mbere Division, Embu." Working Paper, No. 319. Nairobi, University of Nairobi.

Cox, J. Charles. 1905. *The Royal Forests of England.* London: Methuen and Co.

Denman, D.R. 1969. *Land Use and The Constitution of Property.* Cambridge: Cambridge University Press

Desai, M.B. 1948. *The Rural Economy of Gujarat.* Bombay: Oxford University Press.

Elwin, Verrier. 1950. *Bondo Highlands.* Bombay: Oxford University Press.

Hoben, Allan. 1973. *Land Tenure among the Amhara of Ethiopia.* Chicago: University of Chicago Press.

Hoskins, Marilyn. 1980. "Community Forestry Depends on Women" *Unasylva.* 32 (130): 27-32.

Hutton, J. H. 1921. *The Sema Nagas.* London: MacMillan and Co. Ltd.

Lakshmi-Narayana, Sahu. 1942. *The Hill Tribes of Jeypore.* Cuttack: Servants of India Society.

Mukwaya, A.B. 1953. *Land Tenure in Buganda.* Kampala: The Eagle Press.

Penwill, D.J. 1951. *Kamba Customary Law:: Notes Taken in the Machakos District of Kenya Colony.* Nairobi: East African Literature Bureau.

Regmi, Mahesh C. 1968. *Land Tenure and Taxation in Nepal. Volume IV. Religious and Charitable Land Endowments: Guthi Tenure.* Berkeley. Institute of International Studies.

Stanislawski, Dan. 1963. *Portugal's Other Kingdom: The Algarve.* Austin: University of Texas Press.

Stern, Theodore. 1965. *The Klamath Tribe.* Seattle: University of Washington Press.

Williams, Paula. 1985. "(No Longer) Blowin' in the Wind." PJW-15. Hanover, New Hampshire: Institute of Current World Affairs.

The Editors

The Tree Tenure Factor in Agroforestry with Particular Reference to Africa

Louise Fortmann

It is often thought, after the fashion of Gertrude Stein, that once biological distinctions have been made, a tree is a tree is a tree. Fortmann argues to the contrary that attention must be paid to the social meanings of trees and offers a framework for analyzing property rights in trees. This selection should not be read as the definitive work on existing systems of tree tenure but rather as a menu of possibilities. Tree tenure systems may vary considerably within a single society and are constantly evolving.—The Editors.

INTRODUCTION

Agroforestry depends on people's rights to plant and use trees, rights that in turn depend on the prevailing systems of land tenure and tree tenure. While the importance of land tenure in agriculture, forestry, and agroforestry is clearly recognized, the distinction between land and tree tenure often is not. A frequent implicit assumption is that tree tenure is identical with land tenure. Further, the influence of trees on land tenure is often not recognized.

The literature provides many examples of the distinction between land and tree tenure. For example, the principle that trees and land can be sold separately has been reported for Tanzania [6,17,64], Nigeria [47,59], Ghana [63], Uganda [44], and Indonesia [86]. Under Ottoman Land Law, the trees on Cyprus were owned separately from the land and that "the owner of one could not sell his interest without giving a prior right of purchase to the owner of the other." [49] In some cases,

Agroforestry Systems 2:229-251 (1985). Reprinted with the permission of the publishers.

certain uses of trees and tree products are permitted to all regardless of who owns the land on which the tree is growing [5,71].

This article analyzes the components of tree tenure and discusses their importance in the field of agroforestry.

COMPONENTS OF TREE TENURE

Tree tenure consists of a bundle of rights which may be held by different people at different times. Four major categories of rights make up the bundle which comprises tree tenure: the right to own or inherit, the right to plant, the right to use, and the right of disposal.

The Right to Own or Inherit Trees

Murray [56,57] has emphasized the importance to agroforestry projects of the right of the planter to own trees and completely control their usufruct. But in many systems the right to own may be vested in the community or a kinship group larger than the household [27,59,60,84]. In some cases, trees may be owned even when the land on which they are grown cannot be [58,83]. In other cases, as in Niger, forest regulations do not permit individual ownership of trees. [72]. The laws of succession involving trees can be as complex as those involving land. It has been reported that in Sudan palm trees could be subject to complex fractional ownerships due to the laws of inheritance.

The Right to Plant Trees

The right to plant trees, an obvious prerequisite for agroforestry, may be restricted. Particularly in Africa, planting a tree may give the planter rights over the land on which it is planted. The result is that planting trees may be used as a means to get or maintain rights to land. In the 1940s, Basotho chiefs discouraged the planting of trees on arable land for this very reason [49] and the prohibition has carried over into more recent times [22]. Planting restrictions have been reported for the Luguru in Tanzania [10] and the Yoruba of Nigeria [49]. It has been reported that trees may be planted as visible evidence of a claim to land in Kenya [12,76], Upper Volta [79] and Indonesia [86]. In Tanzania, planting permanent trees without permission on the land of another could be construed as "misbehavior" and constitute grounds for eviction [36]. In Zambia, tree planting by the colonial government was regarded as its attempt to seize land [58].

The principle that planting trees establishes a claim to the land was weakened in Tanzanian litigation. In 1965 in *Iddi Juda Omari v. Issa Abdallah*, the court held the customary law "when a person occupies a land and plants sisal or trees of permanent nature on the *shamba* (field), then the *shamba* belongs to him, no matter how long he stays without cultivating it" to be "unreasonable in modern Tanzania" [35] (*cf* also [37]).

But in many places this principle continues to hold currency and affects the ability of people to participate in agroforestry projects.

In other cases, the planter does not obtain land rights but does retain ownership of the tree and with it the right of access to the tree. Such rights of access can be extremely disruptive to other uses of the land.

The Right to Use Trees and Tree Products

1) The right to *gather* may include the right to gather or lop off dead branches or strip off hanging bark and the right to gather things growing on a tree such as fungus, insects, or birds' nests. For example, a Peruvian agrarian cooperative allowed free gleaning of eucalyptus bark [75].

2) *The use of the standing tree* may be necessary for curing hides or for hanging honey barrels. Among the Kamba, honey barrels would be hung in trees on one's own land, on the land of another with permission or in unoccupied trees in the commonage. The owner of the honey barrel then had the right that his bees not be disturbed (62).

3) The right to *cut* all or part of a living tree for timber or building poles can be an important one. The cutting of living trees for fuelwood is generally frowned on unless it is scarce.

4) The right to *harvest produce* such as fruit, nuts, and pods does not necessarily accrue to either the owner of the tree or the owner of the land. In parts of Nepal it has been reported that fruit is considered a common good [8].

5) The right to use produce *under the tree* may be less restricted than other rights. Leaves and twigs and even fallen fruit often may be collected from the ground under trees which are owned by others. Among the Semarang of Malaysia in the 1920's, fallen fruit was a common good even *inside* a private compound [71].

The Right to Dispose of Trees

1) the right to *destroy* the tree by uprooting or chopping down individual trees or by clearing a section of the forest

2) The right to *lend* the use of the tree to someone else

3) *The right to lease, mortgage, or pledge* the tree

Tree pledging, or leasing, is practiced in Nepal [61], Nigeria [2], Sierra Leone [39] and Ghana [60]. (Pledging is distinguished from mortgaging by the fact that the pledgee assumes control of the tree immediately rather than after a process of foreclosure.)

4) The right to *give away or sell* the tree either together with or separate from the land

An Ashanti father in Ghana could give trees to his children before his death [65]. In Tanzania, Abrahams [1] reported the right to sell fruit trees as a recent innovation and Dobson [20] reported that even the planters of trees among the Sambaa did not have the right to sell them. But Meek [49] reported that in Tanzania rights in mango and other trees could be bought and sold.

Who Has What Rights?

Four classes of right holders must be considered separately: the State, groups, households, and individuals within households.

• *The State* exercises its rights in three basic ways.

a) It may regulate (or attempt to regulate) the use of trees owned by others. Certain species may be declared as protected no matter where they are located to be used only with official permission which often involves paying a bribe. This sort of legislation has been reported as detrimental to agroforestry projects in Haiti [57] and Niger [72].

b) The State may prohibit or restrict the use of trees in forest reserves. Forest reserves often are the subject of serious conflict between the State and people living near and within forest reserves. A forest reserve may contain land that is essential to the economy of the surrounding area. This has been reported as a problem in India [28], Nepal [4] and the United States [41] and is known as a problem elsewhere. The State may also allow outsiders to utilize forest resources while prohibiting local people from doing so [54].

c) The State may allow limited use of forest reserve land. In many countries people are allowed to satisfy basic needs for fuelwood, fodder, poles and minor forest products from forest reserves. The taungya system takes this a step farther and actually allows farming on forest land in return for planting and caring for tree seedlings. But where landlessness is acute, the taungya farmer may ensure that the seedlings do not survive, in order to remain on the land. Farmers may also plant tree crops in order to establish a more permanent claim to the land.

• *Groups* need to be considered in three categories.

Groups may be *geographically defined*. All the residents of a certain village may be granted used rights while those enjoyed by "strangers" are denied or restricted. The principle that only "local people of the neighborhood" could harvest palm trees [78] was upheld in a 1926 Nigerian court case [23]. Traditionally among the Nyakyusa of Tanzania, it was residence in a village which gave land (and with it tree) rights [27]. Rules restricting the rights of "strangers" are reported for the Tanzania coast [7,80], the Yoruba of Nigeria [47], and Ghana [60].

Kin groups (which frequently may have a specific territory under their control) may also restrict rights to their members. Tree rights among the Melaban Kantu of Indonesia are vested in such groups [21]. In West Sumatra the decision to cut a valuable tree is made by the extended family [51].

Non-kin groups such as corporations or cooperatives may (usually with the acquiesence of the State) exercise rights over a particular area. Such rights (as those granted logging companies) may in fact conflict with the ancient rights of local people [42]. The establishment of cooperatives on the old haciendas of Peru led to a redefinition of use rights, causing much community conflict. Cooperatives can restrict the right to gather fuelwood to their members and their families, disenfranchising non-members and widows of members of long standing [75].

The tree rights of households may reflect lines of fragmentation such as religion, caste, class, ethnic group or geographical origin [11].

• *Individuals* within a household may also have different rights depending on gender, birth order, or intrafamily status.

FACTORS AFFECTING WHO HAS WHAT RIGHTS

Three general sets of factors affect who may exercise what rights when over what trees: the nature of the tree, the nature of the use, and the nature of the land tenure system.

The Nature of the Tree
Different rules may attach to the tree depending on whether it has been planted deliberately or whether it is self-sown. This distinction is based on the principle that "labor creates rights" [51].

The general rule of thumb is that wild or self-sown trees are community property as shown for Malawi [34], Uganda [30], Zimbabwe [32], Sierra Leone [39], Botswana [69], Lesotho [22], Upper Volta [79], Tanzania [1,17], Kenya [12,85], Zambia [25], Cook Islands [19]. In Ghana and Nigeria, wild trees growing on private land were reported to be the property of the landowner [47,63]. Planted trees generally belong either to the planter or to the owner of the land.

The doctrine of labor creating rights may be extended to wild trees if labor is invested in making the tree usable. Thus the pre-European Ojibwa recognized private rights to wild sugar maples. [31].

The Nature of the Use

The rules that apply to subsistence use often differ from those which apply to commercial use. Trees used for subsistence, particularly those growing on a commons, are often free for use by all. In contrast, the use of trees for commercial purposes may be restricted to trees growing on the seller's property or may be forbidden altogether depending on the particular use [7, 13, 20, 46, 55, 63].

Fuelwood has traditionally been a common good although the rules governing its access may tighten as it becomes increasingly scarce.

The use of trees serving community purposes may be restricted. Particular trees or groves of trees may be considered sacred or the dwelling place of spirits and thus be protected from use or cutting. This protection often also serves a soil and water conservation function. Sacred trees or groves have been reported in Kenya [14,52,81], Uganda [30], Tanzania [18], Indonesia [9], Philippines [16], and Colombia and Venezuela [67].

Trees have long performed a service role in the form of shade. Cutting down shade trees may be prohibited [85] or considered to indicate a lack of intelligence [20,70]. In Botswana it was forbidden to cut trees in the immediate vicinity of a village [69]. On the other hand, shade trees were (and are) sometimes cut down because they were thought to harbor snakes (E. Colson, personal communication).

The Nature of the Land Tenure System

Although tree and land tenure are distinct, each affects the other. As has been shown, planting trees can be used to establish de facto private ownership of land. On the other hand, rights in land also affect rights to trees.

Where land tenure is communal and tree rights are strong, it would appear that tree planters are advantaged in their rights to trees. (It is possible that this is particularly true in the case of shifting cultivation.)

1) *Tree Planters.* The person who plants a tree in many societies is the owner of that tree. This is (or was) the case in Zaire [48], Ghana [68], among the Iteso [43], the Nyamwezi [1], the Hanunoo of the Philippines [16], the Dayaks of Indonesia [86], the Sukuma of Tanzania [17] and among the Ibo of Nigeria [59]. Forest farms in the People's Republic of China own the trees they plant [50]. Among the Ashanti, those who cooperated in clearing virgin forest were joint owners of the fruits of the trees grown in the clearing [65]. Spencer [77] reports as a general principle of shifting cultivation in Southeast Asia that the use of productive trees is the private property of the planter and that the

trees may be inherited. In West Sumatra the inheritance of shares of trees and their produce depend in part on who planted the tree [50].

In contrast, where private rights to land are strong, the strength of one's rights to trees may depend on the strength of one's rights to land. In this case, landowners are relatively advantaged while those with temporary or weak claims to land (tenants, including both share crop- pers and lessees, squatters, pledgees, mortgagees and women) may be relatively disadvantaged. The latter often have restricted rights because of the possibility of using trees to establish a permanent claim to land as discussed above.

2) _Landowners_. In Nigeria the "owner of the land invariably owns the forest on the land" [3]. Among the Buganda all trees eventually became the property of the landowner [55]. In Lesotho the court held that trees belong to the owner of the land whether or not they had been planted with the chief's permission [22]. Among the Fanti of Ghana, the landowner had full rights to trees on the land and could not, "be improved out of his land" with trees planted by someone else [68]. Among the Batswana trees could not be cut on the field of another without permission [70].

3) _Tenants_. In the last century, Kikuyu tenants in Kenya had to cultivate around any trees standing in the field and could not fell trees for construction or manufacture without the permission of the landlord [45].

Among the Buganda, a tenant was not allowed to sell trees of any sort. He could plant economic trees but the landlord got a share of the proceeds and became the owner of the trees upon the tenant's departure (30).

According to Kludze [40] gratuitous tenants in Ghana may not sell or fell economic trees. Under the temporary systems in Ghana the tenant must maintain economic trees which are growing on the land but may not plant any himself. The owner has the right to the fruits of these trees although the tenants may harvest for his personal use, never for sale. Without the permission of the landlord, he may not fell certain trees [60].

In Nigeria, among the Ibo, the share cropper may plant a few economic trees, the number being determined by the number [of trees] which a typical farmer in the community would be growing. Use rights to any trees planted by the owner remain with the owner throughout the share cropping tenancy. However, the use of self-sown trees is vested in the share cropper who also retains the inheritable rights to any economic trees which he has planted even after the tenancy ends

[59]. Among the Ibo, the lessor retained the rights to economic trees but the lessee was permitted to climb them and to prune them to allow cultivation. In practice this meant stripping off all the leaves and branches. The lessee could also cut down non-economic trees if it were "safer and more reasonable in the circumstances" than pruning them. The lessee did, however, have to protect economic trees from fire. If a specific tree was leased, the lessee could not damage the tree [59]. Annual tenants among the Yoruba have neither the right to plant trees nor to use existing ones [47]. In Fiji a lessee could not cut down trees without the consent of the lessor nor could he sell "any forest produce growing on the land" [49].

4) *Borrowers* are under similar restrictions. Among the Gourmantche of Upper Volta borrowers are not permitted to plant trees since this would establish inheritable rights in the tree, and in practice, the land shaded by it [79]. In Costa Rica, borrowers are permitted to plant only annual crops [73].

5) *Squatters* have strong reasons to try to get title to the land. In Costa Rica, squatters who hold the right of access and use try to make their title more permanent by planting trees as the law requires compensation for crops and improvement; producing coffee and peach, and palm trees are generally worth more than the land [73].

On the coast of Tanzania squatters traditionally could plant trees (except cloves) and have rights over the usufruct [6].

A particularly troublesome case of squatters and trees can be found on the coast of Kenya where squatters worked for a small wage and paid rent for land to cultivate for themselves. With the introduction of cashews in 1937, the value of the cashew crop was far higher than the value of the rent. Eventually, an agreement was reached under which squatters could plant cashews in which they had inheritable rights but which protected the interests of the landowners. In eleven of the 296 arbitration cases resulting from evictions beginning in 1957/58, two awarded the trees to the squatters, two split them half-half, and seven awarded them to the landowner. (The legal principles are unfortunately not specified.) [74].

6) *Pledgees or Mortgagees* had rights based on the principle that the usufruct of the trees served as the interest on the loan. Among the Yoruba, it was felt that the pledgee should have use of the trees for a minimum of two or three years in order to be fairly compensated [47].

Under Ibo law the pledgee may not plant economic trees without the consent of the owner. If he does, the owner may destroy them when the pledge is redeemed. Further, since the land and the trees may be pledged separately, obtaining pledge to the land does not automatically imply the right to use the trees [59].

In Ghana, the pledgee (depending on the rights of the pledgor) may use any economic trees including the rights to fell or tap palm trees. He may also grow economic groups. Only if the pledgor redeems the land prematurely must he bear any of the cost of such improvements [60].

Among the Haya of Tanzania a mortgagee could fell trees but could not plant them [18].

Women

Women as a category do not always have restricted rights. Among the Ibo, women have very detailed rights to trees [59]. Tanner [80] found that nearly as many women owned palm trees as did men on the Tanzania coast, reflecting the influence of Islamic law. Meek [49] found that women could inherit rubber land in Malaysia.

But in societies where women are not permitted to own land, their rights in trees may be restricted. Where planting trees establishes rights to land, women may be forbidden to plant trees to prevent them from using this route to obtain land. Or women's rights to both trees and land may be a function of residence and marriage. Where marriage is not a stable institution, women's tree rights may be equally precarious.

THE IMPLICATIONS OF TREE TENURE FOR AGROFORESTRY

In any agroforestry system tree tenure issues must be carefully examined to avoid the following problems.

1) The *loss of rights* may result from an agroforestry project as a consequence of a number of factors:

a) The project may disturb or destroy rights to other uses of the land or the trees on it. Hoskins [33] has described a fuelwood project which involved the clearing of "useless" bush which was in fact the source of numerous products. Agroforestry projects such as alley cropping [38] may involve the loss of the right to use the space where the trees are planted.

b) Certain practices for cultivating and protecting trees may result in the loss of gathering rights.

c) When the value of trees is increased there is a tendency for both land and tree tenure to shift from communal to private holdings. The effect of privatization of land in Kenya was to reduce access rights to trees and certain tree-dependent activities such as the production of honey dropped off [13]. Similar effects may be associated with other shifts in tenure.

It may be useful to construct a table such as the following and determine who may lose what rights as a result of the project (Table 1).

Table 1
Assessing the effect of an agroforestry project on use rights[a]

User Distinctions	—what is sought or produced—								
	Twigs or Leaves	Fuel-wood	Fruits nuts	Fodder	Use of Standing Trees	Timber Construction	Subsistence	Commercial Use	Gain Loss
Gender •Men •Women									
Landed Status •Landless house holds •Temporary land right house-holds									
Farm Size •Small farmers •Large farmers									
Special Uses •Forest Depart-ment •Grazers									

[a]This table has been adopted from [24] at the suggestion of Robert Chambers.

The users category should include whatever groups are relevant in a given project area. For each category of use, their probable gain or loss should be recorded. The loss in rights might be a result of expropriation of land for the project, rising market values of trees and tree-related products, or privatization of land. For example, the commercialization of fuelwood through the establishment of woodlots might lead landless households to lose fuel gathering rights. In the final column a judgment should be made as to which of the categories are net gainers or net losers. This table would allow a project design team to determine what categories of people might be overall gainers or losers as a result of the project and what kind of rights are in greatest need of protection.

2) The *protection of the trees* can be a problem. The ability to exclude others from the use of trees and tree products is essential if tree planters are to reap the benefit of their investment. In the Nepal case cited above, tree owners had no right to exclude others from the use of their fruit trees for religious reasons. In contrast, the religious beliefs of the Dogon of Mali served to protect fruit [26]. While one may have a legal right to prevent others from using resources including trees, in communities based on a system of reciprocal rights and obligations this is often very difficult to do [66,82]. The personal or institutional capacity to enforce exclusionary rights may be very small indeed. In the Sudan, forest officers knew perfectly well that illegal tree cutting was taking place daily on government land, but were totally unable to prevent it [29].

Protection is particularly a matter of concern when agroforestry is undertaken on waste lands. If there are clear communal rights to use such trees either because they are growing on community land or because of the use to which they are put or if there are ambiguous or unenforceable rights to exclude others from their use, the project may be in considerable difficulty.

3) *Certain categories of users may be unable to participate in the project* because they do not have the right to plant or own trees. This is likely to be true of the landless, those with temporary claims to land, and women. In many places, these three categories singly or in combination will comprise the majority of the population. Thus, a project which does not take this into account may end up serving a relatively advantaged minority of the population, or such a project may be destroyed by those who are excluded from it.

4) *Because trees can be used to establish rights to land, it is necessary to monitor who is planting project trees where.* Agroforestry

projects can be used by private individuals to establish private claims to communal land (cf[15]). Similarly, it is necessary to ensure that the community accepts the planting of trees on community land for otherwise disenfranchised people.

CONCLUSION

There has been a perhaps understandable tendency to think of agroforestry in terms of the biological meaning of trees and in terms of land tenure. Yet it is also necessary to consider the social meanings of trees including the norms of tree use and the long-standing body of customary law dealing with tree tenure. Such considerations are essential to understanding the management of resource systems which include trees and in designing agroforestry projects. Identifying who holds what tree tenure rights will help the project designer avoid the unintended destruction of existing rights, the exclusion of certain groups from project benefits, or the capture of the project by an elite for its own purposes.

The identification of existing rights should not be taken as the definitive answer to the problem of tree tenure. Tree tenure rights have been shown to shift over time—often in the direction of privatization as tree resources have become scarce or commercially valuable—affecting land tenure as well [53]. Systems of tree tenure are no more static than other forms of social organization. Indeed, the systematic study of agroforestry which has resulted in refinements such as the alley cropping system may bring about new rights and new pressures on existing tenure. It is with these new directions that future research must be concerned.

REFERENCES

1. Abrahams RG (1967) The peoples of the Great Unyamwezi, Tanzania (Nyamwezi,Sukuma, Sumbwa, Kimbu, Konogo). London: International African Institute.
2. Adegboye RO (1969) Procuring Loan through pledging of cocoa trees.Journal of the Geographical Association of Nigeria 12 (1&2):68-73.
3. Adegboye RO (1979) Impact of land tenure on Nigerian forest ecosystems. Paper presented at the Man and Biosphere Workshop on State of Knowledge on Nigerian Rainforest Ecosystem. University of Ibadan, Nigeria, 24-26 January.
4. Agricultural Information Development Bulletin 4(3):2-9, 38 (1982) Community forestry project in Nepal.

5. Ahn BW (1978) Village forestry in Korea. Eighth World Forestry Congress, Jakarta, 16-28 October. FRG/1-5.
6. Bailey AP (1965) Land tenure: its sociological implications with specific reference to the Swahili speaking peoples of East Africa (Unpublished Masters Thesis: University of London).
7. Baker EC (1934) Report on social and economic conditions in Tanga province. Dar es Salaam: Tanganyika territory.
8. Bennett L (1981) The Parbatiya women of Bakundala. The status of women in Nepal. Volume II Part 7. Kathmandu: Center for Economic Development and Administration.
9. Bompard J, Ducatillion C, Hecketsweiler P (1980) A traditional agricultural system: village-forest-gardens in West Java. Montepellier: Académie de Montepellier, Université des Sciences et Techniques du Languedoc.
10. Brian J (1980) The Uluguru land usage scheme: success and failure. Journal of Developing Areas: 175-190.
11. Briscoe J (1979) The political economy of energy use in rural Bangladesh. Mimeo.
12. Brokensha D, Glazier J (1973) Land reform among the Mbere of Central Kenya. Africa 43 (3):182-206.
13. Brokensha DD, Riley B (1977) Some consequences of land adjudication in Mbere Division. Nairobi: IDS Working Paper 320.
14. Brokensha D, Riley B (1977) Vegetation changes in Mbere Division, Embu. Nairobi: IDS Working Paper No. 319.
15. Cernea M (1981) Land tenure systems and social implications of forestry development programs. Washington D.C.: World Bank Staff Working Paper No. 452.
16. Conklin HC (1975) Hanunoo agriculture. FAO Forestry Development Paper No. 12. Northford Connecticut: Elliots Books.
17. Cory H (1970) Sukuma law and custom. Westport: Negro Universities Press.
18. Cory H, Hartnoll MM (1971) Customary law of the Haya tribe. London: Frank Cass & Co. Ltd.
19. Crocombe RG (1964) Land tenure in the Cook Islands. Melbourne: Oxford University Press.
20. Dobson EB (1940) Land tenure of the Wamsambaa. Tanganyika Notes and Records 10:1-27.
21. Dove M (1976) Tree rights, tree-holding units and tree-using units among the Melaban Kantuq: the factors of scarce land, scarce labor and scarce knowledge in their evolution. Paper prepared for the 1976 Meetings of the American Anthropological Association.
22. Duncan P (1960) Sotho laws and customs. Capetown: Oxford Univerity Press.

23. Elias TO (1971) Nigerian land law 4th edition. London: Sweet and Maxwell.
24. Elliot C (1982) The political economy of sewage: a case study from the Himalayas. Mazingira 6 (4): 44-56.
25. Gluckman M (1965) Ideas in Barotse jurisprudence. New Haven: Yale University Press.
26. Griaule M (1965) Conversations with Ogotemmeli. London: Oxford University Press.
27. Gulliver PH (1958) Land tenure and social change among the Nyakyusa. Kampala: East African Institute of Social Research.
28. Gupta PN (1982) The effects of government policy in forest management in the Himalayan & Siwalik region of Uttar Pradesh, India. In Hallsworth EG, ed Socio-economic effects and constraints in tropical forest management, pp 65-72. Chichester: John Wiley & Sons Ltd.
29. Hammer T (1977) Wood for fuel: energy crisis implying desertification: the case of Bara, the Sudan. Unpublished Masters Thesis, University of Bergen.
30. Haydon ES (1960) Law and justice in Buganda. London: Butterworths.
31. Herskovitz MJ (1952) Economic anthropology. New York.
32. Holleman JF (1969) Shona customary law. Manchester: Manchester University Press.
33. Hoskins M (1980) Community forestry depends on women. Unasylva 32 (130): 27-32.
34. Ibik JO (1971) Restatement of African law: 4 Malawi: II The law of land succession, movable property agreements and civil wrongs. London: Sweet and Maxwell.
35. James RW (1967) Judicial developments in customary law - some reflections. J of the Denning Law Soc 2(1)):41-58.
36. James RW (1971) Land tenure policy in Tanzania. Nairobi: East African Literature Bureau.
37. James RW, Fimbo GM (1973) Customary land law of Tanzania. Dar es Salaam: East African Literature Bureau.
38. Kang BT, Wilson GF. Sipkens L (1981) Alley cropping maize (*Zea Mays*) and Leucaena (*Leucaena leucocephala* Lam.) in southern Nigeria. Plant and Soil 63:165-170.
39. Karimu J (1981) Strategies for peasant farmer development: an evaluation of a rural development project in northern Sierra Leone. Unpublished PhD dissertation, University of London.
40. Kludze AKP (1973) Ghana I: Ewe Law of Property Restatement of African Law: 6. London: Sweet and Maxwell.

41. Knowlton CS (1972) Culture conflict and natural resources. In Burch, WR Jr., Cheek NH Jr., Taylor L, eds, Social behavior, natural resources and the environment, pp 109-145. New York: Harper & Row.

42. Kunstadter P (1980) Implications of socio-economic, demographic, and cultural changes for regional development in northern Thailand. In Ives JD, Sabhasri S, Vorauri P, eds, Conservation and development in northern Thailand, pp 13-17. Tokyo: UNU.

43. Lawrence JCD (1970) The Iteso. In Cotran, E, Rubin N, eds, Readings in Afr Law vol. 1, pp 348-351. London: Frank Cass & Co. Ltd.

44. Leach TA (1919) Date trees in Haifa Province. Sudan Notes and Records 2:98-104.

45. Leakey LSB (1977) The southern Kikuyu before 1903 vol I. London: Academic Press.

46. Liversage V (1945) Land tenure in the colonies. Cambridge: Cambridge University Press.

47. Lloyd PC (1962) Yoruba land law. London: Oxford University Press.

48. Lumpungu K (1977) Land tenure system and the agricultural crisis in Zaire. Afr Environment II(4), III(4):57-71.

49. Meek CK (1968) Land law and custom in the colonies 2nd edition. London: Frank Cass & Co. Ltd. 1949.

50. Lin M and Cai S (1980) A brief account of forestry development in the people's communes in Shao-Qing prefecture Guandong province, China. In Report of the FA/SIDA seminar on forestry in rural community development, pp 121-126. Rome: FAO.

51. Michon G, Lombion R, Mary F, Bompard JM (1983) Shall peasant agroforests survive? Paper presented at the BAPI-Suan symposium on research on the impact of development on human activity systems in Southeast Asia. Institute of Ecology, Bandung 8-11 August.

52. Middelton J, Kershaw G (1965) The central tribes of the northeastern Bantu. (The Kikukyu, including Embu, Meru, Mbere, Chuka, Mwimbi, Tharaka, & the Kamba of Kenya.) London: International African Institute.

53. Millon RF (1955) Trade, tree cultivation, and the development of private property in land. American Anthropologist 57:698-712.

54. Mishra A, Tripathi S (1978) Chipko movement. New Delhi: Gandhi Peace Foundation.

55. Mukwaya AB (1953) Land tenure in Buganda. Kampala: The Eagle Press.

56. Murray G (1981) Mountain peasants of Honduras: guidelines for reordering of smallholding adaptation to the pine forest. Tegucigalpa: USAID.
57. Murray GF (1982) Cash-cropping agro-forestry: an anthropological approach to agricultural development in rural Haiti. Presented at the Wingspread conference on Haiti, present state and future prospects, Racine, Wisconsin.
58. Ng'andwe COM (1976) African traditional land tenure and agricultural development: case study of the Kunda people in Jumbe. Afr Soc Research 21:51-67.
59. Obi SN, Chinwuba (1963) The Ibo law of property. London: Butterworths.
60. Ollennu NA (1962) Principles of customary land láw in Ghana. London: Sweet & Maxwell.
61. Panday KK (1976) Importance of fodder trees and tree fodders in Nepal. Zurich: Unpublished thesis, Federal Technical University.
62. Penwill DJ (1951) Kamba customary law. Notes taken in the Machakos district of Kenya colony. London: Macmillan & Company.
63. Pogucki RJH (1970) Gold Coast Land tenure. In Cotran E, Rubin N, eds, Readings in Afr Law vol I, pp 351-355. London: Frank Cass and Co. Ltd.
64. Prins AJ (1961) The Swahili-speaking peoples of Zanzibar and the East African Coast, East Central Africa Part XIII. London: International African Institute.
65. Rattray RS (1956) Ashanti law and constitution. London: Oxford University Press.
66. Roe E, Fortmann L (1982) Season and strategy: the changing organization of the rural water sector in Botswana. Resource Management Monograph No. 1. Ithaca: Cornell University Rural Development Committee.
67. Ruddle K (1974) The Yukpa cultivation system: a study of shifting cultivation in Colombia and Venezuela. Berkeley: University of California Press.
68. Sarbah JM (1968) Fanti customary laws 3rd Edition. London: Frank Cass & Co. Ltd.
69. Schapera I (1943) Native land tenure in the Bechuanaland protectorate. Capetown: The Lovedale Press.
70. Schapera I (1955) A handbook of Tswana law and custom. Oxford: International African Institute.
71. Schebesta P (1973) Among the forest dwarves of Mayla. London: Oxford University Press.

72. Seif el Din AG (1981) Agroforestry practices in the dry regions. In Buck L, ed, Proceedings of the Kenya National Seminar on agroforestry, pp. 419-434, 12-22 November 1980. Nairobi: ICRAF.
73. Sellers S (1977) The relationship between land tenure and agricultural production in Tucurrique, Costa Rica. Turrialba: CATIE.
74. Shambi MM (1972) The problem of land ownership and cashew nut claims in Malindi coastal belt. Unpublished Paper: Kilifi.
75. Skar SL with Samanez NA, Cotarma SG (1982) Fuel availability, nutrition & women's work in highland Peru: Three case studies from contrasting Andean communities. World Employment Programme Research WEPIO/WP23. Geneva: ILO.
76. Snell GS (1954) Nandi customary law. London: MacMillan & Co. Ltd.
77. Spencer JE (1977) Shifting cultivation in Southeast Asia. Berkeley: University of California Press.
78. Stopford, JGE (1901) Glimpses of native law in West Africa. J of the Afr Soc 1(1):80-97.
79. Swanson, RA (1979) Gourmantche Agriculture Part I Land Tenure and Field Cultivation. Integrated Rural Development Project Eastern ORD, B.A.E.P. Upper Volta Contract AID 686-049-78.
80. Tanner R (1960) Land rights on the Tanganyika coast. Afr Stud XIX 14-25.
81. Tate HR (1910) The native law of the southern Gikuyu of British East Africa. Reprinted from J of the Afr Soc:233-254.
82. Thomson JT (1981) Public choice analysis of institutional constraints on firewood production strategies in the West African Sahel. In Russell CS, Nicholson NK, eds, Public choice & rural development. Cambridge: Harvard University.
83. Tozzer AM (1941) Landa's relacion de las cosas de Yucatan. Papers of the Peabody Museum of American Archeology and Ethnology. Cambridge: Harvard University.
84. Uzozie LC (1979) Tradition and change in Igbo food production systems: a geographical appraisal. Unpublished PhD dissertation, University of London.
85. Wagner G (1970) The Bantu of Western Kenya with special reference to the Vugusi and Logoli, vol II. London: Oxford University Press
86. Weinstock JA (1983) Kaharingan and the Luangan Dyaks: religion and identity in central east Borneo. Unpublished PhD dissertation: Cornell University.

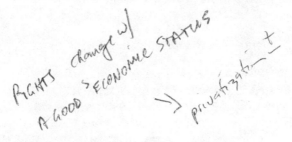

RIGHTS change w/ A GOOD > ECONOMIC STATUS → privatization

Rights in Economic Trees

S.N. Chinwuba Obi

Obi describes customary law regarding economic trees among the Ibo of Nigeria. Under this system rights to self-sown trees differ from those to planted trees. This selection illustrates that rights to trees may be separate from the land on which they are growing. —The Editors.

ECONOMIC TREES

General Principles

One or two general principles stand out clearly in connection with rights and interests over economic trees. We may begin with a short statement of these. It will be noted that these principles are of universal application in two senses of the word: they apply to all economic trees; they also apply to all Ibo societies. The principles are as follows:

(1) If economic trees are self-sown they belong to the owner or owners of the soil on which they grow. But if they are planted by man, they are the property of the person who planted them.[1] It makes no difference on whose land they were planted.[2] Nor is it material that the permission of the landowner was not obtained before the planting was done, bad faith apart. In all cases where a person plants economic trees on another's land, the landowner has no right over the trees or their produce. In normal cases he can only ask the owner to cut the trees down if they interfere with his beneficial use of his land. If this request is refused, he has a legal right to cut them down himself. This happens especially where bad faith is suspected, for example, where the planter is likely to lay claim to the land itself, using the presence

Excerpted from S.N. Chinwuba Obi. 1963. *The Ibo Law of Property.* London: Butterworths. pp. 89-94. Reprinted with the permission of the publisher.

of his trees thereon as circumstantial evidence, or again where a comparative stranger had planted permanent trees on another's land.

(2) Sale or other transfer of land does not necessarily carry with it any rights or interests in economic trees growing thereon. Thus in the absence of express agreement to the contrary, the vendor, pledger or lessor of land retains full rights over all economic plants on it, including the right to go on the land in question for the purpose of enjoying these rights, e.g., harvesting the year's crops. Similarly, on apportionment of communal, or family land, the trees remain in common ownership, unless and until arrangements are made for their distribution.[3] If a person is allowed to live on another's land, and he plants permanent economic trees there (with or without permission), they are his for ever.[4] Even if he ultimately moves to another site, he retains exclusive and heritable rights over the trees and their produce.[5]

Classification of Economic Trees

Ibo law accords differential treatments to different types of trees. It is therefore essential that economic trees be properly classified if confusion on the one hand and tiresome repetition on the other are to be avoided. Various attempts at classification have been made with varying degrees of success... The most ambitious treatment seems to be that of Chubb,[8]...[whose] result may be likened to a number of intersecting circles with not a few perplexing overlappings. He says that trees can be classified as follows:

(1) household palms;
(2) compound palms;
(3) wild palms and groves
(4) scattered palms on farmlands;
(5) plantation palms;
(6) Raffia palms;
(7) plantation trees other than palms;
(8) crop-bearing trees not in plantations;
(9) timber trees.[9]

Thus, the basis of classification is partly territorial (i.e., where the trees grow), partly the origin of the trees (i.e., whether planted by man or self-sown), and partly the source of economic value (i.e., whether fruit-bearing or timber-producing). Since in fact many types of trees do fall into more groups than one at one and the same time, the possibility of confusion is obvious.

Perhaps no single basis of classification can be devised to take care of all economic trees in one swoop. But the classification can easily be done in stages, one basis being used for each stage. The following classification is therefore adopted:

CLASSIFICATION OF ECONOMIC TREES

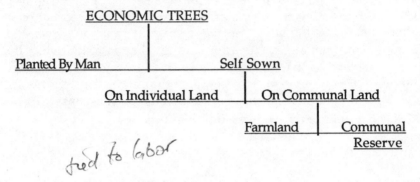

fied to labor

I. <u>Economic trees planted by man.</u>

The most common among these are the oil palm *(nkwu),* the raffia palm sometimes called the wine palm *(ngwo),* the breadfruit tree *(ukwa),* the coconut tree *(aku oyibo, aki bekee),* the pear tree *(ube),* the bana tree *(une, ogede, unele),* the plantain *(jioko, ojoko),* and the oha *(ora)* tree[*] . The general rule about trees of this category is that they are all individually owned by the person who planted them and his heir or heirs... It makes no difference where the trees are planted— whether near the home or away from it. Nor does it matter on whose land they were planted.[10] If the landowner happens to be different from the planter, the only remedy open to the former is to get the latter to remove the tree. In appropriate cases (already discussed) he can do so himself. But he cannot sell, pledge or harvest the trees without the consent of their owner. If a landowner disposes of the land in favour of a third party, whether temporarily or permanently, he retains full proprietary and beneficial rights and interests in all planted trees thereon, unless an express agreement on the matter was reached to the contrary. In the same way, it has been said, even if a man leaves his village, "he may lose his rights over his land, but he does not lose his rights over his trees."[11] But on this rule more will be said *infra* under 2(a).

---

[*] Obi does not provide the Latin name of the *oha* tree. According to Alfred Igboodipe, it is probably *Ceiba Pentandra.*

What happens if a member of a landowning group, say a villager, plants an economic tree on communal land? Does he possess exclusive rights over it, or do different legal principles apply here? The answer is that if he plants such a tree[12] without interference from the group or its head, he acquires and retains exclusive rights over it. These rights are transmissible to his heirs.[13]

II. Trees not planted by man.
The legal rules which govern these vary according as the trees stand on (a) individual holdings, or (b) communal holdings.

a. Self-sown trees growing on individual holdings.
These, like those planted by man anywhere, are individually owned. They are the exclusive property of the landowner. He retains his ownership even after he has parted with ownership or possession of the land itself to a third party. But, and here is the all-important difference which eludes many a foreign student of Ibo law, if a landowner abandons his holding and moves to another socio-political group for good in circumstances wherein the land reverts to his former group, then his rights and interests in both the land *and the trees* terminate. We therefore have the interesting rule that whereas an emigrant can still enjoy the produce of trees which he **planted** before his change of "domicile" he has no such rights over self-sown trees. Similarly, in a dispute over an economic tree which appeared for the first time while A was a tenant or pledgee on B's land, the focal point of interest would naturally be on whether the tree was *akuku* (i.e., a planted tree) or *osis dalu ndam* (a tree that fell "from nowhere"). *Akuku* of course belongs to the tenant-planter, while *osisi ndam* is the property of the landowner.

An exception to the general rule that trees growing on individual holdings belong to the landowner (unless planted by a third party) is said to be found among the people of Ngwa in Aba Division. There, according to Forde and Scott, *palms* growing on "private" land are thrown open to common exploitation for certain periods of the year.[14] But whether this practice is of ancient origin or a modern invention does not appear. Moreover it is not clear whether any distinction is drawn by the Ngwa between palms planted by man and those that are not. It would be strange, to say the least, if plantation palms grown at great expense are thrown open to all comers, along with straggling semi-wild palms.

b. Economic trees growing wild on communal reserve land.

Trees of this class are the joint property of all eligible members of the landowning group. The individual's rights therein are limited to freedom to act in common with others in accordance with recognized rules pertaining to harvesting and appropriation of the produce. These rules vary from place to place. In some places, palm trees are the subject of special rules.[15] In others all economic trees are on the same footing. Thus, in Umucke Agbaja, all palm trees on communal land are open to all members of the village group to harvest. In Ngwa, special days are set apart for the harvesting of palm nuts, while no restriction appears to be placed on the exploitation by the public of other economic trees on communal land. The general rule, however, is that, in the absence of local regulations to the contrary, all rights and interests in economic trees of this class are open and free to all full members of the landowning group. A corollary from this rule is that the group is at liberty to make such rules as to the manner and times of the actual enjoyment of beneficial interests in the trees, as it pleases.[16] But the onus of proving the existence of local regulations which oust the general rule is on the party asserting it.

c. Economic trees growing wild on communal farmland.

Ownership of trees of this kind is also in the landowning group *qua* group. And while the land lies fallow, the same rule as to freedom to harvest subject to agreed restrictions holds good. The only difference is to be noticed where the farmland is actually under cultivation. During this period the individual who actually farms the area around a given tree has exclusive rights over it. This rule probably had its origin in the desire to prevent damage to crops by one member exercising his right of entry among another member's growing crops.

NOTES

1. [Editors' note: Obi's citation system is arcane and somewhat difficult to retrace. Sources are reproduced as is. Citations have been augmented where possible. It was not always possible]
Rowling, C.W. 1948. *Notes on Land Tenure in Benin, Kuruku, Ishan & Asabs Divisions of Benin Province*, (no place, no publisher[eds.]) p. 89;
Meek, C.K.. 1937. *Law and Authority in a Nigerian Tribe* p. 172;
Chubb, L.T. 1948. *Ibo Land Tenure* pp. 99-115;
Green, M.M. 1941, *Land Tenure in an Ibo Village* pp 20-21.

2. Chubb, L.T., ibid. p. 108.
3. Meek, C.K. [no date, eds.] *Land Tenure and Land Administration in Nigeria and Cameroons,,* pp. 172-173;
    Field in *Man,* Vol. LXV, No. 47, 1945.
4. Green, *Land Tenure in an Ibo Village ,* pp. 18-21, especially p. 21.
5. *Ibid.,* p. 32
8. *Op. cit.,* p. 99
9. *Ibid ,* p. 99
10. But see the discussion on *mala fides* and strangers, p. 89.
11. Meek, C.K., 1937. *op. cit.,* p. 171.
12. Meek, *ibid.,* adds "and keeps the ground around [it] cleared of grass."
13. Meek, *op. cit..* p. 1172; Rowling, *op. cit. ,* para. 89.
14. Forde and Scott. 1946. *Native Economics in Nigeria ;* C.F. Chubb, *op. cit. ,* para 103, who includes "compound palms."
15. E.g. Agbaaja, *Vide*
    Green, M.M. 1941. *Land Tenure in an Ibo Village,* p. 18.
16. The landowning group may, of course, decide to "show" these trees to strangers or even to some of its members who would exploit their produce exclusively in consideration of an agreed rent paid in money or in kind.

The Law of Property Rights Regarding Miscellaneous Produce

Hans Cory

> *Cory describes customary law regarding property rights in trees among the Sukuma of northern Tanzania. The system is a good illustration of trees being held separately from the land, of the rights to trees varying with the tenure of the land where they are found,and of differences in the rights of local residents and outsiders. —The Editors*

PRODUCE OF THE BUSH

Fruit, Honey, Beeswax, Gum

Wild fruits in the bush are free to everyone.

Honey and wax of wild bees may be collected by any inhabitant of the area.

A stranger is not allowed to collect honey and wax without the permission of the headman.

The maker of a beehive is the owner of the honey and wax of the bees which have settled in the hive.

The collection of gum is free to everyone, Sukuma or non-Sukuma.

NOTE. To reach a wild bees' nest, pegs are driven into the trunk of the tree to serve as a ladder. Any man who does this has a right to collect the honey and wax.

Excerpted from Hans Cory. 1953. *Sukuma Law and Custom.* London: Oxford University Press. pp. 134, 145-146. Reprinted with the permission of the publisher.

Grass, Building-poles, Fuel

The collection of these commodities is free to everyone, except in areas which are expressly closed, such as *ngitiri* [grazing reserve] or forest reserves.

The collection of fuel is free to everyone, even in another man's holding, except in (the Nyanza group of chiefdoms) where dry branches of a tree are the property of the holder.

Trees

Trees which a man has planted or trees growing on the land allotted to him are his property.

If a man wishes to make a tree plantation he can only do so on the three acres of his *ngitiri* which he is always allowed to retain. . .

NOTE. [These rules] were decided upon by chiefs of the Sukuma Federation and their people in 1949. Formerly no rules existed.

If a man has acquired an *igobe* [big estate] on which are trees (*mihushi* area), he cannot keep more than two acres as his private forest reserve if the community decides to claim the rest of the *mihushi* area from him.

IMMOVABLE PROPERTY

Trees

The same rules are applied with regard to trees which the occupier has planted himself and trees which he found on the land when it was allotted to him.

NOTE. There are no individual trees of ritual importance in Sukuma. There is, however, a superstition that if a man cuts a tree which has been left standing for some purpose by his predecessor he may suffer a loss. Certain species of tree play a part in the rites of some dance societies and a member may be reluctant to cut down such trees.

If a man relinquishes his holding the trees thereon revert, together with the holding, to the community.

• *Trees in the homestead.*

Trees planted in the immediate vicinity of the house are considered to be part of the homestead and therefore cannot be sold separately. If the house is sold in accordance with the [prevailing] rules, such trees may be considered improvements to the house. The occupier, if he relinquishes his holding, can ask for compensation from the new occupier for the value of the trees. If the new occupier cannot or will not pay for the trees, the outgoing holder can cut and sell them.

• *Fruit-trees in the Migunda.*
A man can sell a plot of fruit-trees within his holding unless the trees are planted in the immediate vicinity of his house. . . If he sells the plot, it is understood that he has sold only the trees and not the land. If the buyer does not ask the authority that the land between the trees may be allotted to him, such land can be allotted for cultivation to any applicant.

NOTE. It often happens that one man owns the mango-trees which are planted at wide intervals and another man cultivates the ground between them.

If a man sells trees, either while he is still occupying his holding or when he intends to relinquish it, he must inform the authority about the transaction and name the buyer.

NOTE. If the buyer of trees should be considered by the community to be undesirable as a settler, he is not allotted the land between the trees, or any other land.

• *Sisal and trees other than fruit-trees in the Migunda.*
The occupier can cut such trees and sell them and remain in occupation of the plot. He can also sell the standing trees to be cut within a short time, if he relinquishes the plot.
The plot from which trees have been sold for immediate cutting reverts after the cutting to the community. The buyer of the trees has no right to any trees which may afterwards grow on the plot.
An occupier cannot sell trees for any purpose other than immediate cutting, whether he is retaining occupation of the land or intending to relinquish his holding.
If a man sells sisal poles the buyer has no right to the sisal plants after he has cut the poles.

Date-Trees in Halfa Province

T. A. Leach

Arising out of the author's experience in Sudan, this is one of the earliest detailed descriptions of multiple ownership of trees based on both Islamic rules of inheritance and rules involving tree planting. The author's ethno-centric exasperation with a system different from Anglo-Saxon law permeates the piece. —The Editors.

For a Land Settlement Officer or Inspector in charge of a Date Census in Halfa Province it is impossible to see the wood for the trees; it is even difficult for him to see the trees owing to his preoccupation with the parts thereof.   The present article therefore being written entirely from the point of view of the Land Settlement Officer will deal with no general questions of interest concerning date-trees, such as methods of culture, the different species of dates, the value of a tree's yield or facilities for market or export....

The existing [indigenous] system of ownership and some of the customs... come within the scope of this article, though it will be necessary also to give some account of the ways in which official record is kept of such ownership, and of the method of settling disputes.

The [people] of Halfa Province, with the exception of a few merchants and others in Halfa town and two small outside villages of Gararish Arabs, are exclusively Berberines.

The main characteristics are generally well known. The great majority of the male population are employed away from their homes as servants, *saises, raises*, boatmen, etc., while their women and old men, aided by monetary contributions from those away, eke out a meagre existence on narrow strips of cultivated land squeezed in between the desert and the river, such as may be seen along all the river bank from Halfa to Shellal.

Sudan Notes and Records 2 (1919): 98-104

But the one constant source of pride and object of desire of the absent Berberine is the possession of a share in such a small holding of land, or more particularly in a date-tree.

For these Lilliputian estates are seldom owned by a single individual, and there is nothing in the province too small to be divided.

The question naturally arises. "How can a date-tree be divided up into parts? Or what is the use to a man of owning (say) 3/16 of an indivisible entity like a date-tree?"

The explanation is simple. The principle comes into practical application only when the crop is gathered, and it is the fruit that is divided up each year among the several owners. Even when as will be seen later there are several trees subject to the most complicated cross-division of different partners, the registration of which entails elaborate mathematical calculations to arrive at the proper fractions, the division is probably into three heaps representing the three equal shares of the original owners. One of these thirds is possibly owned now by several heirs of the original owner, and it may be necessary to divide this heap into elevenths. Moh[amme]d Ahmed, one of them, takes his share which is two of these small heaps and goes off with it. Meanwhile the fruit of another tree of which he owns 1/2 has been collected and put in a separate heap for him—and he takes this off and pours it into his own separate individual heap, and so on for all the trees in which he has a share. At the end he has all the dates he is entitled to from different trees collected into one heap, and he has never had to trouble his mind in the least as to the working out of the sum 2/11 of 1/3 of 5 + 1/8 + 1/5 of 1/2 of 7 or whatever it may be. The registration of his ownership is a different thing, but of that later.

The question next arises how did this complicated system of division arise? Why does a man not plant a tree for himself and keep it as his own, at any rate until he dies? Since the land was settled, a tendency to do this is to be noticed. But the number of such trees compared to the vast number of older trees is as a drop in the ocean, and the force of habit is too strong to allow even this practice on a small scale to continue long. One way which would naturally be expected to be a frequent cause of division, is that a man being in need of money, but disliking the thought of parting from the whole of his property, might sell half a tree. This however was a very rare occurrence, and was only resorted to occasionally in cases of real distress and only in Mahas, the poorest part of the Province. It may however have become more common in or since the bad year of 1913-1914. In ordinary circumstances it was a disgrace to sell either land or date-trees. Sale may therefore be ruled out as an important cause of the division of trees, though gifts, as to a son or to a wife for dowry, are not uncommon.

The main causes are as follows:

I.　　The general custom as to planting, especially in former times and before the Land Settlement.

II.　　The Mohammedan law of inheritance.

III.　　The pride of ancestry, and the innate reluctance of the people to part with anything.

I.　The classical method of planting a date-tree is as follows:　A obtains shoot and plants it; B in whose land it is planted receives 1/3 of it; C who waters it (in its early years when it would otherwise never survive till maturity) 1/3, leaving A himself with 1/3 only.

There are, of course, many variations of this basic principle; e.g. A may plant the shoot in his own land and water it himself, in which case he owns the whole of it.　More often B, the owner of the land, having a *Sagia**　waters the shoot and so receives 2/3.　In some cases the land chosen is particularly good for date-trees, and by special agreement B receives 1/2 instead of 1/3 only.

In former days it seems seldom to have been the rule for the land owner to be specially consulted. It would often have been an understood thing that he would receive 1/3 of the tree, but frequently this was not the case, and probably the right to claim the 1/3 was in many cases waived in favour of a friend or in return for the right of planting a tree in the other's land.　During the Land Settlement when claims were put forward in the case of trees of some age, that is at least over 5 years, to 1/3 of any tree on the land purely on the strength of the old custom, the rule followed was that the land-owner must definitely prove that the 1/3 had been actually received in the past or the existence of a specific agreement to that effect.　In more recent times it would have been impossible to plant a shoot in another man's land without his consent.

B (the land-owner) is of course, where every *"sagia"* or plot of land is owned by several partners, frequently not a single individual but may represent all of the owners of a *"sagia."* In that case B's 1/3 has to be subdivided among all the partners in proportion to the shares of each in the land.

This leads us to some description of the different methods of ownership of the land which is occupied specially by date-trees. Such land goes by the general name of *mashghul* (worked, or occupied), or *mashghul el nakhil* (date-trees) and consists nearly always of the

---

* *Sagia* can refer both to a water wheel and to the higher land which is watered by the water wheel, as opposed to land which is watered by flooding for recessional agriculture. (eds.)

foremost strip of the sagia land on the river bank where the roots of the trees when full grown reach to water level....

The *mashghul* is generally an integral part of the *sagia*. Where it is full of old full-grown trees, the sagia owners have little control and as they have nothing to gain out of it they generally, to the detriment of the yield of the trees, take care that they lose nothing either by watering it for the benefit of others. Where there is still space for planting new trees or the trees are mostly the property of the land-owners, the *mashghul* is generally divided up among the partners separately from the rest of the sagia, but as far as possible in proportion to their shares in it. This is a frequent cause of dispute—when one partner is dissatisfied with his portion as being largely occupied by the trees of one or more of his partners, and he claims from the "land-owner's right" to 1/3 of the trees in his own special portion. However he is generally satisfied without resort to this further complication.

The *mashghul* is also frequently a separate plot and not part of any sagia. In many such cases in Halfa District the land is the actual property of the owners of the trees on it, and the owner of every tree or part of a tree is the owner of a share in the land proportionate to the number of trees or parts of a tree or trees he owns. The difficulties which can be raised by a cantankerous partner against any proposal to deal with any portion of such land can be easily imagined. Fortunately in other parts of the Province even where the *mashghul* is a separate plot, it is owned by definite persons whose shares are fixed without reference to the number of trees they may or may not own in it.

To return now to our original shoot which was planted by A on land owned by B and watered by C, we should have little difficulty in recognizing it at any time and tracing its history however much subdivided if it only remained single. But the trouble is that when it grows up it becomes the mother of a clump (Arabic *bura* or *hufra.*) the small shoots which start from its root are seldom cut off by the [indigenous] grower who is more interested in the possession of a large number of trees than in proper palm-culture. In this way one original shoot may grow into a clump consisting of anything up to ten trees, and the clump is always identical as to ownership with the original mother tree. The number of trees in a clump perpetually varies as additional young trees come on, or older trees die off, so that from census to census (an interval of five years) the identification of the trees becomes exceedingly difficult for an outsider.

In the course of the years 1907-1911 the first complete register of individual owners of trees was carried out. Previous censuses had been merely an approximate record for purposes of tax collection only, and trees had been shown in the name of the most important of many partners who were made responsible for the tax. To record all the owners the use of the complicated fractions referred to above was indispensible. But it was impossible to show every tree or clump separately, and for the purposes of the census all the trees in a sagia or similar registered plot of land are shown together. You get thus Mohamed Khalil recorded as the owner of 3 3/4 trees in *Sagia* no. 49, though in fact he has not probably a single whole tree in the world, the 3 3/4 representing the sum of the fractions of single trees or clumps in which he has a share in that *Sagia*. Even if you find Ahmed Ali with one tree to his name in the register, it is probably 1/3 of a clump of 3, or 1/2 + 1/3 + 1/6 of 3 different trees. In spite of these complications however it is generally fairly easy to identify for the purposes of a lawsuit which trees or part of a tree are in dispute, but when it comes to the next quinquennial counting, by which time the number of mature trees is considerably altered, it is unfortunately difficult to obtain much assistance from the older register.

II. The second chief cause of petty divisions, the Mohammedan law of inheritance, is too familiar to require more than the mere statement: the Quadi's documents recording the divisions of an estate are generally very conscientious and thorough, and in order to give no one a share more or less than his due, they employ fractions which are the despair of the Registrar. For strictly correct registration, fractions containing 6 or 7 figures in the numerator and denominator would be nothing.

III. We have now seen how the partition of trees into exiguous fractions arose historically from the customs of the people and the nature of the palm, and how on another side it has been developed to exaggeration by the sanction of ecclesiastical law... The obvious way of getting over these inconveniences would be for the partners and especially co-heirs to come to terms whereby each partner would take a whole tree or trees in one place instead of all retaining fractions of trees scattered all over a village or district, inequalities of value between different trees being rectified by cash payment, or by exchange of chattels or of land in the same way...

However, when all is said and done, it must be remembered that the system practically insures against entire loss of crop by spreading the risks and that the [people] do not feel the inconvenience of the divisions to any great extent, since they are mainly concerned only with the distribution of the dates, and the real sufferers are only the judicial and administrative staff. A register is of no value unless it gives a complete and accurate record of actual ownership, and as the ownership is of the nature explained the register is bound to follow it. The lack of a Register is (*experto crede*) desolation; and an incomplete Register is the worst state of all, causing injustice among the people, for the rights of the deserving may be lost eternally because they are not recorded in the book.

Religious Custom and Tree Rights

Lynn Bennett

*Bennett relates how religious custom in Nepal can have the
effect of turning trees planted on private land into an open-
access resource. This is a classic example of how statutory laws
governing property rights may be overridden by local custom --
religious or otherwise.—The Editors.*

One's rice, wheat, or corn crops are fundamental to survival. There
would be severe sanctions from the village community on any one who
pilfered from the standing grain crop and likewise the "borrowing" of
grain from another household incurs serious obligation.

Fruits and vegetables, on the other hand, do not fall into the same
category as the staple grains. They are somehow "extra." They are
luxuries. Moreover, like flowers, they are considered appropriate
offerings for the gods. Hence, there is intense social pressure on
villagers to distribute these crops to anyone who asks, especially if the
person is going to make a religious offering. By the same token,
villagers must tolerate heavy pilfering of fruit and vegetable crops by
young children. There is no question of expecting a child's parents to
discipline him or her for stealing fruit. It may be annoying, but it is in
the category of a child's prank rather than a theft (as grain stealing
would be). In fact, there is a special festival in celebration of the young
Lord Krishna's fruit stealing when even grown men raid their
neighbor's gardens at night.

As an example of how this attitude discourages horticulture, there
is the case of Jagat Man Thapa, the head of one of our sample households. Eleven years ago he took a loan for Rs. 10,000 from the

Excerpted from: Lynn Bennett. 1981. *The Parbatiya Women of
Bakundal: The Status of Women in Nepal.* Volume II, Part 7: 174-175
Kathmandu Centre for Economic Development and Administration.
Reprinted with the permission of the author.

Agriculture Bank to start an orange orchard. Since the Bakundol climate is apparently good for citrus growing and there are nearby markets where oranges fetch a rupee apiece, the venture should have brought good returns. Part of the problem has been the lack of good extension service to teach him how to prune and fertilize the trees which are now mature. But Jagat Man explains that his main problem is the local children who steal the fruit while it is still green, coupled with his obligation to give fruit to his neighbors for their religious worship. By the time the neighbors have taken their "share" he hardly has any fruit to sell and has actually had to sell land to pay back part of the loan.

This is a rather extreme case—and in fact the women in Jagat Man's household voiced the opinion that he should simply be less charitable—but it does suggest that one of the major constraints to more active interest in kitchen gardening and orchards may be the prevailing social attitudes. In order for horticulture to reach its full potential in villages like Bakundol it may be necessary to expand the conceptual categories of both "food" (to include fruits and vegetables) and "theft" (to include raids on the orchard or vegetable patch)!

A Survey of Customary Law and Control Over Trees and Wildlands in China

Nicholas Menzies

Over the last 150 years prevalent Western perceptions have held that the Chinese failed to manage or protect forestland. Menzies shows that historically, wildland utilization was in fact carefully controlled, and that areas of extensive production were given attention separate from that given to agricultural land. It is particularly notable that common forest lands were sometimes managed specifically by local communities for community benefit.—The Editors.

INTRODUCTION

Wildlands represent two-thirds of China's land base. These are lands unmodified by human activities, or where human intervention has been limited to actions that enhance the productivity of desired components of the natural ecosystem, rather than converting it to another form of production such as agriculture. Wildlands have always been the agricultural frontier of China. Usually they have been dismissed as "wastelands" (*huang di**), of no importance. Marginal lands, though, are rarely wasted Often they are a source of essential resources such as fuelwood and fodder for nearby communities, which regulate their use through a variety of control mechanisms such as village councils, unwritten rules, and internal social pressure. The wildlands of China are no exception to this rule, and they provide examples of customary law applied to the land itself and to other common property resources such as fish and migratory birds.

Written for this volume.

* Author's note: Here, and subsequently, Pinyin Romanizations of Chinese language terms are used.

51

This chapter raises two questions about the management of wild-lands, trees, and tree crops in China over the last century and a half, a period of apparently ubiquitous deforestation. Were property rights in wildlands treated differently from rights in agricultural lands, and more specifically, was a distinction made between rights in trees, and rights in the land on which they grew? Secondly, what form did control and regulation of wildlands take? What were the social fences surrounding the commons? These systems of control appear to be concentrated in several distinct areas of the country. This geographical distribution may be related to a specific set of ecological and socio-economic conditions existing in those areas. The study of Chinese law is hampered however, by the lack of accessible documentary evidence such as parish records and legal archives that researchers in the West find such an invaluable source of information. Information on Chinese wildlands and law is both limited and fragmentary, and any conclusions I have drawn here remain at the level of informed speculation until more sources become available.

PAST VIEWS OF CHINA'S WILDLANDS: DID THE CHINESE HATE TREES?

Erosion and sedimentation following deforestation and the removal of natural vegetation cover are particularly destructive in the rice growing areas of South China. Terraced rice agriculture depends on regular flows from stream-fed irrigation systems. Deforestation disrupts stream flows and may cause springs to dry up, while sediment from eroded hillsides clogs canals and reservoirs, increasing the chances of destructive flooding. As early as the thirteenth century, officials complained of damage being caused to lowland agriculture by forest clearance upstream (Wei Xian, 1242: 1.6b). In later centuries attempts were made, usually with little success, to prevent migrants from planting crops such as maize and sweet potatoes on easily eroded hillsides (Chen Qiaoyi, 1983). When Western naturalists and botanists began working in China during the late nineteenth and early twentieth centuries, they reported widespread deforestation and environmental degradation (Fortune, 1857; Wilson, 1913; Père David, 1949). The situation appeared to be so serious that E.H. Wilson was prompted to write that soon "there will not be an acre of accessible forest left in all central, southern and western China" (Wilson, 1913: I.246).

Many observers, looking at the apparently relentless destruction of the forests and wildlands, blamed the Chinese people, concluding that they suffered from a cultural bias against forests, describing them as 'destructive', 'ruthless', or even as having an innate hatred of trees

(Fortune, 1857: 177-178; Rosenbluth, 1912). An alternative view was that deforestation in China was inevitable due to the pressures of a rapidly expanding population, coupled with what was believed to be ignorance of the principles of scientific forest and land management (Fenzel, 1929). In either case, the assumption was that at no time, and in no place, had the Chinese shown themselves to be capable of regulating and controlling the use of wildlands and their resources.

In a dissenting view, some writers pointed to groves of trees in southern China, protected for geomantic reasons, that were carefully managed to supply timber and to protect water catchments. Lowdermilk noted in a study of land use around the sacred mountain of Wu Tai Shan that over a period of five centuries there had been successive episodes of deforestation followed by careful management (Lowdermilk and Wickes, 1938). Recent research has shown that techniques of forestry have been known and practised in China for millennia (Gan Duo, 1964; Menzies, 1985), and that wildlands were far from always being unregulated, open access commons (Fu Yiling, 1980). Distinct patterns of property rights and tenurial arrangements did exist to accommodate the peculiar characteristics of wildlands and of tree crops. Even E. H. Wilson noted the existence of complex property rights with regard to an economically valuable species such as the lacquer tree (*Rhus vernificula* Stokes) where the trees "are the property of the ground landlord and not of the tenant who holds the land". The tenant had to tend the tree and extract the lacquer exudate which was then claimed by the landlord (Wilson, 1929: 352).

STATUTORY LAW AND CUSTOMARY LAW

In the case of wildlands, the scarcity of documentary records is compounded by the emphasis of Chinese and non-Chinese scholars on agricultural and urban lands. Searches through a variety of different sources have shown, however, that use of wildlands was often subject to controls through the medium of statutory law as well as customary law.

Before considering customary law, it is worth glancing at the status of wildlands, forest lands, and tree crops in statutory law. A seventeenth century legal handbook for magistrates, the *Fu Hui Quan Shu,* classifies land in categories that include 'mountain land' and 'marshland' (Djang Chu, 1984: 35). 'Wasteland,' usually described as abandoned land, is discussed as land to be brought under individual ownership and thus into cultivation (1984: 176-177). Trees and tree crops are mentioned only in passing with a note that "profit from fruit trees is not taxable" (1984: 545), with some traditional Confucian exhortations to plant mulberry trees (for silkworms) and elm trees (for firewood) (1984: 546-547), and with some equally traditional admonitions that magistrates should ensure that roadside trees are planted and maintained (1984: 547).

Allocation of Rights and Tenure in Wildlands

Specialized names are found for many different categories of land in compilations of customary law. 'Mountain side' (*Shan Chang*), and 'wasteland' (*Huang Di*) are terms used in contrast to 'grain fields' (*Liang Tian*), which indicate that it was felt that special tenurial arrangements were necessary at the margins of settlement and intensive agriculture. There was even a special term to designate the owner of wildlands, 'The Mountain Lord' (*Shanzhu*), as opposed to the more common term, landlord (*Dizhu*), the owner of agricultural land.

Where tenants were given the task of clearing land for agriculture, they could be allowed up to three years' free use of the land before they had to pay rent, and they were often granted a share of any revenue from the trees that had to be cut down (Wu, 1962: 2.3. 29b; 2.5. 1b; 2.5. 17a). Of more interest to a study of tree tenure and the management of forested land are the conditions under which tenants held land that was used for valuable forest products such as timber or mushrooms and edible fungi. The most striking difference between tenancy in these areas and in agricultural areas was the length of tenancy contracts. In some areas of Jiangxi, for example, contracts for land to be planted to sweet potatoes and other agricultural crops, were usually for three to five years, with a maximum of ten years. If the land was planted to Pine trees and to Cunninghamia (*Cunninghamia Lanceolata* Hooker) (*Sha Mu*), the contract was open-ended, allowing the security of tenure needed to grow trees (Wu, 1962. 1.3. 25b).

The separation of usufruct rights and property rights to the land itself is common in Chinese customary law. It is seen under many guises, but in all cases, the trees on the land are treated separately from the land itself. Under the system of 'two landlords to one field' (*Yi Tian Liang Zhu*) which was especially common in Fujian province (Fu Yiling, 1961; Morita, 1976), the land itself was the property of the ground landlord who rented it to a tenant. The tenant could not sell the land itself, but was free to mortgage or sell the surface rights on the land. Separate allocation of rights seems to have acted as an incentive to growing crops of timber or bamboo, as in this example from Le'an County, Jiangxi Province:

> In mountainous country, where there is timber and bamboo, there is a distinction between the 'skin' of the mountain and the 'bones' of the mountain. The property rights in bamboo and timber are called the 'skin' of the mountain. The property rights in the land itself,

are called the 'bones' of the mountain. The owner of the rights to the skin of the mountain only needs to pay 'mountain rent' every year to the owner of the rights to the bones of the mountain. There is no time limit. The owner of the rights to the bones of the mountain may not take the land back, nor may he plant trees and bamboo for himself. ... There is no charge to be paid when the land is returned. Furthermore, rights to the skin and the bones of the mountain may be mortgaged and sold separately.

(Wu, 1962: 2.3 27-30)

The economic value of timber and tree crops, together with a recognition of the long rotation period between harvests, led to trees being treated very differently from other crops. When associated with the concept of separate rights to a resource and its produce, this could lead to some intricate accounting arrangements between landlords and their tenants. It was possible, for example, for a tenant to retain at least a share of the rights to trees on the land after giving up tenancy rights to cultivate the land itself, as in one example from Shunchang County, Fujian Province where the planter received sixty percent of the revenue, and the landowner received forty percent (Wu, 1962:2.3.35b).

If land rent was to be paid for some years immediately after trees were planted, tenants would interplant subsistence crops until the tree canopy closed. Where some form of agroforestry seems to have been practiced, there were still more detailed systems for rent assessment. Apparently it was quite common to determine rents separately for the annual inter-crop and the timber, with its longer rotations and greater value (Wu, 1962: 2.4.. 42a; 2.5. lb). A particularly complex system is recorded from Queshan County, Henan Province, where mushrooms and edible fungi were cultivated in the forest. The mushrooms were grown on cut logs set in forest clearings, requiring eight years for a commercial crop to mature. During the intervening years, separate tenancy agreements could be reached for the clearings in which logs were set, for the logs and stumps on which the mushrooms grew, and even for the use of space between the logs (presumably a growing area for annual food crops). The mushroom crop was so valuable that a form of futures market is reported for these clearings, where the expected value of the harvest could be used as collateral in securing loans (Wu, 1962: 2.2. 14a).

Customary Law and Community Control of Wildlands

Since Chinese statutory law paid scant attention to wildlands, effective control or regulation over their utilization was in the hands of the users of the resource. Customary law was especially important as a mechanism by which communities could exert control over land. There is some evidence of common property systems, under which the members of a community had rights to use a specified resource or an area of land, sometimes referred to as "unenclosed" (*Wei She Weizhang*) land. It is worth noting though, that most of the records concern the allocation of rights between individual owners or between owners and their tenants. Where some form of commons did exist, restrictions were imposed on access to and the utilization of these lands, especially for grazing, but mechanisms for monitoring and enforcing these regulations are rarely mentioned[1] :

> In Macheng, whenever people have planted trees or have grazed animals, the custom is to say that there is restricted entry to the mountain (*Jin Shan*). Although scrub and other natural vegetation are not enclosed, outsiders are prohibited from gathering and cutting it. The custom in Zhuxi is that in all unenclosed forests and pastures in the mountains, if someone is currently utilizing [the resources], entering the area to gather them, then no outsiders may enter. Even if the user has not yet taken advantage of cutting the fodder, others may still not enter to cut . . .
> (Wu, 1962: 2.4. 39a/b).

A rare example of an institution established to regulate access to wildlands is the "Mountain Council" (*Shan Hui*) in the Gannan region of Jiangxi Province. The reference to these councils simply states that "There is a Mountain Council in every locality [of the Gannan region]". There is no further information about who served on the councils, and whether their only function was to regulate utilization of the commons, or whether they had other duties within the community. The Mountain Council specified that catalpa, a valuable hardwood, could only be cut for a brief period during the autumn, and that any person

---

1 Most references to common resources are very specific. An interesting case concerns the hunting of migrating wildfowl in Anhui. The guano deposited by roosting birds was so valuable as fertilizer that they could only be killed in exceptional circumstances, with permission from the village head. (Wu, 1962: 6.2. 21b - 22a)

violating the regulation would be "expelled" (*Quzhu*) by the head of the council (Wu, 1962: 2.3. 30a).

Most of the examples of "common lands" might better be described as cases of village or communal ownership. In a study of forest management in Shanxi Province, Ren Chengtong (1925) outlined three categories of ownership: ownership by one village, ownership by several villages managing the land collectively, and clan ownership. He felt that the key to the successful management of village forests was that they had clear and unambiguous rules. In one case in particular, the villagers had devised an intricate management system in which silvicultural and organizational management were linked to ensure a sustainable harvest from the forest. The eighteen villages which jointly managed the area of Mian Shan each selected one officer to their management body. The members were then divided into three groups with six officers in each group. One group was responsible for supervising forest management for one year, on a rotating basis. Within each group, one officer was responsible for business for the year, also on a rotating basis. This gave two cycles: a short cycle of three years (with a different committee each year), and a long cycle of eighteen years (with a different business officer each year). At the end of each short cycle, the three committees jointly agreed to a selective harvest of larger trees, while thinning and maintenance were carried out every year under the supervision of that year's committee (Ren, 1925: 5). Two other villages had written charters which the villagers had had inscribed in stone about a century earlier. According to these charters, revenue from the forest was to be used specifically to run and maintain a school for the village children, and there was a clear system of delegation of responsibilities for management to a committee of village members. Decisions were taken by this committee before the whole village at specially convened temple meetings (it is not clear how the committee members were selected).

Osgood (1970:118-119) described a similar system in Yunnan Province, where the village council selected one person to act as forest manager. Osgood notes that the representatives of dominant lineages had a great deal of influence in the selection of the village council, and that the job of forest manager was considered a sinecure although it carried few material benefits. The manager's authority seems to have rested on links with both the village council and the State Department of Reconstruction in the provincial capital of Kunming. The duties of the forest manager are described as follows:

The forest manager was charged with looking after the trees reserved to supply the wood necessary as timber for building or other village purposes. When someone wished to buy a tree, the price was determined by the manager who then reported it to the council in order to discover if there were any objections ... It was the manager's duty to have new trees planted, and he paid someone to do the work ... The manager had also to see that the grass was burned in the village forest and to report to the government in the event that any trees were stolen.

(Osgood, 1970, pg. 119)

In all these cases, there is a clear distinction between those who are entitled to use the resource and those who are not, with those who may not use it being described as outsiders. The threat of exclusion from the community seems to have been the most important form of sanction, although it is not clear whether a term such as "expulsion" meant exclusion from the community of authorized users, or literal expulsion from the village. It seems that a close-knit community structure would have been needed, both to monitor who was using the resource, and for the threat of exclusion to have any punitive force.

DISCUSSION

Chinese customary law distinguished between wildlands and agricultural lands. Tenancy contracts in these areas were frequently drawn up for a longer period than on agricultural lands and separate rights were allocated to trees and to the land on which they stood. Under these conditions, a distinctive pattern of resource utilization was possible which allowed for both subsistence cropping and for the production of cash crops such as timber.[2]

Conversion of wildlands to agricultural use demands a high input of labor, for small initial returns. It is understandable that a 'Mountain Lord' might feel obliged to offer some incentives in terms of reduced rental payments, in order to attract tenants. It is less immediately obvious why there should be incentives to tenants to manage land for timber and other forest products which do not yield annual revenues. The geographical distribution of most of the recorded examples of customary law may be of some significance in answering this question, although the limited nature of the evidence demands caution in presenting any hypothesis.

---

2 Separation of usufruct rights and rights to the resource base were common in resource systems based on water where rights to the water, to mud (used as fertilizer), and to fish could be held separately (Wu, 1962: 11.3. 17b; 2.4. 35a - 35b).

The majority of the examples in which a distinction is drawn between the 'skin' and the 'bones' of the mountain come from regions of south China, and especially from Fujian, Jiangxi, and Jiangsu provinces. These regions were at the margins of settled agriculture, remote, hilly, and sparsely settled. China as a whole, may have appeared to be densely populated, but labor was scarce in the mountains. To compound the problem, the rebellions of the nineteenth century had devastated these same parts of South China. At least one example of customary law is quite explicit about the need to attract tenants (the example is from Jiangxi Province):

There are two categories of fields in Gannan: Grain Fields, and Rented Fields. . . . In the case of the Rented Fields, the [original] inhabitants fled in the past when the area was looted and burned by soldiers, abandoning their fields. The land was then claimed by settlers from outside who tried to attract people to come and open it up.

(Wu, 1962: 2.3.28b)

Irrigated, terraced rice cultivation was out of the question then, and extensive land use may have been the only possible way for a landlord to realize any revenue at all from these "wastelands."

Finally, the question of enforcement must be examined. I have suggested that the most common way in which the utilization of wildlands was controlled and regulated was through the medium of a distinct set of tenurial conditions that acted as an incentive to produce trees and forest products. Contracts between tenant and landlord defined the obligations of both parties, and any breaches in these contracts were presumably dealt with in the same way as other contracts. There remain the cases of communal or community control of resources. Sanctions against offenders are mentioned but few details are given about the form these sanctions took. Communities that undertook this form of resource management were sufficiently close-knit that social pressure and the threat of ostracism was a deterrent sufficient to guarantee compliance.

If compliance was to be obtained, then the members of the group with access to the resource had to accept the legitimacy of the organization or the institution responsible for management. It follows, then, that this form of management may be more sensitive to major political and ideological changes in which the legitimacy of such traditional institutions is undermined. This, in fact seems to have been the case in China. Contemporary forest law still recognizes some of the principles of separate rights in the resource base and to its products. On the other hand, village forests, temple forests, and clan forests have largely disappeared since the 1911 Revolution and the successive challenges since 1911 to religious authority, Confucianism, and old social hierarchies.

CONCLUSION

In the face of apparently relentless deforestation during the late nineteenth century, observers occasionally noted that there was some evidence that wildland resources in China were not always squandered, but that utilization could be carefully regulated. Chinese sources, limited as they are, confirm that there was a rich body of customary law which addressed the differences between intensive agriculture and extensive land use systems in marginal areas. Where regulation depended on some form of institutional authority, management has been affected by the political and ideological changes of the last century, leading in many cases to further deforestation. Where customary law was concerned with the allocation of rights to trees and wildlands, the patterns of ownership and incentives which evolved have shown themselves to be remarkably resilient to change, and are still encountered today.

LITERATURE CITED

Works in Chinese and Japanese

Chen Qiaoyi, 1983. Lishi Shang Zhejiang Shengdi Shan Di Kenzhi Yu Shanlin Pohuai. "Historical Reclamation of Mountain Land and Destruction of Mountain Forests in Zhejiang Province."*Zhongguo Shehui Kexue*, 1983 (4), pp. 207-217.

Fu Yiling, 1980. Qingdai Zhongye Chuan Shaan Hu San Sheng Bianqu Jingji Xingtaidi Bianhua. "Changes in the Economic Situation of the Sichuan, Shaanxi, Hubei Border Region during the Middle of the Qing Dynasty." *DuoSuo*, 1980 (5),,, pp. 43-52.

--------- 1961. Ming Qing Nongcun Shehui Jingji. "The Rural Social Economy of the Ming and Qing Dynasties." Peking, San Lian.

Gan Duo et al., 1964. Zhongguo Linye Jishu Shiliao Chubu Yanjiu. "Preliminary Researches into Historical Materials on Forest Technology in China." Peking, Nongye.

Morita Akira, 1976. Minmatsu Shindai no "Homin" ni Tsuite. "Concerning the "Shed People" of the Late Ming and Qing Dynasties." *Jimbun Kenkyu* (Osaka), 28 (9), pp. 1 - 38.

Ren Chengtong (C.T. Jen), 1925. Jingying Cunyou Lindi Haochu he Banfa. "Advantages and Methods of Managing Village-Owned

Forests." Nanking, *Jinling Daxue Senlin Xi* (First Published 1925, repr. 1930, 1935).

Shi Nianhai, 1981. Huangtu Gaoyuan Ji Qi Nong Lin Mu Fenbu Diqudi Bianqian. "The Loess Plateau and Changes in Land Utilization Between the Agricultural, Forest, and Pastoral Areas." *Lishi Dili*, 1981 (1), pp. 21 - 33.

Wei Xian, 1242. "Si Ming Tuo Shan Shuili Beilan" "Irrigation Canals of the Mt. Tuo District." (Using Chongzhen 14 edition, 1642).

Wu Xiangxiang, 1962. Zhongguo Minshi Xiguan Da Quan. "A Compendium of Chinese Popular Customs." Taipei, Wenxing Shudian. (Series 6, Volume 1 of Zhongguo Xiandai Shiliao Congshu.)

Works in Western Languages

David, Père Armand, 1949. *Abbé David's Diary* translated and edited by Helen M. Fox. Cambridge, Harvard University Press.

David, Père Armand, 1872, 1873, & 11874. "Journal d'un Voyage dans Le Centre de la Chine et dans le Thibet Oriental . . ." *Bulletin des Nouvelles Archives du Museum d'Histoire Naturelle de Paris V.* III & IV.

Djang Chu, 1984. *A Complete Book Concerning Happiness and Benevolence.* Translation of "Fu Hui Quan Shu" by Huang Liuhong. Tucson, University of Arizona Press.

Fenzel, G., 1929. "On the Natural Conditions Affecting the Introduction of Forestry as a Branch of the Rural Economy in the Province of Kwangtung, especially in N. Kwantung. "*Lingnan Science Journal*, Canton, 7 (1), pp. 37 - 97.

Fortune, Robert, 1857. *A Residence Among the Chinese; inland, on the coast, and at sea.* London, John Murray.

Lattimore, Owen., 1951. *Inner Asian Frontiers of China.* New York, Capitol Publishing Company and American Geographical Society.

Lowdermilk, W.C. and Wickes, Dean C., 1938. *History of Soil Use in the Wu Tai Shan Area.* Peiping, N. China Branch of the Royal Asiatic Society.

Lowdermilk, W.C., 1930. *Factors Affecting Surficial Run-off of Rainfall and Surface Erosion of Soil Profiles.* Stockholm.

Lowdermilk, W.C., 1926. "Forest Destruction and Slope Denudation in the Province of Shanhsi." *China Journal of Arts and Science*, Vol. 4 (3), pp. 127 - 136.

Menzies, Nicholas., 1985. "The History of Forestry in China." In Volume 6 of J. Needham, *Science and Civilization in China.* Cambridge University Press. (In Press).

Moench, Marcus, 1986. " 'Turf' and Forest Management of a Garhwal Hill Village." This Volume.

Osgood, Cornelius, 1970. *Village Life in Old China. A Community Study of Kao Yao, Yunnan.* New York, The Ronald Press Company.

Rosenbluth, R., 1912. "Forests and Timber Trade of the Chinese Empire." *Forestry Quarterly*, Vol. 10, pp. 647 - 672.

Wilson, E.H., 1913. *A Naturalist in Western China.* Vol. I & II. London, Methuen and Co.

----------- 1929. *China, Mother of Gardens.* Repr. New York, Benjamin Blom (1971).

Proprietary Rights to Fruit on Trees Growing on Residential Property

Homer   Aschmann

One of the prerogatives of childhood in many places is raiding local trees, bushes, and vines for their fruit. Aschmann's account from his Southern California childhood establishes that this is not an anarchic activity but rather is a highly socialized activity conforming to rules of tree tenure found across a number of societies. —The Editors.

The planting of fruit trees on urban and suburban residential lots in Southern California is a common practice. In many instances the justification for this effort must be aesthetic or philanthropic. The owner will pick little or no ripe fruit regardless of climatic or soil conditions. Small to middle-sized boys will strip the trees long before the fruit ripens.

If, however, the planter is judicious in his selection of the species to be planted he may fare better as to harvest. Climatic requirements and optima for the various trees are essentially irrelevant except where conditions are completely beyond the tolerance of a desired species. The child culture will allow rights of private ownership for some kinds of fruit. Others are public property. The owner of a loquat tree (*Eriobootrya japponica*) need not worry about his crop. The neighborhood boys recognize it as public property and never permit the fruit to ripen. An orange or an avocado tree is much safer. Only individuals so hardened as to be willing to undertake actual theft will molest his fruit. Other species enjoy intermediate security.

The following mores are based on personal experience, and afford an insight into the fugitive pattern of a child culture which may persist almost indefinitely but never reach the adult level except in the form of vague memories. For comparative purposes it may be well to identify the source in space and time.

1963. *Man* . 63:74-76. Reprinted with the permission of the author.

My observations were made just within the eastern city limits of Los Angeles and in the adjacent Belvedere Township during the early nineteen-thirties. Most of the residents of the district were relatively poor but not impoverished. A high proportion of the modest houses were and are owner-occupied. Almost all were built on separate lots. In ethnic composition there was a mixture of small neighborhoods, a few blocks in extent. Some were occupied by a mixed White American group. Others were definitely Mexican...The practice of planting fruit trees in both front and back yards was nearly universal throughout the district. In the early nineteen-thirties most of the houses were between 10 and 20 years old so that the many fruit trees planted shortly after construction were close the optimum bearing age.

Though during the Second World War this district may have produced a little more than its share of juvenile gang warfare, it could not have been considered a particular trouble spot in the thirties. The youths were scarcely pampered and were almost without money, but, with individual exceptions, they were energetic kids who knew their way around but were happy to act within socially prescribed bounds. Stripping certain of your neighbors' trees of fruit was within these bounds, though it should be done surreptitiously. The owner could chase you away if you were observed, but had no right to claim damages for the fruit taken. Most curiously, the owners' rights varied with the kind of fruit.

The loquat was the most peculiarly public tree. Children of the most respectable families would pick the fruit of any tree of this species they could get their hands on, even those of an immediate neighbor. Since they competed with one another, early picking was essential and the fruit seldom matured beyond a faint tinge of yellow. A fully ripe fruit could be found only in the store. The deciduous fruits, plums, apricots, peaches, and apples, were also subject to raiding, and generally while in a fairly green state. If a peach were ever to ripen it would be fairly safe since it was obviously valuable property, the taking of which would be theft. Figs might be taken, but only in the brief time between ripening and picking by the owner. Green, they are protected by being completely inedible. Oranges and avocados were safely the owner's property.

People being what they are, not all owners approved of this appropriation of their property. There was little that could be done about it. One couldn't watch his trees constantly, and for the public species oral suasion was ineffective. Attempts at vigorous punitive action would arouse the whole neighborhood of boys who could carry out far more damaging operations against the property of a disliked neighbor. It should be emphasized that the fruit was not taken from commercial plantings. If neighborhood boys had not taken it, it would have been eaten by the owner's family or given away, not sold.

Generally, boys between the ages of eight and 14 picked the fruit. Girls in the same age bracket sometimes participated in the activity as well, though they generally only took from trees in front yards. The toughest kid in the neighborhood might for a brief time protect his family's fruit trees by physical threats to other boys. But this capacity was soon lost by disinterest and then the inability to undertake the demeaning enterprise of beating up much smaller children.

Because of the risk of running into someone your own age who might protect his own trees or those of his neighbors as his private poaching preserve, there was some physical risk in picking fruit outside your immediate home district where you knew everyone. Hence when a neighborhood was without boys in the critical age bracket, the owners might enjoy their own fruit. Of course, this would not apply to an extreme case such as a loquat tree in the front yard. As the fruit started to turn color any boy passing by would know that it was not appreciated and appropriate it. One is led to inquire as to the factors which determined the degree to which individual property rights were socially abrogated for particular kinds of fruit. Most of them are apparent in the contrast between the loquat, the most public fruit, and the orange, the most securely private one.

While the prices of the two fruits per pound in a store are roughly the same, commercially grown oranges constitute a major item in the economy of Southern California, and loquats make an almost infinitesimal contribution to the agricultural wealth of the region. Everyone who has driven through the countryside has seen signs offering rewards for information leading to the arrest and conviction of anyone stealing oranges. They are universally recognized as a valuable and salable commodity. Because of its poor shipping characteristics and its unfamiliarity in the marketplace, the loquat is not ordinarily thought of as an article of commerce[1]; it would be difficult to establish a bill against a child's parents for what he had taken. Furthermore loquats could be picked and consumed before they were ripe enough to have value to anyone other than the small boys who did it. A green orange could not be handled even by those boys, and once it had ripened enough for them it had real value.

While the deciduous fruits, plums of several varieties, apricots and peaches (apple trees seldom bear fruit in Southern California) are of importance to the economy of parts of California, this is not true in the immediate vicinity of Los Angeles. Again, there is the aspect of taking something without recognized economic value, supported by the fact that these fruits could be eaten green. Avocados were protected as a fruit of economic worth in the region, by their large size and consequent unit value, and also by the fact that they were not suitable for eating on the run. Taking fruit was for sport not nutrition, and taking home something of value would have been morally reprehensible.

The placement of the trees in the front yards or fenced backyards had a slight effect on their security. The loquat's selection as an attractive front yard ornamental undoubtedly contributed to its vulnerability, particularly to boys wandering outside their immediate neighborhoods. The owner's decision to plant there could be interpreted by any boy who worried about such things as a deliberate invitation. On the other hand the sport of climbing fences into the backyards where figs and deciduous trees were likely to be found was often an end in itself and justified attempts to consume the greenest and sourest fruits.

The preceding remarks are strictly historical, referring to a specific place and time. Such contemporary observations as I can now make, and conversations with adults in various age brackets suggest that a very similar pattern of fruit appropriation has been widespread in Southern California and of considerable duration. A sample reference from a published source is the following remarks by Mary Frances Kennedy Fisher in a footnote to her translation of Brillat-Savarin's *Physiology of Taste*:[2]

> Medlars were called loquats, from the Japanese,[3] when I was a child in Southern California, and they were the only things I ever stole. They always seemed to grow outside the tight-lipped houses of very cross old women who would peck at us marauders and shrill at us. There are very few of the tall, dark green trees left, and most people have never tasted the beautiful voluptuous bruised fruits, nor seen the satin brown seeds, so fine to hold. The last time I saw loquats was in 1947, in the lobby of the Palace Hotel in San Francisco, may of them almost dead ripe, on a long branch which was part of a decoration in the flower shop there. My early experience as a thieving gourmande warned me that they would be at their peak of decay in about six hours.

Her recollection of loquat-stealing seems to date from about 1920 and also comes from Los Angeles; it differs from mine in that she was able to find ripe fruit to appropriate. With variations a similar pattern of fruit-taking can be recognized elsewhere in the United States.

The activities reported obviously are and were illegal, but at the same time had full social acceptance. A person who attempted to gain the protection that the law afforded him could scarcely continue to live in the neighborhood. A crucial but often ignored question for any society, and particularly our own, is whether formal laws and their enforcement constitute an aid or a hindrance to the maintenance of satisfactory relations within social groups. These notes would seem to support the thesis that such laws are a hindrance. Memory of taking a neighbor's fruit seems to make a noteworthy contribution to one's sense of belonging and attachment to a home neighborhood, an important asset in the generally rootless land of Southern California. This is a remarkable return in comparison with the value of the fruit invested.

Unfortunately, effective field work on the problem is possible only at one, and a very early, stage of an individual's career. I would be interested in specific recollections on the topic from other periods and localities. In particular, the development of this pattern in the vast and otherwise nondescript residential subdivision created in the last decade and a half might have some interesting sociological implications.

NOTES

1. The failure of the loquat to establish itself as a commercial fruit in the distant but climatically similar Balearic Islands is noted in a recently published short sketch. Francis Weismiller, 'The Misbro Tree,' *The Atlantic*, Vol. CXCV (March, 1955), pp. 57-60. On Majorca the rights to disposal of the fruit would seem to be similarly uncertain, with the first comer getting away with what he takes. This particular story turns on the right of a pregnant woman to any food she craves, and, of course, her right to loquats was established as soon as she made it known.

2. Jean Anthelme Brillat-Savarin, *The Physiology of Taste* (1825), M. F. K. Fisher translation, The Heritage Press, New York, 1949, translator's footnote 31, p. 457.

3. The word loquat actually comes from the Cantonese dialect of Chinese, and it is likely that Brillat-Savarin, like Shakespeare (*As You Like It, III, ii*), meant *Mespilus germanica* when he said medlar. The medlar looks quite a bit like the loquat and both belong to the Rosaceae, but the former is much hardier and is better known in all but the southernmost parts of Europe.

3

Tree and Tenure Interactions

The literature on land tenure in developing countries is replete with references to the relationship between land tenure and investment in the land. The simplest relationship, most often noted, is that insecure tenure discourages investment because the farmer cannot be confident of the opportunity to reap the returns from investment. While the planting of a new crop is an investment in the land, it is usually excluded from such analysis. Most crops only take a few months to mature, and after all, a farmer must plant crops even in the face of some insecurity if the household is to survive. Where the right to the land is lost, the loser may still have the right to reap the crops in the ground (Bruce and Noronha, 1985).

Trees, however, are so slow-maturing that they must be treated differently from annual crops. Seedling costs may represent a substantial investment, especially where fruit or other economic trees are planted. When trees take up land that would have been used for other crops, there are considerable opportunity costs involved. Different investments in land raise different tenure issues. At least in terms of the relationship of land tenure to investment in the holding, tree planting resembles more closely the digging of a well or the construction of a fence than the planting of annual crops (Bruce, 1986: 28, 87; Brokensha and Castro, 1984).

Authors directly concerned with encouraging agroforestry on farmers' holdings in Nigeria, Haiti and Jamaica have stressed the importance of clear tenure rules, assuring the farmer that the trees planted on the holding will belong to the farmer (Adeyoju, 1976; Murray, 1982; Blaut, 1973:63). The sources of insecurity are varied. A traditional tenure system which involved annual redistribution of parcels, such as that of the Igbo of Nigeria (Uzozie, 1979:344), clearly poses problems for on-farm forestry. Elsewhere, uncertainties about rules of inheritance may pose a problem. In West Java, there has been conflict between three very different sets of rules (Roman-Dutch, Islamic, and customary) which might govern the inheritance of trees (Bompard *et al.*, 1980). Where the state has legislated state ownership of trees or cutting permit requirements to protect trees, the principal consequence has been a loss of incentives to protect trees on the part of the landholder (Thomson,1982; Lai and Khan, 1986).

The positive relationship posited between security of tenure and investment in tree-planting is, however, by no means simple or invariable. There are some tenure situations in which a farmer with insecure tenure may be able to use tree-planting as means of securing the land. This may occur, for instance, where rights in trees are given effective legal protection independent of land, or where rights to land depend largely on the proof of continuous and unambiguous use. Trees prove such use quite nicely. This tenure-enhancing aspect of tree-planting has not been so widely appreciated, nor has another important interaction: the impact which tree-planting on a commercial basis can have upon the general evolution of a land tenure system. The two classic studies of this phenomenon are from cocoa regions of West Africa (Hill, 1963; and Berry, 1975). The readings in this chapter are intended to introduce these interactions between trees and tenure, some of the more important and better documented elements of which are examined in greater detail in subsequent chapters.

Perhaps the most straightforward empirical evidence of the impact of tenure on tree-planting is provided by studies of farmers who have access to a number of parcels of land under different tenures. *Sellers* examines the case of farmers in Tucurrique, Costa Rica, whose cash crops include coffee and peach palm, and whose tenure arrangements include ownership, relatively secure use rights, tenancy, landborrowing and squatting. Sellers breaks these down into situations in which there are rights to crops but not land, and those where there are legal rights to land. His small sample suggests a clear farmer preference for cash cropping trees on land held in more secure tenure and growing short-term food crops on less secure landholdings. A more recent study in St. Lucia (White, 1986:83) shows that tenure considerations may cause trees to be planted on soils and in ecological niches for which they are not best suited.

There is a special relationship between trees and tenure where the farmer enjoys only derivative, temporary rights in land, such as leasehold. Sellers notes that where tenure rights are ambiguous trees can provide a means of lengthening the farmer's possession of a parcel. Even if leasehold rights are of fairly long duration, the landowner will often prohibit or otherwise seek to prevent the planting of trees, regarding it as an attempt on the part of the tenant to tie down the land indefinitely. In Africa the planting of trees by someone other than the owner of the land is commonly seen as a claim to ownership of the land (Elias, 1963; Ng'andwe, 1976; Tanner, 1960; James, 1971:264). When under a communal tenure system individual farmers are seen as "tenants" of their community, which acts as the owner of the land, and their planting of trees may be discouraged (Brain, 1980). In some societies, such as Lesotho, the chief's permission must be sought before a tree is planted (Duncan, 1960:95).

A recent body of economic theory questions whether tenancy should affect investment under perfect factor market conditions (for a summary, see Binswanger and Rosenzweig, 1981), but such market conditions are unusual anywhere. Tenancy arrangements in the developing world are often not impersonal, arm's-length bargains freely negotiated by the parties but instead institutionalized conquest, with those whose ancestors owned the land now working it as tenants for the victorious tribe or clan. *Shambi* relates the history of conflict between African Giriama tenants and squatters and Arab landlords on the Malindi Coast of Kenya. British colonial policy confirmed the appropriation of land by the Arabs, who had established themselves on the Coast in the eighteenth century, during slave-raiding times. Giriama cultivators as early as 1937 began to plant cashewnut trees on Arab-owned land, generating disputes that troubled both the colonial administration and later the government of independent Kenya.

Not only does tenure affect tree planting, tree planting itself affects the evolution of tenure systems. Tree planting has been seen as a major step in the evolution of individual tenure, as in two studies from Mexico (Millon, 1955; Foster, 1966). This is a specific case of a more general phenomenon: as systems of land use change with the introduction of new crops and technologies, so land tenure will change. One of the critical transitions in agriculture in the developing world is that from shifting cultivation to a more stable, rotational agriculture. It is a change which has profound implications for land tenure (Noronha, 1985). *Dove* explores this relationship as he reviews the role of ecology and changing land use on the development of tribal land-rights in the forests of Borneo. Drawing on his research among the Melaban Kantu', swidden cultivators who establish primary land rights through the felling of primary forest, Dove seeks in an integrated appreciation of ecology and culture the explanation of the development of the tenure system.

Such changes in tenure due to the introduction or commercialization of tree crops have a political dimension. They can undermine the land administration powers of traditional rulers and provide the economic basis for the increasing dominance of rural society by a new class of traders and bureaucrats. The *Ralds'* examination of commercialization of banana and coffee and class formation among the Haya of Bukoba District in Tanzania provides an exceptionally well-documented instance of this. They show how the emergence of a market in land spurred by this commercialization has tended to affect land distribution in the decades before and following independence, undermining the semi-feudal *nyarubanja* system of land tenure and family-clan land control.

The instances of tree-tenure interaction discussed so far are of an essentially evolutionary nature, involving the play of farmer subsistence strategies and market forces. But given the profound relationship between trees and tenure, it follows that state action or inaction with respect to tenure systems can block or enhance—at least in the short-term—tree-planting and commercialization of tree crops. There are few studies in this area, but an exception is Burley's comparative examination of India and Kenya, which finds that tree-planting responds to tenure reform (Burley, 1982). In a more localized study from Kenya, *Brokensha and Riley* examine "forest, foraging, fences, and fuel" among the Mbere of Embu District in the late 1970s, during Kenya's major program of tenure individualization, and registration. Prior to the tenure reform, trees on community-owned land had been regarded as a "free good" and were available to community members on an open-access basis. This marginal area was progressively denuded of trees for charcoal production. Brokensha and Riley conclude that tenure change can have a potentially positive but perhaps not sufficient impact on tree-planting, and thus they make an important point: tenure reform may be a necessary but is almost never a sufficient condition for adequate fuelwood production. In the Andes, land tenure reforms often have given smallholders titles in marginal areas and intensive farming for food production here led to deforestation (Ampuero, 1979).

REFERENCES

Adeyoju, S.K. 1976. "Land Use and Tenure in the Tropics: Where Conventional Concepts Do Not Apply." *Unasylva* 28:26-47.

Ampuero, E.P. 1979. "Ecological Aspects of Agro-Forestry in Mountain Zones: The Andean Region." In Trevor Chandler and David Spurgeon (eds.), *International Cooperation in Agroforestry:*

Proceedings of an International Conference. Nairobi: DSE and ICRAF: 77-94.

Berry, Sarah S. 1975. *Cocoa, Custom and Socio-Economic Change in Rural Western Nigeria.* Oxford: Clarendon Press.

Binswanger, Hans P. and Mark R. Rosenzweig. 1981. *Contractual Arrangements, Employment and Wages in Rural Labor Markets: A Critical Review.* New York: Agricultural Development Council.

Blaut, James M. et al. 1973. "A Study of Cultural Determinants of Soil Erosion and Conservation in the Blue Mountains of Jamaica." In Lambros Comitas and David Lowenthal (eds.), *Work and Family Life: West Indian Perspectives.* New York: Doubleday Anchor: 39-65.

Bompard, Jean, Catherine Ducatillion and Philippe Heckseteweiler. 1980. *A Traditional Agricultural System: Village-Forest-Gardens in West Java.* Montpelier: Academie de Montpelier, Université des Sciences et Techniques du Languedoc.

Brain, James. 1980. "The Uluguru Land Usage Scheme: Success and Failure." *Journal of Developing Areas* 14:175-190.

Brokensha, David and Alfonso Peter Castro. 1984. "Fuelwood, Agroforestry and Natural Resource Management: The Development Significance of Land Tenure and Other Resource/Management/Utilization Systems." Paper prepared for USAID.

Bruce, John W. 1986. Land Tenure Issues in Project Design and Strategies for Agricultural Development in Sub-Saharan Africa. LTC Paper, No. 128. Madison: Land Tenure Center, University of Wisconsin.

Bruce, John W. and Raymond Noronha. 1987. "Land Tenure Issues in the Forestry and Agroforestry Project Contexts." In John B. Raintree (ed.), *Land, Trees and Tenure.* Madison: ICRAF and Land Tenure Center: 121-160

Burley, Jeffrey. 1982. *Obstacles to Tree Planting in Arid and Semi-Arid Lands: Comparative Case Studies from India and Kenya.* Tokyo: United Nations University.

Duncan, Patrick. 1960. *Sotho Laws and Customs.* Cape Town: Oxford University Press.

Elias, Taslim Olawale. 1963. *The Nigerian Legal System.* 2nd ed. London: Routledge and Kegan Paul.

Foster, George M. 1966. *A Primitive Mexican Economy.* Monographs of the American Ethnological Society, No. 5. Seattle: University of Washington Press.

Gulliver, P.H. 1958. *Land Tenure and Social Change among the Nyakyusa.* Kampala: East African Institute of Social Research.

Hill, Polly. 1963. *Migrant Cocoa Farmers in Southern Ghana.* London: Cambridge University Press.

James, R.W. 1971. *Land Tenure and Policy in Tanzania.* Dar es Salaam: East African Literature Bureau.

Lai, Chun K. and Asmeen Khan. 1986. "Mali as a Case Study of Forest Policy in the Sahel: Institutional Constraints on Social Forestry." Social Forestry Network Paper, No. 3e. London: Overseas Development Institute.

Millon, Rene F. 1955. "Trade, Tree Cultivation, and the Development of Private Property in Land." *American Anthropologist* 57:698-712.

Murray, Gerald F. 1982. "Cash-Cropping Agro-Forestry: An Anthropological Approach to Agricultural Development in Rural Haiti." In *Haiti: Present State and Future Prospects.* Racine, Wis.: Wingspread.

Ng'andwe, C.O.M. 1976. "African Traditional Land Tenure and Agricultural Development: Case Study of the Kunda People in Jumbe." *African Social Research* 21:51-67.

Noronha, Raymond. 1985. *A Review of the Literature on Land Tenure Systems in Sub-Saharan Africa.* Agricultural Research Unit Report, No. 43. Washington, D.C.: World Bank.

Tanner, R. 1960. "Land Rights on the Tanganyika Coast." *African Studies* 19:14-25.

Thomson, James T. 1982. *Participation, Local Organization, Land and Tree Tenure: Future Directions for Sahelian Forestry.* Paris: Club du Sahel/OECD.

Tiffen, Mary. Forthcoming. *Economic, Social and Institutional Aspects of Shifting Cultivation in Humid and Semi-Humid Africa.* Rome: FAO.

Uzozie, L.C. 1979. "Tradition and Change in Igbo Food Production Systems: A Geographical Appraisal." Ph.D. dissertation, University of London.

White, Marcia. 1986. "Limited Resource Countries and Economic Development: A Methodology Used for the Caribbean." Ph.D. dissertation, University of Illinois.

The Editors

The Relationship Between Land Tenure and Agricultural Production in Tucurrique, Costa Rica

S. Sellers

> *Tenure systems in developing countries are remarkably complex. A farm family may hold some land under several different tenure types, as in Tucurrique. Sellers' study is one of the very few that examines empirically the impact of tenure variations upon where farmers choose to plant perennials. What other factors may be affecting the decision, and does Sellers make adequate allowances for their effect?—The Editors.*

... As in any agricultural community, land in Tucurrique is of vital importance and since many forms of land tenure are logically possible, it is not surprising to find that the people of Tucurrique have terms to cover several prominent forms employed locally. I have used these same terms as a system of classification, formalizing the definitions by referring to rights and obligations.

The different forms of land tenure, roughly in descending order of rights and obligations are as follows.

- *"Titulo"*—holding legal title to the land constitutes ownership in a strict and legal sense. The owner has rights of access, use, and alienation of the land. The title to the land is recorded in the *Registro Publico* and the owner is required to pay an annual property tax which is a percentage of the assessed value of the land. ...
- *"Derecho"*—popularly considered to cover rights of access and use. A *derecho* is sometimes taken to serve *in lieu* of land title when the title cannot be obtained. Strictly speaking, a *derecho* is a negotiable

---

Excerpted from S. Sellers, "The Relationship Between Land Tenure and Agricultural Production in Tucurrique, Costa Rica" (Turrialba, Costa Rica: Centro Agronomico Tropical de Investigacion y Enseñanza [CATIE], 1977). Reprinted with the permission of the author.

document which legally recognizes the crops and improvement on the land. In Tucurrique, local convention acknowledges more rights to the land than does the law. . . .

• *"Alquilada"*—rented land. This involves a formal agreement by which the renter recompenses the owner in money or kind for the use of the land. The renter's rights of access and use would be specified in the agreement. . . .

• *"Prestada"*—borrowed land used with the consent of the owner and with no agreement of rent. . . .

• *"Denuncio"*—by local convention this is the farming of government land, although strictly speaking a *denuncio* involves filing for the right to use the land. Such land is usually classified as forest reserves for water conservation. . . . The farmer with a *denuncio* is a squatter on public land. He has no obligations, and no legitimate rights, although his rights of access and use of the land are acknowledged within Tucurrique. . . .

• *"Precarista"*—a squatter, using land which has a known owner, frequently a *hacienda*, without permission. The *precarista* will usually use the land as long as this right is not challenged by the owner. . . .

Having reviewed the prominent forms of land tenure known in Tucurrique, defined them in terms of incumbent rights and obligations, and referred to some implications of each form, I will now point out the agricultural and economic correlates of these forms of land tenure. For any piece of land in Tucurrique there is a general tendency for the value of the agricultural produce to increase with the security of land tenure.

This generalization may be explained as follows: Forms of land tenure are more secure as they entail more rights and are legitimized by law. For convenience, the six forms defined above can be lumped into three categories: (1) those with no legally recognized rights (*precarista, denuncio, prestado*), (2) those with a legal right to the produce of the land (*derecho*), and (3) those with a legally recognized right to the land itself (*titulo*).

As for the produce of the land, one way of describing it is as ranging from exclusively household-consumed to exclusively marketed. For example, yucca, beans, and some tubers are grown only for household consumption in Tucurrique. Other crops like chayote, squash, and maize are grown for household consumption and for marketing. Finally, coffee, sugar cane, and peach palm are grown mostly for cash income with only minor amounts consumed in the household. Of course in any agricultural enterprise crops may be mixed, so for analysis I separate consumable crops (including chayote, etc.) from cash crops as two extreme categories, and as an intermediate category I note any combination of cash crops and consumable crops in the same field.

For a random stratified sample of 40 farm households in Tucurrique in which I carried out intensive interviews and observations, the relationship between land tenure and agricultural produce is evident. (The N in this analysis is based on the farm plot. Some farm households have more than one plot under different tenure and crop conditions.)

Land Tenure and Agricultural Produce

Tenure Status	Subsistence and Subsistence Market Crops	Mixed	Cash Crops
No formal land rights	10	3	6
Legal rights to crops	3	11	8
Legal rights to land	1	3	11

The major factor which determines this relationship is the fact that the important cash crops are perennials while consumable crops are annual or seasonal. Thus coffee, sugar cane, and peach palm are valuable crops because, while they require relatively large investments of time, capital, and labor to reach maturity, they yield a high return. This means that a farmer who holds title to land and the required time and capital can be reasonably assured of a secure income by planting cash crops. At the same time, reversing the causal relationship, a farmer who wants to assure himself of a solid income with cash crops will do well to acquire titled land and not risk losing his investment.

At the other extreme, the farmer who has borrowed land or is a squatter will probably not plant perennial crops and risk offending the titleholder and losing most of his investment. Of course, there are some farmers who deliberately take the opposite strategy, and as *precaristas* or borrowers try to improve their situation at the expense of the titleholder by gambling with perennial crops. If the titleholder is lax and allows this for a few years it will become increasingly costly to evict the farmer and eventually the *precarista* or borrower may have his labors legally recognized as a *derecho*.

The other condition affecting this situation—and this is really the exception that proves the rule in the relationship between land tenure and agricultural produce—is the borrowing of land from a near relative. This form of borrowing often precedes the inheritance or sale of the land and, as a favor, the father, mother, aunt, etc. will allow the borrower to plant perennial cash crops. Looking more closely at the 19 cases of farmers with no formal title to the land, and distinguishing those who have borrowed land from close kin from the rest, the relationship between security of land tenure and the planting of cash crops becomes clearer still.

Crop and Land Borrowing Patterns

Land Use Situation	Subsistence and Market Crops	Subsistence Mix	Cash Crops
No Kin Relationship	6	1	1
Close Kin-ties Relationship	4	2	5

In conclusion, it is evident that the kind of agricultural produce and value of the crop are closely related to the form of tenure of the land on which the crops are planted. The relationship is mediated by the fact that cash crops tend to be perennials and require greater investments of capital and time, and also by the fact that local custom and Costa Rican law recognize several forms of land tenure. Of particular importance for tenure is the legal distinction between rights to land and rights to crops and improvements of the land. Because of this distinction, a farmer can acquire some degree of security without holding title to the land. This has the felicitous result, both for the farmers and the national economy, of a category of farmers who hold land in *"derecho"* and mix both subsistence and cash crops.

Tucurrique is illustrative of other agricultural communities in that land tenure and the kinds of agricultural produce have an important relationship in all agricultural settings. But just what the relationship is and how it operates will depend on local law, custom, crops, and environmental conditions. Therefore, while the generalization about the relationship can be said to be true, it only acquires meaning as it is interpreted in the particular situations.

Also, I would point out that I have not placed much emphasis on the direction of causality in the relationship as it is found in Tucurrique. What is most important is that elements fit together logically, rather than the sequence in which they occur. I have not tried to argue that the farmer chooses the form of land tenure to fit his crops nor, to take the opposite view, that he chooses the crops to fit the form of land tenure. In fact, I know of cases of both situations and it seems that these factors work in conjunction.

The Problem of Land Ownership and Cashewnut Claims in Malindi Coastal Belt

M.M. Shambi

> *This thoughtful paper by a district officer in Malindi bears no date, but appears to have been written in the early 1970s. When one ethnic group plants trees on land owned by another, it has political as well as legal repercussions. In the event, Kenyan land policy has continued to affirm the land rights of the Arab landowners—no land reform program has been initiated. —The Editors*

. . Land Acquisition by Arabs in Malindi is said to have started in the early 18th Century. There were landlords and landladies in the true sense of Land ownership. The bigger the slave labour force that one had, the more the land that one acquired by virtue of cultivation. The main crop which was grown was millet which was exported to Arabia and India. Maize and cassava were grown for local consumption. . . .

History tells us that the Arab Land-slave ownership was accelerated when Sultan Seyid Said established his capital in Zanzibar in 1840. . . . At this time, more Arabs from Muscat, most of them relatives of the Sultan and clan-members of the "Royal Family" used the cheap slave-labour to cultivate large stretches of land. Having seen that cultivation of *shambas*.[fields (eds.)] produced good results and also because of the more lucrative trade in ivory and mangroves the Sultan was satisfied with the 1886 Agreement which gave him legal rights for ownership of the 10 miles strip. . . .

In the year 1900 all slaves were set free from their Arab Masters through pressure brought about by the British Administration.

Excerpted from M.M. Shambi, District Officer II, Malindi, "The Problem of Land Ownership and Cashewnut Claims in Malindi Coastal Belt" (Nairobi). Reprinted with the permission of the author.

Several of the ex-slaves ran away in an attempt to return to their homes up-country. . . .

Other ex-slaves chose to remain in their former Masters' *shambas*. From about the year 1912 Africans worked for pay in the same *shambas*. that they used to work as slaves. In the same year (1912) Surveyors were sent by the British Government to survey Arab *shambas* in the Sultan's Dominion, and to issue free-hold titles to all those who had claims. . . .

Following the survey of the *shambas*, all the non-Arabs living within the surveyed *shambas*, whether ex-slaves or home-free were automatically squatting on land that was legally owned by Arabs. . . .

At this juncture it is proper to sort out two things: paid labour, and *"ijara."*

a. As aforesaid from 1912 or thereabout, all "free people" working in the *shambas* belonging to Arabs were paid small wages, say a rupee or two. There were no fixed wages though.

b. *"Ijara"* was Land-rent. In a *shamba* of say 300 acres there might have lived fifty families. A big part of this *shamba* was for the master where the tenants worked for wages. At the same time there were little pockets where the tenants planted their subsistence crops in order to support their families. In this case, they had to pay a rent which was called *"Ijara."* At first this was paid in kind. Normally, after harvesting the crop, a portion of it went to the master as a gesture of appreciation for being allowed to dig the land. In the 1930s *"ijara"* was paid in hard cash—Sh.10/- or 15/- per year.

The Landlords thought, quite rightly too, that they could live on *"ijara"* money alone. The tenants could, therefore, cultivate freely, provided they paid the rent regularly. So, between the years of 1930 and 1957 there was no problem because the concept of the land rent was accepted by both parties, i.e., the Landowners and the tenants.

Conflicts began when the cashewnut trees introduced in 1936 as a cash crop began to pay a good profit. . . .

Cashewnut trees were planted as a cash crop in Malindi in the year 1937. Before the years 1912-1936 the main cash crop was cotton. . . .

When the Kenya Cashews Factory was built at Kilifi in the early 1920s there was a long-term plan which was worked out in order to feed the factory and to keep it going. . . .

In the case of Malindi, because the squatters cultivated the land which did not belong to them, it was not easy for the Government to enforce the planting of the nut. Already there were signs of a developing conflict as early as 1937 because:

1. The squatters had already got used to paying *"ijara"* every year. The crops which they planted were seasonal, e.g., maize, cassava,

cowpeas, etc., as opposed to permanent crops such as coconut trees, and cashewnut trees.

2. Some squatters interpreted the extensive planting of cashewnuts as a return to the slave labour.

3. The Landowners on the other hand were also reluctant to allow the squatters to plant cashewnut in their *shambas*.because they sensed that the nut would be more profitable than "*ijara*"—money.

The District Officer Malindi (Mr. Osborn) accused Chief Awade of Ganda that he indulged in secret night meetings to organize the Giriama people for the purpose of defeating Governments' intentions. The chief replied, "Sir, when I told the people not to plant cashewnut trees in this location I did so, not in my capacity as chief, but in my role as a squatter."

In view of the seriousness of this incident, the Administration sought a solution: a public *baraza* [meeting (eds.)] was arranged in Malindi, which was attended by many landowners and squatters. Also present were: the District Commissioner Kilifi, the District Officer Malindi, the District Agriculture Officer Kilifi, the Assistant Agriculture Officer Watamu and chief Awade of Ganda and Gede Locations. In this public *baraza*, an agreement was reached.

The 1937 Agreement

After the dispute between the Arab landowners and the African squatters over the issue of planting cashewnuts as a cash crop, and in view of the fact that the Government was eager to have the nut planted, the following were agreed:

1. The Arab landowners agreed in principle that the squatters could go ahead and plant cashewnuts in their *shambas.*

2. The system whereby the squatters paid Land Rent (*Ijara*) would continue whereas the harvesting and the selling of the cashewnut crop would remain entirely in the hands of the squatters.

3. In the case where a squatter dies having planted some trees, his/her children would claim the ownership of the crop provided they continued to pay the Rent.

4. In case a landowner dies, Rent would be paid to the heirs.

5. When the squatter wants to sell his cashewnut trees he must sell them to the landowner but if the latter was unable to buy the trees, any other person could buy them provided there was proper consultation between the landowner and the prospective buyer.

6. In the case where a squatter dies having owned cashewnut trees and where the deceased leaves no children, the crop becomes the property of the landowner.

Following the 1937 Agreement, the Department of Agriculture provided the seeds distributed both in Ganda and Magarini Locations.

. . . . The Landowner-Squatter conflict started way back in 1957-58. In one word the cause was politics. The Arab Landowners felt insecure at the time the Emergency ended and political parties reformed in the names of Kanu and Kadu.

The land issue was a sensitive one particularly as it was known that political parties were formed (a) to liberate the land held by non-Africans and (b) to give the people their Independence. What had happened to the European population living on the White Highlands during the Emergency might as well have happened to the Arabs at the Mwambao. Therefore, the Arabs decided to evict the squatters; partly because they were "provoked" by the politicians who said that the Sultan's red flag had no place on the Kenya soil.

Following the massive evictions, there was unrest among the African people who had been living on the land . . . .

The conflict lies between the Africans and the non-Africans concerning land ownership in the Coastal Belt. The heart of the matter is, this conflict is between the Arabs and the Giriama (including the other Mijikenda tribes and any other black Africans who fall into the category of "squatters").

1. From a political point of view, one of the Fundamental Human Rights, particularly so in an Independent country, is "Freedom from Want and Fear." This is, and I repeat, *Fundamental*. Research has revealed that the African squatter at the coast is still wanting, i.e., he lacks a . . . [ed.: line illegible] African is living in fear because any time the landowner could evict him.

2. The next point is legal: why does the Arab landowner evict the squatter? As revealed in Chapter II, land was registered and the owners were given Freehold Titles as early as 1912. Their documents have been recognized by the constitution of our Independent Kenya, to be valid and, therefore, legal. . . .

3. From an Agricultural point of view, bearing in mind that Agriculture is the basis of our Country's Economy, it is evident that the land in question has not been fully utilized. Some big stretches of land lie uncultivated, and the ones that are cultivated are planted with Cashewnut trees which are rarely looked after. In other words, there are some *shambas* which are neglected.

Suggestions:

1. All the neglected *shambas* which are currently being registered by the Department of Agriculture under the heading "Mismanaged Farms" whose owners are either living out of the country (e.g., Plot No. 244 of 150 acres—there are two of them in Seychelles, and two of them in Australia), or perhaps not living at all: these *shambas* could be taken over by the Government at no extra cost. They could then be sub-divided for settlement plots for the squatters therein.

2. The Government may, as it shall see need, review the whole issue of Freehold Titles issued to the Arab landowners during the Sultan's reign over Mwambao. I suggest strongly that these Freehold Titles be bought at a minimum cost because the actual development on the land as done by the landowners is little or nil. Given that the cashewnut trees were planted by the squatters, and given that the squatters have spent all their time developing land which is not legally theirs, it follows that the cost of buying out these titles shall be no more than the cost incurred for the survey and, perhaps, in some cases the initial buying price. . . .

The Cashewnut Problem

Let us establish the fact that the Cashewnut trees were, in the majority of cases, planted by the squatters. Let us agree that there are squatters living on the Arabs' *shambas*.. . . . Then:

a. It is possible for a squatter to remain on a piece of land where his 50 or 100 cashew nut trees are growing, through whichever method of acquiring land shall be acceptable by the Government.

b. It is also possible to compensate a squatter for his trees at a maximum cost, and at the same time it may be possible to move him to another piece of land which may or may not have cashew nut trees.

c. Following on point (b) there is a big piece of State Land to the west of Magarini Location which has been recommended for a Settlement Scheme. This is alright but the aim of settling the people there should not be to remove the squatters from the Arab-owned land to State Land. . . .

I have written. Let the readers read, criticize, and judge. But I wish to add this: History repeats itself over the years. That is why it has been important to give a historical narration of events. For example, what happened to Rhodesia might as well have happened to Kenya. Also, the issue over the Kenya "White" Highlands may be similar to that of the Coast "Mwambao."

There are certain facts of life which one must accept. Some of these are political: for example, say boundaries, or land-ownership, or the question of Race. Today the landowners at Malindi's Coastal Belt are said to be Arabs, but in fact they are Kenya Citizens, with fully endorsed Kenya Passports.

The question that must be posed here is: Suppose one evicts an African from an Arab's Land, where does the African go, because he is at home. Similarly, suppose one deprives the so-called Arab (Kenyan) of his land, where does he go because he is not acceptable in Arabia. Therefore, he is also at home.

Finally, I conclude by saying that whatever the solution, it must be a careful one where politics must not over-rule Justice.

The Kantu' System of Land Tenure: The Evolution of Tribal Land Rights in Borneo

Michael R. Dove

This excellent study in the cultural ecology of tenure shows how socioeconomic change interacts with the ecology of the rain forests to affect the evolution of tenure systems. The Melaban Kantu' are longhouse-dwelling, swidden cultivators of dryland rice in West Kalimantan, Indonesia. The article is part of an extended and intriguing academic exchange (see Dove's references) on the interaction of culture and ecology as determinants of land tenure. -- The Editors

There are two major, discrete social groupings in Kantu' society, the *bilek* "household" and the *rumah* "longhouse." The household is partially defined as the group that makes common residence in one section of the longhouse: each longhouse section is built and maintained by a single household. In addition to being a unit of residence, the household is the primary unit of production and consumption. Labor from within each household is used to perform most of the work in the household's swiddens. Similarly, while one household may give rice to another in loan as as a wage payment, it will never share its rice with another: shared consumption occurs only within the household.

The longhouse is the second major grouping in Kantu' society. The most obvious function of the longhouse has to do with settlement. It is a unit of residence, and not merely a *de facto* unit but a *de jure* unit; the

Excerpted from Michael R. Dove, "The Kantu' System of Land Tenure: The Evolution of Tribal Land Rights in Borneo," in *Modernization and the Emergence of a Landless Peasantry: Essays on the Integration of Peripheries to Socioeconomic Centers*, ed. G.N. Appell, Studies in Third World Societies, no. 33 (Williamsburg, Va.: Department of Anthropology, College of William and Mary, September 1985), pp. 159-82. Reprinted with the permission of the author.

residence of individual households in the longhouse is subject to certain constraints imposed by all the households acting together. However, each household owns and maintains its individual section of the longhouse: the longhouse is not, therefore, a "communal" residence (Dove 1982) ...

The Kantu' currently possess a system of land tenure that is very similar to that of the Iban, as described by Freeman (1970). Thus, land rights are established by the first felling of the primary forest on that land.[3] These rights reside in the household of the feller(s). This household continues to hold rights to that land, even after its primary forest swidden has been abandoned and the land has reverted to secondary forest. In fact, once established, these land-rights are potentially unlimited in duration, given also that the household itself, as Appell (1971:18) aptly put it, "exists jurally in perpetuity, through the incorporation of one child and his/her spouse to each generation." When the household undergoes partition, its land-rights are not divided, but simply continue to be shared equally among the siblings involved in the partition. While land rights are primarily held by the household, residual rights are held by the longhouse (*rumah*). These latter rights are activated in the event that a household from another longhouse tries to clear land within the longhouse territory, or in the event that a household from within the longhouse wishes to move out and away. The most important feature of Kantu' land tenure, within the context of the debate on land tenure and ecology, is that cultivation rights are potentially "unlimited" in duration, as among the Iban, Land Dayak, Ma'anyan, and Maloh, as opposed to "limited," as among the Rungus.[4]

The unlimited duration of Kantu' cultivation rights can be attributed to several different factors, among them ecological factors. The pattern of rainfall is arguably the most important of the several ecological factors that have been introduced in the debate on ecological determinants of land tenure.[5] Patterns of rainfall vary considerably through the interior of Borneo, and this variation can be an important determinant of variation in social phenomena. Weinstock dismisses the importance of this variation on the basis that all of the tribal groups in question (Rungus, Ma'anyan, Land Dayak, Iban, and Maloh) receive at least 2,286 mm. (viz., 90 inches) of rain per year, and hence all have "udic moisture regimes" (1979:8). The fact that all of these groups have udic moisture regimes is not questioned here. What is questioned is Weinstock's conclusion that, because this label applied to all cases, any variation among the cases is not important. The range of variation in annual rainfall among these five groups totals almost 80 inches per year. This is shown in Table 1, to which rainfall data for the Kantu' have also been added.[6]

Table 1. Comparative rainfall data for six Bornean groups

	Rungus	Ma'anyan	Land Dayak	Iban	Kantu'	Maloh
Total annual rainfall (mm)	2311	2332	3368	3698	4290	4308
Total rainfall during July, August, and September (mm)	330	236	706	770	1293	762

Of greatest importance is the variation not in annual rainfall, but in rainfall during the months in which the swiddens are normally burned, namely June, August, and September .... [T]he range in variation is over 500 per cent, namely between the Ma'anyan (236 mm.) and the Kantu' (1293 mm.).[7] The significance of this considerable variation is that certain groups (viz., the Land Dayak, Iban, Kantu' and Maloh, each of which receives an average of 883 mm. of rainfall during the burn months) will clearly have a more difficult time (cet. par.) burning their swiddens than certain other groups (viz., the Rungus of Ma'anyan, each of which receives an average of only 283 mm. of rain during the burn months).

For the Kantu' and other high rainfall groups, the greater difficulty in burning the swiddens causes them to place a greater value on secondary forest than would otherwise be the case. Because the average secondary forest tree is smaller than the average primary forest tree, the former type of forest will dry out quicker than the latter type.[8] Hence, secondary forest swiddens can be successfully burned after a shorter period of drought (and following a greater amount of rainfall) than can primary forest swiddens, one consequence of which is that the burns are usually better in the former than in the latter ...

... there are costs and benefits to the farming of both primary and secondary forest. There tends to be a problem with the burn in the former but not the latter, whereas there is a problem with weed growth in the latter but not the former.[10] This is not to say that either forest type is equally desirable, however. It is important to note that the major problem in farming primary forest, namely a poor burn, cannot be remedied by additional labor inputs (the great mass of the timber involved prohibits the performance of any remedial measures, such as stacking and reburning, following a poor burn). In contrast, the major problem in farming secondary forest, namely weed growth, can be remedied through the input of additional labor, in weeding.

In terms of local ecological factors, therefore, the relative desirability of secondary forest is sufficiently great to explain why rights to secondary forest are not relinquished to the community after its use but are held (potentially) in perpetuity by the user, the household. The relative desirability of farming secondary forest is reflected in the fact that, during the swidden years 1974-1975 and 1975-1976, 71 per cent of the households at Tikul Batu made at least one (dryland) secondary forest swidden each year. During the same years, 89 per cent of the households made at least one (dryland) primary forest swidden each year. The ecological value of secondary forest is here counterbalanced by the desire to establish land rights by felling primary forest. In the absence of this latter consideration, the percentages of households making at least one primary or secondary forest swidden would be somewhat lower and higher, respectively.

This case therefore appears to support Appell's (1971) hypothesis relating the permanency of household rights to the value of secondary forest, which in turn is related to high amounts of rainfall and the difficulty of burning the swidden. In the past, critics of Appell's hypothesis have questioned such support on the grounds: first, this same pattern of rainfall and the same system of land rights are not invariably associated elsewhere in contemporary Borneo; and second, the two were not always associated in Kantu' history. In order to understand why these criticisms are not valid as well as to appreciate more fully the role of the ecological factors in the land tenure system, it is necessary to place the contemporary Kantu' situations in historical perspective ....

The system of land tenure described earlier is of comparatively recent origin. Up until the end of the nineteenth century, the Kantu' system of land tenure was quite different. The longhouse seems to have had a delimited territory then as now, but individual households did not hold exclusive rights to given sections of forest within this territory. That is, neither by pioneer cultivation nor by any other means was an individual household able to establish exclusive rights to sections of secondary (or primary) forest. The first change in this system consisted in longhouse recognition of a household's rights of *mudas*. If a *burong bisa* "potent omen" was observed during the planting of a primary forest swidden, the household making that swidden was later required to make an *mudas* offering of one or more pigs. The making of this offering then gave that household the prior right to farm that particular section of land once more, at a time of its own choosing, before the land would become a free good, available for farming to all households in the longhouse. A further dramatic change occurred in the first decades of this century, when the Kantu' consciously and systematically adopted the fundamental tenet of their present system of land tenure: the clearing of primary forest confers upon the household that does the clearing exclusive rights, potentially unlimited in duration, to the secondary forest that succeeds on that site. . . .

As long as warfare was still endemic, there was little pressure for the development of household rights to secondary forest. The Kantu' themselves cite several reasons for this ... the chronic warfare, with the recurrent need to flee or advance against enemy forces, necessitated a semi-migratory settlement system, based upon rudimentary, short-lived, and easily abandoned longhouses (*dampa'* see Dove 1982:40). This settlement pattern mitigated against the development of rights to specific sections of secondary forest, given the possibility that a group would not remain in one area long enough to farm both the primary forest and the secondary forest that would succeed it. In addition, the exigencies of wartime obliged all the households in the longhouse to farm near one another, making their swiddens in a cluster as opposed to in separate corners of the longhouse territory. This particular land-use pattern also mitigated against the development of household rights to secondary forest, since the existence of such rights would have made this pattern more difficult to achieve, by putting the claims of individual households before the overall needs of the longhouse as a whole.

Finally, and of greatest importance, individual rights to secondary forest did not develop at this time because the exigencies of warfare placed a premium on primary forest, not secondary forest (Dove, 1983). As the author has demonstrated elsewhere (Dove 1977), the farming of secondary forest was generally undesirable in wartime, because of the need for such swiddens (unlike primary forest swiddens) to be weeded, which heightened the defensive burden at the same time that it limited offensive capabilities. During this historical period of warfare, therefore, both secondary forest itself and household rights to this forest were of little value. This is not to say that the ecological factor, rainfall, which today makes the existence of rights to secondary forest attractive, was not operable then. It is merely to say that the influence of this variable was largely offset by the overweening importance of other variables, which placed an opposing value on the absence of rights and on the value of primary forest.

As large-scale warfare between Kantu' and Iban gradually diminished, the force of these several factors favoring the absence of rights and the use of primary forest also began to diminish. As this occurred, the relative value of secondary forest (given its higher yields, as well as the rainfall-burn problem with primary forest) began to increase, and pressure began to build for the recognition of rights to this forest. In addition to the change in the military circumstances of the Kantu', however, at least two other factors were involved in this trend, both of which are mentioned explicitly by the Kantu'. These factors bear not upon the differential valuation of primary versus secondary forest, but upon a general increase in the valuation of forest or land of any type. First, the cessation of warfare and the consequent removal of the pressures against sedentarism enabled the Kantu' to start planting rubber groves, a useless endeavor unless a group can remain in the same area for two generations or more. Any land that is planted in rubber is permanently removed from the swidden cycle (with rare exceptions). In addition, its value is greatly heightened which historically led to the first sales of land. For these reasons, the Kantu' say that the development of rubber cultivation generated pressure for the recognition of household rights to individual sections of secondary forest.

The secondary factor creating pressure for the recognition of household rights to secondary forest was, following the cessation of active warfare, the negotiated settlement of Sarawak Iban on three sides of the Melaban Kantu' territory. Shortly thereafter, the Kantu' became aware that the Iban recognized such rights, and they [the Kantu'] say that they followed suit because they feared that otherwise they would be disadvantaged in land disputes with the Iban. This is not to say that the current land tenure system of the Kantu' was simply copied from the Iban. It must be remembered that the Kantu' also speak of other factors that contributed to their recognition of household rights to secondary forest, as well as of factors that mitigated against this recognition prior to their peacemaking with the Iban. Moreover, it is unclear when the Iban themselves first began to recognize such rights. It is possible that they also did not recognize such rights prior to the peacemaking -- for reasons similar to those mentioned for the Kantu' -- and that they modified their system of land tenure at approximately the same time as the Kantu', and for similar reasons; in which case it cannot be said that one group "copied" the other. ... The mere arrival of the Iban in the Empanang Valley may have contributed to this pressure for the recognition of household rights to secondary forest, because it

practically eliminated any possibility for the expansion of the Kantu'
or Iban territory. This contributed to a new image of the forest within
that territory as finite and hence scarce.

Given the new finiteness of the Kantu' territory, population growth
became a third factor in the development of forest rights. Due to the
cessation of warfare, among other factors, the Kantu' population in the
Empanang Valley has expanded rapidly this century.. . . .

This palpable increase in population/land pressure, in addition to
the other changes more directly related to the cessation of
headhunting, has stimulated further developments in Kantu' land
tenure beyond the initial recognition of household rights to secondary
forest based on clearing the original primary forest. One major
development was an adat "law" ruling that household rights had to be
forfeited upon departure from the longhouse ...

When this adat was first promulgated, the land to which a
departed household had held rights reverted to the status essentially,
of primary forest. That is, rights to that land were eventually given to
whichever household first used it (viz., by making a swidden there).
With the further passage of time, however, and as land became
increasingly scarce and more valuable, this treatment of the rights of a
departed household led to too many disputes among the longhouse's
households. As a result, the longhouse headmen began to take all such
rights unto themselves, holding and employing them for personal use.
With the still further passage of time, and again with the increasing
valuation of land, the other inhabitants of the longhouse came to resent
this privileged action by the headmen. Ultimately, the adat was
again changed, this time so that the headmen took over, not the land
rights of departed households, but only the administration of these
rights. Under the headman's administration today, all of the
households in the longhouse ideally farm, in rotation, the forest
sections covered by these rights ...

Several conclusions can be drawn from this preceding analysis
of historical developments in the Kantu' system of land tenure. First,
it is now clear that ecological factors -- specifically the pattern of
rainfall -- played an important role in this development. Other
scholars have questioned this role based on comparative cases in which
this posited association between the ecological factor and the type of
land tenure does not hold for some other group, or historical cases in
which the system of land tenure has undergone change while the
ecological factors have been constant (Dixon 1974; King 1975; Weinstock
1979). With regard to the latter argument, note that among the Kantu'
much of the pressure for the development of household rights to
secondary forest built up, historically, as the result of changes in

critical political, legal, and economic factors. As these changes took place, the absolute values of the ecological variable admittedly did not change -- but its relative value or importance did. That is, as changes took place in the various sociocultural variables, the relative importance of their role in the land tenure system decreased and that of the ecological variable increased. This is why the pattern of rainfall can exert a greater influence over the pattern of land tenure today than it did historically. This example suggests that historical reconstruction of land tenure systems is as fruitful as some scholars have suspected (Dixon 1974:14), but not as problematic as others have feared (King 1975:15-16).

NOTES

3. The phrase "land rights" will be used in this paper, in conformity to usage in the Bornean literature under examination here. However, in the case of the Kantu', as among some other groups, it might be equally accurate to say that they hold and exercise rights to trees, not land.

4. This summary analysis of Kantu' land tenure benefits not only from Freeman's (1970) data on the Iban, but also from Appell's (1971 and n.d.) analyses of that data.

5. It is possible that variation in soils will prove to be as important as variation in rainfall, but the data to substantiate this do not yet exist. Weinstock';s (1979) attempt to use the extant, inadequate soil data in his attempt to refute Appell's initial hypothesis has been rightly criticized by Burrough (1979).

6. This table is compiled from published data for all groups except the Kantu'. the figures for which are based on the author's daily measurements of rainfall over a period of twenty-one months. All figures not originally given in millimeters have been converted to millimeters.

7. The rainfall total for the burn months for the Kantu' may be unusually high because of exceptionally heavy rains during part of the period in which measurements were made. However, the validity of the author's Kantu' data is supported by the similarity of the Kantu' and the Maloch annual totals, given that both groups live along the northwest rim of the greater Kapuas River Valley. In any case, it is clear that the Kantu' typically must deal with more rainfall (even if not 1,293 mm.) during their burn season, compared (e.g.) to the Rungus of Ma'anyan.

8. The author's spot measurements within the Kantu' territory yield average diameters of 24.5 and 12.2 centimeters for single trees in primary and secondary forest, respectively. Based on these

measurements, the trunk of the average primary forest tree has a volume approximately four times as great as the volume of the average secondary forest tree, and hence contains approximately four times as much moisture.

10. The relative costs and benefits of the two types of forest are directly associated with the length of the fallow period. In terms of the difficulty with weeds, a short fallow period is bad, while in terms of the difficulty with the burn, a short fallow period is good. In neither case is the amount of biomass in the forest a consideration. Weinstock (1979:8-9) suggests that the length of the fallow period is important only because it determines the amount of biomass in the forest, and that even this ceases to be a factor after 7-8 years when 90 per cent of maximum biomass has been attained. I agree that the amount of biomass is an important factor among swidden groups forced to farm after short fallow periods (e.g., less than 7-8 years). However, among swidden groups such as the Kantu', who typically farm only after fallow periods longer than 7-8 years, this question of biomass is (as yet) irrelevant; yet the length of the fallow period is not irrelevant, as I have already pointed out. Between the fallow period of ten years and one of one hundred years, there may be little difference in the amount of biomass, but there is a considerable difference in the composition of the biomass (viz., in the number of herbaceous plants present), and this is associated with a critical difference in the severity of the weed problem. Similarly, while there is little difference in the amount of biomass in a ten-year fallow and a one hundred-year fallow, there is a great difference in the distribution of this mass. In primary forest a given amount of biomass is concentrated in fewer and larger flora than in secondary forest, and this distinction is associated with a critical difference in the difficulty of drying and burning it.

REFERENCES

Appell, G.N. 1971. "Systems of Land Tenure in Borneo: A Problem in Ecological Determinism." *Borneo Research Bulletin* 3:17-20.

Appell, G.N. n.d. "Observational Procedures for Land Tenure and Kin Groupings in the Cognatic Societies of Borneo." Duplicated.

Burrough, P.A. 1979. "Soil Maps and Swidden -- A Caveat." *Borneo Research Bulletin* 11:46-51.

Dixon, Gale. 1974. "Dayak Land Tenure: An Alternative to Ecological Determinism." *Borneo Research Bulletin* 6(1):5-15.

Dove, Michael R. 1982. "The Myth of the Communal Longhouse in Rural Development." In *Too Rapid Rural Development*, edited by

C. MacAndrews and L.S. Chin, pp. 14-78. Athens: Ohio University Press.

Dove, Michael R. 1983. "Forest Preference in Swidden Agriculture." *Tropical Ecology* 24(1):122-42.

Freeman, J.D. 1970. *Report on the Iban.* London: The Athlone Press.

King, Victor T. 1975. "Further Problems in Bornean Land Tenure Systems: Comments on an Argument." *Borneo Research Bulletin* 7(1):12-16.

Weinstock, Joseph. 1979. "Ecological Determinism: Is the Appell Hypothesis Valid?" *Borneo Research Bulletin* 11(1):3-13.

Rural Organization in Bukoba District, Tanzania

Jorgen and Karen Rald

Bukoba District is inhabited by the Haya, an ethnic group which in the late colonial period responded enthusiastically to opportunities for commercialization of agriculture. These changes brought not only changes in the rules of land tenure, but as is often the case, changes in land distribution as well. The Ralds examine the role of tenure change in class formation.—The Editors

. . . In Bukoba there existed a feudal system of land tenure (*nyarubanja*), where the pattern of holding land had assumed a hierarchical character, with the king (*Mukama*) at the apex. The hierarchy consisted of institutions of clientship, based on land (*kibanja* land) as the most important property among the Haya (Reining, 1962).

The *Mukama* exercised rights with respect to land, allocating areas of populated *kibanja* to individuals of the ruling class. People living on these areas became tenants (*batwarwa*) of the individual landholders (*batwazi*). There are two main views on the origin of this institution. "The institution arose from the *voluntary* act of many original settlers of Buhaya giving themselves and their properties up to the Bahinda [the ruling dynasty]. The Bahinda were a group of pastoralists who had come to Buhaya from Bunyoro to settle." The other, contrasting theory, which appears more plausible and is supported by Cory [Corry (eds.)], is that of conquest of the indigenous rulers by the Bahinda. "The invading conquerors," he says, "became the absolute masters of the conquered people and their lands" (James, 1971).

Excerpted from Jorgen and Karen Rald, *Rural Organization in Bukoba District, Tanzania* (Uppsala: The Scandinavian Institute of African Studies, 1975), at 39-49. Reprinted with the permission of the authors.

. . . only approximately 10 percent of the holdings in Buhaya were under *nyarubanja* (Mutahaba, 1969). The rest were what Reining calls 'owner-occupants' or what Mutahaba terms 'freeholders'. . . .

The major interest of our study lies in the oral traditions about the exchange of manure and milk and the authority of land allocation between the invading Bahinda and the indigenous people.

The oral traditions hold that at the time of the arrival of the Bahinda, the indigenous people were agriculturalists growing crops like millet and yams—that is, agriculture based on annual crops and even perhaps shifting cultivation methods.

The availability of cattle manure as a supply for the sandy soils of Bukoba apparently facilitated the cultivation of bananas as the staple food. Bananas were certainly grown and appreciated by the indigenous people, but on the unfertilized sandy soils the bananas had such a low yield that they could not form the staple food.[3] By applying manure to the bananas the yield was increased to the point where the households could obtain sufficient food from a small area of banana cultivation.

At the same time the semi-permanent settlements of the millet growers gradually shifted to a permanent settlement pattern. The land tenure also gradually changed from usufructuary ownership to proprietary ownership. Thus, "the effect of Bahinda's settlement was definitely not the suppression of the agricultural culture of the indigenous population. It was to result in the blending of the two cultures, the agriculturalists becoming also cattle herders, and the herders in turn taking on agricultural traits" (Mutahaba, 1969).

With the introduction of coffee as a cash crop interplanted in the banana *kibanja*, the *kibanja* land-use type grew more important and strengthened the proprietary ownership right. Coffee cultivation also encouraged the minority of landholders to extend their control of *kibanja* land through the nyarubanja system. . . .

Pitblado (1970) has observed that: "In general, there is a progression from usufructuary ownership to proprietary ownership as cash crops are introduced, perennial crops planted, and other pressures on the available land increase." This applies to Bukoba, where cattle became an integrated part of the farming system on the arrival of the Bahinda. The cattle manure made possible the shifting from annual crops to the perennial bananas as the dominating food crop and the establishment of permanent fields, the *kibanja* fields. At that time, customary land laws made adjustments to secure the tenure of *kibanja*; the elaborate inheritance rules have further emphasized the importance of *kibanja*.

When coffee was introduced as a cash crop, it was naturally interplanted with the bananas already growing on fertile soil, and proprietary rights within the clan system were protected by demarcating *kibanja* boundaries with plants or trees. The introduction of a cash economy made a major impact on land tenure, as the chiefs manipulated the *nyarubanja* system to obtain tighter control over *kibanja* land and thereby the important cash crop coffee. . . .

The ecological system of Bukoba District, with its variation in soil fertility, increase in population and consequent shortage of fertile land, contains factors which have led to great emphasis being placed on the importance of securing rights to *kibanja* land. At the same time the socio-economic pattern has evolved towards increasing individualism in relation to land.

In post-independence Bukoba the hierarchical control of land executed formerly by the kings and the *nyarubanja* landlords has broken down, but a new rural elite which has strong links with the former hierarchy has emerged. The core of this elite contains businessmen and educated people.

The rapid rise in coffee production, the booming of its price on the world market in two periods and an ensuing drastic fall, and the organization of coffee marketing have given rise to the formation of two particular groups in this elite. The first is a small group of businessmen, who manipulate the coffee economy through trading, smuggling, bribery, and corruption, combined with money-lending at exorbitant interest rates. . . . These people are the real exploiters of the farming system in Bukoba and they are normally not greatly concerned with the acquisition of land. The second and by far the largest section of the economic rural elite consists of a group of rich farmers who are also either small-scale businessmen or wage-earners. The order of the combination should indicate that the rich farmers use an income derived from non-farming activities to expand their farm-unit areas. The wage-earners include people employed outside agriculture, civil servants, clergymen, cooperative officials, managers, shopkeepers, etc. These people invest the surplus from their salaries or allowances in farming in their home areas.

The common feature of this large group is that in one way or another these people have capital available from work outside their own farm unit, and this capital is invested in expansion of the farm areas and/or improved agricultural husbandry. The objectives, apart from an improved standard of living, are basically the same as those mentioned above: to provide for their children in the future, as some of them will have to rely on agricultural production to earn their living. Again, to invest in agriculture, say, by buying *kibanja* land, is also a method of meeting the obligations to family members. Every wage-earner in this country feels the heavy burden of these obligations: the requests for school fees, covering of hospital expenses, repayments of loans, help with clothes and everyday necessities such as salt, sugar, tea, meat, etc. . . .

One way of dealing with these family obligations is to invest money in *kibanja* land in the home area. This land can be allocated to poor relatives, an aunt or divorced sister, who maintain it and at the same time obtain their subsistence.

Furthermore, in a young nation like Tanzania, the land thus bought gives security, like an old age pension. The civil servant can retire to his *shamba* at home and in his old age enjoy the close social contact with his own society after the alienated town life. . . .

This process of class formation in rural areas has a major impact, not only on income distribution, but also on the distribution of the best land.

The importance of the money economy with regard to land tenure and the possibilities of land transfer are shown in Table 13.

Table 13.
Methods of acquisition: per cent *kibanja* plots in sample areas

	Inherited from father	Obtained by purchase	Allocated by Native Authority*	Allocated by VDC**
Ibwera	50	39.5	7	3.5
Nshamba	48	24	21	7
Kanyigo	75	22.5	—	2.5

* Native Authority was the chief's representative dealing with allocation of mainly uncultivated land before independence. Normally a fee of 5 shillings was paid (Ekishembe).
** Village Development Committee.

From the table it can be seen that where land shortage is really an acute problem, there are only two methods of acquisition, inheritance and purchase. As the division of *kibanja* land through inheritance diminishes the size of the units of this land available for the heirs of the coming generations, the only adjustment to this situation within the customary framework is either expansion through purchase of land or migration. . . .

When good *kibanja* land becomes scarce, the price of land goes up. Table 14 shows how the market value of *kibanja* land has increased during the last 20 years.

In the Ihangiro sample 31 farmers out of 52 had bought one or more plots of the main land-use types to expand their farm units. Very few farmers in the sample had sold land. This raises the questions: which farmers are selling land? What is the mechanism in the demand for and supply of land?

Table 14.
Increase in market value of well-established *kibanja* land 1950-1970 *(Ihangiro)**

Year	Shs per hectare	Shs per acre
1954	3000/-	1200/-
1960	4000/-	1600/-
1965	5420/-	2168/-
1968	7400/-	2960/-
1970	10000/-	4000/-

* The prices are average calculations.

Two main reasons exists for a farmer to sell all or part of his land:

1. To move to another area because of population pressure on land. In that case the small holder will often start by selling one-third of his *kibanja* to get some capital on which to survive during the first period of hardship in opening up new land. Over the following period of establishment he will rely on part of his former *kibanja* for food supply and gradually sell the rest. In that way, in densely populated areas in Bukoba District a considerable amount of developed *kibanja* will be available for the well-off farmers to purchase. At the same time the very small holder mainly producing for subsistence will be pushed out towards marginal areas.

2. To clear debts. A lot of short-term loan transactions occur in Buhaya rural society. If the debtor cannot repay his debts at the agreed date (e.g., when the final payment of coffee drops considerably), the loan is normally prolonged for a short period, but at very high interest rates, e.g., equivalent to 200 to 400 per cent per annum.

The final solution to clear the increasing debt may be to sell the land and migrate.

Thus, selling of land is often connected with migration of the poorer farmers as an adjustment to economic crisis. The purchase of land as an adjustment to land shortage works in favour of the rich farmers, who gain more control over the fertile and already developed *kibanja* land. In this way the formation of a rural class structure has been supported and the gap between the rural elite and the majority of common farmers has been growing, creating an inequality in the distribution of not only income but also of fertile land (James, 1971).

NOTES

3. This has been observed in *ujamaa* villages which have planted bananas without manure.

REFERENCES

James, R.W. 1971. *Land Tenure and Policy in Tanzania*. Dar Es Salaam: East African Literature Bureau.

Mutahaba, G. 1969. "The Importance of Peasant Consciousness for Effective Land Tenure Reform. The Problem of Abolishing Nyarubanja Land Tenure in Bukoba District." Political Science undergraduate dissertation, University of Dar Es Salaam.

Pitblado, J.R. 1970. *A Review of Agricultural Land Use and Land Tenure in Tanzania*. Research Notes, No. 7. Dar Es Salaam: BRALUP.

Reining, P.C. 1962. "Haya Land Tenure: Land Holding and Tenancy." *Anthropological Quarterly* 35(2).

Reining, P.C. 1965. "Land Resources of the Haya." In D. Brokensha (ed.), *Ecology and Development in Tropical Africa*. Research Series, No. 9. University of California.

Reining, P.C. 1967. "The Haya: The Agrarian System of a Sedentary People." Ph.D. dissertation, Anthropology, University of Chicago.

Reining, P.C. 1970. "Social Factors and Food Production in an East African Peasant Society: The Haya." In Peter McLoughlin (ed.), *African Food Production Systems*. Baltimore: Johns Hopkins University Press.

Forest, Foraging, Fences and Fuel in a Marginal Area of Kenya

David Brokensha and Bernard Riley

Where individualization of land tenure does take place, as under Kenya's land registration policy, it often involves a new perception on the part of rural people, the perception that land is a valuable, limited good. A similar shift in attitudes may take place with regard to trees. When land tenure is individualized, land distribution patterns will determine the differential impact of the growing scarcity of wood products.— The Editors.

This report deals with changing conditions in Mbere Division, Embu District, Kenya, which is the location for our recent collaborative research.[1] Mbere is a marginal area, representative in important respects of other marginal areas in the tropics, where an increasing population is pressing on a severely limited resource base. Mbere is marginal physically, in that elevation, rainfall and soil make most of it unsuitable for rain-fed agriculture; it is also marginal socially, being on the margins (compared to the more favored areas to the west) of modernization and development.

Mbere Division, which has a wide variety of altitude, rainfall, soils and vegetation, covers about 1600 square km, and can be divided into three ecological zones running from southwest to northeast:

Excerpted from David Brokensha and Bernard Riley, "Forest, Foraging, Fences and Fuel in a Marginal Area of Kenya," Paper prepared for USAID Africa Bureau Firewood Workshop, Washington, D.C., 12-14 June 1978 (Santa Barbara: Social Process Research Institute, University of California). Reprinted with the permission of the authors.

Zone	Altitude	Mean Annual Rainfall
I	1200 meters	1000mm
II	800 to 1200 meters	700-1000mm
III	<800 meters	<700mm

... The Mbeere,[2] who number about 75,000 (estimate for 1978) are culturally and linguistically related to their better-known neighbors, the Kikuyu, Kamba, and Meru. Keeping some cattle and goats, they are primarily agriculturists, in an area subject to recurrent failure of rains and consequent famines. There is a high degree of out-migration of labor.

The title of our paper indicates the main aspects of the problem: *forest* refers to the wooded areas that until recently were regarded, for most purposes, as communal land, where Mbeere people had the right to *forage* for fuel; *fences* are now being erected as a consequence of land adjudication, which is causing a major and dramatic change in land rights and access; *fuel*—firewood and charcoal—has, in the few years (since 1970) that we have known the area, also changed dramatically, in many ways including occurrence and perceptions....

In order to understand the present, we consider first the "traditional" role of firewood in Mbeere society. Three major aspects need to be emphasized: first, firewood was regarded as a free good, abundantly and conveniently available to all.

The notion of scarcity (common in regard to water, or food, or livestock) was inapplicable to firewood. It is a familiar and tragic viewpoint in all societies, when common resources are taken for granted, and people fail to see that they are dwindling.

Second is the importance of firewood in preparing food: "Firewood is the centre of life because it is used to prepare food, the main factor of life."[3]

Third is the symbolic significance of the homestead fire, which was not used for cooking but was the centre of important social activities. Every *mucii* (homestead) had to have a log (*icinga*) fire, outside the compound, especially in the evenings and early mornings. A fire was regarded as essential at night, to keep away hyenas and other wild animals, to deter thieves and intruders, and to serve as a focal point for a range of activities—these included story-telling to children, conversations and visitors, or discussion among the elders....

Land adjudication, introduced into Mbere in 1970, refers to the government of Kenya program for giving individual title to land (see Brokensha and Glazier, 1974 [sic]; Brokensha and Njeru, 1977).

Although the process is not yet complete in all of Mbere, it has already had profound effects on land rights. Before land adjudication, firewood was a "free good" which generally could be gathered anywhere. There were restrictions. Some species (notably *mu-kau*, *Melia volkenskii*, as already mentioned) have for long been private property because of their value as building timber. All vegetation in the *iiri*, the "sacred groves," was once protected, it being forbidden even to collect fallen timber. The Kenya Forestry Department and the Embu Local Council maintained a few forest reserves, the largest being that remnant on the top of Kiang'ombe, the highest hill in Mbere. Some clans had local vegetation conservation rules regarding control of trees along river banks, or on hillsides. But generally a woman could wander off into the bush and collect whatever firewood she wished: this was the case when we first saw Mbere in 1970. As people started getting individual title to land, so did they cut down on others' rights over their land. In decreasing order of importance, these rights included:

- building a house
- planting trees
- planting annual crops
- grazing livestock
- cutting firewood for sale
- cutting firewood for domestic use
- picking up fallen branches for domestic use
- placing bee hives
- crossing the land.

When we left Mbere last, in September 1977, the situation was confused. In some areas (including, but not restricted to, high-value areas in Zone I) land adjudication had resulted already in so much litigation and so many bitter quarrels that practically all rights of others over the land had been stopped: it became common to see fences, and *MBWA KALI* ("Fierce Dog!") signs. In other areas, people said that if they asked permission to gather (not actually cut) suitable firewood, and if they were on good terms with the owner, they would still be allowed to collect. But everyone predicted an increased rate of change, as more owners insisted on exclusive rights over their land. . . .

Firewood first appeared for sale at markets (Siakago and Ishiara) in 1976. Before that date, some salaried people (e.g., male teachers whose wives were not present) and business people had bought firewood by *ad hoc* arrangements, usually made with some poor old woman who was desperate for money. "Selling firewood used to be a poverty sign," said one of our friends, commenting that trees are now seen as an acceptable source of cash revenue by all. . . .

To summarize, firewood played, and plays, a significant part in Mbere society and economy. . . . Until recently, it was regarded as a free good, supplies of which were inexhaustible. By standards of our contemporary energy shortage it was used freely, even wastefully. In recent years, a combination of factors has resulted in drastic changes. These include rapid increase in population and increased clearing of bush for agriculture; decrease in trees available, as they are cut down and not replaced; restriction of access due to land adjudication; acceptance by women (from necessity) of what a few years ago would have been considered inferior species of trees as sources of firewood. Firewood is now a commercial commodity, in ever decreasing supply.

Although in 1977 it was too early to be confident, individual land owners were beginning to recognize that "the other energy crisis" had reached Mbere, and were taking care of their future needs by planting "hedgerow" or "shade plot" stands of *Eucalyptus*, *Grevillea robusta* and other species. The search for firewood is likely to involve most Mbeere people in more time and money, further reducing the time they could spend on more productive activity. . . .

NOTES

1. We are now completing the final draft of a monograph, which will be a comprehensive study of social and ecological change, focusing on changes in occurrence and use of plants, both wild and domesticated.

2. Preferred spelling for the people is Mbeere, although the division is spelt Mbere.

3. Based on note by Samuel Kienge, one of our main Mbeere helpers, who provided much useful information and many insights in this section of our study.

REFERENCES

Brokensha, David and Jack Glazier. 1973. "Land Reform among the Mbeere of Central Kenya." *Africa* 43(3):182-206.

Brokensha, David and E.H.N. Njeru. 1977. "Some Consequences of Land Adjudication in Mbere Division, Embu." Working Paper 320. I.D.S., University of Nairobi.

Riley, Bernard W. and David Brokensha. forthcoming. *People and Plants: Social and Ecological Change in Mbeere, Kenya.* Lanham, Maryland.

4

Communities and Trees

Forests are controlled—either owned or managed—by governments, corporations, communities and kin groups. In this array of social organizations ranging from the nation-state to the individual, professional forestry has tended be a government and private commercial enterprise. In part this is because large acreages are particularly suited to the practice of the large-scale plantation forestry for which foresters are trained (Fortmann and Fairfax, 1985).

In addition, the agendas and preconceived notions of outside observers have often kept community forestry invisible. For example, the Chinese have been concerned with forests and the effects of deforestation for centuries (Menzies, forthcoming). But as Menzies (Chapter Two, this volume) shows, both Chinese and European observers provided only the most fragmentary information on any forest practices, and particularly those of local communities, requiring a heroic effort to piece together even a minimal view of community control. For their part, state and national governments have no particular reason to acknowledge the rights or competence of community foresters since historically central governments have competed with local communities and local people for control of forest land. All over the world, for centuries, peasants and the state have been slugging it out in the forest.

The control of "forests" (not all of which had trees) was such an issue that in the Magna Carta King John was compelled to "disafforest" all the land that had been declared forest during his reign. When land was declared to be forest or "afforested," the right to hunt on it was vested solely in the crown—a reminder to us today that forest use involves much more than just cutting trees for lumber or fuel. "Disafforesting" thirteenth century land had nothing to do with trees but rather was a legal process whereby the right to hunt was no longer vested solely in the Crown and could be exercised by others. Two years later, in 1217, the Charter of the Forests was issued. Under the Charter, all forests except those "afforested" by Henry II (1154) were "disafforested," an act that provided the basis of forest administration for the next century (Cox, 1905:6,12; Hinde, 1985:28). One of Karl Marx's early writings concerned the struggle between national and local powers over the right to use forest land in the Rhineland (Linebaugh, 1976). In the 1870s the Klamath Indians in northern California had to resort to various subterfuges in order to cut and sell timber that the courts held was under trust status and therefore property of the United States government (Stern, 1965:62). Similar struggles continue to the present day (Fernandes and Kulkarni, 1983; Fortmann and Starrs, 1986) and leave their mark on forestry efforts. Communities in Nepal, for example, which witnessed the nationalization of their forests in 1957, have in the wake of denationalization been suspicious as to whether "forest department officials would not just step in again when they thought the community had contributed enough to forest development" (Molnar, 1985:6).

Despite the power of the state, communities continue to play an important role in the use and management of forests and trees. In some places they have become important by the sheer volume of the resources they control; in Switzerland, for example, where in 1955 "communities" (which included administrative communes, non-kin groups holding land in common (commoners), parishes, school communities, guilds and syndicates, and foundations) owned two-thirds of the forests and 72 percent of the forest acreage (Statistiques de la Suisse, 1955). Community jurisdiction can take many forms: communities often control land that foresters need for nurseries; communities make determinations that affect commons projects; communities make decisions about commons use that affect the landless (Panel on Common Property Resource Management, 1986; Netting, 1976), and finally, community control is often exercised over land owned or managed by a multitude of households.

Four kinds of questions arise about the role of community property rights in forest use and management. The first concerns the definition of community. The second develops from the myth of the homogeneous community. The third encompasses mechanisms by which communities exercise control. The fourth involves the factors which lead to shifts from community to state or private control.

DEFINING COMMUNITY AND COMMUNITY MEMBERSHIP

Community control of resources has often been associated with geographically-bounded communities where ties of kinship buttressed territorial ties. But neither community nor community membership is so easily defined. Even if we are conservative and take community to mean a geographically specific place, community membership can be defined by present or previous residence, by property ownership, or by kin ties. Using various definitions, a single individual could, were it advantageous, claim membership simultaneously in a number of communities.

These definitions assume more than academic interest when they are the basis for the distribution of rights to forest resources. The territory and resources over which a community exercises *de facto* or *de jure* control can become a matter of serious, even violent, dispute as when women in the Chipko movement faced off and won against logging contractors, defending the usufructuary claims of their Himalayan villages against the state (Mishra and Tripathi,1978).

Similarly, the definition of community membership determines who may lay what claims against community resources. Such restrictions, if they can be enforced, regulate pressure on the resources. The Yoruba communities described by *Lloyd* distinguished "strangers" as a separate category of residents who had a restricted set of rights to community resources (Berry, 1975). Similarly, the Swiss community studied by Netting (1981:60) restricted access to communal summer pastures and forests to citizens, a category that appeared in written documents as early as 1473. Thus, residence and even private property ownership in the village did not necessarily result in access to communal property.

THE MYTH OF THE HOMOGENEOUS COMMUNITY

Far from being homogeneous, communities are divided by class, caste, religion, ethnicity, gender, geographical origin and length of settlement. This diversity combined with the multiple and sometimes mutually exclusive uses that can be made of trees complicates the equitable distribution of rights of access. Trees cut for timber can not be used for fodder or human food. Lopping a tree for fodder may reduce its value for timber. Thus, to the basic issues of who, when, and how much is added the question "for what."

Different strata of the community or different members of a household or households in different parts of their life cycle have different needs. Jodha (1986) found that the poor were more likely to use common pool resources including village forests for fuel and fodder while the rich used them as a supply of timber. *Hosmer* describes the special gathering rights of the poor. Community attempts to control resources are therefore quite likely to reflect community struggles and cleavages.

Here the myth of the homogeneous community may lead the unwary into simplistic plans that fail to take community diversity into account. Failure to include all groups in decision making can result in untenable decisions. Molnar (1985:8) describes a Nepalese village in which the men decided to protect their village forest from degradation by closing the forest "to all grazing and cutting, only allowing villagers a few days per year to enter the forest and cut small wood and leaf fodder." The result was that the women, who had not been consulted in the decision, were forced to steal wood from the forest of the adjacent *panchayat*.[1] The women of that *panchayat*, whose forest had been placed under a similar system, did the same in the forest of yet another *panchayat*. This domino-effect was a direct result of decision-making without consulting the full range of village users.

As Molnar's observations suggest, community control may also take place at the expense of other communities. Skar and her colleagues (1982) described the exclusion of community members who have traditionally collected wood from an area subsequently taken over by a cooperative.

MECHANISMS OF CONTROL

Communities control forest resources both directly and indirectly. There are a number of advantages to direct community control. First, the resource can be managed as a whole, eliminating the unanticipated cumulative effects of myriad individual management strategies. *Hosmer* and Netting (1981:67) note the importance of maintaining Alpine woodlands intact to prevent avalanche damage. Second, use can be spread over a wide area rather than be concentrated in a single spot. Third, forest products can be distributed more equitably across the community. Fourth, as *Hosmer* shows, the community can use the forest as an asset to meet community needs. *Lloyd* provides a particularly interesting illustration of this in his description of a Yoruba community which harvested oil palms communally, sometimes using them to pay debts incurred by the village as a whole. Finally, the community may be better able than individuals to protect the resource against incursions by outsiders.

An initial question to be answered is how community control is to be enforced. As demonstrated in *Moench*, a community does not have to own forest land in order to control it. Nor does community ownership of a resource automatically lead to community control over it. Community control requires the ability to control the behavior of community members as well as the ability to exclude outsiders. Neither follows automatically from statutory or customary ownership. For example, Eastman and Gray (1987:57) report concern among local residents about over-cutting on community lands in New Mexico. Similarly, a community organized during the 60s in California has been unable to persuade the membership to observe its own tree cutting ban (Don Flickinger, 1987, personal communication). The question for those who would institute or strengthen community management of resources is what community level institutions are necessary and sufficient to initiate and sustain community control of the resource.

Control by a professional forester on behalf of the community as described by *Hosmer* requires that the value of the off-take be sufficient to pay a salary and hence more likely to be found in conjunction with commercial production. Under the control of agents of the U.S. Bureau of Indian Affairs, proceeds from the logging of timber on the Klamath Reservation in northern California were distributed among the residents, rising in the 1930s to over $800 per capita (Stern, 1965: 152-153).

A second mechanism, community control through indigenous institutions, is described by Willan (1967:5) among the Sherpa of Nepal:

> Certain members of the community were designated ... whose function was to report any person who cut trees without permission having been obtained from the village council. Fines were imposed for wrong-doing and were paid in the form of beer.

A notable advantage of such a system is that users and enforcers are in daily interaction. Thompson and Warburton (1985a: 122 and b: 205-206) note that when the Sherpa system was abolished with the nationalization of the forests, deforestation of centuries-old village forests began, since the new system was inconvenient for users and there was no local monitoring of use. Various communities in Mali control tree cutting, at least one to the extent that obtaining official permission from the forest department is merely a formality (Montagne, 1985/1986). Community councils in Swiss villages marked trees to be cut for fuelwood and allotted timber shares by the drawing of lots (Netting, 1981:189). Leaves for fodder are auctioned and the proceeds used for community projects in India (Brara, 1987). Nor is such control confined to distant places. In 1639, in Hampton, New Hampshire, three men were appointed wood's wards to control forest use and to assign a cutting quota to each head of household (Pennsylvania Department of Forests and Waters, 1932).

However, community control does not necessarily pose an easy solution to those trying to reforest or prevent deforestation as the priorities and concerns of local groups may conflict with the agenda of foresters and agroforesters. Agricultural officers in colonial Tanganyika ran afoul of traditional land wardens who forbade the planting of permanent crops because of their concern over the possibility of the alienation of the land from the subclan (Brain, 1980).

Moench examines the management of forest resources through the general process of social control. While such management can be very effective regardless of the ownership status of the land (Moench's villagers managed land that belonged not to them but to the state), this sort of management requires particular conditions if free riding or outside mauraders are not to undermine the system. These include the ability to exclude or control outsiders, community-wide understanding of, and willingness to adhere to, management rules, and effective sanctions for non-compliance. Such management can not work if the resource can not be monitored, if there is no agreement on the rules of management, if the community is split into hostile factions, or if there is no means of sanctioning transgressions.[2]

THE SHIFT AWAY FROM COMMUNITY CONTROL

Changing social relations may shift control of forest resources away from communities. The state may simply seize control for itself as it did in Nepal. Or changing political considerations may lead the state to shift some control into private hands as described by *Chen*. Millon (1955) has speculated that the growth of a commercial trade in coffee and cacao played an important role in the privatization of community land in Mesoamerica. This is similar to the shift documented by Berry (1975). *Cernea* describes how tree planting finalized the transition from community to private control of land, facilitating the exclusion of customary uses such as fodder and grass cutting.

Cernea's discussion is particularly important for those who must deal with communities. Not only does it delineate the differences in interests and resources within communities, it also documents the evolutionary nature of property rights. As McCutcheon (1981) notes, although the ancient rules and processes of the allocation and enforcement of property rights may be solemnly recited, they may no longer affect daily action.

There is likely to be greater effort to bring communities into an increased role in forestry and agroforestry as the dynamics of deforestation and reforestation are better understood. Their integration will require a clear recognition of the diversity and complexity of the rules, processes, and interests involved in community use and management of resources and the effects that government penetration has on the local balance of power and interest.

Notes

1. "*Panchayat*" is a south Asian term referring to a government by a small group of chosen village representatives. In Nepal, the *panchayat* is a unit of nine villages, "wards," administered by a group of eleven elected council members, one of whom serves as a council head. (Molnar, 1985:6).

2. See also Ostrom, 1986; Thomson et al., 1986; Arnold and Campbell, 1986; Messerschmidt, 1986; Blaikie et al., 1986; Jessup and Peluso, 1986; McKean, 1986.

References

Arnold, J.E.M. and J. Gabriel Campbell. 1986. " Institutional Dynamics: The Evolution and Dissolution of Common Property Resource Management" in Panel on Common Property Resource Management, Board on Science and Technology for International Development, Office of International Affairs, National Research Council. *Proceedings of the Conference on Common Property Resource Management*. Washington, D.C.: National Academy Press: 425-454.

Berry, Sara S. 1975. *Cocoa, Custom and Socio-Economic Change in Rural Western Nigeria*. Oxford: Clarendon Press.

Blaikie, Piers M., John C. Harriss, and Adam N. Pain. 1986. "The Management and Use of Common Property Resources in Tamil Nadu,

India." in Panel on Common Property Resource Management, Board on Science and Technology for International Development, Office of International Affairs, National Research Council. 1986. *Proceedings of the Conference on Common Property Resource Management.* Washington, D.C.: National Academy Press. 481-504.

Brain, James. 1980. "The Uluguru Land Usage Scheme: Success and Failure" *Journal of Developing Areas* 14: 175-190.

Brara, Rita. 1987. "Shifting Sands: A Study of Customary Rights in Grazing" Mimeo. Jaipur, India: Institute of Development Studies.

Cox, J. Charles. 1905. *The Royal Forests of England.* London: Methuen and Co.

Eastman, Clyde and James R. Gray. 1987. *Community Grazing: Practice and Potential in New Mexico.* Albuquerque: University of New Mexico.

Fernandes and Kulkarni. 1983. *Towards a New Forest Policy.* New Delhi: Indian Social Institute.

Fortmann, Louise and Paul Starrs. 1986. "Burning Issues: Power Plants and Resource Rights." Report Prepared for the Forest and Rangeland Resource Assessment Program, California Department of Forestry.

Fortmann, Louise and Sally Fairfax. 1985. "American Forestry Professionalism in the Third World: Some Preliminary Observations on Effects." in R.S.Gallin and A. Spring (eds.) Women Creating Wealth: Transforming Economic Development. Selected Papers and Speeches from the Association for Women in Development Conference, April 25-27, 1985. Washington, D.C.: 105-108.

Hinde, Thomas. 1985. *Forests of Britain.* London: Victor Gollancz Ltd.

Jessup, Timothy and Nancy Lee Peluso. 1986. "Minor Forest Products as Common Property Resources in East Kalimantan, Indonesia" in Panel on Common Property Resource Management, Board on Science and Technology for International Development, Office of International Affairs, National Research Council. *Proceedings of the Conference on Common Property Resource Management.* Washington, D.C.: National Academy Press: 505- 531.

Jodha, N.S. 1986. "Common Property Resources and Rural Poor in Dry Regions of India" *Economic and Political Weekly* XXI (27): 1169 - 1181.

Linebaugh, Peter. 1976. "Karl Marx, the Theft of Wood and Working Class Composition: A Contribution to the Current Debate" *Crime and Social Justice* 6: 5-16.

Lloyd, P.C. 1962. *Yoruba Land Law* London: Oxford University Press.

McCutcheon, Mary Shaw. 1981. *Resource Exploitation and the Tenure of Land and Sea in Palau.* Unpublished PhD Dissertation, University of Arizona.

McKean, Margaret A. 1986. "Management of Traditional Common Lands (Iriachi) in Japan." in Panel on Common Property Resource Management, Board on Science and Technology for International Development, Office of International Affairs, National Research Council. *Proceedings of the Conference on Common Property Resource Management.* Washington, D.C.: National Academy Press: 533-589.

Menzies, Nicholas. Forthcoming. "The History of Forestry in China," Vol. 6, J. Needham (ed.) *Science and Civilisation in China.* Cambridge: Cambridge University Press.

Messerschmidt, D.A. 1986. "People and Resources in Nepal: Customary Resource Management Systems of the Upper Kali Gandaki" in Panel on Common Property Resource Management, Board on Science and Technology for International Development, Office of International Affairs, National Research Council. *Proceedings of the Conference on Common Property Resource Management.* Washington, D.C.: National Academy Press: 455-480.

Millon, Rene F. 1955. "Trade, Tree Cultivation, and the Development of Private Property in Land." *American Anthropologist* 57:698-712.

Mishra,A. and S. Tripathi. 1978. *Chipko Movement, Uttarakhand Women's Bid to Save Forest Wealth.* New Delhi: People's Action.

Molnar, Augusta. 1985. "Social Forestry Experiences in India and Nepal." Unpublished Preliminary Draft. Washington, D.C.: General Agricultural Division (ASPAB) World Bank.

Montagne, Pierre. 1985/1986. "Contributions of Indigenous Silviculture to Forestry Development in Rural Areas: Examples from Niger and Mali." *Rural Africana* (23-24): 61-65.

Netting, Robert McC. 1976. "What Alpine Peasants have in common: Observations on Communal Tenure in a Swiss Village" *Human Ecology* 4:135-146.

Netting, Robert McC. 1981. *Balancing on an Alp: Ecological Change and Continuity in a Swiss Mountain Community.* Cambridge: Cambridge University Press.

Ostrum, Elinor. 1986. "Issues of Definition and Theory: Some Conclusions and Hypotheses" in Panel on Common Property Resource Management, Board on Science and Technology for International Development, Office of International Affairs, National Research Council. *Proceedings of the Conference on Common Property*

Resource Management. Washington, D.C.: National Academy Press.: 599-615.

Panel on Common Property Resource Management. Board on Science and Technology for International Development. Office of International Affairs, National Research Council. 1986. *Proceedings of the Conference on Common Property Resource Management. April 21-26, 1985.* Washington, D.C.: National Academy Press.

Pennsylvania Department of Forests and Waters. 1932. "Interesting Forest Facts." Service Letter 3(149, June, 16).

Skar, Sara Lund, Nelida Arias, and Cotarma Saturno Garcia. 1982. "Fuel Availability, Nutrition and Women's Work in Highland Peru: Three Case Studies from Contrasting Andean Communities." World Employment, Research WEP, 10/WP23. Geneva: ILO.

Statistiques de la Suisse, 309 ème Fascicule. 1959. "Forstbetriebe der Öffentlichrechtlichen Körperschaften in der Schweiz" Vol 2 of 4. *Eidgenössiche Betriebszählung 25 August 1955.* Bern.

Stern, Theodore. 1965. *The Klamath Tribe.* Seattle: University of Washington Press.

Thompson, Michael and Michael Warburton. 1985a. "Uncertainty on a Himalayan Scale" *Mountain Research and Development* 5 (2): 115-135.

Thompson, Michael and Michael Warburton. 1985b. "Knowing Where to Hit: A conceptual Framework for the Sustainable Development of the Himalaya" *Mountain Research and Development* 5 (3): 203-220.

Thomson, James T., David H. Feeny, and Ronald Oakerson. 1986. in Panel on Common Property Resource Management, Board on Science and Technology for International Development, Office of International Affairs, National Research Council. *Proceedings of the Conference on Common Property Resource Management.* Washington, D.C.: National Academy Press: 391-424

The Editors

meet needs . . .
defray costs . . .

City, Town, and Communal Forests

Ralph S. Hosmer

Fequently community management of resources is considered to be a phenomenon of the developing world. Hosmer's 1922 letter from Switzerland serves as an excellent illustration to the contrary. Of particular interest are the rules for distribution of forest products, including special rights for the poor, the employment of professional foresters to meet community needs, and the melding of national interests with local control.—The Editors.

A characteristic and striking feature of European forestry is the number of communal, town, and city forests that one sees in each of the several countries. Indeed this class of forest land plays a large part in serving the needs of very many persons who otherwise would be hard put to obtain the supplies of wood that they absolutely require. It is a phase of forestry that should be of interest to Americans, for it holds lessons that could well be taken to heart by many communities in the United States. The purpose of this letter is to give some account of this system, with especial reference to certain forests that are recognized as being classic examples of this class of publicly owned forest land.

The history of many of the communal forests runs back to very early days. Some are the remnants of the land that in pre-feudal times was held for the common use of all the people of the tribe or community in a given locality. More have their origin in prescriptive rights that were secured by the common people during the Middle Ages, under the feudal system. Others, of more recent date, have been obtained through gift, or purchase, or as the result of land adjustments made at the conclusion of a war. But, however they came into being, forests of this class are now distinctly a factor to be reckoned with in all the European countries...

Excerpted from Ralph S. Hosmer. 1922. *Impressions of European Forestry*. Chicago: The Lumber World Review.

As to the reasons for the desirability and necessity for communal forests, we find the answer in two words, fuel and transportation. As conditions became more settled in the European countries and as population increased, the accessible forests were naturally the first to begin to show the effects of exploitation. With the difficulties of transport it became evident that the local wood supplies must be conserved and continued. Especially was this true with regard to fuel wood.

THE SIHLWALD

Unquestionably the most noted forest of this class in forestry annals is the city forest of Zürich, Switzerland, the Sihlwald...

The Sihlwald is a forest of 2580 acres (1044.8 hectares) in area, situated on the east slope of a range of hills, known as the Zürichberg, that runs south from Zürich. The highest point is Albishorn (2974 feet). The forest lies in the valley of the Sihl river...

The history of the Sihlwald as a forest supplying the needs of Zürich runs back to the year 853, when the German king, Ludwig, gave it, with other lands, to his daughter Hildegarde, the first abbess of the nunnery at Zürich. During the succeeding centuries it continued to supply construction timber and other wood required by the people of the city. In 1524, with the political changes incident to the Reformation, the Sihlwald became the property of the city of Zürich, in whose ownership it has since remained.

The old chronicles record various ordinances in regard to the use of the Sihlwald and indicate that there was a more or less definite plan of management, at any rate from about the beginning of the sixteenth century. The appointment of two foresters was definitely authorized in 1460, and there are many other indications that the forest was carefully looked after. Modern working plans for the Sihlwald date from 1834, the years of grand revisions being 1860, 1880, 1900 and 1920. [This selection is dated 1922, (eds.)] There are periodic revisions every 10 years...

It was interesting, at the headquarters of the forester on the Sihlwald, to see the manuscript copy of this working plan with its subsequent revisions. One point of especial value is that this particular plan has an appendix in which is recorded the reasons why certain pieces of work were done on the forest. By this means subsequent foresters have the opportunity to check up more accurately on the projects initiated by their predecessors. Especially is this true if the project was somewhat experimental in character and turned out badly;

knowing all the facts in the case, that particular mistake is not likely to be repeated...

The forest of the Sihlwald is predominantly beech, managed on a rotation of 100 years. The silvicultural method is shelterwood, where the final crop is removed in a series of cuttings, so spaced as to years, as to induce natural reproduction of the new crop. The wood and timber from the thinnings of course form an important part of the annual proceeds from the forest...

For transporting the logs down the slope there has been constructed a narrow gauge railroad, in part with movable tracks, that seems well to serve the purpose. Log shoots are also in use for both timber and fuel wood. The smaller wood, branches and the like, is usually brought down on sleds over prepared tracks, the sleds being carried up the hill by the laborers...

The area of the Sihlwald is hardly great enough profitably to support a local wood-using industry, but a small mill established in earlier years is still maintained and actively operated. Lumber, railroad ties, tool handles of various kinds, stakes and poles are the main products, together with that from an excelsior machine that turns out four grades of this material, called in Europe "woodwool"... There is also an impregnating plant for the preservative treatment of railroad ties. Some 30 men are employed in the mill, and about 120 more in the forest, so that the Sihlwald supports directly a comfortable little community. In connection with the Sihlwald there is maintained in Zürich a city woodyard from which the people of this city can be supplied with fuel wood. At the mill in the Sihlwald bundled kindling wood is also prepared for sale at this market.

The normal annual yield of the Sihlwald, including both the thinnings and the final cut, averages around 8.5 cubic meters per hectare (2.47 acres)... In general it may be said that in normal times the Sihlwald is an investment that yields a satisfactory revenue. The memorable thing about this forest is that it has been supplying Zürich with wood for over one thousand years.

THE FOREST OF WINTERTHUR

Not far from Zürich, to the northeast is the forest of Winterthur, ... that city being an important manufacturing center where especially are made various kinds of machinery. The forest lies on the rising land immediately behind the town.

Whereas the Sihlwald is predominantly a beech forest (60 percent), Wintherthur is a coniferous stand...

The forest of Winterthur covers an area of 2984 acres (1208 hectare). It has long been a city forest and for more than a century has been managed under a definite working plan. The rotation normally in use is 100 years, but there are numerous stands older than this and in certain places over-standards of pine are being allowed to remain into or through the second rotation. The silvicultural method followed is group-wise shelterwood. Small openings are made in the mature forest, which as reproduction begins are gradually enlarged by the removal of more and more of the old trees, until finally the old stand is replaced by the new crop... Winterthur, in common with the other forests with which this letter deals, has a system of permanent forest roads, so that with the ready market for all forest products even a few trees can be removed from a given place at a profit.

Particularly close utilization is a feature of this forest. Even the small branches of the spruces and firs are sold for use in covering garden beds... Somewhat larger branch wood, especially of the broadleaf species, is made up into bundles... The larger fuel wood is corded and sold alongside the roads... Dead branches and cones are collected by poor persons on certain days of the week, so absolutely nothing which can be used is allowed to go to waste...

In Winterthur, as in other of the city forests visited in Switzerland and in Germany, ample provision is made for those who repair to the forest for recreation. All the crossings of the forest roads have sign boards, seats are provided at frequent intervals, trees are cut out to make vistas where there is a chance for an outlook, and on the top of the hill in the center of the forest is a tall steel tower from which one can get an admirable view over the surrounding country.

FOREST ADMINISTRATION IN SWITZERLAND

... Switzerland is divided politically into 22 cantons, each of which preserves a large share of autonomy. Each, for instance, has its own forestry organization, all generally similar to that of Zürich, although differing in details and in the titles borne by the foresters.

The cantonal forest services are independent of the federal government and of one another, much as are our own state forestry organizations. But there is this exception: Under the Swiss forest law areas that are required to be kept under forest for protective purposes, as torrent and avalanche control, are declared to be "protection forests", and then come under the supervision of inspectors who make up the staff of the Forestry Bureau of the Confederation, that has its head-quarters at Berne. All work on these forests is, however, done, co-operatively with the cantonal foresters...

THE COMMUNAL FOREST OF GRINDELWALD

...There is one other Swiss example that deserves mention, the mountain forests of the commune of Grindelwald, in the forest district of Interlaken, in the canton of Berne. Grindelwald, ... is a little town nestling in a high valley in the Bernese Oberland, under the shadow of the high peaks of the Wetterhorn and of the Jungfrau. The commune is made up of seven mountain villages, each of which has its forest. Three-fourths of the forest land in the valley belongs to the commune. From their location these forests all fall into the protection forest class. They are managed under working plans, drawn up by one of the assistants in the district forester's office and supervised and administered by the local ranger. No trees can be cut until they have been marked by the ranger, and strict care is taken not to exceed the allowed annual limit.

The interesting point is, however, the way in which the timber so cut is distributed among the people, for there is not enough to permit any to be shipped out of the valley. Applications for timber and wood may be made only by bona fide residents of the commune, landowners. They are divided into six classes. First served are those who want lumber for repairing the little cabins that shelter the cattle in the high pasture lands, or for the construction of new cabins. In local usage these mountain pastures are "the alps," not the mountain peaks as we normally use the term. Second, comes wood for building and repairing fences on the mountain sides. Third, repairs to cattle stables in the valley. Fourth, repairs to houses in the valley. Fifth, lumber for new houses—which are usually put up by all the neighbors joining in a house raising "bee," just as used to be the custom in America, when the Ohio valley was still on the frontier. (Likewise the owner of the house sets up drinks for the crowd, the only payment, just as did our own worthy forbears.)

When all these needs are served, if there is any wood left, the sixth-class applicant comes to be considered, the man who wants fuel. Often he does not get any, for the allowed cut has been exhausted; but he seldom goes cold, for almost every landowner has a little patch of private woodland and also the right to gather dry wood and branches in the communal forest. Of course all of this is on a very small scale and rather primitive as to methods—the lumber for the repairs to the alpine cabins has for instance all to be packed on men's backs, up slopes where one plank makes a good load—but it serves to show the value of communal forests and the need of exercising the great care in their perpetuation. . . .

One point in the Swiss forest law regarding privately owned forest land may perhaps here be noted. In the federal enactment that applies to all the cantons it is made specific and mandatory that the existing forest area of Switzerland shall not be reduced. Consequently, when the private owner of forest land cuts his forest he must either do it in a manner approved by the local forest officer, or within a specified time, two years, replant it artificially with nursery stock. If he fails to do so the government does the planting and sends him the bill. Payment or imprisonment are the remaining alternatives. This provision of the law applies even to areas in the agricultural valleys where the owner desires to transform his forest into farming land. He may be permitted to do this after due consideration by the local officials, but he must still afforest an equal area somewhere else. The present proportion of forest land to total area must be maintained.

During [World War I], owing to the high prices that could be got for lumber shipped to France or to Italy, all the forest lands of Switzerland were temporarily declared protection forest and thus made subject to inspection and more effective control. In this way wholesale exploitation of private forest land was prevented, for with wartime prices the owner who clear cut could well have paid his fine and still made a very handsome profit. The government did not wish to see the local supply so much reduced.

CONCLUSIONS—APPLICATIONS OF THE PRINCIPLE

The conclusions which an American may draw from visits to the city, town, and communal forests of Europe may perhaps be summarized somewhat as follows: It is quite obvious that the economic conditions that obtain in Europe do not hold for the United States. . . . . [In Europe] nearby markets and dense population justify highly intensive forest management, with permanent roads and absolute utilization. With us there is another set of conditions altogether, to say nothing of differences in climate, in the species that make up the forest, and above all in the customs and habits of the people. But notwithstanding all this, it is borne in upon the visitor that these European communities have got hold of a principle, and are using it to their advantage, that could equally well be applied in other countries.

In a few of the smaller German villages, it is said that the annual net proceeds from the community forest are sufficient not only to pay all the local public expenses, such as schools, roads, official salaries and the like, but also to permit of a cash dividend to all the land owners, in place of a tax levy. That this is exceptional is true; also it is true that it is only found in a few very small communities. But in many European towns the net revenue from the town or communal forest is enough materially to reduce the yearly budget of the town, which would otherwise have to be raised wholly by taxation...

And further with a community forest there is bound to be development of local industry; small perhaps, but nevertheless of value. The more persons who are employed in permanent, stable industries the better it is for any community.

Now for the application. Almost every American city, town, and village has in its neighborhood areas of waste land, of little or no value for agriculture or for any other productive use except the growing of trees. But it can do that. And moreover it can be bought very cheaply. Very often there is already enough young growth on the land to make, under proper care, the beginning of a forest. Refinements and intensive practice of forestry can come later when the forest begins to pay a revenue. A very small investment by the town at the start will set things going.

And so the lesson that the writer believes America can gain from these European town forests is not the importation of European methods or systems, but rather the adoption in practice of the principle that has led to such beneficial results of the other side of the Atlantic.

*Communal oil palm resource -
Customary Courts*

Land Rights in Ijebu

P. C. Lloyd

> Lloyd depicts two forms of community control of trees among the
> Yoruba of Nigeria. Cases from customary courts confirm
> community protection of sacred groves. An unusual form of com-
> munity management is the arrangement by which some or all of
> the oil palms are harvested communally.—The Editors.

Around most villages is a ring of thick forest useful alike for
defense and in keeping sheep and goats in the village. In this forest,
or in other nearby clumps of trees, are the shrines to the village's
peculiar deities, the *oro* grove[*] and the 'bad bush.' Such land is held
by the *olori ilu* [head of the town (eds.)] and the elders—the *ekeji
ilu*,[**] [led by]the *oloritun* [the oldest man of sound body and mind
living in the quarter of a village (ed.)]—on behalf of the whole
community.

> *Samuel, Bale of Idona* v. *Abiodun Koya* Ilugun Native Court
> 85/1956, transferred to Ijebu Ode Native Court:

Excepted from P.C. Lloyd. 1962. *Yoruba Land Law*. London: Oxford
University Press. pp. 174- 175. Reprinted with the permission of the
publisher.

[*] The center of the oro cult where "malefactors were usually killed and
the bodies of witches and those dying unnatural deaths were thrown
without burial." (p.153) [ed.]

[**] Titles such as *eketa ilu* were held by "the oldest men of each segment
of the dominant descent group (or of the several groups themselves in
larger villages) and the titles were held in rotation-on the death of
the *olori ilu* he was succeeded by the *ekeji ilu*, whose title in turn went
to the *eketa ilu*. In some villages and especially those formed by the
amalgamation of villages, the most senior title holder is known as the
bale" (p149)

The defendant entered the *igbo oro*, the sacred grove of Idona, and uprooting the *peregun* [*Dracena fagrans* (ed.)] trees, started to cultivate the land. The plaintiff ordered him to leave the land as cultivation of the grove was prohibited; he reported the matter to the *Elerunwon*, the priest of the grove, who also ordered the defendant to leave and to make a sacrifice in atonement. The defendant claimed the land as 'family land'— it was not disputed that his family land was adjacent to the grove. The court found, however, that the land was part of the *oro* grove, and vested therefore in the Bale and people of Idona. The defendant was ordered to leave the land.

Disu Onisanya v. *Gabriel Adeshina* Ijebu Ode Native Court 1033/1955:

The defendant was Bale of Idotun village, near Ishonyin, and the plaintiff a member of the community. The plaintiff sought from the court a declaration that the land which the Bale granted to the Aladura Church was vested in the whole village and used for *agemo*[cult name (ed.)] dances. He claimed that the Bale had not consulted the people of Idotun. The land had had an olden building on it but none of the descendants of its owner were known living. The members of the village had for many years cleared the land by communal labour. The Church gave 30 s[hillings] for the land which was used to buy gin for the elders—it was not shared *per stirpes* among the members of the village (all of whom traced descent from a common founder).

The court held that the land was not part of the *agemo* grove and that the Bale granted the land with the concurrence of the majority of his people. The grant was therefore valid.

The plaintiff seems to have fallen out with his village— hence this action; the villagers later revenged themselves by trying to deprive him of his own building plot—he had planted kola on it instead of building upon it—and the elders granted the land to another person. The court (Ijebu Ode Native Court 826/1956) sensing the nature of the quarrel, upheld the defendant's rights to the land—though they had no legal grounds for so doing—and advised him to make peace with his village.

In many villages the *olori ilu*, or (where such a title exists) the *oloja*, have their own *orubo* [farm land of the chiefs (ed.)]. The use of this land is governed by the same rules as those applying in Ijebu Ode.

A feature which seems peculiar to Ijebu villages is the communal reaping of the oil palms. In some villages all palms, in others only certain areas rich in palms, are embraced in this scheme. Palms are not allocated to individuals by the elders; instead, a certain day is appointed, usually once a month, on which every man is entitled to reap as many trees as is physically possible. Only full members of the village may enter this contest—those who reside elsewhere or who have not fulfilled their duties (such as clearing paths, supporting village contributions) are not allowed to participate. A man may employ one labourer to reap on his behalf. If any debt is owed by the whole village, such as the costs of a land dispute in the courts, it is usually these palms which are pawned to raise money. Frequently an individual member, anxious to gain prestige in his village by redeeming its honour, will repay the debt; when he feels that insufficient deference is paid to him he insists on his undoubted right of reaping the palms himself—they are in fact in pawn to him by the village. Such actions seem a frequent cause of disputes. Title to the palms is vested in the *olori ilu* for the whole village.

Fuel & Fodder

{ Comm. rights clear
{ Indiv. rights fuzzy

"Turf" and Forest Management in a Garhwal Hill Village

Marcus Moench

Moench undertook field research in a village in Teri Garhwal, India in 1984. This selection describes a system of locally recognized and respected inter-village and intra-village customary rights to land and trees ("turf") that supersedes national statutory rights and results in a reasonable level of forest management.—The Editors.

This chapter outlines a customary system of land and tree tenure, herein called "turf", and the system of forest management in a Sub-Himalayan Indian village, examines the theoretical connections between turf and the management system, and examines the implications of turf and village management systems for forestry projects.

The customary system of land and tree tenure described here is termed turf because of the informal and geographically defined nature of the tenure system. For the purposes of this chapter, turf is defined as a system of resource tenure that is: 1) geographically based (e.g. territory that is claimed on the basis of proximity to points of use or with boundaries that follow natural divides) 2) associated with a distinct social unit such as the village, clan, or family and 3) not incorporated into or recognized by any official, statutory tenure system. In the case study which follows, turf and forest management are examined on inter-village and intra-village levels.

Because turf is by definition associated with a social unit such as the village, the group with use rights is clearly delineated and generally small. Given the intimate nature of life in a village-like social group, information concerning resource use tends to be available, exclusion of non-members is relatively straightforward, there may be a relatively high degree of assurance between members, and informal social mechanisms exist for the control of free riders. Information

---

Written for this volume.

availability, exclusion, and assurance are also aided by the geographic nature of turf areas. Thus, turf includes elements often noted as fundamental to successful management of common resources (Ciriacy-Wantrup and Bishop, 1975; Gilles and Jamtgaard, 1981; Runge, 1981; Popkin, 1981; Oakerson, 1985).

THE VILLAGE STUDY

Munglori is 12 kilometers north-east of Mussoorie in Tehri Garhwal, India. The predominant local culture is Hindu Pahari (Berreman, 1972). Typical of many villages in the area, Munglori is a medium sized, Rajput (a relatively high cast) dominated, agricultural village with access to extensive oak forests, grassland and rain-fed agricultural lands but owning relatively little irrigated land (Table 1). Despite close linear proximity to the major center of Mussoorie, Munglori is isolated by the area's steep topography, and village production activities are primarily directed at subsistence needs rather than external markets. These subsistence activities are based on locally available resources, of which fodder and fuel are key elements.

Forest and grassland resources are critical to maintenance of village agriculture. The only source of fertilizer readily available to most villagers is farmyard manure. This fertilizer is in turn dependent on a continuous supply of fodder derived from overgrazed grasslands and leaves lopped from the forest. Roughly one third of the fodder (excluding the three month monsoon season) given to stall-fed stock is oak (*Quercus incanna*) leaf cut from the forests. In addition, as in most Himalayan villages, wood is the primary fuel. In Munglori, roughly half of the total wood fuel required comes from the small twigs remaining as a by-product of fodder collection. Thus, fodder, fertilizer, and fuel supplies are closely linked and the condition of forests is central to maintenance of village agriculture. Oak is the dominant species used to meet these needs and all references to "forests" in the rest of this paper refer to oak areas.

Forests in the Munglori region are owned by the state and under control of the Forest Department. Officials of the Forest Department are few and their presence has little influence on day-to-day patterns of forest use. Each village has a clearly defined "turf" area in the forests over which it claims use right. This use right has no legal standing but is explicitly recognized by other villages and serves as an effective, if unofficial control on access to forest. Turf in Munglori is ownership of resources that are officially in the public domain. In addition, within each village's forest families or small groups of families have hazily defined areas of regular use adjacent to outbuildings. These areas are <u>not</u> explicitly recognized by other members of the village but do provide a basis for limited management.

Field information was collected during a nine month period in 1984 via a series of semi-formal group interviews and through discussion with key individuals within the village. Extensive confirmation (i.e. by at least two independent groups or three separate individuals) was required prior to inclusion of the information in the data set. See Moench (1985) for details of the methodology and in-depth information on the village.

Table 1
Basic Village Characteristics

Population	254	Agricultural Lands*	78.4 *ha*
Rajput	206	Irrigated	7.5 ha
Scheduled Caste	48	Rainfed	70.9 ha
Livestock Total	351	Privated Grasslands	4.8 *ha*
Buffalo	89	Village Grasslands**	30.0 *ha*
Cattle	148	Forest Surrounding	
Goats & Sheep	106	Village***	485.0 *ha*
Bullocks	56	Portion of Forest	
Mules/Horses	9	Lopped for fodder***	98.0 ha

* All land areas are in hectares; data from local Patwari (land officer) records.
** Estimated from field measurements as the area of village common grassland.
*** Forest within the immediate watershed above Munglori.

OAK FOREST MANAGEMENT

Forest management in Munglori is not an active system involving organized cooperative action by the villagers but is defined by use (Roe & Fortmann, 1982). In this way it is quite different, for example, from the traditional village management systems in Nepal described by Messerschmidt (1985). These involve organized community action on the part of the villagers with the explicit goal of protecting or improving local forest resources. In Munglori the lack of organized community action around forests does not, however, reduce the importance of the de facto forest management that occurs. This *de facto* management is central to both the production of leaf fodder and the maintenance of forest condition.

The starting point with regard to forest management is the distinction between lopped areas and the full canopy forest. Lopped areas are essentially production forests directed at the supply of fodder and to a lesser extent fuel. Unlopped oaks do not supply fodder. Regular lopping is a prerequisite for the production of fodder. There are at least two reasons for this. First, villagers indicate that stock prefer fresh tender leaves from trees which have been regularly lopped because older leaves from previously uncut oaks are hard and dry. Second, larger branches tend to have a lower leaf-to-wood ratio than smaller ones. If the primary objective is fodder, collection of smaller branches from regularly lopped trees is, within limits, more desirable. As a result, the unlopped portions of the forest can not be considered as part of the primary leaf fodder production area. This implies that total production of the forest is irrelevant to fodder and fuel supply. Since demand is focused on a limited area, degradation can occur in conditions where aggregate forest production far exceeds demand (Moench and Bandyopadhyay, 1986).

Analysis of the branches collected for fodder can also provide an estimate of lopping frequency. The villagers' stated goal in fodder collection is to find a tree with branches that are easy to collect and have a large amount of leaf. They avoid cutting very small branches because these are difficult to collect and because cutting all the branches can kill the tree. The range in basal diameter of branches collected by villagers is narrow. In a random sample of 40 headloads, branches between 0.8 cm and 1.5 cm in diameter comprised 72 percent of those collected. Less than 1% of branches were smaller than 0.6 cm and less than 4 percent were greater than 2.1 cm. This size range corresponds to an age range for the branches. Ages for a large sample of branches of varying diameters were estimated via nodal point and ring counts. The weighted mean age for the branch size range collected by villagers is nearly five years. This is equivalent to a lopping frequency for the oaks of 2-3 years because branches younger than 2-3 years are in size classes smaller than those which appear in headloads.

Villagers' stated goals and the branch analysis indicate that lopped portions of the forest are managed for fodder production. This management is directed at the production of easily collected branches which can supply a large amount of leaf fodder relative to wood while maintaining the forest for sustainable fodder production. By avoiding cutting all of the branches, particularly small ones, from any tree and by selecting trees with "a good crop" of branches on them, killing the tree by overlopping is avoided. The result of management to meet these goals is a *de facto* lopping rotation in oaks of 2-3 years and an average branch harvest age of roughly five years.

In addition to the lopping system an explicit element of management is the reservation of oaks in the vicinity of *chans* (out-buildings near or in the forest where stock are kept) for cutting during periods of high labor demand. These *chans* belong to individual families in the village. The leaf fodder available on oaks near the *chans* is not collected except during periods, such as the harvest, when little time is available for the collection of fodder from other areas. At these times, *chan* owners use the fodder which has been saved for their stock.

Other elements of use which occur in the lopped forest and can be regarded as part of the management system include grazing and the entry of fires from adjacent grassland areas. Grazing in the lopped forests is, for the most part, uncontrolled. In many grassland areas management is present and grazing is controlled, however, description is beyond the scope of this paper. Fires also are a major factor within lopped areas. These fires are set in grassland areas during the period prior to the monsoon to ensure a good grass crop. Given the dryness of the season they frequently spread to adjacent lopped oak areas and even into the main forest.

The *de facto* management occurring in forests is not resulting in rapid degradation of the resource. Regeneration of the oaks in some portions of the lopped and browsed area is good. In these locations, regeneration under continuous lopping pressure has resulted in a very dense growth of roughly two meter high oak bushes.[*] These areas are regarded as prime fodder collection locations by the villagers.[**] The soil in these areas is also in good condition, the organic content is high and there is a heavy covering of leaf litter. In contrast, the general pattern, particularly in exposed locations, on dry south-facing slopes, or

---

[*]   Regeneration in this case refers to both "seed originated" and "coppice originated." In general, regeneration is good in moderately lopped and browsed forests which are not south-facing and which are a fair distance from grasslands. Singh *et al.* have noted similar high levels of regeneration in moderately disturbed mixed oak forests and a shift toward "coppice originated" regeneration and away from "seed originated" with increasing disturbance (Singh *et.al.*, 1985).

[**] These sites tend to be in locations not prone to frequent burning and where moisture availability is better than average. In the most dense areas as many as 40-50 two meter high oak bushes occur in a 10x10 meter quadrat.

in locations where village grazing and lopping demand appears to be concentrated, is gradual degradation. Regeneration of *Quercus incanna* has declined and the soil is devoid of leaf or other organic litter. As a result the forest appears to be gradually retreating along its margins. The current management thus appears to result in good fodder production characteristics and to avoid *rapid* degradation, it does not, however, ensure the forest's long-term stability.

Despite the fact that this management system is a function of use and not based on an explicit set of rules, several elements basic to its functioning require control over access to the resource or more specifically, the exclusion of outsiders. These elements are 1) the ability to lop on an effective rotation which produces branches of the most desirable characteristics; 2) the ability to limit lopping to a point where the productive characteristics of the trees are not damaged and 3) the ability to reserve fodder in the vicinity of *chans* for use during periods of high labor demand. A number of adjacent villages are extremely limited in their access to good sources of leaf fodder. Without limitations on access to the forests near Munglori these forests would be subjected to much greater utilization pressure and the system of management would probably change. Overuse occurs in forests near villages on the opposite side of the watershed from Munglori that are near large towns and the road. Forests there, despite their extensive nature, are more heavily lopped than in the Munglori area. Furthermore, villagers complain that people from a market town which has recently grown at the end of the road enter "their" forests and lop indiscriminately without care for the condition of the forest.

"TURF" IN ACTION

Officially, all forest areas surrounding Munglori are reserved, owned by the government and under Forest Department control. Villagers are granted concessions in the forest which permit them to lop trees for fodder and fuel, graze animals, and collect minor forest produce. They are not permitted to cut trees except with forest department permission and there is no specific demarcated area for each village's use. As a result, the official position is one of access for all villagers living in the general area to the forests for permitted uses.

Inter-village

Turf in the Munglori area operates both between villages and within village areas. On the inter-village level, villages have clearly defined areas of forest regarded as their own and which other villages recognize. This forest area has clearly defined boundaries which generally follow natural features. Munglori's forest is bounded by the ridge crest above the village and by a spur of land between it and the next village downstream within the main watershed. Within the area recognized as "belonging" to Munglori, the village has exclusive "right" to collection of fodder, grazing of stock and the cutting of fuel. These rights are carefully guarded by the village — particularly in the accessible lower portion of the watershed where infringements may result in fights. Infringements are, however, rare and no fights occurred during the period of research. The upper ridge crest boundary of Munglori's forest, although clearly defined, is not enforced to the same extent as the lower boundaries near to the village. Members of other villages, from across the ridge where forest is limited, often enter this upper area for fodder collection without objections. The area is, however, clearly acknowledged as "Munglori's". Its limited use by outsiders is tolerated because of its inaccessibility and because forest areas close to Munglori are sufficient for village fodder needs.

A primary function of turf on the inter-village level is, thus, to control access. The experience of villages near large towns and the road indicates that management activities, particularly those involving control of lopping, would not function if numerous villages had access to "Munglori's forests."

Intra-village "locational turf"

Within the village turf area villagers have equal access and equal right to all portions of the resource. That is, there are no areas where individuals or groups have an explicit use-right. When asked which portion of the forest they can use, villagers indicate that they could go anywhere within the village area. At the same time, they indicate that fodder in the forest immediately adjacent to agricultural outbuildings (*chans*) is saved for periods of need. Each family owns between two and four *chans* where stock are kept within easy access of fodder sources and where the dung produced can be distributed on family agricultural fields. Stock are rotated between *chans* on a seasonal basis depending on fodder availability and agricultural work requirements. When stock are kept in a given *chan*, the owner tends to collect fodder from the portion of the forest in the general vicinity of that chan but not immediately adjacent to it. All individuals are viewed by the village community as having equal access to all portions

---

Villagers also plant farm trees such as *Grewia oppisitifolia* (*bhimul*), *Celtis australis* (*kharik*) and *Ficus nemoralis* (*dudhala*) near outbuildings. These trees are explicitly owned by the planter and the fodder they produce is used as a supplement to other fodder.

of the village forest. Actual use patterns tend to be more localized and are constrained by local norms defining appropriate use.

Chans are frequently located in small groups and there are no explicit rules to control the cutting of fodder in their vicinity. Still, convenience, courtesy, informal social control, and, possibly, the potential for retaliation serve to protect use rights. Villagers refrain from cutting fodder in parts of the forest far from their *chan* because of the difficulty of carrying it back. They refrain from cutting fodder immediately adjacent to *chans* except during seasonal periods of high labor demand because of their need for accessible fodder sources at that time.

The net result of the patterns of use within the village is hazily defined turf areas where individuals and small groups manage the forest to meet their specific needs. This locational turf encompasses the general area where individuals collect fodder during periods when stock are kept in *chans* and a more clearly defined core where fodder cutting is limited to periods of need.

In summary, turf as it operates in the Munglori forests has two basic elements. These are: 1) a clearly defined area of forest use for the village as a whole and 2) hazily defined areas of individual or group use within the village area. The first of these elements, although unofficial, is explicitly recognized by other villages. The second element is implicit in patterns of use but is not explicitly recognized by village society.

TURF AND VILLAGE MANAGEMENT— DEVELOPMENT IMPLICATIONS

The concept of turf can be useful in designing forestry projects. Unofficial village level control over forest resources is common and much of this can be viewed as a form of turf. In many areas, traditional forest management systems are also common at the village level. These factors provide basic opportunities for and place fundamental constraints on community forestry programs and other rural development activities.

Turf controls forest use and access. If intra or inter-village turf rights are ignored in the development of afforestation projects there is a high potential for conflict between the project and the village. Given the importance of forests to village life and the effective control which villagers can exert over activities in local forests any conflict is likely to result in project failure. Furthermore, if conflict does not arise there is a significant chance that project benefits will be skewed to the rich (Cernea, Chapter Six, this volume). On the other hand, turf represents an opportunity. The successful introduction and development of new institutions is one of the most difficult features of any development project. If turf rights could be acknowledged by government or development agencies, even in an un-official manner, they might provide a basis for the introduction of improved management activities without requiring the development of a new institutional base.

The same types of opportunities and constraints that exist in the case of turf occur with village management. As Messerschmidt (1985) has noted as a general case in the northern border districts of Nepal, replacement or change of existing management practices tends to be resisted. This appears to be particularly true where new management systems are perceived as a threat to local control over the forest and/or are introduced from the outside with little understanding of village level goals and concerns. Successful integration of village forest management practices with project forest improvement goals has occurred, despite initial village opposition, where project officials and villagers have been willing to negotiate on the techniques of management and joint goals to be met (Thompson & Warburton, 1985b, pp. 217-218, quoting Jeff Romm). Thus, the presence of village level management limits the possibility of introducing any new system. At the same time, if handled carefully, it may provide a basis for the introduction of management elements which improve forest conditions from the perspectives of both forester and villager.

ACKNOWLEDGMENTS

This paper is based on research conducted during 1984 under a fellowship from the Berkeley Professional Studies Program in India and in association with the Doon Valley Ecosystems Project headed by Dr. Jayanto Bandyopadhyay. My support while writing the paper was provided by the Environment and Policy Institute at the East-West Center.

BIBLIOGRAPHY

Berreman, G.D. 1972. *Hindus of the Himalayas: Ethnography and Change.* Second edition, expanded. University of California Press, Berkeley and Los Angeles; Oxford University Press, Bombay.

Chambers, R. 1983. *Concept and Issues Paper: People and Common Property Resources in Land.* Paper prepared for a staff meeting, Rural Poverty and Resources Program, The Ford Foundation, Cairo, May 9-13.

Ciriacy-Wantrup, S.V. and Bishop R.C. 1975. "Common Property as a Concept in Natural Resources Policy," *Natural Resources Journal* 15: 713-727.

Gilles, J.L. and Jamtgaard, K. 1981. "Overgrazing in Pastoral Areas," *Sociologia Rurals* 21(2):129-141.

Hardin, G. 1968. "The Tragedy of the Commons." *Science* 162: 1243-1248.

Messerschmidt, D.A. 1985. "Conservation and Society in Nepal: Traditional Forest Management and Innovative Development." A paper prepared for the Workshop: *Lands at Risk; in the Third World: Local Level Perspectives*, Institute for Development Anthropology, Binghamton, New York, Oct. 10-12.

Moench, M. 1985. *Forest Utilization and Degradation: An Integrated Analysis of Biomass Utilization Patterns in a Garhwal Hill Village, Northern Uttar Pradesh, India..* M.S. project, Energy & Resources Group, University of California, Berkeley.

Moench, M. & Bandyopadhyay, J. 1986. "People-Forest Interaction: A Neglected Parameter in Himalayan Forest Management," *Mountain Research and Development* 6(1):3-16.

Oakerson, R. (1985). "Common Property Resources: An Analytic Framework." in Feeney, D., Gilles, J., Oakerson, R., & Thompson, J.T., *Workshop on Management of Natural Resources Held in Common*, December 5, Unpublished paper prepared for A.I.D. , Washington D.C. by Associates in Rural Development, Inc. Burlington Vermont.

Popkin, S.L. (1981). "Public Choice and Rural Development—Free Riders, Lemons and Institutional Design." In Russell, C.S. & Nicholson, N.K. (eds.) *Public Choice and Rural Development*. Research Paper R-21, Resources for the Future, Washington D.C., pp. 43-80.

Roe, E. and L. Fortmann. 1982. "Season and Strategy: The Changing Organization of the Rural Water Sector in Botswana." Special Studies on Resource Management, No. 1. Ithaca: Cornell University, Rural Development Committee.

Runge, C.F. 1981. "Common Property Externalities: Isolation, Assurance, and Resource Depletion in a Traditional Grazing Context," *American Journal of Agricultural Economics* 63: 596-606.

Singh, S.P., Ralhan, P.K. & Tewari, J.C. 1985. "Stability of Himalayan Climax Oak Forests in View of Resilience Hypothesis," *Environmental Conservation* 12 (1): 73-75.

Thompson, M. & Warburton, M. 1985. "Knowing Where to Hit It: A Conceptual Framework for the Sustainable Development of the Himalaya," *Mountain Research and Development* 5 (3): 203-220.

Land tenure ≠ tree tenure

planting creates tree tenure

Stabilize Wildland Rights and Consolidate the Responsibility System

Chen Zhimin

Individual rights within the context of community land owner-ship and management are illustrated by these changes in rights to trees. Land in this case remains the property of the collec-tive, while individuals obtain rights to plant trees on the land and the rights to those trees.—The Editors.

The Central Committee of Communist Party of China and the Peoples Congress have published the "Decisions on Questions Relating to Forest Protection and the Development of Forestry."

....The Decisions state clearly that commune members must be allo-cated private plots of wildland, to grow trees and forage in perpetuity, and deeds of ownership should also be issued. The area of wildland allocated (which includes wasteland and marshland) will depend on the situation of the commune. In general, five to fifteen percent of a brigade's wildland suited to forestry will be allocated. In areas with a large area of wildland, or wasteland, or marshland, and where the people are willing and able to manage them as forest land, a larger area may be allocated.[*]

Allocation of private wildlands does not mean "dividing the land up between each household." Ownership of the land remains with the collective. Commune members have rights of usufruct and may only use the land to plant trees and grow forage. They are not allowed to clear

Excerpted from *Chinese Forestry*, Beijing, May 1981, and translated by Nicholas Menzies. Used with the permission of the translator.

[*] The commune system has been replaced since this article by a system of government divided according to the older system of counties and municipalities. The legal arrangements pertaining to trees and wildlands remain in force as outlined in this article.

137

land for grain crops. If they do not follow this rule, the right to use the land reverts to the collective.

...The Decisions state: "All trees planted by commune members around their homes, on their private plots, or any other place specified by the collective, shall remain the private property of that individual and may be inherited." This decision was made because of the characteristics of trees which take a long time to grow and to yield a benefit. This carries on the tradition of caring for one's descendants expressed in the proverb, "The first generation plants trees, their grandchildren enjoy the shade."

.. . . . In forestry run by the collectives, we will popularize a responsibility system that will be based on specialized contracts the nature of which will be determined by circumstances. The exact form of contract will be decided on a case by case basis. In general, for wildlands owned by communes or brigades, anything that may appropriately be managed at the production brigade level should be contracted out to the production brigade. Otherwise, management may be undertaken by the commune, the brigade or by specialized groups, specialized households, or to individuals specialized in this work. Individual trees may be the responsibility of individual commune members. Trees at the edges of fields or intercropped with agricultural crops shall be contracted out together with the fields. Some mountains suitable for planting trees, owned by the production brigade, can be contracted out to specialized reforestation groups or may be managed on the principle of "the household that plants is responsible."

reforestation creates land tenure —

land grab

diversity of land uses - diverse needs

Land Tenure Systems and Social Implications of Forestry Development Programs

Michael M. Cernea

> Cernea describes a World Bank project in Pakistan in which despite assumptions to the contrary, community control of the project land had over time been supplanted by individual wealthy families who now controlled the land and therefore were the project beneficiaries. The project is a clear warning about the necessity of determining the **de facto** as well as the **de jure** status of land. —The Editors.

THE CHALLENGE: POPULATION GROWTH AND FUELWOOD CONSUMPTION

Given the high rate of population growth (around 3 percent *per annum*), fuelwood usage in Azad Kashmir represents by far the largest need to be met by reforestation. A prime cause of the large scale deforestation which has taken place over the last 20 years is the local shortage of fuelwood. But deforestation is not merely an environmental, economic or a technical problem. It is a sociological and a behavioral phenomenon. In addition, the general shortage of timber for construction and general use in Pakistan (Draper *et al.*, 1978) is also exerting a strong pressure to over-exploit the natural forests in order to maintain a minimum essential flow of timber into the national economy.

Population pressure has accelerated the deforestation process considerably. Under customary rules, the people of the area are enti-

---

Excerpted from Michael M. Cernea. 1981. *Land Tenure Systems and Social Implications of Forestry Development Programs.* World Bank Staff Working Paper 452. Washington, D.C. : World Bank. Reprinted with the permission of the author.

139

tled to remove deadwood, branches, and noncommercial species without payment, primarily for personal consumption. The exception is those areas declared by the Forest Department to be closed for rehabilitation purposes. Closed areas cannot, however, exceed 25 percent of a forest block at any time. In practice, they are well below this maximum, thus slowing down the rehabilitation process.

Similarly, in actual practice the loosest interpretation is given to the expression of this customary right. Virtually all trees within several miles radius of habitations are debranched more than permissible by silvicultural recommendations. In many locations, debranching has reached the stage where only the top 10 to 20 percent of the crown remains. Outright topping of trees also occurs, with the consequent death of the tree. In the Chir pine areas, long thin vertical slices of the bole of the tree are removed at stump level to be used like a candle for home lighting purposes. These practices are significantly depleting the value of the forest resource. Roadside avenue trees are similarly molested. In the Mirpur district, for example, miles of avenue trees were being uniformly hacked to death, and a large proportion had already been removed.

Adverse effects on forest resources are also occasioned by grazing. This is generally exercised without adequate control and extends to nomadic populations who enter from the Punjab and the North West Frontier Province to herd their livestock in the Azad Kashmir Alpine rangeland during the summer season.

The abuse of customary rights and of the concessionary agreements granted for timber effectively limit the role of the Forest Department (FD) as the agency of government in the exercise of management of the forest. The resultant situation is one in which the Department is in open conflict with a high proportion of the population. At the time of the appraisal of the Hill Farming Project it was reported that there were more than 50,000 cases of forest offenses pending in the courts. This amounted to about one family in six being involved in a reported forest offense and is directly relevant to many farmers' reluctance and/or suspicions regarding participation in development schemes managed by the Forest Department...

At the time when the pilot Hill Farming Project was prepared, it was thought that the most likely successful strategy would be a blending of the private users, or social, approach with the public approach. The objective was to ensure that both private and public needs were met through a set of coordinated activities which were to provide the much needed fuelwood (and fodder) and at the same time protect the environment.

DEVELOPMENTAL ASSUMPTIONS AND PROJECT DESIGN

The strategy of the forestry component of the Project was designed to experiment with solutions addressing *both* the technical and the *social* aspects of developing forestry resources. Specifically, the project was to finance a pilot program of fuelwood plantation. This was to test not only improved tree species and planting techniques under field conditions, but also to develop suitable social strategies for involving local people in the planting, protecting, and maintaining of the reforested areas. Community acceptance of the obligations involved in replanting denuded areas, and in protecting the new tree blocks, was to be crucial for the success of the project.

Assumptions about Land Tenure: the Role of *Shamlat*

The assumptions about the tenurial status of the land to be reforested under the project played an important role in the project conception and design. The experimental planting of fuelwood on the 3,000 acres was supposed to take place mainly on community land (*Shamlat*), and also a much smaller portion on *government* and *private* land. The emphasis on community land was intended to conserve a flow of benefits (mainly fuelwood), primarily to the smaller farmers who constituted the great majority of these communities. Project planting on government, and on limited private, land was expected to demonstrate to the farmers the benefits of fast growing tree species, and thus to induce more tree-planting by the farmers on their private lands.

A professional sociological analysis of the land tenure system in Azad Kashmir was not undertaken during the preparation of the Hill Farming Project. According to the explanation given at that time by various officials, *Shamlat* land was regarded as community land. The various village communities would have decision-making authority over it, and implicit rights to share in the use of it. The Project Appraisal Report used a working definition, according to which *Shamlat* is "land generally left uncultivated, owned jointly by a number of families." Quantitatively, the Appraisal Report assessed the *Shamlat* area as a major resource, totalling approximately 325,000 acres. This is equal to no less than 60 percent of the total cultivated farm area in Azad Kashmir, which is about 500,000 acres, and more than twice the size of the combined nonarable farm areas.

Given such an understanding of *Shamlat*, it was then quite logically assumed that fuelwood planting under the project on *Shamlat* land would:

(1) require community consent:

(2) promote and allow for direct community participation: and

(3) eventually produce tangible benefits for the communities involved.

The general assumption was that the small farmers in Azad Kashmir, particularly those with little land and, implicitly, less access to firewood, would be the primary beneficiaries of project planting on land belonging to the communities.

At the project design stage, it was anticipated that the involvement of farmers in this reforestation program would take four main forms:

(a) Making village community lands available for fuelwood plantations;

(b) Volunteering plots of privately owned nonarable land for forestry plantations;

(c) Providing support for protecting the tree seedlings and for enforcing the temporary closing of reforested areas to indiscriminate grazing; and

(d) Contributing toward the costs of reforestation by certain payments for seedlings, by labor contributions, or through other forms of assistance.

The actual innovation embodied in the project's forestry component was of both a technical and a social nature. On the technical side, the project departed from the routine approach of having the Forest Department plant only on government land, attempting this time to involve the farmers' lands. It designed a new approach. Under this, the state foresters would attempt to induce planting on non-governmental land as well, to introduce fast growing species, to expand the total area under fuelwood, and thus to respond to the growing needs of the small farmer for wood for heating and cooking.

As to the role of the farmers themselves, the project was to promote a change in farmer's land use strategy for nonarable areas. Farmers were currently emphasizing fodder production and grazing, whereas the project proposed to convert some nonarable lands to fuelwood growing,[*] and sought the direct participation of farmers in its implementation. In sum, the project was setting objectives that partly required a modified productive behavior. The question was:

Would the target farmer population respond as expected?

---

[*] The project included other components in order to compensate for the conversion of certain grazing land into forest through intensified fodder production.

A SOCIAL ANALYSIS OF PROJECT IMPLEMENTATION

Project Progress

The actual implementation of the Hill Farming Project began in 1978... With respect to physical targets, the progress of the forestry component of the project was quite satisfactory. The reforestation target of the first year was accomplished: fuelwood trees were planted on 500 acres of identified land and the first project nurseries were established successfully. The positive support received by the forestry component from farmers involved was quite significant. This was especially so given the rather unfortunate tradition of suspicion and conflicting relationships between farmers and the Forestry Department. While the objective in the first year of the project was to plant 500 acres exclusively on government land, the project staff succeeded in identifying 100 acres of community and private land in addition to the 400 acres of government land, which were relatively easy to find. As reported by the project staff, the owners and users of the private and community land agreed to dedicate the land for fuelwood plantation, although no formal contract was signed.

The second year of the project had an increased planting target of 1,250 acres. Other landowners came forward and volunteered their nonarable lands for tree plantations. After reviewing the available areas, the project's forestry staff tentatively identified for planting about 750 acres of community and private land, and 500 acres of government land. This was a much larger proportion of non-government land than that of the most optimistic assumption at appraisal stage ...

The implication of this progress was that if it was feasible to identify and plant with fuelwood large areas of non-governmental land, then prospects for a large scale follow-up reforestation project were really good. The positive response of the farmers under the pilot project suggested that there was potential for incorporating significant tracts of private and community (*Shamlat*) land into the fuelwood production circuit. It was therefore necessary to assess and to understand the mechanism and implications of this progress, which was faster than had been anticipated at appraisal.

The social analysis of the implementation of the forestry component of the project was accordingly undertaken to ascertain whether or not the identification of land for fuelwood plantation was in tune with the initial social, technical, and economic assumptions, and whether or not it was likely to lead to the expected distributional benefits...

Forest Tenure Systems and Social Stratification

The social analysis first sought to ascertain the main legal land tenure systems operating in Azad Kashmir both on forest land and on land that was potentially usable for reforestation purposes. Three basic categories were identified:

(a) *Khalsa*, or Crown land, which belongs to the state and is accordingly government land; under *Khalsa* land there are two categories of forests: (i) demarcated and (ii) undemarcated *

(b) *Shamlat* land itself, which derives its name from the concept of "getting together" and is land belonging to the village communities: the uses of these lands are varied, including grazing areas, forest areas, sites for village public buildings, village graveyards, and so on; and

(c) *Malkiat* land, which is privately owned; ownership rights on this land are recorded in the Revenue register and are validated by it.

The social stratification of private (*Malkiat*) landowners ranges over a broad spectrum. In addition to a large number of smallholders (about 65 percent of the total) there is a significant group of farmers with medium size holdings and a smaller group (less than 5 percent) which controls large or very large holdings. More precise information on forest holdings for the entire Azad Kashmir is not available as the Agricultural Census of 1972 recorded only arable lands.

---

* The official definitions of "demarcated forest land" and "undemarated forest" valid in Azad Kashmir date from 1930 (see "The Jammu and Kashmir Forest Regulation Act" No. 2) and are as follows:

"Demarcated Forest" means forest land or waste land under the control of the Forest Department, of which boundaries have already been demarcated by means of pillars of stone or masonry or by any other conspicuous mark, or which may hereafter be constituted as a demarcated forest;

"Undemarcated Forest" means and includes all forest land and waste land (other than demarcated forest and much waste land as is under the management and control of the Revenue Department), which is the property of the Government and is not appropriated for any specific purpose."

As a rule of thumb, the demarcated forest areas are high density and better quality forests, while the undemarcated forest areas are low density forests, often located between the demarcated forests and the cultivated lands.

The Historical Cycle of Partitioning-Appropriation-Privatization of Community Land

Given the critical importance of the land tenure pattern for the strategy of the project, special attention has been given to (1) an in-depth analysis of the status of *Shamlat* land and (2) to ascertaining the social mechanism of community decision-making and the profit-sharing procedures resulting from investments in forestry development. This assessment led to the identification of significant differences between the legal/formal status of the land and the *de facto* situation. This finding has important consequences for the implementation and impact of the project.

Given both the existing social stratification of forest landowners in Azad Kashmir and the coexistence of several tenurial systems on forestry land, the social issues which arise refer to the distributional consequences of project investments in forestry development. The socio-logical analysis revealed that the elicitation of farmers' cooperation with the program has led to formerly unanticipated consequences in the flow of benefits to various social groups.

Contrary to expectations, *Shamlat* land appeared not to be truly community land in the cases examined during field work. Significant changes have taken place gradually over time in most of Azad Kashmir. These have resulted in a dual and a divergent status: while, legally, *Shamlat* continues to be considered community land, in real life it is operated and used as private land. This finding is bound to modify the assumptions about the project's developmental consequences that were made when the planting of *Shamlat* land was originally planned.

Specifically, the limited interviews carried out with farmers in different villages and districts produced two main findings: (1) that there is a discrepancy between the official (legal) and *de facto* status of *Shamlat*; and (2) that usufruct benefits from the so-called *Shamlat* land accrue to precisely identifiable individuals, rather than to communities as structured groups.

How did this major change in the forest tenure and land tenure system come about? Essentially, it accrued over a long period of time and is not yet fully completed. Reconstructing the social and political processes which have led to this change, it appeared that *Shamlat* land was, indeed, historically and initially, allocated to villages for communal use for their grazing and fuelwood needs. Subsequently, the following tripartite cycle of processes occurred, leading from informal partitioning through appropriation to eventual privatization:

(a) *Informal partitioning* of *Shamlat*, for use among certain village families whose lands adjoined the Shamlat areas. The *Shamlat* plots so partitioned were proportional to the amount of cultivatable land of the respective family farm, and numerous small and more remote farms were excluded from this process.

(b)*Progressive appropriation* of *Shamlat* by these families. Rights to *Shamlat* became transferable through inheritance (or sale) of fractions of the cultivatable areas, which carried with them rights to proportionate fractions of the *Shamlat* plots. At the same time as these procedures were becoming increasingly prevalent, *Shamlat* still formally maintained its status as community land and was not entered in the Revenue records as belonging to private families. In consequence, the families concerned did not have to pay land taxes on"their" *Shamlat* plots.

(c)*Gradual privatization* of *Shamlat*: since 1974, when the tax on land was abolished in Pakistan, the pressure has increased to have *Shamlat* plots entered in revenue records in the names of the families who appropriated them, thus validating them as privately owned lands. The interested families use various forms of pressure to obtain such re-registration of lands, in spite of existing legal regulations.

The historical cycle of partitioning-appropriating-privatizing of community land developed at different speeds in various districts of Azad Kashmir. It is reported that the status of land registration and tenure differs, for instance, in Mirpur district from, for example, Poonch district. Some areas and communities still maintain pieces of *Shamlat* as truly community possessions.

In its main lines, however, the historical cycle described above seems to be an ongoing one. For instance, current regulations continue to permit, under certain circumstances, the transfer of areas of *Khalsa* (Crown) land to village communities, where it should become community land. Slower or faster, however, the processes analyzed in the preceding paragraph develop. Thus yesterday's piece of *Khalsa* land becomes, through transfer or through encroachment, today's *Shamlat* land, which, in turn, is likely to become tomorrow's *Malkiat* land.

Farmer's Response to Fuelwood Planting

The gradual change in the tenurial status of community land into private land has had several consequences on reforestation activities. To secure *Shamlat* or private land for forest plantation, the project has had to secure the support of individual farmers, who are the relevant decision makers under these circumstances. For the time being, no community decision making process, and/or community administration/ protection of plantations, are involved. Benefits are therefore bound to accrue to the individuals involved, rather than to the community.

An analysis of the social composition of the farmers who offered their private (*Malkiat*) land for project reforestation, and of the farmers who are in real control of the plots of nominally *Shamlat* land, reveals that it is the larger landholders who tend to take advantage of the project forestry component. This finding is contrary to the initial assumptions on which the project was based. It appears that the tracts of *Shamlat* land being offered for planting—and assumed by the project to generate benefits for village communities—have surreptitiously changed their tenurial status, and in fact are managed on a strictly private basis. Their *de facto* owners hope to get their "Shamlat" lands planted at full government expense, and without making any repayment commitments.

Currently, the government bears all the costs of the fuelwood planting program... Interviews with farmers indicated that the wealthiest landowners, who do have the economic resources to contribute, at least in part, towards the costs of establishment and protection of trees, have not done so, nor, in their present thinking, do they intend to do so in the future. For instance, at one of the project's reforestation sites, the main contribution to the 100 acres (75 private and 25 *Shamlat*) planted in the first project year was made by one influential family of six brothers—landowners, of whom only one is an "almost" full-time farmer, while the others are absentee landlords operating shops and small enterprises in Muzaffarabad and owning lands operated with tenants in other villages as well.

Another landowner, who offered about 125 acres of land for planting in the second project year, flatly refused to contribute any payment, arguing that the government should provide for the citizens. A third large farmer, who also wanted his 56 acres planted also in the second project year, requested in particular government-paid watch guards to protect the proposed plantation. Protection against fodder and grass cutting by adjoining small farmers seems to be an additional advantage expected by the larger farmers, because once the private or *Shamlat* nonfarm land is tree-planted, it will also be protected, thus restricting the access and customary rights of smaller farmers to collect grass, tree branches, etc.

Interviews with numerous farmers in the area revealed that their attitudes *vis-a-vis* reforestation of their lands and cooperation with the Forest Department are differentiated along socio-economic lines. Virtually all farmers interviewed realized the severity of current and foreseeable shortages of fuelwood, and were supportive of reforestation efforts. But the smaller farmers are currently more hesitant to actually accept project planting on their lands than are the larger farmers, for reasons which will be mentioned below. At the same time, the smaller farmers appeared more prepared to contribute towards the costs of project planting than did the larger farmers.

The hesitations of the smaller farmers stem from their suspicions (1) that they may lose possession or control over their land to the government once it has been planted with trees by the Forest Department, and (2) that they may be deprived of access to fodder collection and grazing, which is critical for them. Most of the smaller farmers interviewed indicated that they would, if they could, offer small plots for project planting, provided they receive convincing assurances that the Forest Department will not alienate their lands and that they will be able to cut grass for their cattle. The non-contiguous nature of these plots would raise technical difficulties for the Hill Farming project and the Forest Department in undertaking the planting.

Thus, it would seem to be in the interest of the small farmers to develop some flexible, yet clear, pattern for contractual arrangements, addressing the technical difficulties of planting on small plots as well. On the other hand, it appears necessary to relax the project's requirement for tree-blocks of a minimum of 50 contiguous acres adjusting the requirement more appropriately to the circumstances of very fragmented land ownership.

The larger landowners have displayed a consistent positive response to the project, except for not being willing to participate in contributing to its costs. Being confident in the political power that they are wielding, they do not regard tree-planting by the Forest Department as a threat to their ownership on land and trees, and tend to manipulate available project opportunities and resources to their benefit. This attempt is facilitated by the current absence of a legal framework which would define the obligations, not merely the rights, of the farmers whose land is being reforested through government contribution.

REFERENCES

Draper, S.A., A.J.. Ewing, J. Burley, C. Graym. 1978. "Pakistan: Forestry Sector Survey. World Bank Staff Working Paper No. 284.

5

Tenure and Deforestation

In the Amazon Basin, on the archipelagos of the Pacific, and on the fringes of the Sahel, farmers, among others, are destroying forests at an alarming rate. They may be drawn to the forests by the burgeoning urban demand for fuel or by land-hunger, or they may be driven by drought or famine. They are commonly too constrained by the short-term demands of survival to avoid the long-term environmental degradation caused by their actions. Tenure arrangements can accelerate or retard this process.

Deforestation has been promoted by laws or customs that confer land rights on the person who first "clears" the land, and this is still the legal situation in many developing countries today. This legal concept developed in a less crowded world, appearing across centuries and in cultural situations as diverse as seventeenth century England, which gave rise to John Locke's concept of the origin of property in the mixing of labor with the soil, and seventh century Arabia, in which the Koran enunciated the concept of *ihya al-mawat*, which grants title to vacant land to the one who clears it and places it under cultivation (Schacht, 1964:141).

The processes of deforestation now underway in the Third World took place centuries ago in Europe. The history of the clearing of the woodland in Europe makes clear the importance of the legal principle of assartment—a seventeenth century term meaning the appropriation of land through clearing of the trees—in the destruction of European forests, both in post-Domesday Britain and on the continent (Darby, 1956: 191-195). The process has gone on into relatively recent times in some parts of Europe, as in Ireland (Regan, 1982). This, however, is where the similarity stops. The climate and soils of Europe have permitted relatively easy reforestation but in many developing countries the destruction of the natural forest initiates processes which lead to serious soil degradation and, in arid regions, desertification. Much of North Africa was once covered in forest.

Jones discusses the land tenure elements in the clearing of large areas of pine forest in Honduras. The situation is archetypical: a land-hungry rural population clears forests and initiates cultivation, only to learn that the soils are of poor quality and will not sustain a permanent agriculture under available technology and inputs. The farmers move on to clear other forest land, selling or abandoning that cleared earlier to export-oriented cattle ranching. The pattern has repeated itself elsewhere in Central and South America, as in Panama (Bishop et al., 1981) and Mexico (Nations and Nigh, 1978).

The article by *Maurer* provides a particularly vivid picture of this process in the Brazilian Amazon. To the ecological damage noted by Jones and others is added an even more sinister note: the genocidal effects of the clearing of the forest on the Amazonian Indians, their tenure systems, and their way of life. Here the impact of population growth and market forces is actively promoted by a government as "development." In forests throughout the world there exist unique cultures that now find their refuge imperiled, and the destruction of forests is often a human rights issue as well as an ecological concern (Grasmick, 1979, excerpted in Chapter 8 of this book).

Denevan summarizes the causes of deforestation and forest and woodland degradation in tropical Latin America in his 1982 report to the United States Congress' Office of Technology Assessment. His analysis examines land tenure in relation to other factors that have given rise to precipitous destruction of new world forests, and is particularly helpful in its insights into the macro-economic forces behind these trends. While the immediate agents of deforestation may often be peasant populations, the forces behind the policies to open these areas to settlers may be the ultimate beneficiaries, including the local cattle industry and multinationals. Peasants are hardly the only agents of deforestation: international timber firms have often abused their concession rights, ignoring their responsibility to replant and departing with profits (Riddell, 1982).

These processes of internal colonization and deforestation are pervasive and have been under way in Africa and Asia as well. Riddell has described the process in West Africa (Riddell, 1982). In the African development literature, divergent viewpoints are sometimes evident. In the case of Ivory Coast, a land tenure policy that gives secure title to those who place land under production has been praised by one author as having contributed to the tree crop expansion which fueled the Ivorien "economic miracle" (Hecht, 1983:33), while another has critiqued the policy as having encouraged extensive operations that resulted in unnecessary destruction of natural forests, through land grabbing by clearing (Tiffen, forthcoming). The balancing of important but not always consistent policy objectives is not easy in such cases. Tree clearing is sometimes associated with very valuable programs such as eradication of tsetse fly and sleeping sickness (Nshubemuki and Mugasha, 1983).

In Asia, too, farmers clear forest to establish land rights. Bajracharya (1980) has described the process of peasant land grabbing through tree clearing in eastern Nepal. *Colfer* examines the interaction between land rights and deforestation in East Kalimantan, Indonesia, in a marginal area of an American timber concession along the Telen River where Kenyah Dayaks have been resettled. They practice swidden cultivation of dry rice but also gather food and other products from the forest, and work for the firm holding the concession as intermittent wage and contract labor. The concession is itself a tenure conferred by the Indonesian government on the American firm for a specified term and purpose, which must be integrated with local land rights. Colfer focuses on tree cutting by the local villagers to answer the question, "Why do Kenyah cut down trees?" Colfer's "situational analysis" involved the preparation of land use histories for each household in the study community of Long Segan. She seeks a balanced assessment of the relative impacts of more traditional land clearing and acquisition patterns on one hand and the commercialized harvesting of timber products under the timber concession on the other.

The pressure on the forest and wooded areas may be increased because of peasant land-hunger caused by maldistribution of land in already settled areas, and some authors have stressed the impact of inequitable tenure patterns in the "sending" areas. Eckholm (1976), in his classic *Losing Ground*, indicates how in El Salvador the radically skewed distribution of land in the fertile valleys and the conversion of land to commercial production have driven peasant subsistence cultivators up onto the hillsides. There peasants clear the steep slopes of trees to cultivate, but soon face soil exhaustion and declining fertility, and initiate disastrous erosion. Tenure considerations have been critical throughout the Third World in the clearing and cultivation of fragile lands, where cultivation can often not be sustained and long-term ecological damage results (Thiesenhusen, 1979:254). Both maldistribution and an inadequate reform response can create this problem. Agarwal (1980) has noted the critical role of maldistribution in forcing peasants onto marginal land, and Barnett et al. (1982) have characterized peasant-led deforestation as a "last desperate act" of peasants in an intolerable position. On the other hand, reforms that appropriate the landlords' agriculturally marginal lands and place the costs of reform on them can equally promote deforestation, as in some areas of the Andes (Ampuero, 1979). And when a reform throws off "excess labor" or reduces income, as Tuazon (1984) asserts was the case in the Philippines, it can lead to a resurgence of shifting cultivation and consequent deforestation.

If law or custom defines the forest as a resource open to all—and the woody matter there as a good free for the taking—one has a "tragedy of the commons" situation, in which individual woodcutters lack incentive to restrain their cutting (Hardin, 1968). This theme has been raised again and again in recent work on the Sahel (e.g., Thomson, 1982), and is accented in the *Hammer Digernes* study of desertification through fuelwood cutting around the town of Bara in the Sudan's gum arabic producing region of Kordofan. There, 1970 legislation claimed title to most rural land for the government, and the powers of the village *sheikhs* to control tree cutting have thus been in decline. The breakdown of social control of land use, which led to the situation that the author describes, was brought about by the replacement of traditional "native authorities" with less effective "people's councils" by the post-independence governments (El-Arifi, 1978). In the face of a growing market for charcoal and a declining market for gum arabic, social control of tree cutting largely collapsed. Even where *Acacia Senegal* survived, population pressure forced the telescoping of the traditional cultivation cycle from seventeen to nine years, resulting in declining fertility and increasing wind erosion.

Traditional authorities have not been indifferent to the destruction of the resources upon whose continued productivity the livelihood of their subjects depend. While their efforts at conservation have most often been overwhelmed by the great weight of economic forces, it is important to note that they have sometimes used their powers as traditional land managers in attempts to conserve trees. These efforts have only rarely been described in the literature, but the few examples include legislation by Tswana chiefs in the interest of conservation of trees in early twentieth-century Botswana (Schapera, 1943:416) and similar restrictions on tree cutting in the Law of Lerotholi in Lesotho (Duncan, 1960:95). In some traditional systems, chiefs or even private landholders, in the case of the Kikuyu of Kenya, could establish tree reserves (Leakey, 1977). There is a growing demand among students of Third World forests, dealt with in greater detail in Chapter 8, for maintenance of traditional styles of limited and sustainable forest exploitation and management as the solution to deforestation.

Tenure arrangements obviously are not the only factor affecting rates of forest clearing in large parts of the Third World, but tenure emerges as a key element. Failure to understand its impact will seriously undermine any attempt to grapple with the complex processes of deforestation.

REFERENCES

Agarwal, Bina. 1980. *The Woodfuel Problem and the Diffusion of Rural Innovations.* Sussex: Tropical Products Institute, Science Policy Research Unit, University of Sussex.

Ampuero, E.P. 1979. "Ecological Aspects of Agro-Forestry in Mountain Zones: The Andean Region." In Trevor Chandler and David Spurgeon (eds.), *International Cooperation in Agroforestry: Proceedings of an International Conference.* Nairobi: DSE and ICRAF: 77-94.

Bajracharya, Deepak. 1980. "Fuelwood and Food Needs vs. Desertification: An Energy Study of a Hill Village Panchayat in Eastern Nepal." In *Energy for Rural Development Program Report PR-8-20. Part 3.* Washington, D.C.: USAID.

Barnett, Andrew, Martin Bell and Kurt Hoffman. 1982. *Rural Energy and the Third World.* Oxford: Pergamon Press.

Bishop, John, Robert Hudgens and David Gow. 1981. *Dynamics of Shifting Cultivation, Rural Poor, Cattle Complex in a Humid Tropical Forest Life Zone.* Research Note, No. 2. Washington, D.C.: Development Alternatives.

Darby, H.C. 1956. "The Clearing of the Woodland in Europe" In William L. Thomas Jr. (ed.), *Man's Role in Changing the Face of the Earth* Volume I. Chicago: University of Chicago Press: 183-216.

Duncan, Patrick. 1960. *Sotho Laws and Customs.* Cape Town: Oxford University Press.

Eckholm, Eric. 1976. *Losing Ground: Environmental Stress and World Food Prospects.* New York: W.W. Norton and Company.

El-Arifi, Salih. 1978. "Some Aspects of Local Government and Environmental Management in the Sudan." In J.A. Mabbutt (ed.), *Proceedings of the Khartoum Workshop on Arid Lands Management.* Tokyo: United Nations University.

Grasmick, Joseph. 1979. "Land and the Forest Dwelling South American Indian." *Buffalo Law Review* 27:759-800.

Hardin, Garrett. 1968. "The Tragedy of the Commons." *Science* 162: 1243-1248.

Hecht, Robert M. 1983. "The Ivory Coast Economic 'Miracle': What Benefits for Peasant Farmers?" *Journal of Modern African Studies* 21(1):25-53.

Leakey, L.S.B. 1977. *The Southern Kikuyu Before 1903.* Vol. 1. London: The Academic Press.

Nations, J.B. and R.B. Nigh. 1978. "Cattle, Cash, Food and Forest: The Destruction of the American Tropic and the Lacandon Maya Alternative." *Culture and Agriculture* 6:1-5.

Nshubemuki, L. and A.G. Mugasha. 1983. "The Modifications of Traditional Shifting Cultivation Brought about by the Forest Development Project in the Dada Area, Kondoa, Tanzania." Lushoto, Tanzania: Forest Division, Silviculture Research Station.

Regan, Colin. 1982. "Colonialism and Reforestation: A Case Study of Ireland." Maynouth, Ireland: Department of Geography, St. Patrick's College.

Riddell, James C. 1982. *Causes of Deforestation and Forest and Woodland Degradation in Tropical Africa.* Washington, D.C.: U.S. Office of Technology Assessment.

Schacht, Joseph. 1964. *An Introduction to Islamic Law.* London: Oxford University Press.

Schapera, Isaac. 1943. *Tribal Legislation Among the Tswana of the Bechuanaland Protectorate.* London School of Economics and Political Science, Monographs on Social Anthropology, No. 9. London: Percy Lund, Humphries and Co.

Thiesenhusen, William C. 1979. "Hill Land Farming: An International Dimension." In J. Luchok, J.D. Cawthon and M.J. Breslin (eds.), *Hill Lands*, Proceedings of an International Symposium held in Morgantown, West Virginia, 3-9 October 1976. Morgantown: West Virginia University Books: 254-263.

Thomson, James T. 1982. "Participation, Local Organization, Land and Tree Tenure: Future Directions for Sahelian Forestry." Davis: Club du Sahel/OECD.

Tiffen, Mary. Forthcoming. *Economic, Social and Institutional Aspects of Shifting Cultivation in Humid and Semi-Humid Africa.* Rome: FAO.

Tuazon, Raul. 1984. "Land Tenure, Agrarian Reform and Upland Deforestation in the Philippines." Unpublished manuscript.

The Editors

Handwritten margin notes: No secure tenure – no improvements

Cashcrop vs other prod. systems (migratory denudes (cashcroppers))

Socio-Cultural Constraints in Working With Small Farmers in Forestry: Case of Land Tenure in Honduras

Jeffrey Jones

> In situations of land scarcity, peasants need few tenurial
> incentives to clear forest land. But when such rights are not
> conferred it can only encourage unsustainable land use and lead
> to the eventual abandonment of the farms in favor of newly
> cleared forest land. What factors lie behind campesino move-
> ment upon the forests, and what factors render it so destruc-
> tive?—The Editors

Introduction

... The list of socio-cultural constraints on small farmers in forestry is
quite long, and this paper will only focus on one, land tenure, specifically in Honduras. Land tenure is a socio-cultural problem in the most
basic sense: the judgement of who has access to what resources and under
what conditions is a fundamental value judgement. It involves the
perception of the social worth of different social groups, and the
evaluation of the national (community) well being. It reflects the
social organization of the society through the constellation of forces
which form the political and economic determinants for different
patterns of land use. The objective of this presentation is not to analyze

---

Excerpted from Jeffrey Jones, "Socio Cultural Constraints in Working
With Small Farmers in Forestry: Case of Land Tenure in Honduras,"
Prepared for "Short Course in Agro-forestry in the Humid Tropics,"
held at CATIE, March 16-25, 1982 (Turrialba, Costa Rica: Centro
Agronómico Tropical de Investigación y Enseñanza, CATIE, Department
of Natural Renewable Resources, 1982). Reprinted with the permission
of the author.

the socio-cultural bases of land tenure, but rather to consider how land tenure affects the possibilities for social forestry. . . .

In 1974, the Corporación Hondureña de Desarrollo Forestal (COHDEFOR) was created by *Decreto Ley* [decree law (eds.)] 103. This law gave COHDEFOR jurisdiction over production and marketing of all wood, although in practice controls are focussed on pine. This jurisdiction includes control of firewood, charcoal, and all activities which affect forest areas, such as clearing and burning for agricultural production. The law puts all national forests under direct COHDEFOR administration and gives extensive authority even over privately owned forests. This sweeping legislation was developed to begin with a massive reorganization of forest use along more rational lines and to insure the maintenance of the forest as a productive system, but to some extent these goals are not achieved, and are even impeded by this same legislation.

Land Tenure in Honduras

Access to land is a major problem for Honduran campesinos. Only 20 percent of the rural population owns land, while 40 percent have no access to land. The rest of the population either rents or squats on land (Table 1). The problem has led to the development of a number of campesino organizations which specialize in land invasion to force action from the National Land Reform Institute (INA) (Parsons 1975). Most important are ANACH (Asociación Nacional de Campesinos Hondureños) and UNC (Unión Nacional de Campesinos).

The 80 percent of the rural population which has no land creates obvious pressure on the forest resource. While some of these farmers admit to squatting on national land, it is likely that many more occupy or exploit the forest without acknowledging this to census takers. Many of these farmers are migratory, to a greater or lesser extent. The best soils have been occupied by the first settlers in all regions, and the soils in pine forest are generally of poor quality and will not sustain a permanent agriculture. A common pattern is to fell the forest, cultivate a few years and sell the land as cleared pasture. The migratory farmer then moves on to other forested land (Murray 1981) which will be able to sustain intensive agricultural production for a few more years.

The low number of land-owners also has the effect of encouraging "squatting" by farmers who do not own land. COHDEFOR officials are preoccupied with the phenomenon of annexation of national lands contiguous to titled property. Since there are no other owners present to dispute their claim, farmers extend their fences, and claim the additional land as part of their titled parcel. This annexed land is usually part of the national forest.

Even in cases where farmers do not actively occupy forest land, they may utilize it. As in all third world countries, the firewood market presents an economic opportunity for poor, and especially landless, peasants. Nearby pine forests can be easily exploited by local farmers with a minimum risk of COHDEFOR control in most of the country. The production of charcoal is possible in even more remote areas, due to its light weight and ease of transport. A more extensive use of the forest is for grazing, where cattle are simply set loose to forage. While grazing itself causes a minimum of damage to the pine forests, fire is used to maintain the quality of the "pasture." Burning off is said to control ticks, and clears away dead (or live) vegetation so it can be replaced by grasses. What can be safely concluded is that the campesinos, both as legal owners and as squatters, occupy and use forest lands much more intensively than COHDEFOR. This situation creates some obvious problems, but also offers important lessons and possibilities.

Table 1.
Number and Percentage of Rural Families in Honduras by Land Tenure, 1974

| | Total | Occupied National Lands | *Single forms of Tenure* | | | Mixed Tenure Own & Rent | Without Land |
			Own	Rent	Other		
Number of families	325,106	72,272	65,518	44,054	2,516	10,981	129,765
Percent	100.0	22.2	20.1	13.5	0.8	3.4	39.9

Source: *Censo Nacional Agropecuario, 1974.*

The Forest-Peasant Conflict

In tropical America, the relationship of the peasants to the forest has been one of antagonism. This is not an inevitable relationship from a biological standpoint, but has been promoted by the objectives and policies of economic development implemented in most countries. As pawns in the development process, peasants find themselves irresistibly pushed toward programs of colonization and deforestation. Attempts to change colonization and deforestation policies and practices represent changes in the "rules of the game" for the peasants. This human dimension of the problem of forestry presents the greatest challenge of social forestry.

The mainspring of peasant pressure on the tropical forest is commercial agriculture. In Central America, one of the most successful development strategies has been the expansion of export crops. Sugar, cotton, sesame, and most of all cattle, have experienced important increases in their production areas in recent years to meet the opportunities of foreign markets, which promise good prices paid in "hard" currencies (Nations and Nigh 1978).

One unfortunate side effect of increased commercial agriculture is the pressure it puts on the production of food crops. The higher incomes generated from export crops tend to displace food crops and peasant farmers away from traditional areas of cultivation, which are in the most accessible and most developed areas of the country. The displaced peasant farmers are the spearhead of agricultural colonization, staying on cleared land for a short time only before selling out to commercial agriculture interests (Murray 1980 [sic]; Heckadon 1978 [sic]).

Colonization and deforestation have been encouraged as methods for absorbing displaced farmers, and for accommodating the increase in total (food and export) agricultural production. One of the strongest incentives for colonization is the promise of land access; most Latin American countries recognize land rights on the basis of usufruct (use rights) and do not rely on the documentation of "legal" acquisition (Clark 1971). Deforestation is also encouraged by laws which penalize "unused" lands, i.e., forests, by making them susceptible to higher tax rates or to expropriation. . . .

Problems of Peasant Farm Forestry

There is sharp contrast between campesino attitudes and government attitudes toward forestry. Law 103 explicitly recognizes the forest as a highly valuable resource, and much of COHDEFOR activity is directed toward preserving the forest. The peasants, on the other hand, seem to have an indifferent and even hostile attitude toward this in general. The distance between these attitudes is a measure of the problems currently faced by social forestry.

A comparison of Central American countries shows a surprisingly low incidence of trees on Honduran small farms. In most countries, trees planted in agroforestry combinations are an important component of farm activities. Prunings from living fence posts provide posts to renew fences or for sale. Fruit and timber species are scattered around the farm, or concentrated in home gardens, and provide fruits, wood, shade, etc. These agroforestry systems allow a diversification of farm activities without competing directly with other crops, and are common in most Central America (Budowski 1981 [sic]). Nevertheless, Honduran farmers are involved in these systems to a very limited extent (Table 2), which is probably a reflection of the land tenure situation. Since farms are generally temporary due to the migratory farming pattern, and lack land titles, the plantation of slowly maturing crops is less likely (Sellers 1977), despite the potential for economic benefits.

Of course, the principal motivation for deforestation is land acquisition by campesinos who are landless, or who find their soils exhausted. Such clearing activities have a double motivation. They present the opportunity for farming for several years, and may be closer to new forest areas for exploitation. Another motivation is the cash from the sale of "improvements" when the land is abandoned, which represents a capital reserve built up by the farmer's own work. It may represent one of his few possibilities for capitalization of his farm activities.

Table 2.
Land Use in Central American Small Farms

	Country			
Tree Use	Costa Rica (percent)	Panama (percent)	Nicaragua (percent)	Honduras (percent)
Living Trees	84	87	50	19
Fruit Trees	98	94	78	53
Timber	40	44	42	16

Sources: Jones, J.R. 1982; Jones, J. y Otárola, A. 1981; Jones, J. y Pérez, L.A. 1982; Lemckert, A. y Campos, J. 1981.

At a more profound level, the lack of campesino interest in the forest reflects the low level of benefits they are likely to obtain from it. The control of all forest exploitation by COHDEFOR is a disincentive. Burning off forest to improve pasture, or cutting it down to create cropland are the activities which promise the highest return to peasant farmers. . . .

Conclusion

. . . In the case of Honduras, patterns of land ownership and current forestry laws combine unintentionally to discourage an optimal forest use by the peasants. The lack of security of land tenure discourages improvements such as fruit trees or plantations. Furthermore, since peasant use rights are based on clearing the forest, reforestation diminishes the value of the improvement they might otherwise sell. . .

The success of forestry programs which involve small farmers depends on an accurate understanding of the peasants' adaptation to the ecological and socio-economic situations they face. The extent to which program designs address the peasants' adaptational needs will determine the degree of peasant support and cooperation in these programs.

REFERENCES

Budowski, G. 1980. "The Socio-Economic Effects of Forest Management on Lives of People Living in the Area. The Case of Central America and Some Caribbean Countries." Turrialba, Costa Rica: CATIE.

Clark, S. 1971. "Arrendamiento, aparcería y otras formas indirectas de tenencia de la tierra en Costa Rica; análisis jurídico y económico." San José: Universidad de Costa Rica, Proyecto de Derecho Agrario.

Heckadon, M.S. 1980. "La colonización campesina de bosques tropicales en Panamá." s.n.t. Presented in symposium "La Flora de Panamá," Universidad de Panamá, 1980.

Jones, J.R. 1982. "Diagnóstico socio-económico sobre el consumo y la producción de leña en fincas pequeJas de la Penfinsula de Azuero, Panamá." Turrialba, Costa Rica: CATIE. In press.

Jones, J. and Otárola, A. 1981. "Diagnóstico socio-económico sobre el consumo y la producción de leña en fincas pequeñas de Nicaragua." Turrialba, Costa Rica: CATIE.

Jones, J. and Pérez, L.A. 1982. "Diagnóstico socio-económico sobre el consumo y la producción de leña en fincas pequeñas de Honduras." Turrialba, Costa Rica: CATIE. In press.

Lemckert, A. and Campos, J. 1981. "Producción y consumo de leña en las fincas pequeñas de Costa Rica." Turrialba, Costa Rica: CATIE. Serie Técnica, Informe Técnico No. 16, 1981. 69p.

Murray, G.F. 1981. "Mountain Peasants of Honduras: Guidelines for the Reordering of Smallholding Adaptation to the Pine Forest." Tegucigalpa, Honduras: USAID.

Nations, J.B. and R.B. Nigh. 1978. "Cattle, Cash, Food and Forest: The Destruction of the American Tropic and the Lacandon Maya Alternative." *Culture and Agriculture* (Bulletin of the Anthropological Study Group on Agrarian Systems), no. 6:1-5.

Parsons, K.H. 1975. "Agrarian Reform in Southern Honduras." LTC Research Paper, No. 67. Madison: Land Tenure Center, University of Wisconsin.

Sellers, S. 1977. "The Relationship Between Land Tenure and Agricultural Production in Tucurrique, Costa Rica." Turrialba, Costa Rica: Centro Agronómico Tropical de Investigación y Enseñanza (CATIE).

Land Scams

ranching wins

The Amazon: Development or Destruction?

Harry Mauer
. . .

Mauer's article captures the play of interests among early settlers, newcomers and those who victimize them in the clearing of the Brazilian Amazon. Legal confusion reigns. Where new land is free for the clearing, how effective would tenurial incentives be in encouraging the investment and sound husbandry necessary to create a sustainable agriculture?—The Editors

The Pioneers

A visit to the Amazon immediately reveals that Amazonia is being occupied by two antagonistic groups: the *paulistas* (a word that literally means people from Sao Paulo, but in the Amazon has come to mean any investor from the South) and the peasants.

In the hotels of Porto Velho, a city in the Federal Territory of Rondonia that has doubled in size to 70,000 during the last decade, the *paulistas* sit and wait for a deal to close, for a bribe to reach the right hands, for the local bureaucracy to budge. A typical example is Otavio Levanti, the grandson of Italians who emigrated to Brazil and settled in the fertile southern state of Parana. He has taken advantage of government fiscal incentives to buy 17,000 hectares of land [one hectare is 2.471 acres (eds.)]. As soon as the papers are processed he plans to return to Parana, leaving a partner to look after the Amazon land. At the beginning of the dry season they will burn off the forest, plant pasture and bring in cattle from Mato Grosso. It should be a good investment, he says, but in the meantime he is sick with longing for the cool weather and quasi-European amenities of Parana.

Harry Mauer, "The Amazon: Development or Destruction?" NACLA Report, May/June 1979, pp. 27-37. Reprinted with the permission of the author.

162

Another contingent of pioneers stands in small clusters outside the local headquarters of the National Institute of Colonization and Agrarian Reform, or INCRA. Their floppy, stained shirts, ragged trousers, shapeless straw hats and their silent, diffident manner identifies them as peasants. Most of them are hoping to discover whether the state, as embodied by INCRA, will give them legal title to 100 hectares of forested land—land that in many cases they are already occupying.

To a large extent, the future shape of Amazonia lies in INCRA's hands. A series of laws has placed ownership of the bulk of Brazil's Amazon with the government and INCRA administers the distribution of that land. In Rondonia, INCRA's role is particularly crucial. The territory contains large tracts of extraordinarily good soil for Amazonia, which suddenly became accessible in 1960 with the completion of a rudimentary highway from Cuiaba to Porto Velho. The BR-364, precursor of a network of roads that has been feverishly cut through the forest, inaugurated the era of the truck in Amazonia—an event as significant as the great railroads were to the American West.

Now trucks struggle up the dirt road by the hundreds, bringing migrants by the thousands: rural laborers thrown out of work by the mechanization of agriculture, or small farmers forced by drought or market collapse to sell out their ever-large agribusiness competitors. They are destitute, often illiterate. They arrive in ramshackle pickups or panel trucks, several families riding in the back sheltered only by tarpaulins. Amazonians have sardonically dubbed these vehicles the "parrot's perch"—the name of one of the most notorious forms of torture perfected by the Brazilian military regime. (The victims slung over a bar, head down, and then beaten, shocked, or raped.)

The rush up the BR-364 began in earnest in 1972; by 1974, according to official figures, more than 900 families were entering Rondonia every month. Belatedly, INCRA moved to channel this massive influx into orderly "colonization" projects.

Five such projects are now under way in Rondonia and in theory, they exemplify simplicity and social justice in action. The landless peasant arrives in Rondonia and registers with INCRA. He is assigned a plot, usually of 100 hectares, in one of the designated areas. INCRA provides financing, infrastructure, health care, education, technical assistance, marketing facilities—all this is theory. But lower-echelon INCRA employees make no secret of the fact that the agency's resources don't remotely match the requirements of the situation. What actually happens, in a typical case, is that a peasant family arrives and may or may not register with INCRA; in either case, they search out some attractive land, clear the forest, and pray to obtain legal title some-day.

By 1978, the legal status of 12,000 colonizing families in Rondonia had been "regularized," with 16,000 more registered and waiting; how many are unregistered in anyone's guess. And since INCRA cannot actually provide the services that might make the projects thrive, occupation tends to be unstable. The result is a maelstrom of drifting peasants and violent frontier towns on the BR-364.

The Speculators

INCRA also has the job of unraveling a byzantine tangle of land tenure, since no one bothered to survey property boundaries in the Amazon for centuries. But with agriculture and ranching now a possibility, land has become a valuable commodity. The *grileiro*, or real estate swindler, has become one of Amazonia's classic characters. Petty *grileiros* prey on the peasants; they trek a mile or two into the forest, clear a plot, build a hut and then, claiming ownership, sell out to one or more gullible newcomers. The large-scale *grileiros*, many of them lawyers, are more ambitious. They set up storefronts in town and deal in huge parcels of land on the basis of titles that at best are doubtful and at worst are printed for the occasion. Since INCRA usually must go to court to have the titles declared invalid, and since the new "owners" may well be rich and powerful groups of *paulistas*, property questions are often settled by what one official politely called "extraofficial means."

The pattern is repeated throughout Amazonia. In response to an advertising campaign in southern Brazil, concocted by the governor, a horde of speculators descended on the state of Acre. Between 1972 and 1974, they sold and re-sold an estimated two-thirds of all the lands in the state. Investors now own about 80 percent of the state, much of it concentrated in the hands of Sao Paulo companies like the Grupo Atlantico/Boa Vista and the Grupo Atalla, who together hold title to nearly two million hectares.

The real victims of the speculative outburst are the descendents of Acre's original settlers. Their forebears migrated from the blighted northeast to the Amazon during the rubber boom in the late nineteenth century, and it was their occupation of Acre, then part of Bolivia, that made possible Brazil's annexation of the area in 1903. If they did not tame the jungle, they at least learned to live in it; and from the rubber trees they extracted the milky liquid that built the cities of Manaus and Belem. When the boom collapsed, those who had survived the unimaginably brutal conditions of the *seringais* (where the rubber trees grow wild and are dispersed in the jungle) stayed on, eking out a living by planting subsistence crops and tapping the trees on a more or less independent basis. Then the speculators arrived, wanting to rid the land of "squatters"—the laborers that had been there for decades, and some for a hundred years. . . .

May to November is the time to clear the land of both forest and squatters. Houses and crops are burned. Barbed wire is strung. But it is also time when those doing the clearing may be ambushed. One man who has worked to organize the peasants was pessimistic: "The government wants large-scale ranches in Amazonia. The *paulistas* come in here with planes, tractors, defoliants, private armies, bank loans, subsidies. And the local police, the judges, the soldiers—they look after the people who can pay the price."

Those who are forced from the land often return to it as peons on ranches owned by the *paulistas*. Generally, they are hired by a labor contractor, whose stock in trade features tempting promises about pay and working conditions. Once he assembles his herd, the peons are driven or flown to the ranch, often deep in the forest, to do backbreaking labor for ten hours a day or more. Not infrequently they are treated as prisoners, subject to beatings for infractions, with armed guards posted to prevent escape. Equally often the contractor vanishes at the end of the season, without paying his men. And with the apparatus of justice notoriously for sale, the peons have little hope for redress. Benedito Travares, an Acre landowner who was among the very few ever brought to trial for conditions amounting to slavery on his ranch, boasted publicly that he could buy any local policeman in the state for five dollars. . . .

Polamazonia

The generals' concept of "development" has been through many stages. First came Operation Amazonia in 1966: the free trade zone, the creation of SUDAM—a giant agency to direct the flow of investment projects—and fiscal incentives. Soon afterwards came another plan, President Medici's dream of a Trans-Amazonian Highway, a 3,000-mile road to run from the Atlantic coast to the Peruvian border, largely through virgin forest. Medici predicted that peasants would pour into the Amazon and build prosperous farms, towns and cities along the highway, thus narrowing the gulf between Brazil's modernizing south and its poverty-stricken north.

But the Trans-Amazon was a failure. Five million colonists were expected by 1980, but no more than 50,000 came, and of those many gave up and went home. The colonists received so little of the financial and technical help they had been promised that many Brazilians now wonder if the plan was meant to fail. Lately, they call the highway the "Trans-miseriana."

In 1974, yet another military president, General Ernesto Geisel, bestowed still another plan on the Amazon—this one giving short shrift to the problem of poverty. Called *Polamazonia*, it established 15 development "poles" where financial resources would be concentrated, each involving massive industrial, mining or ranching projects. The Amazon was no longer seen as worthy of development for its own sake; rather it would serve as a satellite region, charged with furnishing raw materials for the modern area of Brazil, the center-south, earning foreign currency through exports.

This change in strategy coincided with the end of the Brazilian "miracle," and the onset of the worldwide recession. Brazil was experiencing 40 percent annual inflation rates, a growing balance-of-payments deficit and a mounting foreign debt of some $41 billion. The Amazon would have to make its contribution to the drive to raise exports, by producing goods in demand on world markets.

Unfortunately, for the forest, one of those goods is meat. Through SUDAM's fiscal incentives, the government (and therefore, indirectly, the Brazilian public) has subsidized the creation of hundreds of cattle ranches. Many of the subsidized ranches are enormous, adding to the concentration of landholdings in Brazil, and many are owned by foreigners. Among these are the King Ranch, a 180,000-acre spread in Para; the Suia-Missu Ranch in Mato Grosso, which covers over a million acres and is owned by the Italian firm Liquigas; and the 300,000-acre ranch in Para acquired by Volkswagen.

Watching the ranches spread, Amazonians mutter what is fast becoming a proverb in the region: "Onde o boi entra, o home sai." (Where cattle enter, man exits.) And SUDAM's own figures bear out the saying. It takes few workers to run a large ranch; though agroindustrial projects absorbed half the subsidies distributed by SUDAM between 1966 and 1976, they created only 17,000 of the total 70,000 jobs.

Ranches are highly efficient, however, when it comes to destroying forest. An American agronomist working for several ranches in Para described the modern system of clearing land: "They take two Caterpillar D-8 tractors, run a 24,000 kilogram chain between them, and just drag it through the forest. It pulls up everything by the roots." According to her, many ranches have already been abandoned, their soils useless, their fields smothered by weeds, only to repeat the process in newer ranching areas.

Such apparent short-sightedness reflects the investment mentality of the Amazon, where the goal is to make a quick killing and get out.

Not a few ranches, in fact, are set up solely to siphon off fiscal incentives from SUDAM, a practice that has given rise to the shell-game known as the "tourist cow," whereby a herd of cattle is rented to occupy a phantom ranch on the day that SUDAM officials come to inspect.

But whether the ranches are well-managed, ill-run or largely fictitious, they have the same effect on the forest. No one knows precisely how much of the southeastern Amazon has been devastated since the ranchers moved in, but the area is substantial. Figures from the Brazilian Insititute for Forestry Development (IBDF), the agency responsible for protection of the ecology, show that in the state of Para alone, between 1973 and 1977, the government authorized the clearing of some 4.5 million acres of forest. And that is only the expanse cleared with government permission. Brazilian law governing deforestation forbids any proprietor to clear more than 50 percent of the land and requires payment for the reforestation of an equivalent area. But the law, like so many others, is rarely enforced. . . .

Causes of Deforestation and Forest and Woodland Degradation in Tropical Latin America

William M. Denevan

Looking at tropical Latin America as a whole, Denevan seeks to generalize the causes of deforestation and relate them to one another. In the face of strong economic incentives for unsound land use, does the solution lie in regulations and other legal solutions, or in the development of new technologies which make sustainable land use more profitable?—The Editors

. . . .

Ranching Tradition. Cattle ranching, with roots in Spain and Portugal, has always been a prestige occupation in Latin America (Parsons 1976:126; Myers 1981b:7). A person with pasture and livestock (a *hacendado* or *ganadero*) is a person of status and respect, regardless of production and profit. In fact, to this day many ranches are inefficiently operated, in part because of the tradition that ownership is what is important, not profit. While this has largely changed with pressure for land reform on under-used properties and greater incentives for modernization, the social desirability of having even just a few cattle persists.

Land tenure. There is a tradition in Amazonia and elsewhere in Latin America that it is the act of deforestation, or other "improvement," which gives one the right of possession of land. Given land tenure injustices, this is a means of allowing the poor to use and/or

Excerpted from William M. Denevan, "Causes of Deforestation and Forest and Woodland Degradation in Tropical Latin America," *Report to the Office of Technology Assessment*, Congress of the United States, July 16, 1982, Assessment of "Technologies to Sustain Tropical Forest and Woodland Resources," at 25-43. Reprinted with the permission of the author.

obtain land. The legal system often recognizes this. Many squatters thereby obtain land and many apparent legal owners thereby lose land or have to compensate the deforester; even corporate owners can lose land this way (Fearnside 1979b:340). As a result, there is great incentive to clear as much land as possible as quickly as possible.

Economic viability. Other than the initial purchase of livestock, for which credit can often be obtained from agencies encouraging cattle production, costs of ranching are low compared to commercial crop production. Clearing and pasture planting costs are minimal, the labor required for ranch management is very little, and cost of land is low—as low as $1.18 in the Brazilian Amazon according to Fearnside (1979b: 340). In contrast, expenditures for fertilizers and pesticides for intensive agriculture are high, labor costly, and the market unreliable for both basic crops and for export crops. The market for beef, in contrast, is steady or expanding. These differences are described by DeWalt (1982) for Honduras, where land for pasture is increasing, land in forest or fallow is decreasing, and basic crop land is only holding steady despite rapid population growth.

Negative resource perception. There tends to be an attitude by colonists, ranchers, and development agencies that tropical forest land is so poor that it might as well be used to produce beef rather than not at all, even though cattle carrying capacity is low.[7] The option of land recovery (after brief cultivation) under forest fallow is long term and hence not attractive to most land owners, and more intensive forms of land use are seen as too expensive compared to ranching. . . .

Shifting Pasture

Shifting cultivators have been criticized as consumers of vast amounts of forest, only a portion of which is cultivated at one time. Cattle are seen as a means of utilizing all of a land area. In reality, however, in areas of wet forest pasture is seldom stable. Pasture is abandoned and rotated with forest fallow just as are swiddens and for similar reasons: declining fertility, erosion, soil compaction, invasion of unpalatable weeds, and low productivity. The utilization phase is longer than that for swiddens, but it is not unusual for pastures to be abandoned after only 10-15 years of grazing. Fallows are likely to be short, so that a degraded shrub forest is produced. Reduced pasture productivity often leads to overgrazing and even more severe habitat deterioration. Hecht (1981a:83) reports pasture degradation exceeding 50 percent in parts of the Brazilian Amazon and ranches only five years old failing and being sold or repossessed.[9]

In areas of seasonal forest it takes less pressure from grazing, weeding, and particularly burning to maintain a permanent grassland, or scrub savanna, usually however with degraded soils, poor forage, and a low livestock carrying capacity.

The result of pasture instability, degradation, and shifting is even greater pressure to clear new forest for pasture. It can well be said that cattle "eat" the forest (DeWalt 1982:4), or that the consumers of cattle "eat" the forest, or that cattle "eat" people when a few cattle for beef for the privileged are raised on land that could produce food crops, especially when on the better tropical soils as is often the case. . . .

Cattle ranching is considered to be the most important factor causing deforestation. It is expanding rapidly, particularly in Central America, responding to the U.S. market, and in the Brazilian Amazon, responding to the national market with a probable major future market in Europe. The growth of cattle ranching, however, reflects not only markets but government and international assistance, low cost loans, and other incentives.

Lugo and Brown (1982) argue that Myers and others exaggerate the role of the United States and Europe in the conversion of tropical forests. This role does not seem exaggerated for Central American cattle ranching. Otherwise, the U.S./European influence may be greatest in terms of financial assistance and incentives. Clearly the majority of actual utilization of tropical forests and deforested land in Latin America is for national needs, not international markets. . . .

NOTES

7. Fearnside (1979a) has demonstrated that cattle yields in Amazonia are much lower than often thought. He cites previous estimates of up to 4 head per hectare. His own calculation is 0.32 head per hectare of unfertilized pasture for the first three years and 0.21 for the next two years (5 hectares per head), with further declines thereafter.

9. For a more optimistic view of the ecological viability of cattle raising in Amazonia, see Alvim (1980:31-34) and Sanchez (1978).

REFERENCES

Alvim, Paulo de T. 1980. "Agricultural Production Potential of the Amazon Region." In F. Barbira-Scazzocchio (ed.), *Land, People and Planning in Contemporary Amazonia.* Occasional Publication, No. 3. Cambridge: Centre of Latin American Studies: 27-36.

DeWalt, Billie. 1982. "The Big Macro Connection: Population, Grain and Cattle in Southern Honduras." *Culture and Agriculture* 14:1-12.

Fearnside, Philip M. 1979a. "Cattle Yield Prediction for the Transamazon Highway of Brazil." *Interciencia* 4:220-225.

Fearnside, Philip M. 1979b. "Deforestation in the Brazilian Amazon: How Fast is it Occurring?" *Interciencia* 7:82-88.

Hecht, Susanna B. 1981a. "Deforestation in the Amazon Basin: Magnitude, Dynamics and Soil Resource Effects." *Studies in Third World Societies* 13:61-108.

Lugo, Ariel E. and Sandra Brown. 1982. "Conversion of Tropical Moist Forests: A Critique." *Interciencia* 7:89-93.

Myers, Norman. 1981b. "The Hamburger Connection: How Central America's Forests Become North America's Hamburgers." *Ambio* 10:3-8.

Parsons, James J. 1976. "Forest to Pasture: Development or Destruction?" *Revista de Biología Tropical* 24 (Supl. 1):121-138.

Sanchez, Pedro. 1978. *Pasture Production in Acid Soils in the Tropics.* Cali, Colombia: CIAT.

Kenyah Dayak Tree Cutting: In Context

Carol J. Pierce Colfer

This study from Indonesia examines tree-cutting in an unusual context: a peasant community resettled within a foreign timber concession. Colfer asks, "Why do Kenyah cut down trees?"—The Editors

Long Segar—Part of the Context

Long Segar was formally designated as part of a Resettlement Project[*] in 1972. It is populated by about 1000 Uma' Jalan Kenyah Dayaks who began migrating out of the remote interior (from Long Ampung) in 1963. They came to Long Segar because of localized population pressures (and resulting land land scarcity in the immediate vicinity), and religious and political differences in Long Ampung; and because they wanted the access to trade goods, education, medical services, and wage labour that a location like Long Segar afforded. Other groups from Long Ampung have formed six other satellite villages for similar reasons. . . .

The village is situated within an American timber concession area, composed of primary forest. The topography varies from flat to gently undulated and is criss-crossed with rivers of varying sizes (all subject to flooding). Located inland and squarely on the equator, the weather is hotter than the 30° to 32° centigrade averages of Samarinda (near the

---

Excerpted from Carol J. Pierce Colfer, "Kenyah Dayak Tree Cutting: In Context," in *Final Report: Interaction Between People and Forests in East Kalimantan* (Washington, D.C.: Indonesia-U.S. Man and Biosphere Project, 1982).

[*]Also included in this project are an adjacent Kutai Muslim community and an Uma' Kulit Kenyah Dayak community about 20 minutes downriver by outboard-motor driven canoe.

coast). Rainfall is high—3253 mm or 128 inches and 127 days of rain in 1979-80, at Muara Marah (LEAP 980:6) with no clear dry or wet season. Soils are generally poor, the best being judged "marginally suitable" for continuous dry land arable agriculture (Ibid).

Wage labour opportunities are available in agriculture, but the more lucrative employment involves sub-contracting with the timber companies, with the pilot plantation, or providing lumber milled in the forest with a chainsaw to Samarinda-based buyers. Almost all wage labour opportunities involve forest clearing or forest-harvesting.
. . . .

Why do Kenyah Cut Down Trees?

If we want to understand the dynamics of human-forest interaction in this region, it is important to ascertain for what reasons the people participate in forest harvesting and clearing. They fall into the following broad categories:

—To make ricefields and gardens.
—To clear land for plantations, roads, or construction for wage and contract labor.
—To harvest merchantable timber for wage or contract labor.
—To sell as lumber or shakes.
—To construct houses, granaries, fieldhuts.
—To make canoes, mortars, and other implements.
—To burn as firewood.
—To harvest edible internal portions of the trees.

The above order very roughly parallels both the degree of human involvement and impact on the environment. Of the top four activities, only the cultivation of ricefields and gardens was possible . . . . The relevance of these four activities to money-making opportunities—a series of opportunities that was entirely absent in the context provided by their remote, interior homeland—is immediately apparent. Kenyah integration into the "modern" money economy is an important factor in the changes that have occurred in their interaction with the surrounding rainforest. Let us, therefore, examine these activities to clarify the decision-making set that influences people in their allocation of time and energy to one activity or another.

Ricefields and Gardens

Dry rice provides the traditional subsistence base for all Kenyah groups. The Uma' Jalan Kenyah consider themselves to be rice farmers, and rice cultivation is the core of important symbolic systems. Kenyah ethnic identity and women's roles are directly connected to the cultivation of rice; and in the recent past, their animist religious system included a proliferation of taboos and proscriptions believed to influence the success of rice crops.

Swidden or shifting cultivation is their mode of operation, and the Uma' Jalan Kenyah, unlike some other Kenyah groups (e.g., Jessup 1981) prefer to plant rice in primary, or very old secondary forests. This means that, ideally, every family opens a new section of primary forest every year for their ricefield (uma). . . .

. . . Although the American timber company has legal rights to harvest trees in the area (an activity that is incompatible with swidden cultivation), the rights of indigenous populations to continue their traditional land-use practices are also recognized by the Indonesian Government. This right, combined with the fact that Long Segar is located in a section of forest with few marketable trees (as determined by a forestry survey), has meant that the people could essentially do as they liked. Traditional land-tenure rules may also contribute to large ricefields. The household which first clears a portion of virgin forest retains the right to use that area. So, clearing large sections of forest would also function to "reserve" large landholdings. A sense of land scarcity does not, however, seem to be very important in traditional Kenyah daily life. The traditional situation has been characterized by sparse populations and high overall land-person ratios. . . .

Forest Cutting for Money

In the Long Segar setting, forest cutting for money provides an important economic supplement to rice production. East Kalimantan is a boom region. Almost the entire province has been leased to timber companies, and it is far and away the largest timber-producing province in Indonesia (Ruzicka 1979). Opportunities for Kenyah men to participate abound. Men can clear forests for the construction of logging roads, logging camps, transmigration sites, plantations, and houses. They can also hire themselves out to the lumber companies as *sensas* (chainsaws—a term which refers to both the man and his machine), and cut timber on a contract basis. Or, they can arrange informal agreements with longboat operators and others, to provide specified sizes and lengths of lumber, felled and milled by chainsaw in the forest. A final possibility is the production of shingles made of ironwood, for sale. . . .

The men who participate in forest clearing are usually between the ages of approximately 20 and 40. Young men go, before they are married or in the early years of marriage; and as their responsibilities at home increase with age, they tend to seek moneymaking opportunities closer to home. Also, as their physical strength diminishes, forest harvesting and clearing cease to be open to them.

Unlike the American situation, where logging is seen as a romantic profession, at least by the participants (Colfer, with Colfer 1978), the Kenyah consider it dangerous and do it primarily because they deem it necessary for subsistence (the definition of which broadens with people's perceptions of what the world has to offer). There is a sense among the Kenyah that physical labour as demanding as logging saps a person's strength and leads to a diminishing lifespan—whether by an abrupt logging accident or by the gradual draining of one's life energy. .

Now that development theory and practice are moving increasingly into a participatory framework, trying to involve people in their own development, this body of knowledge takes on a significant role. If development is being decentralized, and people are to take active part in the process, the knowledge and experience that they have (or do not have) are important factors. In Long Segar, agricultural and forestry-related activity must be somehow merged into a development strategy that can protect the forest, both for short and medium-range harvesting, and for its long-term role in protecting the environment for future agroforestry exploitation. Such a goal can be served most directly by tapping the knowledge of the forest and agriculture system that the people possess, and forging with them new strategies. . . .

REFERENCES

Colfer, C.J.P. with A.M. Colfer. 1978. "Inside Bushler Bay: Lifeways in Counterpoint." *Rural Sociology* 43:204-220.

Jessup, Timothy. 1981. "Why Do Shifting Cultivators Move?" *Borneo Research Bulletin* 13(1):16-32.

Ruzicka, I. 1979. "Rent Appropriation in Indonesian Logging: East Kalimantan 1972/3-1976/7." *Bulletin of Indonesian Studies* (July):1-74.

Wood for Fuel—Energy Crisis Implying Desertification: The Case of Bara, The Sudan

Turi Hammer

In arid areas of Africa clearing of woodland initiates desertification, a process of resource degradation that is extremely difficult to reverse. Traditional authorities may once have had the power to restrain such cutting, but often authority over land has been reassigned by national legislation to relatively ineffective modern local government institutions. Turi Hammer recounts this process around a town in Sudan's western province of Kordofan.—The Editors

. . . The Unregistered Land Act of 1970 says that land is not liable for sale, and reaffirms the formal laws as laid down in 1925, that all unregistered land, i.e. outside village boundaries, is to be regarded as government property. Land inside village boundaries is divided into land under utilization and hence occupancy by residents, and land under the trusteeship of the local leader. Due to lack of officials the Government approaches the traditional local leaders to act as their civil servants. These leaders bear the title of *sheikh*, and are heads of prominent families, often akin to those who founded the villages. As only loose guidelines for control over land are given to the *sheikhs*, practice differs between villages according to tribal customs and rules as well as to the *sheikhs'* knowledge about and evaluation of factors like population pressure, animal pasture, farming demands, soil quality and so on.

Excerpted from Turi Hammer Digernes, "Wood for Fuel--Energy Crisis Implying Desertification: The Case of Bara, The Sudan," Thesis in Geography, for the Cand. Polit. degree, University of Bergen, Norway, November 1977, at 52-53 and at 107-110. Reprinted with the permission of the author.

The general system is that each village has the right to cultivate and collect gum from within a demarcated boundary around the village. From this land plots are distributed among the inhabitants. Each family usually has three or four plots where they alternate cultivation, fallow, gum tapping, and charcoal burning in a rotational cycle. The cycle starts with clearance of trees and bushes that have grown up naturally. Some *Acacia Senegal* trees are usually left to give seeds for new trees as cultivation of sesame (*Sesamum indicum*), *dukhn* (*Pennisetum typhoideum*), water melon (*Citrullus vulgaris*) and perhaps a little *durra* (*Sorghum vulgare*) starts. When the soil becomes too exhausted to yield more profitable crops, the farmers start to clear and cultivate another of their plots, leaving the first to fallow for a period. During the cultivation period *Acacia Senegal* is allowed to grow, and during the fallow period gum is tapped until the trees cease to give satisfactory yields. When the plot is cleared for new cultivation, the trees are felled and made into charcoal. This land use is based on watering by rain only, with no fertilizer added. The plots are inheritable, in practice from father to son only. It is rare to find women owning land. If the village has land exceeding the claims of the inhabitants, the *sheikh* may allocate this to adults of the village or to new-comers who want to settle. In practice new-comers are allowed to cultivate for crops only, as their right over the gum exuded from the *Acacia Senegal* trees on the plots they cultivate is not recognized. Gum tapping on such land should revert to the communal ownership, but in practice the *sheikhs* rent out the right to tap gum against payment. When people move to settle elsewhere, their plots should revert to communal property. Trespassing to tap gum from trees on plots under the rotational cultivation cycle is regarded as a serious offence, and cases are usually brought to court.

On land outside village boundaries there is limited grazing by cattle, sheep, and goats owned by settled families in Bara and villages, and by the herds of camel-owning nomads who pass through the vicinity of Bara on their way between dry-season pastures to the south and rain-season pastures to the north. On such government land, here called open land, *Acacia Senegal* trees are often controlled by wealthy Bara citizens or village *sheikhs*. This system of 'crop ownership' on waste land is based on local custom and tradition as developed from the latter part of the 19th century, when gum trade became of economic importance, as individuals then began to demand the right of gum forests. They claim to own the trees, and rent out the right to tap trees from their forests, or they hire labourers to tap the gum which they themselves sell at the Bara Auction market. Especially since the export of gum from Northern Kordofan started to decline in 1967/68 there has been less control by the tree 'owners,' and a remarkable increase in trespassing by people who tap gum or cut trees illicitly for fuel. Some of the charcoal sellers interviewed said they had cut trees on land that did not belong to anybody, as far as they knew. When outside village boundaries they thought they could carry out any activity they pleased without annoying anyone. These sellers were probably new in the area, and had been informed neither about central nor local rules. According to Forest Laws no tree whatsoever should be cut, except for the purpose of clearing ground for cultivation, without permission from the local forest office. When asked, the Forest Office people in Bara admitted that nobody ever comes to ask permission, although they knew that lots of trees were cut daily on government land....

In the first part of this century the *goz*[clay soil (eds.)] farming cycle used to take about 17 years, with 4 to 5 years of intensive cultivation. When cultivation ceased because of decreased soil fertility, coppice shoots of *Acacia Senegal* could quickly form a stand of trees to be tapped for gum after 3 to 5 years. Trees from new seedlings would mature later, so that the gum after 3 to 5 years. Trees from new seedlings would mature later, so that the gum garden formed could yield good gum for 7 to 10 years (A.G. Seif el Din 1972).

Figure 15
Traditional Cultivation Cycle

Cultivation----Fallow----Gum Tapping---------Clearing & Burning	Mean of Cycle**
[4-5 Years------->[3-5 Years----->[7-10 Years-------------->circa 17	years

---

** Mean according to information from the farmers.

During my field work farmers from eight villages explained in detail about the present 8 to 11 years' cycles. After 2 to 3 years of cultivation and growth of *Acacia Senegal*, 1 to 3 years of fallow is allowed before gum is tapped for 3 to 5 years. They said, however, that the trees gave good quality gum for 2 or 3 seasons only.   The findings of the field study in the Bara area are supported by satellite images of the Sahel zone. They show that Sahelian farm lands once left fallow for 10-15 years to allow a regeneration of fertility and moisture are frequently now left to rest only for three years or even less (AMBIO 1975).

Figure 16
Present Cultivation Cycle

	Clearing &	Mean of
Cultivation---Fallow--Gum Tapping-----Burning	Cycle**	
[2-3 Years--->[1-3 Years-->[3-5 Years---->	circa 9 years	

** Mean according to information from the farmers.

This intensified use of land leads to general decline in fertility, as the soil gets less rest than that needed for rehabilitation, and farmers have to abandon plots for good after three such short cycles. Such bare land is exposed for wind erosion, and in the traditional village cultivation areas it is quite common to see extensive deflation hollows bordered by a thorn fence. The wind-borne sand is laid down on plots under cultivation, hindering good crops there.

This intensified, shortened cycle is probably caused by a complicated set of factors, resulting from both climatic and human conditions.
Climatic data from Bara indicate that there might have been a general decline in precipitation from 1908 to 1976 and that the years 1965 to 1976, with the exception of 1972, had rainfall far below the last 25 years' average. . . . With diminished rainfall less gum is produced by the *Acacias,* and because of low returns people feel that they might as well cut the trees and start growing crops again on the plots. When dry periods last for some years, swarms of white ants arise and feed on the roots of trees in the area. They damage the roots, and this leads to the premature death of the trees. The existence of these white ants were [sic] held to be the main reason for the extensive decrease in gum yield by a man owning a large number of gum trees south of Bara. In general, the reduced gum yields may lead to owners of gum trees on open land lessening their control efforts, thus making it easy for trespassers to cut trees for charcoal.
However, I think the climatic conditions are only supporting factors to the impact on the ecology of the social, political, historical and demographic conditions under which the people in the area live. . .

The pressure on land increases as the population grows, and the ecological system gets disturbed. As there is no demographic record for the area, details about population cannot be established. However, many factors indicate a recent rapid increase in population due to in-migration to Bara town and its vicinities . . . , the new-settlers being either villagers who have given up their farms and animals because of the drought, or nomads who have lost their herds and become seden-tary. The out-migration is reportedly lower from Bara . . . and also village *sheikhs* said that few people moved away for good. Some youngsters left for the Gezira or Kashm el Girba irrigation schemes to become wage earners, but approximately half of them returned to settle in the villages, while some became only seasonal labourers on the schemes.

Many people who have lost animals or fields try to take up farming in areas of better fertility. Although huge areas lie waste, it is very difficult for new-comers to obtain land to start cultivation. It seems that the *sheikhs*, under whose jurisdiction land not claimed by the long-established villagers rests, by and large are rather unwilling to allocate plots to new-comers. He admits their right to set up their tents or build huts in the outskirts of villages, and might give them the right to cultivate for some years. However, their rights over gum trees, arising from the plots they cultivate, are not recognized. The trees are supposed to revert to the communal ownership of the original settlers, but the profits from such trees often goes to the *sheikhs* themselves (A.G. Seif el Din 19?) [eds. in original]. One might expect that such a practice forces the troubled new-settlers either to cultivate the plots beyond the sound limits as set by the soil quality, thus over-using the soil so that it needs even longer time than traditionally to recover, or they possibly cut the trees and make charcoal for sale as soon as the cultivation period is over, to earn something from them as a replacement for gum. When getting new plots they leave the old one desolated and exposed for wind erosion. . . .

People reported on the lack of interest, understanding or help from the governmental agencies in Bara, El Obeid, and Khartoum. Some experienced soil deterioration with decreasing yields and increasing prices on products that become more and more scarce. Others lost their animals because of degrading pastures. Quite a number of men got involved in the extensive cutting of trees and charcoal burning to meet the ever-increasing need for fuel. In some areas people saw moving sand dunes encroaching over their fields or pastures. And they all said, "Representatives from the government never come to see us and our living conditions. How can they help us?"

The intensified use of land in the Bara area, compelled by population pressure and carried out without any effective control, leads to desertification. . . .

REFERENCES

AMBIO Vol. IV, NO. 4, 1975. Eckholm, E.P.: "Desertification, a World Problem."

A.G. Seif el Din. 1972. The Future of Gum Arabic in the Sudan. El Obeid.

A.G. Seif el Din n.d. The Future of Gum Arabic in the Sudan, unpublished paper

6

Tenure and Afforestation

There is wide recognition of the need to place more land under trees in developing countries, to meet both fuel production and conservation objectives. Afforestation is the name for this process and is used here to refer to the intentional planting of trees (and not to include sustainable use pattern which permit natural regeneration). Tenure affects afforestation efforts, because tenure is one determinant of incentives for farmers to plant trees. Some of the ways in which tenure affects the planting of trees have already been examined in Chapter 3, which introduced tree and tenure interactions. In this chapter, Sellers made the point that security of tenure increases incentives for the long-term investment involved in tree planting, and Brokensha and Riley noted the potential of security-enhancing tenure reforms to promote tree-planting. If rights to tenure can be earned by use, this may promote both clearing of natural forest and planting of commercial tree crops such as cocoa and coffee (Harbeson et al., 1984:6; Tiffen, forthcoming; Hecht, 1983:33). The four cases on palm planting as proof of ownership from *James and Fimbo* show the operation of several customary laws in Tanzania in this regard. The planting of trees is used by the courts to sort out conflicting claims to land where documentary proof is unavailable or ambiguous.

Noronha (n.d.) has gathered a multitude of cases to demonstrate that rural people around the world have planted trees on their holdings. Planting of trees by individual farmers for fuelwood occurs on a large scale in Kenya, where a high percentage of farm families collect and replant with seedlings on their holdings (Kenya Woodfuels Survey, 1984:10), in Rwanda (Winterbottom, 1985:3), and on a more modest but significant scale in Lesotho, where fruit trees are planted (Turner, in this chapter). It is another question whether enough is being planted to meet future needs. A study in Tanzania (Fleuret and Fleuret,

1978) found that the village of 200 peasants studied would have needed to plant 1,360 trees per year to keep pace with their consumption!

The material covered in Chapter 3 and above examines the incentives of individuals to plant trees on their land, or land they covet. There are other options, such as planting on community land, which involve other units of social organization. These options have been explored in the past decades in afforestation projects instituted by developing countries and donors. These projects have often foundered due to failures to frame rights in trees and land so as to provide economic incentives for planters, and failure to frame effective institutional arrangements for the protection of the trees and distribution of their benefits. This chapter first examines some of the alternative units of social organization for afforestation, then examines the experience with these options in several development projects.

The range of institutional options is broad. *Cernea* explores them from a sociological perspective in his article on "Alternative Units of Social Organization Sustaining Afforestation Strategies": communities, small groups, associations, age groups, and women's groups. Tree planting is an activity that may be organized in certain societies by any one of those groups. Land tenure systems in developing countries offer a variety of alternative tenure "niches," categories of land that are to be used by certain groups in the society and for particular purposes. The land on which trees are to be planted may be owned by a group defined by common residence, such as a village, or a group defined by common descent, such as a clan, or by a family or individuals within a family. The selection of a particular area of land for tree-planting can, by virtue of the tenure niche in which the land falls, determine who in the community will benefit from the trees. Planting trees on the village commons, for instance, may permit the village landless to benefit from the project along with property owners (Mukhoti, 1986).

Over recent years, a great deal of largely unsatisfactory experience has been acquired with "village forestry." In some cases the trees are to be planted for erosion control purposes; in other cases, in "community woodlots" as a source of fuelwood. Trees for community woodlots are generally planted on common land near the village, but if erosion control is the objective, planting may be on mountain slopes used primarily as common pasture. Organizing the protection and eventual disposition of trees on community land has been difficult, though often the matter has been approached with a surprising naiveté (Noronha, 1980; Noronha, 1981; Blair, 1982; Hoskins, 1982). In his paper on Lesotho, written for this volume, *Turner* examines a continuing dilemma in community woodlot projects: should the project rely on state forestry personnel or on traditional chiefs to ensure the survival of the seedlings? The former often have little local presence and less authority, while the latter may abuse their authority, cutting the trees for their own use. Only a small fraction of the trees planted in the woodlot program has survived.

The Lesotho experience is unfortunately representative of the experience with many village forestry programs in other developing countries (e.g., Brain, 1980). The difficulty of what was being attempted was clearly underestimated. Noronha (n.d.) makes the point that there is little evidence that there were community planting schemes before the advent of modern community forestry programs. *Thomson*, writing of the Sahel, examines what he refers to as the "village woodlot fallacy," focusing on villagers' perceptions of the feasibility of local collective action. This feasibility seems to be quite limited, and Thomson urges clearer definition and privatization of rights in trees. He concludes that the institutional and managerial problems of afforestation on community land are so serious that a stronger emphasis on tree-planting on individual or family holdings is required, and that tenure must evolve in a manner supportive of tree-planting on those holdings.

Development agencies have come to regard community-based forestry initiatives with great skepticism. While community resource management systems may be impressive, development project planners have not proved at all adept at reproducing them in the context of their projects. Opinion has swung heavily in favor of "farm-forestry," due both to the problems that have plagued village woodlots and to some impressive results in on-farm forestry. *Murray* describes a successful project in Haiti which involves tree-planting on the farmer's holding with a strong cash-crop emphasis. It is this emphasis on cash income and clear farmer rights to the trees, Murray emphasizes, that account for the success of the project. The project has sought to convey two messages in particular to the participants: "You will be the owners of any trees planted;" and "You can cut the trees when you want." But, of course, farm forestry may not be an effective approach where farmers do not have secure and untrammeled tenure (Ng'andwe, 1976; Ogunforwara and Heady, 1973; Francis, 1986).

There have, it should be noted, been some very effective community afforestation programs. *Gregersen* examines the "New Community Movement" in South Korea, in which community initiatives, supported by national law, have compelled individual landowners to contribute their lands for reforestation. If the landowners concerned fail to reforest, the Village Forestry Association undertakes the reforestation on a proxy (cost-sharing) basis. Contracts set production shares for the owners and the VFA. The program has been highly successful.

Compulsion, of course, has often failed, as in the compulsory tree-planting program in post-Mao China (Ross, 1983).

No institutional options should be foreclosed. It is clear that many community forestry experiments to date have suffered from both a poor theoretical appreciation of common property management issues and a grossly inadequate understanding of the particular institutional arrangements and potentials in the communities concerned. Some of the theoretical bases for sound common property management have been set out in Chapter 1, and could be revisited at this point. Secure tenure can be provided by institutional arrangements other than private individual ownership.

REFERENCES

Blair, Harry (ed.). 1982. *Report on Community Forestry Workshop.* Washington, D.C.: USAID.

Brain, James. 1980. "The Uluguru Land Usage Scheme: Success and Failure." *Journal of Developing Areas* 14:175-190.

Bruce, John and Louise Fortmann. 1986. "Tenurial Aspects of Agroforestry: Research Priorities." In John B. Raintree (ed.), *Land, Trees and Tenure: Proceedings of an International Workshop on Tenure Issues in Agroforestry.* Madison and Nairobi: Land Tenure Center, University of Wisconsin, and International Council for Research in Agroforestry: 387-400.

Fleuret, Patrick and Anne K. Fleuret. 1978. "Fuelwood Use in a Peasant Community: A Tanzania Case Study." *Journal of Developing Areas* 12:315-322.

Francis, Paul. 1986. "Land Tenure Systems and the Adoption of Alley Farming." Ibadan, Nigeria: International Livestock Center for Africa.

Harbeson, John W. et al. 1984. *Area Development in Liberia: Toward Integration and Participation.* AID Project Impact Evaluation, No. 53. Washington, D.C.: USAID.

Hecht, Robert M. 1983. "The Ivory Coast Economic 'Miracle': What Benefits for Peasant Farmers." *Journal of Modern African Studies* 21:25-53.

Hoskins, Marilyn. 1982. "Social Forestry in West Africa: Myths and Realities." Paper presented at the American Association for the Advancement of Science Annual Meeting. Washington, D.C.

Mukhoti, Bela. 1986. "Forestry Projects and Landless Farmers—A View of Issues from within a Donor Agency." *Culture and Agriculture* 30:7-12.

Ng'andwe, C.O.M. 1976. "African Traditional Land Tenure and Agricultural Development: Case Study of the Kunda People in Jumbe." *African Social Research* 21:51-67.

Noronha, Raymond. 1980. "Village Woodlots: Are They a Solution?" Paper prepared for the Panel on the Introduction and Diffusion of Renewable Energy Technologies, National Academy of Sciences, Washington, D.C.

Noronha, Raymond. 1981. "Why Is It So Difficult to Grow Firewood?" *Unasylva* 33:4-12.

Noronha, Raymond. n.d. "Why Do People Grow Trees." [mimeo Washington D.C., about 1982 ed.].

Ogunforwara, O. and Earl O. Heady. 1973. "Integrating Short-Term Farm Enterprises with Perennial Tree Crops: An Application of Recursive Programming to a Tree Crop Settlement in Western Nigeria." *Nigerian Journal of Economic and Social Studies* 73:81-94.

Ross, Lester. 1983. "Obligatory Tree Planting: How Great an Innovation in Implementation in Post-Mao China." In *Joint Committee on Chinese Studies of the American Council of Learned Societies and the Social Science Research Council Workshop on Policy Implementation in the Post-Mao Era, Ohio State University, Columbus, Ohio, June 20-24, 1983.* Purdue, Ind.: Purdue University Press.

Tiffen, Mary. Forthcoming. *Economic, Social and Institutional Aspects of Shifting Cultivation in Humid and Semi-Humid Agriculture.* Rome: FAO.

Winterbottom, Robert. 1985. "Rewards Integrated Forestry and Livestock Project; Report of the Phase II Rural Forestry Pre-preparation Mission." Washington, D.C.: World Bank.

The Editors

Customary Land Law of Tanzania: Planting Trees as Tantamount to Ownership

R.W. James and G.M. Fimbo

> *While in some tenure systems clearing land of trees creates rights, in others planting trees establishes rights. In yet others, mature trees provide the best evidence of long use, upon which may hinge the establishment of rights. James and Fimbo illustrate this with four cases decided under the customary laws of different ethnic groups of Tanzania.—The Editors*

. . .

Mariam bint Chaulembo v. Hamisi Waziri [8]

Kilale, Rufiji law. Plaintiff claimed the disputed land by inheritance. 400 coconut trees were on the land and it was established that these were planted by the defendant who had been on the land for a long period, including a period during the lifetime of the deceased owner. At the time when the defendant took possession there were eight coconut trees on the land. The plaintiff claimed that the defendant was a trespasser and must vacate the land on receiving compensation for the improvements which he had effected. Held under native law and custom in this part of the Territory, land can only be acquired by effective cultivation, and cultivation to the extent only of eight trees cannot be permitted to establish a claim to an area containing four hundred.

JUDGMENT. The plaintiffs in this case claim ownership of an area of land to which they say they are entitled by inheritance from Mwanaisha bint Mwichande. The area has never been demarcated but is described as a fairly large area on which some four hundred coconut

---

Excerpted from R.W. James and G.M. Fimbo, *Customary Land Law of Tanzania: A Source Book* (Nairobi: East Africa Literature Bureau, 1973), at 301-302, 353-358. Reprinted with the permission of the authors.

trees have been planted and, except for these trees, there is no other material cultivation upon it. It is admitted that during a long period, including the lifetime of Mwanaisha, who died about fourteen years ago, the defendant has been in occupation of the area in dispute and that the only effective cultivation at the time when he assumed possession was the existence of eight coconut trees. Except for those eight trees the defendant claims to have himself planted all the four hundred or so trees by virtue of which the area in dispute is now capable of identification. There is no effective rebuttal of this claim, and the courts below have rightly assumed that this is the case. The decision from which appeal is now made was that the defendant was a trespasser and must vacate the land on receiving compensation from the plaintiffs for the improvements which he has effected, and this compensation has been assessed at one thousand shillings, which sum the plaintiffs have paid into court. The Board is unable to agree that this decision is right. Under native law and custom in this part of the Territory land can only be acquired by effective cultivation, and cultivation to the extent only of eight trees cannot be permitted to establish a claim to an area containing four hundred. Since the exact situation of the original eight trees cannot now be ascertained, the defendant must be regarded as in lawful possession of the whole area now in dispute, but he must compensate the plaintiffs in respect of the eight trees which were in existence when he assumed possession. This compensation has been assessed by the District Commissioner at three hundred shillings and the Board sees no ground for rejecting that computation. The appeal is allowed and the appellant is declared to be the rightful occupier of the land in dispute by virtue of his beneficial use thereof. It is further ordered that the appellant must pay three hundred shillings to the respondents to be divided between them in accordance with their respective shares of inheritance as already determined by the District Commissioner. The respondent will pay all the costs incurred by the appellant in the present appeal in the courts below, which costs are to be determined by the District Commissioner and should be deducted from the amount of compensation payable by the appellant under this judgment. . . .

Jeremiah s/o Anthony v. Ramadhani s/o Saidi [22]

Haya law—Dispute as to ownership—planting of boundary trees is tantamount to and indicative of ownership. Customary tenant has no right to plant trees to mark boundary.

SPRY, J[udge]: This is a case concerning the ownership of land. It is not in dispute that the plaintiff/appellant bought the land in 1956, and the only real issue is whether the man who sold the land to him, one Issa s/o Selemani, was the owner. Clearly, if Issa was not the owner, the sale could not change the ownership.

It appears from the evidence that the defendant/respondent leased the land to Issa in 1939, that Issa and his brother Salimu went into occupation, that there were disputes over the next three years and that some settlement was reached in 1942. The only witness who could give personal evidence of this settlement was one Kilyobamu, who said that it was a sale of the land for Shs. 60.

The local court found for the defendant/respondent, mainly on two grounds; first, that certain trees on the land had been planted by him and, secondly, because the sale by Issa was not witnessed by the neighbours. With respect, neither of these was a good reason. As regards the first, it is not disputed that the defendant/ respondent was formerly the owner of the land. As regards the second, Issa's son acknowledged the sale to the plaintiff/appellant.

The Buhaya Appeal Court allowed an appeal by the plaintiff/appellant, mainly because the land had been demarcated by the planting of boundary trees.

This decision was reversed by the District Commissioner, in a short judgment which does not deal with the real issue.

Additional evidence was called for by the Local Courts Appeal Officer, of which the most important element is testimony that customarily no landowner would allow a tenant to plant trees to mark a boundary; this is an indication of ownership.

The assessors who sat with me were of the opinion that this appeal should be allowed. From their knowledge of local conditions, they regarded Kilyobamu's evidence as credible. Secondly, they confirmed that the planting of the boundary trees indicated ownership, as against tenancy. Thirdly, they noted that the defendant/respondent had failed to explain his inaction during the years since the sale by Issa.

I agree with the assessors. I think the weight of evidence was all in favour of the plaintiff/appellant and that the District Commissioner was not justified in reversing the decision of the Buhaya Appeal Court.

I accordingly set aside the judgment of the District Commissioner and restore the judgment of the Buhaya Appeal Court in favour of the plaintiff/appellant, Jeremiah Anthony, and he is awarded the costs of this appeal and the costs in the courts below.

Mbwana Nassoro v. Alli Jongo [23] (Kisarawe)

SPRY, J[udge]: This is an appeal from the judgment of the Regional Local Courts Officer, Dar es Salaam, allowing an appeal from two decisions of the Local Appeal Court of Kisarawe, reversing a decision of the Local Court of Mkuranga.

The proceedings concern the ownership of a *shamba* at Mwandege. The appellant, Mbwana Nassoro, who was the plaintiff in the original action, asserted that this *shamba* had fifteen years before been mortgaged by his father to Alli Selemani Jongo, the respondent, for Shs. 40 and he was seeking to redeem it. Alli claimed that he had bought the land by three separate transactions. He also said that he had bought two other *shambas* twenty-five years previously and I understand this to mean that it is Alli's case that all three *shambas* were amalgamated. Alli also said that he planted many trees on the land, which, he said, he would not have been permitted to do had he been only a mortgagee.

Before this court, Mr. Desai for the appellant argued first that three of the documents were unsatisfactory, because they had not been signed by the witnesses named and he argued that they ought to have been proved by the evidence of the Wakili. I would certainly agree that it would have been better had the Wakili been called, if he is available, but I certainly do not regard the failure to call him as fatal to Alli's claim. It was open to Mbwana to call the Wakili, if he thought fit, in order to rebut Alli's defence.

Secondly, Mr. Desai pointed out discrepancies between the description of the property in the documents and that in Alli's evidence. With respect, I do not attach any great significance to these discrepancies. The appellant was testifying to events that happened between fifteen and thirty years ago; the number of trees on the land and even the names of the neighbours will have changed during that time and there were, I think, bound to be discrepancies unless the respondent had refreshed his memory from the documents.

Thirdly, and in the alternative, as I understand it, Mr. Desai argued that three of the documents on which Alli relies related to sales of trees only and not land. Mr. Desai relied not only on the wording of the documents themselves but also on an article of Mr. A.A. Oldaker on Tribal Customary Land Tenure in Tanganyika, published in Tanganyika Notes and Records, Nos. 47 and 48 at page 117.

As regards the documents, there are two points to be noted. First, as Mr. Desai pointed out, they are expressed as sales of trees. They include, however, the names of adjoining owners, which it may be argued indicates an intention to sell *shambas*, rather than trees. Furthermore, it is within judicial knowledge of this Court that documents such as these have been used in connection with the sale of *shambas*. It is, in my opinion, a matter to be decided on the facts of each particular case whether the intention was to sell trees or a *shamba*.

As regards Mr. Oldaker's article, I do not think with respect that great weight can be attached to it. While Mr. Oldaker was a very experienced officer, his article is a broad generalization and cannot therefore be regarded as authoritative in determining the customary law of any particular area. Mr. Desai is, however, to be complimented on the diligence he has shown in seeking authority on these difficult questions.

The assessors who sat with me were both firmly of the opinion that the sales were sales of *shamba*. They said, as did the Mkuranga Court, that according to local custom in the Kisarawe area a mortgagee of trees is only allowed to take the fruit of those trees; he is not allowed to plant other trees. In this case it is quite clear on the evidence that Alli planted trees, not just once, but from time to time over the years. The assessors considered that this was a clear indication that Alli had bought *shambas* and not trees.

Mtefu Mtau v. Abel[24]

Chagga law—Nature of grant by landowner to Forestry Department. Held, that as the defendant who had received the land from the Forestry Department had produced development of a permanent nature on the land without protest, such acts are indicative of ownership having been granted by the original owner.

KIMCHA, J[udge]: This is a claim for a developed *Kihamba*. The undisputed facts are that the piece of land in dispute originally belonged to Mtefu Mtau, the Appellant in this case.

In 1946 the Appellant was approached by a representative of the Forest Department and was requested to allocate a portion of his land to the Forestry Department for establishing a Forest Camp. He agreed and a piece of his land was demarcated by Ex Mangi John and transferred to the Forest Department.

This is the piece of land now in dispute. The Camp was first occupied by a representative of the Forest Department named Makibonza who was later replaced by the present Respondent Rumishael.

Rumishael has continued to live there to this date and has produced development thereon of a permanent nature.

In 1954, Usseri 13/54, the appellant, claimed the same piece of land without success.

The Kilimanjaro District Council Appeal Court held that the Appellant having sued the Respondent unsuccessfully in Usseri 13/54 for the said piece of land the case is now res judicata. To this observation the Regional Local Courts Officer added that "It is a remarkable fact that Rumishael, Respondent, should have been permitted to carry out the extensive development for a period of years without protest from the Appellant." It was not until 1954, eight years afterwards, that an attempt was made unsuccessfully to displace him. I think the Appeal Court below came to the right conclusion, although it had not the benefit of the belated admission (admission did not belate the suit in Usseri 13/54) now made by the Appellant.

I dismiss the appeal accordingly with costs.

To these observations I would add that the Appellant lost the rights over the disputed piece of land when he consented to its transfer to the Forest Department. In fact he is now suing the wrong party, he should have earlier sued the Forest Department or the Forest Department and the Respondent jointly because the respondent got it from the Forest Department.

I also doubt whether the Appellant would have succeeded even if he had sued the Forest Department as it appears that the transfer was permanent and not for a term of years.

For these reasons I find that the Kilimanjaro (Original Appeal Court and Regional Local Courts Officer, Moshi) came to the right conclusion in dismissing Mtefu's appeals.

Notes: An appeal court would not lightly set aside findings of fact of lower court. Where the evidence upon which an inference of fact is made is documentary evidence, an appeal court can, however, reappraise the findings. . . .

NOTES

8. (1946) App. to the Governor No. 140 (No. 24/1946).
22. (1963) L.C.C.A. 63/1962.
23. (1964) Digest, 255.
24. (1965) L.C.C.A. 8/1964.

Alternative Units of Social Organization Sustaining Afforestation Strategies

Michael M. Cernea

Social forestry has often come to grief through lack of fore-thought and caution with respect to the unit of social organiza-tion to sustain afforestation. Hard choices must be made among existing social units and between those units and units which might be created to manage afforestation. Cernea explores some of the pros and cons of putting new wine in old wineskins or building a better wineskin. —The Editors

. . . Although commercial and industrial forestry projects are not a recent invention, social forestry projects are. In the conventional type of forestry development, large corporations or government agencies hire workers to establish or expand plantations on large tracts of land the businesses and agencies control; the wood is harvested for use in indus-try or construction. The new approach, social forestry, is to induce a large number of small farmers systematically to plant fuelwood trees on their own lands. . . .

Several social conditions are necessary if these innovations are to succeed. This chapter discusses a few of the substantive social prerequisites for every social forestry program, whether they are explicitly identified or ignored. Financial investments alone cannot make the program a success. These prerequisites often go beyond the dynamics of individual adoption of innovations regarding tree-growing

Excerpted from Michael M. Cernea, "Alternative Units of Social Organization Sustaining Afforestation Strategies," in Michael M. Cernea (ed.), *Putting People First: Sociological Variables in Rural Development* (New York: O.U.P. for the World Bank, 1985), pp. 267-293. Reprinted with the permission of the publisher.

194

to the more complex processes of collective adoption. Although adoption of innovations by individuals has been the subject of an entire stream of sociological research spearheaded by Rogers and others,[1] the collective adoption of innovation, as correctly pointed out by West, has received far less attention.[2] Yet processes such as reforestation, environmental protection, watershed rehabilitation, and in general the group management of natural resources require sociologists to be more concerned with the dynamics of collective behavior and with the prerequisites for the systematic diffusion of collective innovations.

Central among these social prerequisites is the existence of a unit of social organization or a structure capable of sustaining an innovation. Financial inducements alone, however important, are not sufficient and their impact is not automatic. Other social factors whose functions must be recognized include purposeful patterns of social organization for conserving natural resources or for producing new resources, existing land tenure systems that are either conducive to or restrictive of the given innovation, ownership rights to and distributive arrangements for the newly developed resources, authority mechanisms for collective decision making and for mobilizing group (or even individual) action, social perceptions and attitudes, political power that affects the distribution of generated benefits, and the influence of external change agents. . . .

Perhaps the most important factor in designing the social strategy of forestry programs is the adequate identification of the unit of social organization likely to undertake the program and able to do so successfully. For a while, various forestry projects have lumped together, under the broad umbrella of social or community forestry, various objectives and different approaches. This resulted (as in the Azad Kashmir project) in an unclear or mistaken identification of the social unit which could perform the intended activities.

Contributing to this insufficient clarity was the fact that the concept of community forestry was at a certain point loosely defined by some major agencies as "including *any* situation which intimately involves local people in a forestry situation" (emphasis added).[8] Contrary to this overly encompassing definition, the operational challenge is to disentangle the broad term "people" and to identify precisely *who* and *how*: what social units of organization among the people can and will do afforestation, and which social units and definable groups can act as sustaining social structures for long-term production activities.

Such social units of organization can be either natural (existing) social groupings, such as the family household, or groups organized specifically to plant and protect trees. Examples of deliberately created groups (discussed below) are tree growers' associations or women's groups. Creating such social units—organizing them—is, however, a task that requires both correct social understanding of what is to be done and appropriate methods for social organization. The need to establish social units introduces a clear sociological dimension in forestry development projects and in the work of forestry departments.

Establishing a functional social group means, of course, much more than simply lumping together a set of individuals into an artificial entity labeled "group." It implies a process of selection and self-selection of the members, a willingness to associate and participate, a perception of both self-advantage and co-responsibility, and the establishment of an enduring social structure with well-defined functions. This will in turn help mold patterned behavior among members and is the essence of grass root, purposeful institution building.

Forming enduring units of social organization is particularly important in the case of tree growing, given the long production cycle, which requires structured support over an extended period. Such small-scale organizations enhance the capacity of their members; they maximize the cumulative impact of the contributions of individuals and enable them to perform activities and achieve objectives that otherwise might not be attained.

The social arrangements that need to be designed and established for social forestry will vary with the technologies envisaged for reforestation in different ecological areas. The technical and physical characteristics of a forestry program and the socio-structural characteristics of the unit that is its social actor should be compatible.

When forestry programs are designed, it is essential to realize that there are a number of different potential "social actors," but that they are not equally fit for different technical (silvicultural) approaches to forestry. The appropriateness of various tree-planting technologies to one or another local situation is not neutral to social structure. Such technologies refer to species selection, nursery development, planting technology and configurations, plantation managing, protection, marketing, and so on. For instance, to determine which of three basic types of tree arrangements—block planting, linear planting, or mixed associations of trees and crops—is the most adequate in a particular case would require identification of the socio-economic characteristics of the farmers themselves and assessment of the local land tenure systems and land availability. The proper fit between the technical elements of afforestation and the social units around which an afforestation strategy can be built is at the core of the cooperation between forestry experts, planners, and sociologists.

The range of structurally different social actors in forestry development projects is quite broad: communities, villages, village governing bodies, farm families, groups of farmers, cooperatives, schools, private companies, and public institutions. . . .

NOTES

1. See Everett Rogers and F. Shoemaker, *Communication of Innovations: A Cross-Cultural Approach* (New York: Free Press, 1971); see also E. Rogers, *Diffusion of Innovations*, 3rd ed. (New York: Free Press, 1983).

2. Patrick C. West, "Collective Adoptions of Natural Resource Practices in Developing Nations," *Rural Sociology*, vol. 48, no. 1 (1983); and Patrick C. West and S. Light, "Community Level Change Strategies for the Management of Fragile Environments," in K. Shapiro, ed., *Science and Technology for Managing Fragile Environments in Developing Nations* (Ann Arbor: University of Michigan Press, 1978).

8. See Y.S. Rao, "Community Forestry: Requisites and Constraints," in *Community Forestry: Some Aspects* (Bangkok: United Nations Development Programme, East-West Center, and RAPA/Food and Agriculture Organization, 1984).

REFERENCES

Rao, Y.S. 1984. "Community Forestry: Requisites and Constraints." In Community Forestry: Some Aspects. Bangkok: United Nations Development Programme, East-West Center, and RAPA/Food and Agriculture Organization.

Rogers, Everett. 1983. *Diffusion of Innovations*. 3rd ed. New York: Free Press.

Rogers, Everett and F. Shoemaker. 1971. *Communication of Innovations: A Cross-Cultural Approach*. New York: Free Press, 1971.

West, Patrick C. 1983. "Collective Adoptions of Natural Resource Practices in Developing Nations." *Rural Sociology* 48:1.

West, Patrick C. and S. Light. 1978. "Community Level Change Strategies for the Management of Fragile Environments." In K. Shapiro (ed.). *Science and Technology for Managing Fragile Environments in Developing Nations.* Ann Arbor: University of Michigan Press.

Land and Trees in Lesotho

S. D. Turner

As in Highland Ethiopia, the mountains of Lesotho in recent generations have been largely deforested. Spectacular erosion has resulted. The country has a long history of remedial tree planting with few visible results. In recent years much effort has been invested in village woodlots. Turner examines some of the institutional dilemmas.—The Editors

In customary Sesotho law, all land was held by the King on behalf of the Nation. Private ownership did not exist. On behalf of the King, chiefs allocated arable and residential rights to adult men. On the death of the land holder, all rights in the land reverted to the chief for reallocation. The requirements of widows and some preferential interests of descendants were commonly recognized. Individual rights of usufruct on arable land were suspended each year after harvest for a period of communal grazing of crop residues. All other land and its resources, notably pasture and trees, were held and administered by the chief for the communal use of his people. An effective system of control, *leboella* (Sheddick, 1954, 116) was administered by chiefs and their advisers. It permitted the monitoring of grazing and other resource conditions, the (seasonal) opening, closing and restriction of areas so as to protect resources, and the punishment of offenders by village courts. Although customary land law has been superseded by the Land Act of 1979, some of the principles upon which it was based remain largely effective in the day to day functioning of rural land use and administration.

The principal purpose for which Basotho have traditionally planted trees is fruit production for home consumption. Planting is

---

Revised for this volume from S.D. Turner, "Land and Trees in Lesotho" (Institute of Southern African Studies, National University of Lesotho, 1984), written for this volume. New version November, 1987.

mainly around the homestead. As Sheddick notes, "Private ownership of trees is most complete where they are grown on a parcel of land over which the holder has uninterrupted control" (1954, 125). This is the homestead. Occasionally, the residential site is large enough to permit the planting of a small orchard. A recent response in the lowlands to the increasing pressure on arable land and the declining availability of 'fields' has been a substantial increase in the area of some of the residential sites allocated, so that a small field crop can in fact be cultivated in the 'garden'. This also has potential for fruit production under relatively secure tenure. The holder of a residential site has exclusive rights to the produce of trees growing there. On the holder's death, however, the rights to the trees traditionally reverted with the rights to the land to the chief, for reallocations ...

Although a few self sown peaches can often be found in the fields, the planting of trees in field areas was traditionally discouraged. Partly this was because of the birds they would harbour. A more fundamental reason was the seasonal tenure of crop land, under which individual holders' rights were suspended each winter after harvest for a period of communal grazing of residues. Furthermore, reversion of rights to the chief on the holder's death did not encourage the planting of a long term crop of trees ...

While private tree ownership was traditionally a minor feature of Sesotho land use and tenurial patterns, the arrangements for communal tree resources were more significant. As indicated, trees fell under the *leboella* system of resource management, Ashton (1967, 152) suggested that "Today, the natural bush or forest is regarded as the highest form of *leboella* ." While the principles of *leboella* control and resource management are as clear for wooded areas as for pasture, their enforcement was more liable to local variation, depending upon administrators' perceptions of the need to protect the trees. Most commonly, collection of a headload of dead wood did not require special permission. the chopping or felling of wood required the chief's approval and was subject to traditional regulations....

Policy for fuelwood and pole production has clearly recognized the links just described between control, management and income. Production was designed on a community basis, however, and income was intended to accrue to the community. At the same time, control and management were to be vested primarily in government. Although indigenous institutions for communal resource management exist, these were judged inadequate for the efficient woodlot production urgently needed to redress Lesotho's biomass deficit. Control of village woodlots is vested in the Forest Division under the Forest Act, 1978.

The Lesotho Woodlot Project began with normal tenure and *leboella* arrangements for woodlots, but in his 1973-74 annual report the Project Manager noted that

> "Since forestry is such a long term operation, O.D.A. [one of the LWP donors] are insisting that the ownership and control of land given for woodlots shall be taken away from the local authorities and vested in the Ministry of Agriculture" (LWP Project Manager's Report, 1973-74, 5) ....

Subsequent reports indicate the desire of the LMP to assign direct control over woodlots to the Forestry Division so that forest officers would have the absolute authority over these areas thought necessary for adequate protection of the young trees and proper management and ultimate harvesting of the maturing crop.

The Forest Act provides for this. Following inspection and approval of a woodlot area by the Chief Forest Officer and its demarcation, it is gazetted as a forest reserve.

> "As from the effective date of a declaration ... the forest reserve shall be managed, maintained and controlled exclusively by the Forest Division in accordance with the Act" (Forest Act, 1978, section 5).

Within the forest reserve, the Forestry Division is authorized by the Act to demarcate, erect buildings, install equipment, construct roads and "do all such things as may be necessary for planting forests and for their exploitation, management, maintenance and control" (Forest Act, 1978, section 6) ... The Forestry Division is to decide (section 17(2)) when and how much forest produce may be removed from the reserve. The Act also makes provision for the establishment of the Forest Fund into which the proceeds from sales of forest produce are to be paid, and from which a proportion (currently 20%) is to be returned for local development activities in the communities whose areas forest reserves lie.

Like the soil conservationists before them, the foresters have thus sought to manage communal resources on behalf of rural communities, and to impose the necessary control through the law. As enabling legislation, the Act was not intended to accomplish as total an exclusion of rural people from their village woodlots as the wording may suggest. Bureaucratic and political problems have led to several years' delay to payment to villages of their share of proceeds from the Forest Fund, causing some discontent. But application of the Act has not in practice discouraged communities from applying for woodlots. Furthermore, even when legally excluded from responsibility, some chiefs and village courts continue to take spontaneous action to protect their woodlots. Nevertheless, the administrative burdens of the programme as administered under the Forest Act are substantial. The LWP has tried to increase community involvement in the management of the forest reserves, notably by awarding chiefs and other prominent villagers the status of 'honorary forest officers' so that they can help prevent damage. As more woodlots mature, the Forest Division will need extra staff to handle harvesting and marketing. The Forest Act offers government effective management and control of woodlot resources, but at a high price and a rate of implementation too slow ever to bridge the widening gap between wood supply and demand.

In a society where trees and other land resources have traditionally been owned and managed by the community, and where community mechanisms for such management remain comparatively strong, village woodlots have an essential role. As with land administration under the 1979 Land Act, however, woodlot administration under the 1978 Forest Act will have to be simplified, and the role of government reduced. Because of the tradition of community resource management and its residual strength, rural people do feel a collective incentive to manage forest resources, conserve soil and water, and profit from forest produce. But, as with other forms of resource conservation, the incentive is strongly linked to profit perceived. Even if proceeds from the Forest Fund were paid out promptly to approved village projects, this sense of profit would inevitably be diluted by the communal nature of the venture. Foresters rightly doubt whether there would be adequate incentive for the systematic replanting of harvested woodlots. They therefore retain this responsibility under the Forest Act.

As in the case with soil and water conservation on crop land (IFAD, 1986), (agro)forestry production is more attractive to rural people when it offers direct individual profit, without a Forestry Division or a village committee as intermediaries. People making money from trees on their own land will replant them. Some of the tenure trends discussed earlier present new opportunities for tree and shrub cultivation by individuals. On the other hand, the time has not yet come for allocation of sections of marginal grazing land to individuals for (agro)forestry. Whereas the community can agree to convert such an area to tree planting, reduction of the grazing resource by its allocation in parcels to individuals would not be acceptable -- for planting or for grazing purposes. Again, therefore, the community woodlot has an essential contribution to make.

REFERENCES

Ashton, H., 1967. *The Basuto*. 2nd edition. Oxford University Press.
  IFAD (International Fund for Agricultural Development), 1986. *Soil and water conservation in sub-Saharan Africa: issues and options*.

Lesotho. Forest Act, 1978.

Lesotho Woodlot Project. Manager's Report, 1973-74.

Sheddick, V.G.J., 1954. *Land Tenure in Basutoland*. London, H.M.S.O.

Participation, Local Organization, Land and Tree Tenure: Future Directions for Sahelien Forestry

James T. Thomson

> *Thompson is one of the few analysts to examine local communi-
> ties' own perception of their ability to make rules to govern
> resource use. The implications of his evidence from Niger and
> Upper Volta are not encouraging for community-managed
> forestry in the Sahel. —The Editors*

... *Avoiding the "Village Woodlot" Fallacy.* Popular participation in
identifying resource management opportunities *and* constraints is
imperative if foresters are to avoid future repetitions of the "village
woodlot" fallacy. That fallacy lay in foresters' often unexamined
assumption that villagers shared their perceptions. *Foresters saw
village woodlots as a resource management opportunity.* But their
analysis of the problem, predominantly administrative and technical,
took little account of social factors villagers had to confront. *What
foresters saw as a management opportunity often looked to villagers,
for political reasons, like a highly risky investment.* The interest
many rural Saheliens express in individual woodlots confirms foresters
initially failed to focus on all relevant elements in the local resource
management scene; they thus directed much effort to promoting socially
or politically infeasible solutions [NFPA: I, 68, P.4.5.1.2.; UVFPA: 28,
P.2.2.4.; Thomson, 1979: 1-2]. ...

Social And Technical Constraints. As has been widely recognized,
social factors played a major role in the village woodlot debacle

Excerpted from James T. Thomson, "Participation, Local Organization,
Land and Tree Tenure: Future Directions for Sahelien Forestry,"
Prepared for Club du Sahel, OECD (Silver Spring, Md., December
1982). Reprinted with the permission of the author.

[Hoskins, 1979b: 18-20; Winterbottom, 1980: 10-13; Thomson, 1979: 22-24]. These factors also influence other woodstock management efforts (live fences, bush fires, exploitation of state forests, etc.). They can be usefully analyzed as a series of potential constraints on innovation in resource management activities. Four general categories of constraints exist: *technical, economic and financial, legal* and *political*. Because technical factors interact powerfully with social factors, the general discussion of constraints begins with the former. . . .

Economic and Financial Constraints. Resource management must make economic sense and be financially feasible before rural people will cooperate in efforts at reforestation. Most Saheliens operate on a narrow margin of security, and so try to minimize risks. But this is not tantamount to saying they will never take risks [Popkin 1979: 18-22 provides an extremely interesting analysis of this problem]. Especially those who have a bit of surplus, be it land—temporarily fallowed fields—labor or capital, may invest it in woodstock management if wood scarcities become apparent or wood prices rise in area markets (both are increasingly common phenomena in the Sahel [MFPA: 88-89, Ps.4.4.1.1.3.-4.; NFPA: II, 17, P.2.2.; Winterbottom, 1980: 2-3, esp. Table 1]). . . .

Legal Constraints. Land tenure and tree tenure rules may create major barriers to investments in new supplies once local people begin to feel the pinch of wood shortages. So may legal processes by which disputes are resolved concerning these rules [for a fuller discussion of these issues, see Thomson, 1981a: 126-45; UVFPA: 95-96, P.8.4. raises a number of the issues in a succinct fashion].

Defining Tree Tenure: A New Necessity. Until quite recently, abundant supplies of land and trees justified use rules which treated these resources as free goods. Anyone could collect wood in the bush commons, usually without authorization [UVFPA: 21, P.2.1.5.1., *"d'ordre politique foncier,"* 60, P.6.1.1.; NFPA: II, 62; Thomson, 1983b: 175-76]. Access to land, under either grants or loans, usually took place with minimal limitations on the user's right to exploit both land and trees as he saw fit [MFPA: 119, P.6.1.1.].

Given abundant resource conditions, such rules fittingly promoted exploitation of otherwise under-utilized production factors. But when resources grow scarce, and when investment in new supplies becomes imperative, permitting uncontrolled exploitation of common property resources ceases to be a functional rule. Uncertainty about who will reap results of investment in reforestation and land fertility must discourage local investment in either case [UVFPA: 67, P.6.2.1.3.]. *Ambiguity about control of benefits from investment in resource management* (e.g., more wood, less water or wind erosion, improved soil fertility or water availability) *will exist where* goods are legally treated as unregulated common properties; *or where* regulations governing common properties can be easily manipulated; *or where* land is loaned for an indeterminate period of time; *or where* ownership and use rule conflicts exist within a single jurisdiction (based on "customary" law differences in inter-ethnic situations, or divergences between local and national rules). *Unpredictability of the legal process often also raises doubts about the value of resource use rights.* National forestry codes and land tenure codes often run counter to local rule systems [MFPA: 121, P.6.2.1.; NFPA: II, 60-62, P.5; UVFPA: 67, P.6.2.1.3.]. Uncertainty about which version might be applied in some potential future dispute can easily discourage people from investing their limited surplus of land, labor or capital in production of new supplies of now scarce resources.

Political[1] Constraints.   In many contemporary Sahelien communities, local political conditions render long-term collective activities impossible. (The Swiss-financed village woodlot program in Upper Volta implicitly recognizes this [UVFPA, 1982, 149-50].) Table 1 suggests both the generally low levels of local competence residents perceived in these four sites in 1979 and the marked inter-village variations which may exist among adjacent communities (Villages 1 and 2 shared a common border, as did 4 and 5). These villages ranged in resident population from 500 to 1,500.

Sahelien communities which approximate even the "best" of these four illustrative cases (Village 5) in terms of perceived low level of policy-making competence face a real dilemma. *Implications for participatory renewable natural resource management on a collective basis are devastating.* In such milieux, local political conditions dictate that villagers cannot, for lack of effective local political frameworks, jointly protect and culture village woodlots, live fencing or windbreaks during critical initial years until they become established. They *cannot* as a group police woodstock or pasture use on village lands. They *cannot* develop and systematically maintain watershed management by collective action over the lands of all holders in a single watershed. Joint soil conservation operations and the like are *impossible where these depend on the capacity to enforce collective decisions, because that capacity does not exist.*

Table 1.² "About what sorts of things can you make laws?"

Villages' Reported Areas of Local Competence Totals	Niger 1		Upper Volta 2	4	5
None	6 (16%)	24 (71%)	0 (0%)	0 (0%)	30 (20%)
Marital Problems	21 (55%)	3 (9%)	36 (69%)	22 (71%)	82 (53%)
Marital Problems Plus Other Issues (alms, livestock control, well-digging, etc.)	10 (26%)	6 (18%)	12 (23%)	9 (29%)	37 (24%)
Any Problem	1 (3%)	0 (0%)	4 (8%)	0 (0%)	5 (3%)
N=	38	34	52	31	154

Collective Action Conditions. Collective action possibilities will be greater whenever local communities enjoy both *rule-making capability*, including taxation and resource use regulation, and *rule enforcement capability*. Where a small, or even a large number of local decision makers (with or without state authorization) can effectively establish binding local regulations concerning resource use, taxation and other such critical building blocks of sustained collective action, long-term management operations are feasible. Autonomous local resource management operations become possible and indeed probable, if popular opinion supports them, where local communities can enforce their own locally-made rules in village or quarter moots, at low cost. This appears to have been the case, for instance, in pre-colonial Mossi society [UVFPA: 21, P.2.1.5.1. *("d'ordre social et traditionnel,"* 65,66, P.6.2.1.1.], where earth priests *(tengsobanamba)* exercised general control over allocation of land and regulated bush fires.

By contrast, in communities where local cohesion is lacking [NFPA: II, 57, P.4.; UVFPA: 21], it would be naive to assume local initiative will suffice to sustain effective collective action over the long run. *If making and enforcing resource use and management rules depends on the willing consent of each and every person affected, locally-initiated collective efforts become practically impossible to sustain. Under such circumstances, if environmental problems are to be dealt with to any extent collectively, either outside leadership in policy-making, and in implementation, and in enforcement must be constantly provided, or the conditions of local public collective action must be modified.* (It is *highly problematic* whether all environmental management problems can be resolved by individual efforts unaided by collective backup at the local level, at least to provide a framework for coordination and enforcement of rights and duties.)

Top-Down Implementation Unlikely. The former approach—outside policy-making, implementation and enforcement—seems excluded by limited government manpower as well as by bureaucratic inefficiencies. Many administration and extension tasks are now badly executed for lack of manpower, or for lack of responsive manpower. What likelihood then is there these same organizations and individuals can successfully shoulder the burden of *daily supervision* of renewable natural resource management activities *in local milieux throughout the Sahel where management has become imperative*? The answer in a word? None.[3]

Can Local Collective Action Conditions Be Changed? That leaves the other option: improving local-level collective action conditions in those communities now too "under-governed" to envisage sustained collective activities. In many areas, increasing capacity for autonomous collective action will be difficult for a variety of reasons [see, e.g., Thomson, 1983c: *passim*]. One is often lack of authority to raise taxes, at local initiative, to finance environmental management activities (payment of woodlot guards, production of seedlings, establishment of soil erosion control structures, etc.), as is the case in Niger [NFPA: II, 59, notes the *arrondissement* (two levels above the village, three above the quarter) is the lowest level rural jurisdiction with any taxing authority].

Yet if national governments do not begin seriously experimenting, at least in selected sites, with efforts to create really viable, effective local (i.e., village and quarter) governments, solutions will not be found. Government invitations or exhortations to villagers to participate either on a voluntary basis in local operations, e.g., cooperatives or village development groups, or on a non-voluntary basis under the direction of outside government officials, are not adequate responses.

A brief example may illustrate this point. No one would expect citizens to pay state taxes voluntarily, were it clear those who refused to pay would face no punishment. Why then should all villagers be expected to comply voluntarily with environmental management regulations, many of which may be onerous for particular individuals in the short or even in the long term, if it is well and widely known non-compliance is not punished? If some can flaunt regulations, benefit from resource-maintaining investments of others and yet refuse to bear their fair share of the costs, is it reasonable to expect those otherwise willing to participate with cash, time or effort, to do so? Hardly. This suggests increased attention to conditions of local non-voluntary collective action will be necessary where individual initiative and individual activities do not suffice to ensure adequate environmental controls.

Organizational Reform Criteria. What is needed under such circumstances are local *non*-voluntary jurisdictions responsive to local interests and local needs. Villagers must acquire the capacity to make decisions with minimum expense in time and effort necessary to acquire appropriate authorization, i.e., through duly constituted local governments or special districts which can make binding and enforceable rules concerning environmental management. Such rules must be enforceable on a non-voluntary basis, by appropriate local judicial actions, against recalcitrants and violators.

Constraints Interdependent. Changes in one constraint may influence impacts of others. Technical innovations, such as genetic engineering to increase thorn species growth rates, may make live fencing—enclosures—much more attractive than at present. This might obviate the current need for collectively-implemented dry season grazing controls to promote reforestation. Enhanced collective action capability could make windbreaks or hydraulic erosion control structures economically feasible where they may not now be. Localizing the tree tenure legal process may enhance the value of trees, promoting reforestation.

RECOMMENDATIONS . . .

"Decoding" Tree Tenure Rights. This is a complex topic, fraught with problems. Most "solutions" will impose costs on some or all users. It is unlikely that a single formula denationalizing tree tenure will be appropriate for the entire Sahel, or even for all regions of a single country.

Private Rights in Trees: An Alternative to Code Controls. Privatization of tree tenure rights offers an alternative to national forestry code controls as a solution to the problem of insuring sustained-yield woodstock management. The current system of national ownership and subsidiary usufructuary rights could be replaced by village, quarter or individual ownership of specific parts of the woodstock (woodlots, trees located on fields, common bushlands, state forests, etc.). *Such a tree tenure system assumes the more direct property rights would give user-owners a strong incentive to control exploitation and provide for adequate future supplies* [UVFPA: 95-96, P.8.4., clearly states this position]. . . .

Is This Assumption Justified? The evidence suggests it is in some places, but not in others. Where supplies still exceed demand, it often is not. There, relaxation of code restrictions would probably simply substitute uncontrolled use of local woodstocks for uncontrolled use of national woodstocks. Relaxation might also legalize the current widespread devastation of remaining natural forests by farmers in search of new, fertile lands. Under such circumstances, abolishing national controls seems ill-advised. (Note, however, that maintenance of national authority over such threatened woodstocks may hardly delay their destruction if forestry departments cannot mobilize the manpower necessary to enforce use regulations.)

The assumption of better woodstock management through tree tenure privatization appears more justified where (a) villagers *perceive wood shortages*, (b) would be *willing and able to enforce property rights*, and (c) would *invest in creating new supplies* if they could be reasonably sure they would reap benefits of their investments. In some Sahelien areas these three conditions are already met. Private woodlots in Niger's Tera and Bouza *Arrondissements*, and at various locations in Upper Volta and Mali, as well as pronounced interest in individual or family woodlots remarked on in the Nigerien and Voltaic Assessments, confirm this. In some areas field owners now with increasing frequency prevent others from cutting trees on their land

[NFPA: II, 120]. This also lends support to the contention *if* their purpose is to defend existing trees rather than merely to escape having to pay a fine if a passing forester notices a cut tree. Table 2, below, shows that both motivations are possible—though defense of trees predominates—and that respondents' projected reactions to this hypothetical situation vary somewhat.

Table 2. "What would you do if you saw someone trimming branches or cutting a tree on your field?"

Villages' Projected Reaction	Niger		Upper Volta			
	1	2	3	4	5	Totals
Do Nothing; Inform Individual He Will Pay Any Fines Assessed by Forester	7 (20%)	4 (12%)	5 (20%)	4 (7%)	0 (0%)	20 (11%)
Forbid Trimming or Cutting; Lodge A Complaint Against the Individual	28 (80%)	29 (88%)	20 (80%)	50 (93%)	33 (100%)	160 (89%)
N=	35	33	25	54	33	180

All five villages have experienced decreasing wood supplies since the drought, which probably explains the overall high proportion of respondents projecting positive action to defend trees on their fields. Such positive action responses may, however, be somewhat inflated by some Nigerien villagers' perceptions that defense of trees was the "appropriate" response, i.e., desired by foresters. Foresters never visited the Voltaic villages, so their opinions would not have affected responses there.

Privatization Problems. Problems must be expected from privatization if tree tenure rights are at variance with land tenure rights. Vesting control over trees in he "who works the land" risks eviction of tenants where the *effective* land tenure rule accords property rights to those "who first cleared the field" and their descendents. Landowners may seek to prevent tenants from establishing property rights either to newly-planted trees or to natural regeneration which the latter may protect. Those whose fields are already treeless may likewise generate problems if no nearby bush land remains where they can exploit a common woodstock. Common land woodstocks would also pose a problem: who is to decide who owns them and how they should be exploited?

Localizing Tree Tenure Legal Process. Privatizing tree tenure rights implies as a practical corollary localizing legal recourse and enforcement. This would markedly reduce costs to tree owners of defending their woodstock rights. A villager can generally find his quarter head, village chief, earth priest, or local Muslim cleric much more easily than he can track down a roving forestry agent. Thus authorizing local notables to handle tree tenure disputes would encourage litigation in defense of tree property rights. Such proceedings would slowly clarify those rights in local moots open to all. Decisions would be publicly debated rather than being handled in administrative proceedings between forester and violator. The latter often exclude non-interested parties. Moot proceedings would help inform locals of the new system of tree tenure rights, as well as defining content of rights.

Translating Forestry Codes. Wherever forestry codes are to remain in force, it would be extremely useful to translate them into local languages, as the Maliens are reportedly doing [MFPA 121]. This would permit rural Saheliens to inform themselves about their rights and responsibilities under the codes, something which is now, for most, impossible. . . .

NOTES

1. "Political" as used in this context derives from the word *policy*. A policy is defined as a decision which can be enforced by sanctions. "Political constraints" thus refer to difficulties which arise from sanctioned decisions, or from the *inability to make sanctioned decisions at certain political levels, e.g., the local level.*

2. Table presents results of surveys administered in three villages of a canton in Niger's south-central Mirriah Arrondissement, and in two

villages of an arrondissement in Séguénéga Subprefecture in the Yatenga region of northern Upper Volta in 1979 by James Thomson under a Rockefeller Foundation International Relations fellowship. In the third Nigerien village, 11 respondents (43%) reported no local competence, 15 (58%) some competence; interviewing errors preclude a detailed break-down of degrees of competence.

3. The para-statal forestry development corporations now operating in Mali [MFPA: 93-94, P. 5.1.1.2.2.] and proposed for Niger [NFPA: I, 126, P.7.2.2.4.] and Upper Volta [UVFPA: 109-11, P.8.6.2] might engender greater agent responsiveness by making rank, reward and advancement more dependent on job performance than on academic diplomas. But foresters will still be too few to deal with all, or even with a major portion of environmental management problems on a direct basis. *

REFERENCES

Hoskins, Marilyn W. 1979b."Women in Forestry for Local Community Development." Prepared for Office of Women in Development, Agency for International Development, Washington, D.C.

MFPA. 1982. *Etude du secteur forestier au Mali. (Provisoire).* Ouagadougou: CILSS; Paris: OECD. SAHEL D(81).

NFPA. 1981. *Analyse du secteur forestier et propositions: Le Niger.* 3 vols. Ouagadougou: CILSS; Paris: OECD. SAHEL D(81).

Popkin, Samuel L. 1979. *The Rational Peasant; The Political Economy of Rural Society in Vietnam.* Berkeley: University of California.

Thomson, James T. 1979. "Bois de Villages (Niger); Centre File 3-P-72-0093/Report of an Investigation Concerning Socio-Cultural and Political-Economic Aspects of the First Phase of the Project and Design Recommendations for a Possible Second Phase." Prepared for International Development Research Centre, Ottawa, Canada.

Thomson, James T. 1981a. "Public Choice Analysis of Institutional Constraints on Firewood Production Strategies in the West African Sahel." In Clifford S. Russell and Norman K. Nicholson (eds.), *Public Choice and Rural Development.* Washington, D.C.: Resources for the Future: 119-152.

Thomson, James T. 1983b. "The Precolonial Woodstock in Sahelien West Africa: The Example of Central Niger (Damagaram, Damergu, Aïr)." In Richard P. Tucker and J.F. Richards (eds.), Global Defor-

---

* MFPA, NFPA, UVFPA, and GFPA are Forestry Programme Assessments for Mali, Niger, Upper Volta, and Gambia by Club du Sahel/CILSS in 1981-82.

estation and the Nineteenth Century World Economy. Durham, N.C.: Duke University: 167-179.

Thomson, James T. 1983c. "Politics of Sahelien Desertification: Centralization, Non-Participation, Inaction." In H. Jeffrey Leonard (ed.), *The Politics of Environment and Development*. New York: Holmes and Meier.

UVFPA. 1982. *Analyse du secteur forestier et propositions: la Haute Volta*. Ouagadougou: CILSS; Paris: OECD. SAHEL D(82).

Winterbottom, Robert T. 1980. "Reforestation in the Sahel: Problems and Strategies; An Analysis of the Problem of Deforestation, and a Review of the Results of Forestry Projects in Upper Volta." Paper presented at African Studies Association Annual Meeting, Philadelphia, October 15-18.

The Wood Tree as a Peasant Cash-Crop: An Anthropological Strategy for the Domestication of Energy

Gerald F. Murray

> *The strength of on-farm forestry is the direct and simple proprietary relationship between the farmer and his or her trees. The Haitian experience cited by Murray is encouraging. The profit motive rather than disinterested environmental awareness is harnessed to achieve reforestation and erosion control.—The Editors*

Though differing in emphasis from each other, several attempts to explain rural Haitian poverty, including the field studies of Moral (1961) and the more recent literature searches by Zuvekas (1978) and Lundahl (1979), have concurred in their identification of deforestation and soil erosion as major impediments to economic well-being in rural Haiti. Largely in response to Zuvekas' findings, several planners in the late '70s, aware that large sums of money had been wasted on unsuccessful reforestation and erosion control projects in Haiti, asked whether the root of the failure might not lie in Haitian peasant land tenure insecurity, in an unwillingness on the part of the Haitian peasants to make long-term investments in land in which they felt they had little long-term security.

Though such reluctance would make perfect anthropological and economic sense among a truly landless peasantry, this hypothesis appeared at odds with much existing anthropological research which

Excerpted from Gerald F. Murray, "The Wood Tree as a Peasant Cash-Crop: An Anthropological Strategy for the Domestication of Energy," in Charles R. Foster and Albert Valdman (eds) *Haiti Today and Tomorrow: An Interdisciplinary Study* (Lanham: University Press of America, 1984), pp. 141-160. Reprinted with the permission of the publisher.

indicates that Haitian peasants not only consider themselves owners of much of their land, but demonstrate their security quite concretely by investing thousands of hard-earned *gourdes* [ed.: local currency] in the purchase of new plots whenever the opportunity arises (cf. Herskovits, 1971; Métraux, 1951; Underwood, 1964; Murray, 1977). In 1978, and at greater length in 1979 (Murray 1978; 1979), I proposed an alternative anthropological approach to the erosion problem, one that laid the blame for failed reforestation projects not on "Haitian peasant land tenure" or on the conservatism of a frightened peasantry, but rather on several crippling flaws that weakened the very design on which most of these projects had been based. The problem resided neither in the culture nor the psyche of the Haitian peasant, the argument went, but in the behavior of planning and implementing institutions.

This general critique was accompanied by a specific series of alternative recommendations. The conceptual cornerstone was the suggestion to cease promoting the tree among peasants as a sacred, untouchable legacy for future generations (a message which is ignored at any rate) and to begin promoting the planting of fast-growing wood as a privately owned cash-crop planted by peasants on their own land. The marketability of wood as a fuel has been evident for decades in Haiti and had been discussed or documented in a series of studies specifically addressed to that issue (Earl 1976; Ewell 1977; Conway 1979; Voltaire 1979). During a prolonged visit to Haiti, the forester Michael Benge (1978) was particularly instrumental in acquainting local planners and implementers with the technical possibilities of fast-growing wood.

My own recommendations as an anthropologist focused principally on the institutional, organizational, and motivational dimensions of the task. I argued that if certain anthropological insights were applied and certain institutional barriers removed, a flow of resources would be activated, and Haitian peasants would plant millions of trees on their own land. These claims were put to test when an $8 million project, based directly on these recommendations, was prepared by USAID. . . .

The project has now been underway for over two and a half years. In view of the newness of the project and the controversial character of some of its design features, definitive judgments about its success must be deferred to the future. But the unprecedented and unexpectedly rapid planting of over five million project trees by Haitian peasants on their own land has given preliminary validation to several of the basic anthropological hypotheses. This burst of voluntary, unremunerated tree-planting by perhaps ten thousand peasant families all over Haiti renders the project at least worthy of description. It will be the purpose of these pages to provide such a description. . . .

Cash Flows

The curtailing or elimination by Haitian peasants of the restorative fallow phase can clearly be attributed on the one hand to demographic stress. Enough land is simply not available to cultivators to permit them or their family members to maintain the 15 or 20 year fallow cycle that would permit natural regeneration of the soil. But demography is only part of the story. Involved in the drama is another factor: the dependence of the Haitian peasant on *steady flows of cash*.

Field research by anthropologists, geographers, and economists has exposed the weaknesses of the traditional stereotype of the "subsistence peasant." Though pop articles may still talk about "subsistence farming" in rural Haiti, it is not at all clear that the Haitian peasants "produce most of what they consume and consume most of what they produce." Even allowing for regional variation, it appears more accurate to say that most Haitian peasants produce largely for a cash market, to which large percentages of each harvest are consigned. Furthermore much of the contents of their cooking pots are similarly purchased from that same cash market throughout much of the year. The model of the self-sufficient peasant is generally inaccurate and constitutes a faulty theoretical base on which to found development projects.[3]

This involvement of the peasant in a cash economy activates three mechanisms which impede the tree-mediated regeneration of the soil.

1. *Intensive cropping independently of food needs*. Where a farming system's goal is to feed its members directly (as was the case in many former tribal systems) there is no incentive to produce substantially more than can be directly consumed. Food storage constraints and food spoilage problems make systematic overproduction irrational. But where there is a cash market, there is no such built-in ceiling to the intensity with which land will be worked. The pull of additional cash will be much more vivid and compelling than the much vaguer and fainter negative payoffs from degrading soil.

2. *The cash-oriented livestock economy*. As is true of many other peasantries, the Haitian peasant uses livestock as an important element in his cash-generating repertoire. Livestock often serve as a bank. One tactic is for cash profits from food harvests to be invested in animals. Interest to the investment comes in the form of weight increases in the animal purchased and in terms of the offspring of female animals. But livestock must be fed. And the current practice of many peasants is to picket cattle in recently cropped fields. But this in

turn profoundly alters the course of the regenerative process. Even if the land is left out of cultivation for a long period, the brush and tree species that would otherwise emerge are destroyed by the livestock. The land is rapidly taken over by grass, the regenerative cycle is broken, and the landscape changes to a barren savanna.[4] This tragic sequence has already led to the removal of uncounted thousands of hectares of Haitian soil from agriculture. That is, in addition to population growth *per se*, cash-oriented livestock raising can provide a partially autonomous impediment to the reappearance of the soil restoring tree.

3. *The commercialization of wood.* But in addition to these factors, the general growth of the population and the appearance of an urban sector which depends on purchased charcoal for fuel energy had endowed the tree with a rapidly increasing economic value. The ancient practice of ignoring dead or fallen trees has disappeared forever. Even in the 19th century there was a vigorous lumber extraction industry (spearheaded not by the peasants but by lumber exporting companies). This industry continues, especially in pine regions. But more recently the growing charcoal market has triggered off feverish tree cutting behavior among poorer peasant groups who, during much of the year, have no other option for ensuring the continual flow of cash on which the Haitian peasantry as a whole has become so irrevocably dependent.

These observations can be rephrased in the idiom of resource flows. The current agrarian system in Haiti emerges as one in which major cash flow mechanisms operate in a manner which unleashes destructive downward soil flows and which subsequently impede the tree-mediated soil-recuperation flows that characterize tropical horticulture under more benign conditions. And let nobody underestimate the importance of the cash flows to the peasant himself. The peasant's awareness of and concern for this vital cash flow are much stronger and more pressing than his concern about destructive soil flows or about the missing flows of nutrients back to the soil. What is central to the consciousness of the agronomist is present but *tangential* to the daily concerns and maneuvers of the peasant. And sadly, what is primary to the peasant—the need for a short term flow of cash income—is often poorly perceived or even dismissed as "short sightedness" or "inability to delay gratification" by many well-paid technicians presumably hired to help him. . . .

Constructing Messages for Haitian Peasants

With the assistance of the collaborating PVO, Project staff will meet with farmers in potential tree-planting communities. Several messages are generally included in the presentation: *"Tree planting need not be for your children or your grandchildren only. You can make money from trees you plant."* The trees provided by the Project grow rapidly. Under proper conditions, they can yield charcoal harvests in four years time. Even conservatively speaking current market conditions are such as to yield $1.50 per tree (gross revenue) if the trees are harvested for charcoal. If the trees are planted at two meter by two meter spacing (to permit two or three seasons of continued food cropping among the trees), a hectare of land can hold 2,500 trees. Assuming replanting of trees that do not survive the transplanting trauma, this means a potential gross revenue of $3,750 from each hectare of land over a four-year period from the trees alone, not counting the additional revenue from the crops which can continue to be planted until shade competition becomes too great, and the revenue from animal grazing once the crops have been removed and the trees are large enough to permit grazing without damage to the trees themselves.

The general response of the peasants to this message has been unexpectedly positive. The negative experiences which many communities have had with some reforestation projects (especially those in which tree planting has been imposed from without) have not sufficed to blind peasants to the economic value of trees. What most surprises the ordinary peasant group to whom this presentation is made is:

1. the large number of widely spaced trees that can fit onto a unit of land;

2. the manner in which cropping can continue for the first two or three seasons and in which livestock grazing can subsequently be reintroduced.

That is, an effort is made to present fast growing trees which can mesh with and enhance rather than compete with the preexisting cropping and grazing patterns on which the Haitian peasants currently depend. . . .

"You Will be the Owners of Any Trees Planted."

During the preliminary community visit, and during subsequent visits to the nursery and established outplantings, repeated assurances are given that the peasant who accepts and plants these trees is the owner of the trees. The project forfeits all rights in the tree once the peasant accepts it and plants it on his land. This reassurance is of incalculable importance

One of the fears that has undermined the effectiveness of many reforestation activities has been the fear on the part of peasants that the trees planted are not theirs. Even peasants who plant the trees on their own land are more often than not unsure, when questioned, as to who owns the trees. Many will say they belong to *konpanyia*—i.e., "the company," a common and revealing way of referring to organizations such as FAO, USAID, and other project organizers, to distinguish them from *leta*, the State. In other regions peasants have been heard to refer even to trees planted on their own land as *pyebwa leta*—the government's trees. To deal with this problem, peasants are assured— by us and by local PVO—that they, not the Project, are the owners of the trees.

"As Far as We're Concerned, You Can Cut the Trees When You Want."

Another message that is repeated frequently during initial contacts and site visits is the message that our project, far from considering the tree to be a "sacred" object which must never be touched, views the tree rather as something which *should* be harvested when it is mature. This raises the issue of laws regarding tree cutting.

Most Haitian laws which deal with the tree emphasize prohibitions against cutting trees, or the need to secure permission and/or pay a tax for the privilege of cutting a tree. In general the use of the tree as a source of cash has generally been viewed by authorities and planners as a type of destructive irrationality on the part of peasants. One reforestation program after another has come in with the finger-wagging message that the tree should be seen as a sacred soil-conserving, rain-drawing object which the peasant should plant but never cut. Tree cutting is viewed, not as a legitimate economic behavior, but as a type of economic misbehavior. This has produced a situation in which the peasant's use of the wood tree as an element in his cash-flow regime has been done in an implicitly surreptitious fashion. The peasant is aware of the existence of laws which in one manner or another would tend to restrict his tree-cutting behavior were the laws obeyed. And local forest agents are becoming stricter in forcing would-be tree-cutters to pay the required taxes. Despite the legal impediments, peasants do *"regle afè yo"* --settle matters-- with local authorities and continue to cut trees, sell the wood, and generate cash income.

The Project openly discusses—with PVOs as well as peasants—the Haitian laws concerning the cutting of trees. It is stated clearly and repeated several times that the Project can make peasants the owners of the trees that are planted, but that they must continue to deal with local authorities as they have always done. They need not ask the Project for permission to cut the trees. But neither can the Project free them from the "tax" that local forest vigilantes currently charge, even for wood that a person cuts from his own property.

Despite open discussion of this matter, the Project has yet to encounter a peasant community that hesitates to plant trees because of fear of future government restriction in cutting. The virtually unanimous opinion of peasants consulted on this matter is that a person who plants wood will be able easily to *"regle afèli avèk l'eta,"* settle matters with local authorities. The key variable in Haiti is ownership of the tree that is planted on one's property. Once the ownership right is guaranteed, the peasant feels free to plant trees.

To emphasize this ownership the Project goes so far as to insist that if, after a year or so, the peasant changes his mind about the trees, he is perfectly free to pull them out. He will never get more trees from the Project. But he is free to do to the tree whatever he wants. The function of such an unusual message is to remove any fear in the peasant's mind that the Project retains any ownership rights in the tree which the peasant plants on his land. . . .

Preliminary Project Results

1. The effectiveness of this approach in stimulating the planting of trees by peasants must be judged as impressive in any quantitative measure. The original goal was the planting of three million trees in four years. The three million trees had already been planted before the Project had reached its second year. As of current writing, the Project is in the middle of its third year and has already planted nearly six million trees. In terms of sheer numbers of trees, then, the results are promising.

2. Numbers of trees planted is by itself a potentially deceptive measure of project output. An anthropologist would in fact reject this output as one more failure if the six million project trees ended up on the property of two or three landowners. Of great importance, therefore, is the fact that the trees of Project Pyebwa stand on the property of over ten thousand peasant families in hundreds of Haitian villages. The Project has succeeded in stimulating unprecedented peasant interest in tree planting and in structuring resource flows in such a way that the outputs do in fact reach their intended peasant beneficiaries. . . .

5. Tree survival rates vary by region, the principal determining factor being the amount of rainfall. In some regions a project will have to plant 120 trees to have 100 alive after two years. In drier regions a Project may have to plant 300 trees to have 100 remain alive. But what is important is that mortality appears to be associated, not with

livestock depredation, but with climatic stress. That is, the peasants are not only planting trees; they are also according them the same protection against livestock which they accord to their other crops. This suggests that the central objective of the project is being met: the introduction of wood as one more crop in the agrarian inventory of the Haitian peasant. . . .

NOTES

1. The project to be described in these pages is funded principally by USAID/Haiti, though additional grants have been made directly to the field office by the governments of Canada (through the Mission Administered Fund of the Canadian Embassy in Port-au-Prince), Switzerland (through Helvetas, a developmental organization that also operates with private funds), and Belgium (through its support of a volunteer Belgian technician working in the Project). ...

3. Perhaps the strongest argument for the "non-subsistence" nature of the rural Haitian economy can be found in De Young (1958). But evidence for the cash-orientation of peasant life is also present in Simpson (1940), Métraux (1951), Moral (1961), Schaedel (1962), Murray (1977), and other descriptive studies of rural life. The bulk of "cash-crops" produced are not export crops, but crops consumed internally in Haiti. For descriptions of the market system through which these crops move, see Mintz (1960), Underwood (1970), Locher (1975), Murray and Alvarez (1975), Girault and LaGra (1975).

4. For an analysis of changing Haitian landscape patterns see Palmer (1976). The evolution of landscape in the Dominican Republic had earlier been analyzed by Antonini (1968).

REFERENCES

Antonini, Gustavo. 1968. "Processes and patterns of landscape change in the Lines Noroeste, Dominican Republic." Ph.D. dissertation, Columbia University.

Benge, Michael. 1978. *Renewable energy and charcoal production.* Port-au-Prince: USAID

Conway, Frederick J. 1979. *A study of the fuelwood situation in Haiti..* Port-au-Prince: USAID.

De Young, Maurice. 1958. *Man and Land in the Haitian-Economy.* Gainesville, FL: University of Florida.

Earl, D.E. 1976. *Reforestation and the fight against erosion: Haiti--Charcoal as a renewable resource* Romm:FAO

Ewel, Jack. 1977. *A report on soil erosion and prospects for land restoration in Haiti.* Port-au-Prince: USAID

Girault, C. and J. La Gra. 1975. *Characteristique structurelles de la commercialisation interne des produits agricoles en Haiti.* Port-au-Prince: IICA.

Herskovits, M. 1937. *Life in a Haitian valley.* New York: Knopf.

Locher, U. 1975. "The market systems of Port-au-Prince. *Working papers in Haitian society and culture.* New Haven: Antilles Research Center.

Lundahl, M. 1979. *Peasants and poverty: a study of Haiti.* London.

Métraux, R. M. 1951. "Kith and kin: A study of Creole social structure in Marbial." Unpublished Ph.D. dissertation, New York: Columbia University.

Mintz, S. 1960. Peasant markers. *Scientific American* 203: 112-118, 120, 122.

_____. 1960. A tentative typology of eight Haitian market-places. *Revista de Ciencias Sociales* 4:15-57.

Moral, P. 1959. *L'économie haitienne.* Port-au-Prince: Imprimerie de l'Etat.

Murray, G.F. 1977. "The evolution of Haitian peasant land tenure: A case study in agrarian adaptation to population growth. Ph.D. dissertation, Columbia University.

_____, 1978a. *Hillside units, wage labor, and Haitian peasant land tenure: A strategy for the organization of erosion control.* Port-au-Prince: USAID.

_____. 1978b. *Informal subdivisions and land insecurity: An analysis of Haitian peasant land tenure.* Port-au-Prince: USAID.

_____. 1979. *Terraces, trees, and the Haitian peasant: An assessment of 25 years of erosion control in rural Haiti.* Port-au-Prince: USAID.

Murray, G.F. and M.D. Alvarez. 1975. "Haitian bean circuits: Cropping and trading maneuvers among a cash-oriented peasantry.' *Working papers in Haitian society and culture.* S. Mintz, ed. New Haven: Antilles Research Center.

Palmer, E.C. 1976. "Land use and landscape change along the Dominican-Haitian border." Unpublished Ph.D. dissertation, University of Florida, Gainesville.

Schaedel, Richard. 1962. *As essay on the human resources of Haiti.* Washington, DC: Agency for International Development.

Simpson, George Eaton, 1940. "Haitian peasant economy." *Journal of Negro History* 5:489-519.

Underwood, Frances W. 1964. "Land and its manipulations among the Haitian peasantry." *Explorations in Cultural Anthropology*, Ward Goodenough, ed., pp. 469-482. New York: McGraw-Hill.

_____. 1970. "The marketing system in peasant Haiti. Papers in Caribbean Anthropology," S. Mintz, ed. New Haven: Human Relations Area File.

Voltaire, Karl. 1979. "Charcoal in Haiti." Port-au-Prince: USAID.

Zuvekas, C., Jr. 1978. *Agricultural development in Haiti. An assessment of sector problems, policies, and prospects under conditions of severe soil erosion* (mimeo). Washington, DC: USAID.

Village Forestry Development in the Republic of Korea: A Case Study

H.M. Gregersen

> *Not all village forestry programs are failures. The New Community Movement in South Korea has had important successes with Village Forestry Associations. What distinguishes this effort from the less successful instances of village forestry reviewed in this chapter?—The Editors*

Summary of Historical Developments Leading to Action

In ancient times the abundant forests of Korea were considered an obstacle to human development. They hindered agricultural expansion and harbored wild animals which attacked people. Somewhere between the 14th and 15th centuries, the situation began to change. With rapid population growth and consequent increase in wood fuel consumption, concern mounted in many areas regarding wood availability. Felling restrictions were established and the holding of forest land by private citizens was prohibited under the Yi Dynasty (1392-1910).

After the prohibition of private ownership of forest land there developed a strong tradition of communal access to the forest for wood and litter to meet the fuel requirement of the (then) new *"ondol"* heating system. This tradition continued down through the centuries to the present. After the Japanese invasion, the King granted forestland to loyal subjects. This started again the tradition of private ownership of forestland. Thus, toward the end of the Yi dynasty, private ownership rights were held over most forest land. "The modern private ownership

Excerpted from H.M. Gregersen, "Village Forestry Development in the Republic of Korea: A Case Study," FAO/SIDA Forestry for Local Community Development Programme, GCP/INT/347/SWE (Rome: Food and Agriculture Organization of the United Nations, 1982). Reprinted with the permission of the Food and Agricultural Organization of the United Nations.

system was established over forestland following the enactment of the Forest Law (1908) and under the Chosen Forest Land Survey Decree (1918) and the Assignment Decree of Forests for Special Preemptive Rights (1926)" (Storrs, 1973: p. 3). However, even after the system of private ownership was firmly established again, the tradition of communal use of forests—both public and private—continued with almost total disregard for ownership. . . .

As population continued to increase, the pressure on remaining forests intensified. Little effort was made to regenerate and manage the forests. Problems became more acute with the overfelling which took place during the Japanese occupation in World War II and during the Korean War. Wood fuel, so necessary to carry villagers through the cold winters, was difficult to find. Wood imports increased dramatically. More fundamental problems developed. Farming in the lowlands and plains depended on a steady flow of water in rivers originating in the once forested upland watersheds. As forest destruction intensified, river flows became more erratic, giving rise to serious problems of drought and flooding.

For decades, Korea experienced progressively worsening problems of erosion as all forms of organic matter were removed from the hillsides for fuel. Erosion and loss of soil caused productivity of agricultural lands to diminish. Shifting cultivation increased and many rural inhabitants became poorer and in many cases suffered severe hardship. . . .

Despite concerted efforts in the 'fifties and 'sixties to reverse the situation and to rehabilitate denuded areas and increase the forest growing stock, conditions in general worsened. Population growth, which led to increasing fuel demands and requirements for agricultural land, put additional pressures on the environment, particularly since local inhabitants continued to live with the age-old tradition of free access to the forest and had little regard for the forest as a sustainable source of goods and services and income. Private forest land owners had little incentive to invest in their lands. This was a serious obstacle to forest improvement since 73 percent of forest land was in private hands in the early 'seventies.

The exact evolution of the mounting concern over the problems is somewhat unclear, particularly in terms of the chronology of events which led up to the major and drastic changes which were instituted in 1972 and 1973. Whether the initial pressures to "do something" came from the bottom up or the top down is open to question. We do know that the formal initiation of the *Saemaul Undong* (or "new community movement") in 1970 and efforts to establish local forestry cooperatives before 1970 laid the foundations for events in 1972 when formal recognition of the problem and a decision to do something about it were made a matter of top national priority through the Forest Development Law and the First Ten-Year Forest Development Plan. These bases for action are discussed in the following chapter. . . .

The Saemaul Undong or "New Community Movement" . . .

Saemaul Undong means literally "a movement to make new village or new community," but it is also interpreted to mean "a movement for great betterment or modernization" (Ministry of Home Affairs, 1980: p. 2). The movement deals with spiritual as well as material prosperity. It provides a modern variation on the philosophies of Confucianism and Buddhism, which have played such an important and prominent role in the traditional life of villages.

Experimental projects were started in rural villages in 1971, and by 1972-73, the movement was in full progress in most villages. Projects were in three areas: spiritual enlightenment, environmental improvement, and income generation.

Saemaul Undong projects are selected and undertaken according to the following principles (Ministry of Home Affairs, 1980: p. 26, 27):

> Firstly, the *Saemaul* projects should be decided by consensus of villagers at village assembly and implemented with their total participation.
>
> Secondly, the projects should be linked to common benefit of village, not to particular participants' interest. If a project is planned only for some specific people, it is sure to fail because other villagers are reluctant to participate in that project. The income gained from the project with people's total participation should be equitably returned to the participants, who are encouraged to deposit some amount of income for village common fund.
>
> Thirdly, the projects should be selected in consideration of specific conditions of village. Accordingly, topographical and natural conditions as well as socio-economic specifics should be fully taken into account in selecting the projects.
>
> Fourthly, the projects should be selected in consideration of potentials of village. A project could not be implemented without sufficient money, labor and skills required for it, even though it is well planned in view of its contribution to common benefit of village or its appropriate procedures in process of decision making. In our experience it is found those villages with failure in the *Saemaul*

Undong have not fully taken into account their conditions or potentials and technical problems.

Fifthly, the projects should be directly or indirectly linked to the increase in participants' income. Without any connection with income-increasing of the villagers, they would hesitate to participate in those projects, and consequently the *Saemaul Undong* could not continue to grow.

The project development and implementation process set up was as follows (Ministry of Home Affairs, 1980: p. 28):

a) Programmes at village level are formed and organized by the village development committee which consists of about fifteen members. Here the *Saemaul* leaders usually take an active role in forming a programme.

b) Plans and programmes are adjusted at the township levels in consultation with the community *Saemaul* council and sent to the Mayor or the County-Chief.

c) The Mayor of a city or the chief of a county regulates the programmes from lower level organization, with the consent of the city or county Council of *Saemaul Undong*. If any problems cannot be solved at the county or city level, they can be sent to the government of the province.

d) The Governor, advised by the Provincial Council, coordinates project plans submitted by cities and counties; he sends more complicated problems to the National Council.

e) Finally, the National Council confirms plans and gives directions for implementation. The council also coordinates other related projects and decides investment scale on the basis of national budget. . . .

Legal Basis for Community Forestry Programme Action . . .

Of primary importance is the Forest Development Law of 1972, which provided the main legal basis for the community forestry effort discussed in this case study.

This law was established to promote an accelerated forestry development program to contribute to national economic development. Under the law:

a) The Director General of the OOF [Office of Forestry, Ministry of Home Affairs, (ed.)] must classify all forest lands into one of the three types of "development regions" based on forest conditions and likely uses and requirements for land. The three types of regions are:

1) *"Timber forest development regions."* These are mainly remote forest areas where timber forests can be established on a large scale.
2) *"Forest recreation development regions."* These are areas which should be maintained for recreation and health purposes, e.g., parks, green areas around cities and so forth.
3) *"Farm forest development regions."* These are the areas of most concern in the present case study. They include forest areas in and around villages which can be used by the villages for fuelwood, growing of fast yield tree species (for income) and fruit, nut and other species for village use.

b) The law gives the OOF the power to require reforestation and forest management on private forest lands within development areas established in the regions. This is a critical provision, given the high percentage of forest land in private hands (73 percent of the total). Required work on private lands is carried out in two common ways, "execution by proxy" and voluntary agreement between owners and local VFA's [Village Forestry Associations (ed.)]. In the former case, if an owner cannot or does not comply with government orders within a specified period (generally one year) the OOF may designate an executor—a VFA or private individual—to undertake the work. The owner of the land can compensate the executor, or, if compensation is not forthcoming within six months of completion of the work, then the law provides that the executor shall receive 90 percent of the output and the owner 10 percent. (In the case of fruit or nut bearing trees the profit share rate shall be 80 percent to executor and 20 percent to owner.)

What this meant, in effect, is that the government (OOF) was given the right to require forestry development on private lands. This opened the way to overcome the earlier difficulties encountered because of the great number of owners of small forest areas. It provided the means for rapidly increasing the area of productive forest plantations particularly for fuelwood.

c) The Law recognized the need for funding for private forestry activities. Thus, a "Forest Development Fund" was set up under the law. This provided long term, low interest loans for VFA's and private individuals. . . .

Selection of Planting Sites

Villagers and government officials jointly determine the best sites for the needed fuelwood plantations. As discussed earlier, if such land happens to be private—as it often is—the OOF, through powers given to it under the 1972 Forest Development Law, can require the private owner to plant or to enter into a production sharing contract with the VFA.

Once the site has been determined, the FAU [Forestry Association Union, (ed.)] and government officials prepare a "reforestation plan" including total area to be planted, species, number of seedlings required, expenses by financial sources (self-inputed, loan of subsidy), time schedule for the work, labour supply plan, and a reforestation planning map. All this information is needed in order for the government to have the time to organize seedling supplies, materials, transportation to sites, etc. . . .

Forest Protection

A main function and aim of VFA's is forest protection. Hundred of thousands of hectares of forest have been damaged by insects, diseases, fires and illegal cutting. To prevent further damage, VFA's voluntarily participate in various protection programmes.

The main voluntary activities in which the VFA's participate include:

• Village patrols of forest areas to prevent illegal cutting and to identify early problems of insect and disease attacks;

• Cooperative forest pest control;

• Forest fire control and prevention.

• Patrols of one or two men are active in many village areas. Some VFA's hire full time patrol men, particularly if they have sizable valuable forests under their jurisdiction. The patrols report insect and disease problems, timber trespass and illegal forest destruction. If forest fires are spotted, the village can be called out on short notice. . . .

Examples of Village Forestry Projects . . .

Establishment of Fuelwood Plantation. The village of Suelchi-Ri (Gwanchon-Myeon, Ismil-Gun, Jeonbug-Do) has a population of 428 persons (58 households) and an area of 273 ha, of which 217 ha are classified as forest land (Establishment of Fuelwood Forest, n.d.) . It is a primarily agricultural village, with an annual income per household of some 1.8 million won.

Fifty-two of the households are entirely dependent on wood fuel. Total demand per year was estimated to be 189 mt., or an average of 3.25 mt. per household. Present supply comes from forest fuel (67 percent) and agricultural residues (33 percent).

In the early 1960s a fuelwood project was conceived to prevent pending serious fuel shortages. The plan was developed by the Ismil-Gun FAU and the plan was approved by the provincial government. Since the land involved was in private hands, the county government had to order the private owners to establish plantations. This was in 1964. Since the owners failed to meet their obligation, the VFA was authorized to undertake the project on a "proxy-execution" basis (i.e., a cost sharing basis). The VFA followed the process described earlier in this chapter. Upon completion of the project, the county government duly ordered the land owners to reimburse expenditures. The owners failed to comply and instead entered into a production sharing contract with the VFA, whereby the owner would get 20 percent and the VFA would get 80 percent of the output. (Note that share rates have since been altered to a 10-90 percent basis.)

The project took place during the period 1964-77, i.e., it started considerably earlier than the First 10-Year Plan. This is pointed out here to again stress the point that cooperative forestry activities were taking place on an isolated village basis before 1973. The First Plan served the function of consolidating isolated planning and production efforts to make sure that all villages got involved in forestry activities. The successful experience of the isolated villages which had been involved in earlier years was incorporated into the planning for the major national forestry development drive starting in 1973. . . .

Erosion Prevention and Timber Production. A final example is taken from an account provided by the Ministry of Home Affairs:

Wolsong 3-ri, Pyonghae-myeon, Uljin-kun
Kyongsang Pudko

Saemaul leader Ju-Shik Kim has been a simple-hearted farmer. He believed that the village can benefit from planting trees on the barren land because it raises the incomes of the villages and prevents frequent flood and land erosion. He began to convince them of the need for planting trees and persuade them to join in reforestation.

But most of the poor people would not listen to him. Persistent effort at persuasion eventually brought some of the villagers to respond to his appeal. In the first year of his campaign, the villagers planted 15,000 pine trees and big cone pines.

Unfortunately, however, most of the trees planted in that year died because of poor soil fertility and management techniques.

He did not give up despite the ridicule and indifference shown by his fellow villagers, and kept up his drive to plant trees with the aid of his close friends and relatives.

The flow of Typhoon Sara caused landslides and washed away farm fields and homes. It made the villagers realize the importance of forestation and regret having ignored the exhortation of their leader in the past. They started planting and taking good care of trees on the hills. The community afforestation campaign thus resulted in covering the 41 hectare hillocks behind the village with luxuriant 100,000 pine trees. The trees will soon grow up to be worth hundred of million Won.

Inspired and elated by the success in the afforestation project, the members of the community joined the project of widening the village road up to five meters for the passage of trucks. In a few months, back alleys were reconditioned and 160 houses had their thatch roofs replaced by slate or tile. Such a rapid completion of the project to ameliorate the basic environments of the community has completely changed the look of the village.

Four work teams are organized to specialize in sericulture, animal husbandry, seedling growing and cash crops. A method of agricultural extension was introduced to have a high-income for farm households. It served greatly to raise the status and farming techniques of farmers in the low-income group.

In keeping with this principle, a four-hectare mulberry farm was acquired and a two-acre silkworm rearing room was built in 1973. Early in 1975, a new collective pigpen was constructed with a special Presidential grant of 850,000 Won to house a new breed of 82 Berkshires [the number is an actual count of pigs, not the descriptor of a new strain of Berkshire, (ed.)]. The number of cows which is now 93, will be gradually increased and the 10-hectare grassland by the seaside will be turned into improved pasture on which more oxen and cows will be grazing, making this village the largest and foremost cattle-raising community in the province.

Aside from providing an interesting example of how projects are often the result of determination of one or a few individuals in a village attempting to stimulate cooperative efforts, this project also indicates how the cooperative spirit can spread from one activity (in this case the initial tree planting) to other village activities. This spread of enthusiasm and confidence in the ability of villagers to do something for themselves is central to the spirit of the Saemaul Undong. The forestry activities truly became part of the total community development effort, not an isolated activity which had no relevance to other functions and desires of the community. ...

REFERENCES

15. Establishment of Fuelwood Forest, n.d. Suelchi-Ri, Gwanchon-Myeon, Ismil-gun, Jeongbug-Do.
45. Ministry of Home Affairs, Republic of Korea. 1980. *Saemaul Undong.*
65. Storrs, C. 1973. *Forestry for Community Development.* 10th Session Asia-Pacific Forestry Commission.

7

The Gender Division of Tenure

Descriptions of rural livelihood systems have with rare exceptions given only passing notice to two elements—trees and women. Finding sources on either prior to 1970, the year Ester Boserup published her classic *Women's Role in Economic Development,* is not easy. Even after 1970, references to the two together are usually restricted to a single line, or at best, a paragraph, unless the focus is domesticated economic trees. Indeed, this section has the fewest selections for the simple reason that there are no other sources of publishable length on the subject. The citations in this introduction generally refer to the single sentence or paragraph in the works in question that mentions property rights, women, and trees. The implicit assumptions in the literature that either only men are producers and users of trees or that what applies to men applies equally to women are both erroneous. The resulting knowledge gap is unfortunate, not only because women have been involved in tree utilization and tree-raising for centuries,[1] but also because they experience particular problems in regard to access to forests, trees, and tree products.

Women, trees, and forests are important to each other in three ways. First, women are major users and managers of trees. The division of labor in many societies places on women the responsibility for obtaining food, fuelwood, and fodder, products that are obtained, at least in part, from trees (Cecelski, 1985; Chen, 1986; Fortmann, 1986; Hoskins, 1979; Hoskins 1980; Hoskins, 1983; Molnar, 1985; Williams, 1984). Second, no matter who plants trees, women's cooperation and labor are crucial for keeping them alive. It is often women in their role as livestock managers who teach their children to keep small stock from eating the young saplings (Molnar, 1985). Third, it is women who suffer the most from forest degradation—their work loads rising beyond what is manageable as they must go farther and farther in search of wood, fodder, and water (Molnar, 1985).

Three property issues emerge from these connections. First, women need the *right to use* trees and their products. Women's cooperation and labor for tree and forestry projects are unlikely to be forthcoming unless they receive part of the benefits. This also has ecological implications. Where men control tree products, women may hold out for planting annual crops from which they benefit, rather than ecologically beneficial trees (Blaut *et al.*, 1973). And if women are to fulfill their responsibilities, they must have access to trees in convenient places. Potentially, the more restricted women's access, the greater the amount of time they must spend obtaining tree products and the less the time available for other tasks. Convenient access is so important that in some parts of Uttar Pradesh parents use the proximity of a forest to the groom's village as a criterion for choosing a husband for their daughter (Czech, 1986:6). Simple access is not, however, enough. A second tenure issue is *security of access*. Women with access but no control over trees may suddenly find their supply destroyed by those who control the trees. Finally, if the resource is to be sustained, women must have the *right to plant and protect trees*.

This raises a series of practical questions. Can women use the full range of tree species that grow locally or are they prohibited from using certain kinds of trees that might be useful in fulfilling their responsibilities? Do women have access to all trees in the area or are they restricted to certain localities—roadsides, reserve forest and so on. *Obi's* unusually detailed enumeration of the tree rights of women is an excellent example of gender differentiation of property rights in trees.

At a more general level, *Rocheleau* elaborates the point made in Fortmann (Chapter Two, this volume) that women's rights to land and trees are often restricted by customary or statutory law or by practice. She summarizes the position of women in respect to statutory, coded, and uncoded customary property law; describes how changes in law have affected women, often adversely; and outlines the niches where women farm or gather and may have or need property rights.

Security of access poses a particular problem for women whose access to trees depends upon their relationship to a man. Insecurity of access is a result both of lifecycle changes (marriage, childbirth, divorce, widowhood) and changes in national policies such as land registration (*Rocheleau*), in technology, and in value of tree products.

Widowhood is probably the most significant life cycle event in terms of security of property rights. A widow may retain certain of her husband's land and tree rights (Chubb,1961; Hoben, 1973: 146-148; *Obi*) or she may lose them altogether as in the case of a Peruvian cooperative (Skar *et al.*,1982). Even during her husband's lifetime, a woman can not necessarily depend on him to protect her property rights. Women in the Dominican Republic who used trees controlled by men for hog food lost their supply of palm fibres for handicrafts when, after a swine fever epidemic, the men cut down the trees.(Fortmann and Rocheleau, 1985). Commercialization may pose a threat to women's rights. In Burkina Faso, village woodlots have not eased the burden of women as the wood is controlled by men who sell it in the city or use it for their own purposes in the village (Skutsch, 1986; Williams, 1985b).

Women may therefore want to increase the security or convenience of access by planting their own trees. This raises additional practical questions. Will they be allowed to plant trees at all? Will they be allowed to plant the species they want? Will they control the trees they plant? Does this depend on where they plant them? Will they control them after they are widowed or divorced? Upon divorce, women in Cameroon lost all rights to personal possessions, food supplies and unharvested crops, hardly a property system conducive to tree planting by women (Brain, 1972:162). *Chavangi et al.* describe cultural restrictions on women's tree planting and means for circumventing them. They demonstrate the need for understanding trees as social as well as biological constructs.

The very paucity of literature on the questions raised here indicates the need for undertaking serious research and policy analysis. As has been repeatedly noted, people who do not consult or consider women cut themselves off from women's specialized knowledge and skills, ignore the poorest section of the community, and may harm the on-going activities of women (Fortmann, 1986; Hoskins, 1979; Hoskins, 1980; Hoskins, 1983; Williams, 1985a). Many social forestry and agroforestry projects address women's problems—e.g. the scarcity of fuelwood and fodder—but they do not necessarily benefit women. Better project design would have to take into account the responsibilities of women in livelihood systems that rely on trees and tree products, the rising importance of female-headed households (Colfer, 1985; Buvinic and Youssef,1978), the existence of separate, gender-differentiated production systems within the household (Fortmann, forthcoming), the ways women's needs, resources and abilities differ by class, ethnic group and life cycle stage; and the areas of conflict between customary and statutory law.

NOTES

1. Cox (1905:8) mentions in passing that in 1231 Henry III granted the privilege for an itinerant forge in Dean Forest to Mabel de Cantilupe for life. The following year she was granted the right to cut an oak on each of any fifteen days of her choosing for the rest of her life in order to support the forge.

REFERENCES

Blaut, James M., Ruth P. Blaut, Nan Harman, and Michael Moerman. 1973. "A Study of the Cultural Determinants of Soil Erosion and Conservation in the Blue Mountains of Jamaica." in Lambros Comitas and David Lowenthal (eds.) *Work and Family Life: West Indian Perspectives*. New York: Doubleday Anchor: 39-65.

Boserup, Esther. 1970. *Women's Role in Economic Development*. New York: St. Martin's Press.

Brain, Robert. 1972. *Bangwa Kinship and Marriage*. Cambridge: Cambridge University Press.

Buvinic, Myra, Nadia H. Youssef, with Barbara von Elm. 1978. "Women-Headed Households: The Ignored Factor in Development Planning." Washington, D.C.: International Center for Research on Women.

Cecelski, Elizabeth. 1985. *The Rural Energy Crisis, Women's Work and Basic Needs: Perspectives and Approaches to Action*. Geneva: International Labour Office.

Chen, Martha Alter. 1986. *A Quiet Revolution: Women in Transition in Rural Bangladesh*. Dhaka: BRAC: Prokashana.

Chubb, L.T. 1961. *Ibo Land Tenure*. Ibadan: Ibadan University Press.

Colfer, Carol J. Pierce.1985. "On Circular Migration: From the Distaff Side" in Guy Standing (ed.) *Labour Circulation and the Labour Process*. Geneva: International Labor Organization: 219-251.

Cox, J. Charles. 1905. *The Royal Forests of England*. London: Methuen and Co.

Czech, Horst J. 1986. *The Truco Concept*. Eschborn: GTZ.

Fortmann, Louise and Dianne Rocheleau. 1985. "Women's Role in Agro-forestry: Four Myths and Three Case Studies" *Agroforestry Systems* 2: 253-272.

Fortmann, Louise. 1986. "Women's Role in Subsistence Forestry" *Journal of Forestry*. 84(7): 39-42.

Fortmann, Louise. Forthcoming. "Women's Role in Small Farm Agriculture" in Miguel Altieri and Susanna Hecht (eds.) *Agroecology and Small Farm Development*. Boca Raton: CRC Press.

Hoben, Allen. 1973. *Land Tenure among the Amhara of Ethiopia*. Chicago: The University of Chicago Press.

Hoskins, Marilyn. 1979. "Women in Forestry for Local Community Development: A Programming Guide" Grant No. AID/otr-147-79-83. Washington, D.C.: Office of Women in Development, USAID.

Hoskins, Marilyn. 1983. "Rural Women, Forest Outputs, and Forestry Projects" FO: Misc/83/3. Rome: FAO.

Hoskins, Marilyn. 1980. "Community Forestry Depends on Women" *Unasylva*. 32 (130): 27-32.

Molnar, Augusta. 1985. "Women and Forestry: Encouraging Participation." Draft Manuscript.

Skar, Sara Lund, Nelida Arias, and Cotarma Saturno Garcia. 1982. *Fuel Availability, Nutrition and Women's Work in Highland Perus: Three Case Studies from Contrasting Andean Communities.* World Employment, Research WEP, 10/WP23. Geneva: ILO.

Skutsch, Margaret McCall. 1986. "Participation of Women in Social Forestry Programmes: Problems and Solutions" *Bos Newsletter* No. 13 5(1): 9-18.

Williams, Paula J. 1984. "The Women of Koundougou." PJW-11. Hanover, New Hampshire: Institute of Current World Affairs.

Williams, Paula J. 1985a. "Women and Forestry." Invited Special Paper, Theme III.6.1. Ninth World Forestry Congress, Mexico City, Mexico. 1-10. July.

Williams, Paula. 1985b. "Women's Participation in Forestry Activities in Burkina Faso (Formerly Upper Volta)." PJW-17. Hanover, New Hampshire: Institute of Current World Affairs.

The Editors

Women's Rights and Interests in Trees

S.N. Chinwuba Obi

Obi lays out the rights to trees that women enjoy under the customary law of the Ibo of Nigeria both directly in their own right and derivatively in their status as a wife or ward of a male. These rules suggest that women play a significant role in the ownership and management of economic and other trees.— The Editors.

A woman's rights and interests in economic trees may be said to fall into two classes, viz. direct and derivative. "Direct" rights and interests are those which a woman has and enjoys (or could enjoy if she chose to) as of right and independently of her status as a wife or a ward. "Derivative" rights and interests we define for present purposes as those which attach to a woman by virtue of her legal position as wife, widow, mother, or ward.

WOMEN'S DIRECT RIGHTS IN TREES

Nkwu ana[*]

As already stated, a baby may acquire property rights in a palm tree, and this baby may be a girl.[19] A woman retains her rights over *nkwu ana* for as long as she lives. It is tapped for palm wine for her benefit and at her request. Its nuts are reaped for her, also at her initiative. Of course, she cannot do the harvesting herself. But this reflects no defect in her property rights. She cannot because the law of

Excerpted from: S.N. Chinwuba Obi. 1963. *The Ibo Law of Property.* London: Butterworths. p. 96-98. Reprinted with the permission of the publisher.
[*] Palm tree under which the umbilical cord or first hair cuttings of a child are buried. The tree belongs to the child.

crime says so. Finally, it must be noted that marriage does not in any way affect the legal position of a woman in respect of her *nkwu ana*. She retains all her former rights and interest in this tree after marriage, and usually continues to visit her place of birth from time to time in order to harvest it. Where she is married a long way from home, however, or where she resides abroad, she normally appoints a beneficiary in her place.

Other trees

As for planting trees, it is unusual for women to do this before marriage.[20] There is no telling what distance will lie between a woman's place of birth and her matrimonial home, since marriage is both exogamous and virilocal. On the other hand a woman may, and often does plant economic trees in her matrimonial "home." If she does, they are her exclusive property. Common examples are such food trees as banana, plantain, paw-paw, breadfruit and "bitter-leaf" trees.

Just as a woman may purchase land either before or after marriage, so may she purchase economic trees either with or without the land on which they grow. Similarly she can lease a tree or take a pledge of them or accept a gift of them. Provided the purchase, pledge, or acceptance was done by or on behalf of the woman and for her exclusive benefit, her guardian, parent, or husband has no legal claims to the trees or their produce.

WOMEN'S DERIVATIVE RIGHTS IN TREES

Children and Wards

As a child or a ward,[21] a woman can claim the right *vis-a-vis* her guardian to be maintained out of the proceeds of the sale (or other disposition) of economic trees which were once her parent's, now deceased. This is so even if, as a woman, she has no right of inheritance over those trees. As long as she is being reasonably well maintained by her guardian, she cannot claim the exclusive use or benefit of any such trees. But she has an action (before a Native or Customary Court) against a guardian who exploits her late parent's trees for his own benefit while neglecting to satisfy her reasonable needs and demands.[1]

Wives

As a wife, a woman has a right over certain economic trees of her husband's.[2] What exactly these trees are varies from society to society. Thus, in Umeueke Agbaja, a wife is entitled to the fruit[3] of such trees as the breadfruit tree which is looked on as a woman's prerequisite and will belong to the wives of the men who own the trees,[4] and the *oha* tree.[*]   In this society, too, women are entitled to the kernels (but not the oil) where man and wife co-operate in winning these articles from the palm nut. In most other Ibo socieites, however, both oil and kernel belong to the woman. The Ibo saying on this point is, "*Akwu dalue ani nwanyi enwelu*" (literally, "If a bunch of palm nuts falls to the ground, woman becomes owner"). Indeed, it may be stated as a general rule that timber trees belong to the husband while food trees belong to the wife as far as **beneficial interests** are concerned. But to this rule there are some exceptions. Notable among these are the pear tree , the coconut tree, the citrus tree, and the kola nut tree. These, though food trees, are the exclusive property of husbands *a propos* their wives.

<u>Widows</u>
    Widows with or without children surviving are entitled to their late husband's economic trees during their life, so long as they reside among his people. In the words of Green, "a widow with no son has the right to her husband's palm trees during her lifetime."[5] This is true of all but timber trees. In the case of timber trees, she has a right to cut as many as she actually needs for her own use. Her late husband's lateral heirs too can help themselves at will if the deceased man left no male children as heirs. So may his children, if he left any.

NOTES

19. As its *nkwu ana*
20. But if they do, the trees will be their individual property
21. Of any age

1. This principle also applies to land and other forms of property
2. Green, M.M. 1941. *Land Tenure in an Ibo Village* pp 18-23.
3. Including edible leaves
4. Green, *Ibo Tenure....* p. 21
5. Ibid. p. 20

---

[*] The Latin name for *oha* is not provided. A.J. Igbodipe suggests that it is probably *Ceiba pentandva*.

Culture as the Basis for Implementation of Self-Sustaining Woodfuel Development Programmes

Noel A. Chavangi
Rutger J. Engelhard
Valarie Jones

The restriction of women's rights to trees may be reinforced by cultural beliefs as it is among the Luhya of Kenya described here. Such restrictions constrain women's ability to meet their own needs for tree products by planting trees. Because biological and social definitions of trees are not synonymous, the problem can be resolved in the short run by giving women fuelwood species to plant which are not defined locally as "trees." Long term effectiveness will also require changes in the attitudes of men toward women.—The Editors

The Kenya Woodfuel Development Programme (KWDP) carried out a survey of cultural attitudes and traditional practices of the people of Kakamega District to find out how they are used to define the status of men and women within the household with respect to woody biomass production and utilization...

The survey of more than 300 Luhya people was conducted over a period of four months in 1984 by means of open discussions with groups of men and/or women from seven selected areas within the district (see Chavangi 1984, 1985). Due to the sensitivity of some aspects of the subjects under discussion separate meetings were held for men and women.

Excerpted from "Culture as the Basis for Implementation of Self-Sustaining Woodfuel Development Programmes," Kenya Woodfuel Development Programme. Nairobi: Beijer Institute. Reprinted with the permission of the authors.

243

ACCESS TO CONTROL OF HOUSEHOLD RESOURCES

It is generally understood by the Kakamega community that men, as the heads of households, have overall control over all household resources. Women are expected to seek their husbands' opinions and consent before doing anything that may affect the allocation of those resources. In theory, joint ownership by man and wife is implied, but this is generally interpreted as meaning that the wife belongs to her husband alongside all the other household resources or 'assets'. Indeed, in Kiluhya, the same word is used for 'to marry' and 'to cook'.

By tradition only men are able to have permanent rights of owner-ship of land. Trees are often planted to demarcate farm boundaries and thus serve to demonstrate ownership. Since trees are regarded as permanent features of land, only men are able to plant them and to have sole rights to the use of them. A woman does have certain rights of access to her husband's land, but not to the trees growing on it.

This situation has been very effectively sustained through well-manipulated social taboos, which are used to rule out the possibility of women's active participation in tree-planting activities so that they will not be able to claim ownership of land. Examples of these taboos are:

• If a woman plants a tree she will become barren. Since child bearing is traditionally the only guarantee of stability in marriage, no woman would dare plant a tree lest she become barren and hence a social misfit.

• If a woman plants a tree her husband will die. Since the life of a widow is a miserable one, no woman would take actions that could threaten her husband's life.

• Certain tree species are believed to be sensitive to women, and if a woman were merely to carry them from the nursery to the planting site it is said that the seedlings will wither and die.

If a woman plants a tree it is viewed as a direct challenge to her husband's supremacy in the household, and thus is viewed as grounds for divorce. Moreover, trees planted by women cannot be used in the construction of houses. Thus women are prohibited from planting trees in case those trees are used inadvertently.

Although the strength of such taboos has in recent times been weakened through female contact with religion and education, the influence they still have on women's activities should not be underes-timated. Women who do manage successfully to get round such restric-tions get their sons or even hire male labor to plant trees for them, often without telling their husbands. This usually happens if the husband is employed outside the district.

THE DIVISION OF RESPONSIBILITIES

There exists a very distinct division between the responsibilities accorded to men and women at the household level, and this is rigidly maintained. The women deal with the day to day running of the household, child rearing, tending food crops, fetching water, cooking, and providing woodfuel. Men only very rarely involve themselves with these tasks, and indeed would be afraid of the ridicule of other men if they were seen to be helping their wives. Fuelwood has until recently been regarded as a common and free good that could be collected from areas of natural vegetation near or on the farms in the district, but as these traditional sources have dwindled, primarily as a result of increasing population pressure, the workloads of women have increased tremendously (Staudt 1975/76, Boserup 1970, Fortmann and Rocheleau 1985).

Women are gradually becoming more aware of their disadvantaged position and are attempting to create some degree of independence, while at the same time still maintaining the necessary respect required of them by the community. The factors that affect the status and role of women, and their efforts to increase their influence within the household, can be summarized as follows:

• The traditional husband-wife relationship within the household. Some men are more willing to allow their wives a certain degree of individualism than others - the role of religion in this respect is important since it often has a neutralizing effect on the traditional acceptance of male supremacy.

• Whether or not the husband lives on the farm. Women whose husbands are employed away from home tend to have greater access and control over household resources and decision making.

• Widows seem to be in a peculiar position. Their actions are usually dictated by society at large, their sons, and the immediate relatives of their late husbands. Older widows tend to have a greater degree of control than younger ones.

In general, men dominate most aspects of life within the household, and so their support and involvement are seen as essential to ensure the success of any envisaged intervention.

In order to obtain the fuelwood they need for cooking, the women are now having either to walk longer distances in search of free fuelwood, or are having to rely to an even greater extent on the household land to which they do have access, using hedges, remnants of bush, and crop residues such as maize stalks. But these materials provide only very low-quality fuel and large quantities are required (Barnes *et al.* 1984).

But despite the growing desperation of women in their search for new sources of energy, they can not plant trees for that purpose. Such an action would be considered almost as an act of rebellion against the conventional acceptance of male control of household resources; in fact many women at present would be too afraid of social censure even to consider doing it openly. Also, because the provision of fuelwood has always been women's responsibility, it is generally felt that if they admitted they could not cope it would be tantamount to admitting to being a failure as a wife.

In the high-potential smallholder agricultural areas where almost all the available land is fully utilized, acute shortages have led to a situation where woodfuel is becoming increasingly a commodity. Women are thus being forced to engage in activities such as growing vegetables for sale or handicrafts (either individually or in groups) to raise money to buy fuelwood or charcoal from the market.

As the prices of woodfuel rise in response to the demand, women are devising their own methods of reducing the effects of the shortage by reducing their energy consumption. Wood may be used much more sparingly, fewer meals cooked, or foods that require shorter cooking times used instead. Such foods tend to be less nutritious than traditional staple foods, with the result that the general level of nutrition of the household may fall. Some women have started to use improved fuel-efficient stoves, but so far these have not been very successful in that they are often inconvenient to use and sometimes require even more fuelwood than the traditional three-stone hearth to cook the same meal (Hosier 1984, Cecelski *et al.* 1984).

The planted trees on the farms, being the sole property of the men, are very rarely felled specifically for use as fuelwood within the household.

THE USES OF TREES

Trees are planted and managed by farmers in Kakamega District for many purposes, such as poles or timber for construction, split wood for sale, wood for making charcoal, and for use in rituals and religious ceremonies. There is a distinct preference for exotic tree species, such as eucalyptus, cypress, and pine, which are regarded as cash crops, or as a form of investment, to pay for school fees, etc. Indigenous tree species are rarely planted because they are thought to be able to grow on their own. In only a few areas are indigenous tree species such as *Sesbania sesban* deliberately grown in agricultural land. *Sesbania* is generally not regarded as a tree, but rather as a plant that enhances soil fertility (by nitrogen fixation), and so is tolerated by farmers. This species has been effectively adopted as a source of fuelwood by the women in these areas.

Although the men plant large numbers of trees on their farms, those trees are not used to supply fuelwood to the household. The provision of fuelwood is regarded as being of very low priority in relation to other, seemingly more pressing, needs of the household. Nevertheless both men and women admit that there are shortages of fuelwood, and these appear to be occurring regardless of the size of the landholding or the amount of woody biomass that is growing on the farms. The cause of the shortage in Kakamega District must be seen to be directly related to the traditional division of responsibilities between men and women, and the rules that determine who has access to and control over the wood produced on the farm.

Since fuelwood collection outside the farm is no longer possible, and since the indigenous knowledge of trees and agroforestry techniques is considerable, it seems obvious that the farmers should be encouraged to increase household wood supplies either by planting more trees themselves for that purpose, and/or by allowing their wives to do it. This would help to fill what appears to be a 'missing link' in the procurement of household fuelwood supplies: fuelwood is either collected or, when this is no longer possible, it is purchased from the market. The deliberate production of fuelwood on the farms has so far not been considered as a way of alleviating the problem.

TREES AND LAND TENURE

In any development programme that involves tree planting, whether on private or communal land, the complex issue of land ownership and tenure must first be fully researched and taken into account, since any misunderstanding of its possible implications could seriously jeopardize the project. The issue of land tenure was raised during discussions with farmers in one part of Kakamega District that had previously been occupied by white settlers who had felled almost all of the trees to make way for extensive plantation agriculture. The white settlers had left, and the area is now being resettled, but many of the new residents were unsure whether their occupancy was guaranteed, and were therefore reluctant to make any permanent improvement to the land, including planting trees. Their fear was that the KWDP might be trying to plant trees in order later to lay claim to and maybe even to confiscate the land.

The point is an important one. The situation in Kenya is described here to illustrate the possible impacts that systems of land administration could have on afforestation or agroforestry development programmes today and the future.

Land ownership in rural Kenya can be said to be on a private tenure basis, supported by legal and traditional provisions. The traditional concept of land was that it was a collective and functionally homogeneous asset that must be preserved for the benefit of present and future generations. The right of allocation of land use was usually entrusted to the recognized male head of the clan, who consulted with other family members before taking decisions. Private 'user rights' to land were therefore very strong. Trees were viewed as permanent features in relation to land (reflecting the long time they take to mature), so that only the entrusted user of a piece of land could plant trees on it. Land 'ownership' disputes were traditionally resolved in favor of the (male) party who could claim ancestral ownership of the most mature trees on the land.

Under the British administration a very different system of land tenure was introduced, based on the concept of individual ownership that excluded all other rights of access, supported by title deeds issued by the land registration office. Individuals were thus enabled to buy land outright and to have full and exclusive use of it.

In recent years, however, there has been a resurgence of litigation over who holds what interests in what land, particularly in areas of Kenya that are experiencing severe population pressure. This development has been encouraged by judicial attitudes that now tend to regard the land tenure reform programme as an exercise in the rationalization of land administration rather than the privatization of land rights. Indeed, the prevailing view in Kenya's High Court is that "the adjudication, and registration of any land formerly held under indigenous law cannot free it from the community trust obligations inherent in that law" (Okoth-Ogendo 1985). Cases of land disputes are now being passed back to clan elders to make final decisions as to who owns or has rights of access to the land in question.

The relationship between land tenure and tree tenure has far-reaching implications for plans for developing agroforestry systems, especially if the tree species to be introduced are those that by tradition are regarded as evidence of intention to claim ownership of the land. Existing stocks of trees could disappear as a result of either wanton destruction or the conversion of land to uses that appear to meet more immediate—usually agricultural or pastoral—needs (see also Brokensha and Glaszier 1973, Brokensha and Njeru 1977, Fortmann 1985).

The farmers in rural areas of Kenya are thus justifiably very suspicious of all tree-planting programmes, in that they fear that they may be a tactic on the part of the government or development agency to claim title to the land or deprive them of the right to cultivate the land on which the trees are planted. In fact, KWDP enumerators who were to observe the performance of tree seedlings distributed free to farmers, were refused entry to some farms. Investigations revealed that farmers who had not been given seedlings had spread the rumor that the real intention of the KWDP was to claim ownership of the land on which the seedlings had been planted, and only after considerable efforts to assure the farmers that this was not the case was it possible to continue the monitoring.

THE NEW APPROACH

Constraints

The major obstacles to introducing a project aimed at increasing female participation in tree planting are of course the traditional attitude to and of women, and their rights and responsibilities with respect to land, trees, and fuelwood. Such attitudes are both the product of and the mechanisms that serve to perpetuate the cultural and social system, so that efforts to intervene by advocating the involvement of women in tree-planting programs are likely to evoke strong resistance from the men, as well as fear of repercussion on the part of the women. The issue is a controversial one in that it could lead to serious conflicts between husbands and wives, and ill feelings among the men towards the objectives of such programmes. Such reactions would obviously jeopardize the success of any intervention strategy no matter how well intentioned.

Since fuelwood is considered to be solely a woman's problem, when the idea is advanced that women should be allowed to plant their own trees for fuelwood the men cite many reasons why they think this would not be acceptable. Such a development would appear to erode male control within the household by excluding male participation and is therefore perceived to be threatening. In particular, if women were allowed to plant and therefore to own their own trees, then the men might have to request their wives' permission to use them. Women often help each other out in times of hardship, such as in sharing fuelwood, and believe that in doing so they are providing a valuable service to the community, whereas the men think that such actions are mere extravagance, and if women were given a free hand there would soon be no trees at all on the farms.

These decidedly negative attitudes toward women planting and controlling the use of trees were considered the most important obstacles that would have to be overcome before any intervention could be implemented. The question then was how to develop a more positive attitude to encourage both men and women to explore new possibilities that would benefit both.

Tree planting has always been an individual activity arising from the traditional relationship between tree and land tenure. The strength of the cultural, economic, and spiritual values attached to trees planted on farms in the district would also make it difficult, if not impossible to change these values to allow women access to those trees for use as fuelwood.

An additional constraint was that if the project was to focus on the diversion of the present planted woody biomass form the market to the household (a very unwelcome proposition to the men!) this would have the undesirable effect of reducing the supply of tree products to the market, thus increasing prices. This would then increase the burden on the women in some areas by aggravating the fuelwood shortage at the household level. It was therefore necessary to consider the possibility of planting trees for fuelwood in addition to or replacing part of the existing woody biomass on the farms.

Possible approaches

In view of these many considerations, the KWDP was forced to rethink its original programme strategy (to encourage decentralized group nurseries), taking into account all of these cultural factors relating to the roles and responsibilities of women within the household. If the ultimate objective of helping most, if not all, of the farms in the district to become self-sufficient in fuelwood was to be achieved, then both men and women would have to be heavily involved in tree-planting and harvesting activities. Only then would beneficial effects be seen at the household level.

The awareness programme

The most obvious problem that had to be avoided by the KWDP was the possibility of creating strife within households if the project appeared to be encouraging women to break long-standing cultural taboos. A new line of approach to the problem was needed, one that embraced the needs of the whole community to help them deal with the problem together, yet which would be flexible enough to meet individual needs. A new idea was developed in the form of a mass "awareness programme" that addressed the community to bring the issue into the open so then it could be discussed and pragmatic solutions sought. A change in male attitudes is required, since without the full cooperation of the men, the programme's activities will almost certainly lead to areas of conflict (between husbands and wives, as well as between the community and the KWDP) that will not be easy to resolve. Given that fuelwood has always been the women's responsibility, a situation needs to be created in which men, if they actually help their wives to obtain fuelwood or allow them to plant trees, will not be subject to the ridicule of other men in the village. This can only come about if the community at large is made aware of the extent of the overall problem, and is fully involved in formulating and implementing a solution from the outset.

The trees normally planted by men on the farms are exotic species such as eucalyptus, which have many uses, but take many years to mature. One avenue that is being explored is based on the observation that some species, particularly *Sesbania sesban*, are not considered to be trees by either men or women. *Sesbania* is already intercropped with food crops by women in a few parts of the district to improve soil fertility. Since it is not regarded as a tree, and so women cannot claim ownership to land through it, then the men do not see it as a threat to their standing in the community. The KWDP is developing this line of approach, by introducing similar tree species that can serve the same purpose, but which bypass the cultural blockages.

Multipurpose species

Both men and women agree that to plant trees that will be used solely for fuelwood would be impractical, for several reasons. Men will not tolerate a situation in which their wives have sole access to the trees, and in any case many farms are far too small to support a woodlot of women's fuelwood trees in addition to the trees the men already raise for other purposes. The problem is therefore being approached from several angles simultaneously. The suitable species identified by the KWDP agroforesters (*Sesbania, Leucanea, Calliandra, Mimosa*) have many advantages: they have no traditional connotations, they grow very quickly, allow for close planting, they can provide animal fodder, act as windbreaks, improve soil fertility and help prevent erosion, in addition to providing a continuous source of high-quality fuelwood. One potential drawback of *Mimosa*, however, is that its stems are tall and straight, making them ideal building poles so that they might be monopolized by the men, but even this could be turned to advantage if all four species are marketed as a package that can within a very short period of time provide a significant contribution to the total needs of the household in relation to wood.

Male migration

Traditional rules of land inheritance in Kakamega dictate that on the death of a man, his land be divided among his sons. But as the population density has increased, the farms in some areas have been divided to such a degree that they are now incapable of providing the subsistence needs of the families living on them. Large numbers of men are thus being forced to leave their families on the farms while they move to other areas in search of paid employment. In the most densely settled areas of Kakamega, up to 50 percent of the farms are being run by women *in absentia*. While the men's consent still has to be obtained in some matters, these women do tend to have a greater degree of control over household resources and decision making. Some of them do plant and fell trees for their own use and for sale, but only to a limited extent, and often without their husband's knowledge and consent or, where the traditional taboos are particularly strongly enforced, some get their sons or pay male workers to do it for them...

Groups

Numerous women's groups already exist in the district, many of them church-affiliated, whose members strive to work together to earn cash for household needs, or simply to help each other in times of hardship... With some groups, some women were barred from further participation by their husbands, who considered their increased involvement in tree planting as acts of rebellion. Other women appeared to be more willing to take risks and intended to use the project as a lever to lessen their husband's control. In view of the observation that the effects of the cultural impasse were being most strongly felt within the households, the KWDP decided that this was where its efforts should be directed. In order to keep potential conflicts to a minimum the project chose to concentrate on the mass awareness programme treating the household as a unit, rather than to focus on the women alone. The KWDP could therefore best be described as a women's project in which the men are the prime target group!

REFERENCES

Barnes, C., Ensminger, J., and O'Keefe, P. (eds) (1984) *Wood, Energy and Households: Perspectives on Rural Kenya*, Energy, Environment and Development in Africa, Vol. 1 (Stockholm: Beijer Institute/ Scandinavian Institute of African Studies).

Bosserup, E. (1970) *Women's Role in Economic Development* (London: Allen and Unwin).

Brokensha, D. and Glazier, J. (1973) "Land reform among the Mbere of Central Kenya." *Africa.* 43(3):183-206.

Brokensha, DD. and Njeru, E.H.N. (1977) *Some Consequences of Land Adjudication in Mbere Division.* Working Paper 320 (Nairobi: IDS).

Cecelski, E., Dunkerley, J., and Ramsay, W. (1987) *Household Energy and the Poor in the Third World* (Washington, DC: Resources for the Future).

Chavangi, N.A. (1984) *Cultural Aspects of Fuelwood Procurement in Kakamega District.* Working Paper No. 4 (Nairobi: Kenya Wood-fuel Development Programme).

Chavangi, N.A. (1985) *Agroforestry Potentials and Land Tenure Issues.* Paper prepared for the International Conference on Land Tenure and Agroforestry, Nairobi, May 1985.

Eckholm, E., Foley, G., Barnard, G., and Timberlake, L. (1984) *Fuelwood: The Energy Crisis That Won't Go Away* (London: Earthscan, International Institute for Environment and Development).

Fortmann, L. (1985) "The tree tenure factor in agroforesry with particular reference to Africa." *Agroforestry Systems* 2(4):229-251.

Fortmann, L. and Rocheleau, D. (1985) "Women and agroforestry: Four myths and three case studies. " *Agroforestry Systems* 2(4):253-272.

Hosier, R. (1984) "Domestic energy consumption in rural Kenya: Results of a nationwide survey," in C. Barnes *et al* (eds) *Wood, Energy and Households: Perspectives on Rural Kenya*, Energy, Environment and Development in Africa, Volt. 6 (Stockholm: Beijer Institute/ Scandinavian Institute of African Studies) pp. 14-60.

Okoth-Ogendo, H.O. 1985. "Tenure of Trees or Tenure of Lands?" Paper prepared on the International Conference in Land Tenure and Agricultural. Naivete, May, 1985.

Staudt, K. 1976/76. "Women Farmers and Inequities in Agricultural Services." *Rural Africaner* 29:81-94.

In Whose Trees? Proprietary Dimensions in
Forestry. Fortmann, Bruce (eds). Westview
Press, Boulder, Colorado 341 pp. 1988

Women, Trees, and Tenure:
Implications for Agroforestry

Dianne E. Rocheleau

*Rocheleau raises three important points regarding women's
access to trees- the difference between customary and statutory
law; the difference between **de jure** and **de facto** rights; and the
spatial distribution of women's rights. National legislation
and policies dealing explicitly with women's rights to trees
and tree products is needed.—The Editors.*

POINTS OF CONTRAST AND COMPARISON

Women participate in forestry and agroforestry in ways different
from men. Women may work side by side with men, or separately;
always, however, there are effective differences in rights and responsibilities. This is especially true with regard to access to land (Black
and Cottrell, 1981). Control of agroforestry system components and
products is subject to rules distinct from those governing men's actions.

While differing women and men's roles may limit some kinds of
tree culture and agroforestry, there are also special possibilities for
women's agroforestry taking advantage of their separate domains of
space, time, activities, interests and skills. Women have special
knowledge, rights, obligations, and abilities. Agroforestry can
validate women's land and tree use rights. In women's use of trees are
embedded their claims to ownership, to increased production, their
rights to decreases in gathering time, and their authority to reconcile
conflicting objectives for shared household or community plots (e.g.
changing the conflict between cash crops and fuelwood to a possibility
of *both* cash crops and fuelwood).

Revised for this volume from a paper presented at "Land, Trees and
Tenure: An International Workshop on Tenure Issues in Agroforestry"
Nairobi, May 27-31, 1985.

254

Nowhere are the special problems and opportunities for women so clear as in the arena of land use and ownership. Even in countries where traditional law (e.g. Moslem law, Mayer, 1984) or modern legal reforms have provided for equality in most spheres, strong gender inequality often exists with respect to use and ownership of agricultural land (Ahooja-Patel, 1982; Mazumdar, 1982; Fortmann, 1981). This has obvious implications for women's adoption of agroforestry technologies that depend on secure access to land on a permanent or long term basis.

DIFFERENCES IN STATUTORY AND CUSTOMARY LAW

Sometimes differences in men's and women's land and tree rights are clearly stated in statutory law (FAO, 1979). More often these codes defer to (coded) customary law in matters of "marriage" and inheritance, which include most of the cases relating to women's land rights. While civil and statutory law usually applies to all people of a given state, customary law may vary by region, religious affiliation, or ethnic origin, adding to the complexity of interpretation and administration. Within statutory, and customary law, women's rights are often tied to marital status (FAO, 1979) though the most independent group under one customary code may be the most powerless under another body of customary law (married *vs.* widowed, divorced *vs.* single). The result is a complex array of types of rights within parallel legal codes, nested within social units ranging from the individual to the kin group.

The process of customary law interpretation is riddled with judgments attempting to reconcile culturally incompatible rights, obligations, property, and units of social organization. Many outsiders point accusingly at the discriminatory nature of traditional systems, yet women often lose out in the translation of custom to "modern" systems (Onger-Hosgor, 1983; Etienne and Leacock, 1980; Muntemba, 1982). In Tanzania and Malawi, customary law was standardized at the national level after independence, resulting in a uniform patrilineal system. This deprived women from matrilineal groups of former land use and residential rights in their own villages by allocating land to households through male heads (Fortmann, 1981; Brain, 1976).

In other cases the interpretation of the customary law during the implementation of land reform and settlement programs undermines women's access to land. For example, Luo women in Kenya lost their rights and security of access to lineage land (in the commons and in the household plots) when land adjudication officers judged the inherited right to allocate land as synonymous with land ownership, ignoring all other rights. Male heads of household and male relatives of women heads of household were allotted exclusive rights of ownership, with few exceptions. By contrast, the actual categories of traditional rights included ownership (vested in the lineage), the right to allocate land (vested in married men), membership in the patrilineage (passed on to sons through the mother), and rights of usufruct and residence, including access to common lineage lands as well as to own plots within husband's allocation (acquired by women through marriage) (Pala Okeyo, 1980; Okoth-Ogendo, 1985).

Luo women did not lose their access to all the lands they previously used, but they have lost some lands, all *security* of access, and the status they formerly had. With each succeeding generation women may be less able to rely on tradition to protect their autonomy as farmers and their access to communal lands as gatherers (Pala Okeyo, 1980). This case typifies the loss of prior customary rights and suggests the elements of ambiguity, dependence, and insecurity that replaced a fairly definitive, complementary, and stable land using and owning relationship between men and women. While the men's rights and inter-household distinctions were legally well defined, women's rights and intra-household distinctions were left to customary law, much modified and circumscribed by the new tenure system. This opened a wide gap between *de jure* and *de facto* rights and responsibilities, and made women's farming and gathering activities dependent on the permission of individual men.

The erosion of women's customary rights under modern legal reforms (colonial and post-independence, capitalist and socialist) is a widespread phenomenon (Etienne and Leacock, 1980; Onger-Hosgor, 1983; FAO, 1979; Cultural Survival Quarterly, 1984a). It has been reported for many ethnic groups, throughout Africa (Fortmann, 1981; Barnes, 1984; Afonja, 1981; Muntemba,1982), Asia (Nowak, 1984; Endicott, 1984; Cultural Survival Quarterly, 1984b; Palmer, 1978; Mazumdar, 1982), and Latin America (Arizpe, 1982; Deere, 1981; Deere and De Leal, 1981; Mickelwait *et al.*, 1976). Sometimes this has been done on the pretext of formalizing customary tenure systems; in other cases it has simply been imposed by colonial powers or by national governments on ethnic minorities. This was particularly pronounced during the colonial period with respect to matrilineal groups, extending to de-registration of women's ownership or use rights in Zimbabwe, Zambia (Muntemba 1982) and Malaysia (Boserup, 1970).

The tendency of most land tenure reforms has been to expand and legalize men's access to land, while decreasing and "informalizing" women's rights of ownership and use rights. Rights of usufruct in general, and overlapping multiple-use rights in particular, have been largely ignored in favor of individual or state ownership. In both cases the titles or allocation of land are made on a household basis to male heads, or to associations whose members are exclusively or predominantly male heads of households. Even where a separate commons recognized as part of the reform process, as in India and Pakistan, unregulated overuse and privatization by influential individuals (Cernea, 1985) reflect the inadequacy of legal and administrative infrastructures vis-a-vis maintaining women's access to land and trees.

However, the evidence does not indicate an unmitigated disaster for women. There are also some examples of women (Nigerian and Ghanaian) gaining more secure rights to land after privatization (Afonja, 1981), although the questions then arise "how many?" and "which women?" (Mazumdar, 1984). In many cases the wealthier rural farm women have benefited most from such reforms. The cases cited in Ghana and Nigeria involved the recognition of women's ownership of commercial tree crop plots (usually cocoa). Some governments have also implemented reforms-of-reform, as in Mexico where the government changed the rules of membership in *ejidos* to allow women to retain their own plots after marriage (FAO, 1979). Some recent land reform programs, as in Nicaragua, have also incorporated special provisions for sharing of benefits by women (Deere, 1986), while others have simply perpetuated prior *de facto* exclusion of women from land ownership and management (Onger-Hosgor, 1983). In other cases, landless women have gained access to land through revolutionary or liberal land reforms, although the terms of access are limited by marital status, administered by male relatives, or vested in associations of male heads of household, as in Ethiopia (Onger-Hosgor, 1983; Whelan, 1984).

Gaps Between Women's *de jure* and *de facto* Rights

In addition to formal legal differences between men's and women's land and tree rights, there is often a widening gap between women's *de jure* and *de facto* rights and responsibilities. As men benefit from land reform, their legal rights often envelop and exceed former customary rights; men then have less interest in the recourse of customary law. Women's rights, by contrast, are either subsumed within rights legally ascribed to male relatives and community groups with recourse to coded customary law, or they are part of a growing body of uncoded, evolving customary law, outside the formal legal system. In the latter case, women's rights of use and access as currently recognized by the community may differ from previously coded customary law as well as from national statutory law. Women's rights are subject to two distinct systems of customary and statutory law, and are also often embodied in an evolving version of customary law that is recognized by legal institutions and national authorities.

The disparity between *de jure* and *de facto* rights in many areas is a land reform crisis in the making, particularly for women, but also for landless people in general. It may well be that rights of residence, and informal access to land, however insecure legally, are what keep many women and landless people in the countryside. For women the inability to dispose of property is of little consequence, as long as they have farmland to work. However, as urban-dwelling sons and other relatives inherit and take possession of the land, they may change the terms of access (Haugerud, 1983) as well as the land use and land cover. In one case in Embu District, Kenya, three co-wives agreed not to register the death of their husband so as to protect their control over their coffee fields and their harvest from competing heirs and bureaucratic interference (Haugerud, 1983). While customary law would have protected their right of residence, their rights to cropland and resulting profits would have been entirely at the discretion of the heirs. The complicity of neighbors and relatives in the widows' maintenance of their husband's legal existence may, in this case, indicate a shift in customary law toward recognition of expanded rights for widows with absentee sons.

While rights of residence and gathering may persist, guaranteed by coded customary law, land use changes made by heirs may drastically reduce availability and quality of tree, shrub and crop by-products, not to mention the women's control of the major products. The legal heirs may sell multipurpose trees for timber or charcoal, unless women residents have legal tree ownership or well-defined use rights. Such rights have been safeguarded in some cases. For example, in groups on the Kenyan coast, widows retain exclusive rights to harvest fruits and nuts from trees, while the land itself may be inherited and managed by another relative. Women's tree rights are also recognized among the Ibo of Nigeria (Fortmann, 1985; Obi, 1963) and among Tanzanian coastal people observing Islamic law (Fortmann, 1985; Tanner, 1960).

Where more egalitarian or separate-but-equal rules currently apply (as in some groups of pastoralists, forest dwellers and hill people), women may lose their rights under poorly conceived land tenure reform or land settlement projects. In many areas development projects have set precedents for subsequent survey and land allocation/registration procedures by dealing only with male heads of household and community leaders (Nowak, 1984; Endicott, 1984).

Strengthening or improving women's tree ownership and rights of usufruct might well provide a means to reconcile women's needs for secure access to trees and tree products with men's legal ownership of the land. Where such rights are not well-defined there may be a gradual shift from women's land uses to men's land uses and from women's tree species to men's species as the legal distribution of land and trees is increasingly reflected in actual use and management.

The causes for these trends and for the widespread imbalance between rural women's needs, responsibilities and rights are a topic of hot debate (Etienne and Leacock, 1980; Arizpe, 1982; Deere and De Leal, 1981; Afonja, 1981; ICES ,1985; D. Jain, 1984). Varying degrees of blame have been placed on traditional, colonial, neo-colonial, nationalist, and capitalist or socialist political economies. The fact is that rural women's responsibilities are often out of balance with their legal status and formal rights to land, trees, and the products of both. Discrepancies between women's rights, responsibilities, and authority, between *de jure* and *de facto* rights, and between coded and uncoded customary law, all must be faced by agroforestry and social forestry planners and project personnel.

Division of Space, Time and Responsibility

In most rural areas of the Third World, men and women have distinct domains of activity, responsibility, control and knowledge. The extent of this division varies from almost nil, as among the Dayak forest dwellers of East Kalimantan (Colfer, 1981), to very strictly defined separation of men's and women's domains, as maintained in some parts of India and the Middle East, particularly where purdah and other forms of seclusion are observed (Ahooja-Patel, 1982). The degree, type, and terms of division vary substantially between regions, ethnic groups, and classes, based on differences in customary law and practice.

Whether clients are following long-established customary practice or recently-adopted role definitions, men and women in any given household or community are likely to have distinct interests, needs, and capabilities in agroforestry or social forestry. Division of labor, expertise, authority, and spatial domains influence the participation of women in new types of technology and land use systems. For settlement or agroforestry projects committed to women, these role differences can also determine: areas available to women; the potential patterns for mixing trees, crops, pasture, and animals; the types of trees and tree products to be included; types and amounts of labor and management inputs; and the tenure arrangements needed.

Spatial Niches in the Rural Landscape

Visible landscape patterns are an excellent point of departure for determining the spatial distribution of men's and women's domains, and potential niches for shared, separate or interlocking agroforestry technologies. Given the cultural and environmental diversity of land use systems and the dynamic nature of community development cycles and land use, little can be assumed as to which niches will be used, managed, shared, or owned by women. While live fences are the major opportunity for women's agroforestry technologies in some parts of western Kenya, the external boundary fences are the exclusive domain of male heads of household among neighboring groups. In some areas women still manage separate food and cash crop plots of their own, and in still others men and women cultivate and harvest separate plants within the same multi-storied agroforestry systems.

While there are no niches universally used and managed by women, there are some spaces that are more often their domain. Strangely enough, the areas most important to women are typically those closest to home and the farthest away. Home gardens are located near the center of household activity, while common gathering areas (forests, bushland and grassland) are usually at the outer periphery of home, croplands, or an entire settlement, depending on population and land use intensity (Raintree and Warner, 1985). While the nearby gardens are located so as to minimize time away from home, the distant location of peripheral gathering of the commons minimizes opportunity cost of land and actual labor and management inputs on-site.

Home Gardens. The cultivation and management of home gardens by women is a widespread phenomenon among settled groups the world over (Buch, 1980; Niñez, 1985). This is particularly pronounced in Latin American areas where women do not traditionally till the land. The woman's domain in the home garden acts as a way around taboos that forbid tilling the main cropland. Moreover, by definition such plots are located close to the home, accessible to women whose mobility may be limited by custom, or by the complex logistics of mixing travel with child care, food processing, and food preparation. Home gardens increase production through intensive labor input, without adding time away from home, and within a flexible schedule shaped around other household responsibilities (Chaney and Lewis, 1980).

Some features of home gardens may also be applicable to community or social forestry approaches (Chakravorty, 1980), particularly the features of location near the home and of species and product diversity. If fuelwood or tree products are the main objectives and women have landscape niches available close to home, they may be better able to plant and utilize such trees in a home-garden or in a block planting of equivalent size close to home. Women's groups in some projects have specifically requested combining vegetable gardens with tree nurseries (Rocheleau, 1985), particularly where sufficient water was not available at the household level, but was available at a community site. Establishment of valuable horticultural crops in a home garden plot can identify the site as one of value, strengthening "social fences" against grazing and browsing. While trees are respected as property in some places, elsewhere crops may be more valued and respected. Although the problem shifts from one of damage due to neglect to losses from theft, participants are more motivated and capable of solving the latter.

The Commons. While the commons is rarely their exclusive domain, it is often a major source of subsistence and commercial products for women. In some stages of land use intensification it may become the major source of women's livelihood or of their contributions to the household and community (Roy, 1980; Dahlberg, 1981). Where land is plentiful, as among some forest dwellers, shifting cultivators, and pastoralists, the forest or rangeland is a shared domain of men and women, with division more likely to occur on the basis of labor, expertise and security. Women are usually, but not exclusively, responsible for gathering food and fuelwood, as well as fiber, some medicinal plants and other "minor" forest and range products. They may also manage grazing or browsing animals.

The communal grazing and gathering areas deserve special attention since they may bear on tree and land tenure. When men take up wage labor or intensified agricultural and livestock production, the group may continue to rely heavily on forest and range products gathered by women. Safeguarding or expanding women's tree ownership and rights of usufruct in surrounding forests and rangeland may help to prevent environmental degradation and to maintain important sources of food and other products, as well as maintaining women's status and customary rights to use and protect forest and rangelands of adequate extent and quality.

As village development cycles and land use conversion and intensification proceed, the commons may become a residual domain, left to women by default. In the process of land use intensification from bush fallow to multiple cropping women's use of gathering areas may change substantially, and the commons itself may shift from one spatial niche to another over time. This transition is also marked by constant adjustments between use of the commons and use of interstitial niches on-farm.

Women may eventually find their access to household or lineage fallow lands preempted by permanent cropping, and even their access to seasonal fallows may be curtailed by multiple cropping and/or irrigation. Changes in crop and reduction of crop and weed diversity can remove valuable sources of cropping system by-products. This process has been documented among landless gatherers in some parts of India (Das Gupta, 1984). It has also been reported, in various stages of development, by women in Kenya (Barnes, 1984; Fortmann and Rocheleau, 1985), the Dominican Republic (Rocheleau, 1984), and Zambia (Huxley et al., 1985). Unless gathering remains an activity of the landowners themselves, its products are liable to be relegated to the status of by-products with no niche of their own, unless the plants or the niche are re-defined as gatherers' property.

Agroforestry technologies can either reinforce or ameliorate this problem (Hoskins 1983). For example, a new alley-cropping system could displace shrubs or weeds that provide leafy vegetables (Fortmann, 1985). But, enrichment planting and more intensive management of selected woody species in cropland and grazing lands could provide forest or range products for women within a system compatible with men's crops or pasture. This would require a clear statement of women's tree ownership or rights of use

In areas where a commons does not exist as such, women often rely on the "borrowing" stick wood, grazing privileges, and other non-commodity goods and services from private woodland or pasture lands of a neighbor, relative or patron. This practice is widespread in Kenya among neighbors and clan members. In Latin America the patron-client relationship prevalent in rural areas often includes such arrangements.

Women's tree and land ownership and rights of usufruct for common lands may apply to individuals, households or groups. However, the issues of group ownership and distribution of rights and products between group members are likely to be more important than in on-farm approaches. While the "tragedy of the commons" (Hardin, 1968) is an oft-invoked (and perhaps over-used) concept, there are several points that favor helping women consolidate and maintain well-defined conditions and terms of tree ownership or rights of usufruct in village commons, in public forests and rangeland, or in "unclaimed" interstitial niches such as roadsides, gullies and boundaries.

The use of home gardens and the commons illustrates how land use change can modify women's access to land and trees as well as how women's involvement in decision-making and planning may be the key factor in site choice and technology when women are the clients of agroforestry and social forestry programs. Tree ownership and contractual use agreements develop diverse and managed agroforestry systems, systems that range in size from plots to whole watersheds.

Authority and Decision-Making. The exact form and degree of women's decision-making power and authority varies substantially. In many cases men's and women's authority and decision-making powers are interlocked in a complex system of household, kin group, and community governance that recognizes sexual division of skills, knowledge, and interests. Among the Luo in Kenya, while men as a group always had more authority over the allocation of land and now have even more control as individuals through title deeds, women still retain ownership of the harvested crops from their sub-plots and have full authority over the disposition of the grain in their stores and the profits from its sale (Pala Okeyo, 1980; Chakin, 1985).

Another critical point is the choice of organizational units to mobilize public participation and decision-making, or to work/facilitate between the whole client group and research and development programs (Max-Neef, 1982; Thomson, 1983; Weber and Hoskins, 1983). Much of the basis for evolving common law, as well as for land tenure reform and environmental law, rests with a variety of decision-making groups ranging from the Forest Department to peasants' associations to councils of village elders and kin groups.

The scale and type of social organization chosen for program-client liaison can radically affect the results (Chambers, 1983). The results of tenure reform among the Luo in Kenya, reflected the absence of women among the adjudication officers and local advisory committees (Pala Okeyo, 1980). Likewise the decisions of village *Panchayats* in the Indian Himalayas often show a strong bias toward men's interests in the disposition of the village commons and in the terms of village participation in development projects, although women have begun to demand membership and a voice in the *Panchayat* (S. Jain, 1984; Berreman, 1984; Bhatt, 1980; Mishra and Trepathi, 1978).

In many forestry and agroforestry projects, species choices, planting niches and management plans are made by outside technical advisors in consultation with male household heads or local headmen in the community, resulting in loss of women's information about their own particular working environments, plants, and plant use and management (Hoskins, 1979). Women's involvement in a Honduran agroforestry project through local women's groups has made a positive difference in the success of a new technology (Wiff, 1984), influencing as well the eventual disposition of the land and trees currently owned, used or managed by women. If women's participation and benefits are to have any widespread impact, women must be involved in the planning and management of agroforestry and social forestry strategies, programs, projects, and technology development.

While many researchers and practitioners of social forestry are disillusioned with the undifferentiated community as a unit of organization, and with the commons as a unit of design and management (Cernea, 1985), the undifferentiated household is no panacea. While Palmer (1978) states that the "gravitational center of development is shifting to the cooperative, the farmers' association, and the village unit organization," in other areas these structures are breaking down and households are the strongest unit of organization. In yet other cases, clan groups or small women's groups are the predominant units of organization for rural development (March and Taqqu, 1982; Wijngaarden, 1983; Rocheleau, 1985). Moreover, it is not only the strongest unit of organization that is of interest, but also, the one that gives most voice and scope for women. The appropriate unit of organization will vary from place to place and with the type of technology and tenure question involved. It will also depend on whether women are considered as priority clients or as part of a larger client group.

Indications for Policy, Research, and Development Action

The problems and opportunities inherent in the sexual division of labor and rights require special consideration and types of action not yet part of the mainstream approach to agroforestry and social forestry programs. The implications of these differences extend to the content of *technology designs* and *social contracts* for management, as well as to the way that research and development activities are carried out with women clients. The gender-based differences in legal status, use of land and access to space, types of activities, and control of labor, all have a direct bearing on *what* type of plants can be planted, managed, used and harvested, *where*, *by whom*, for *what purpose*, and, for *whose benefit*.

Policy Formulation

If women are to secure access to the production and products of agroforestry and social forestry systems, policy interventions may be required on five key points:

 • 1) *The concept of tenure security* must be broadened. Since women's rights often are nested within social structures dominated by men, the failure to treat the complexity of multiple rights and multiple uses will usually leave women with no formal legal rights to land or trees. Legislative and regulatory powers could be used to formalize the separation of land and tree tenure, while refining use rights and access to trees.

 • 2) *Gathering and the products of gathering warrant recognition within the law and regulations* that define the uses and users of land.

The role of gathering in subsistence and commercial economies may need to be documented, in order to justify such formal recognition, but in many cases the information is at hand (Fleuret, 1979; Livingstone and Zamora, 1983; Lee, 1979; Ayensu, 1983; Williams, 1984; and 1985; Hoskins, 1979; Surin and Bhaduri, 1980; Cernea, 1982; Christophersen and Weber, 1981; Weber and Hoskins, 1983; Flores-Paitan, 1985; Rocheleau et al., 1986; Wachira et al., 1987) and has only to be interpreted and acted upon. This is a concern of landless people in general, as well as of most women in farming, herding, and forest-dwelling communities (*Unasylva*, 1984; *Cultural Survival Quarterly*, 1982). Where rights of access can be modified to accommodate gathering and reserve especially fragile or valuable trees and source areas for exclusive use by gatherers, then environmental, equity, and production objectives can be combined to the mutual advantage of women gatherers and the community at large.

• 3) *Promoting women in processing and marketing* through national and regional policy initiative can also increase women's access to the products and benefits of agroforestry and social forestry systems. Such an approach could transform a current marginal activity with no security into a major, secure source of income for women. Further legal or regulatory provisions might be required to maintain women's control, and to prevent expropriation of newly profitable enterprises into men's domain or into the hands of local elites.

• 4) *Giving women access to decision-making about land and trees* may require changes in the interpretation and enforcement of legal codes. Women's ability to secure rights of land and tree ownership and access is conditioned by the scope of their overall legal status, and by the conflicting interpretations of parallel systems of coded customary law, national laws and regulations, and actual practice. National legislative reform to improve women's legal status as property owners and claimants may be required. Or a change in interpretation of existing national laws in order to facilitate internal reforms of customary law to broaden and/or protect and formalize women's rights of ownership and access to land and trees may suffice.

• 5) *Strengthening the status and power of organizations that represent rural women* can be accomplished with national policy initiatives. While this sometimes results in government or elite manipulation of non-representative groups, it is also possible to empower authentic, popular women's organizations from grass roots to the national level. Legal legitimacy and widespread official recognition can allow such groups to deal with credit, project administration, access to the factors of agroforestry and social forestry production, directions of research and development, and formulation and enforcement of local codes or project contracts that protect women's rights to land, trees, and their products.

Such policy shifts and interventions would provide conditions for women's full participation in agroforestry and social forestry. The process also requires appropriate technologies, responsive organizations for local planning, implementation, and enforcement of programs for the benefit of both men and women.

Where women's tree and land tenure and direct access to decision making are unduly constrained, agroforestry and social forestry programs may serve women clients best by working to adapt existing organizations toward a greater voice for women in agroforestry and social forestry decisions controlled by men. Another alternative would be to introduce new types of agroforestry and social forestry activities, sites, and plant types that are not yet defined as men's domains (Fortmann and Rocheleau, 1985), and to promote profitable roles for women with as much control by them as possible over the production process and/or the final products.

One of the key elements in the action research programs will be the choice of organizations to represent women and the style of interaction within and between organizations. Adequate information for these decisions will not always be available nor will it necessarily be consistent over large regions. Perhaps the most practical approach to this issue is to work toward the best unit and terms of organization through participatory research (Uphoff et al., 1979; Max-Neef, 1982; Lowdermilk and Laitos, 1981; Messerschmidt, 1983; Woods, 1983) in representative areas allowing women to identify, create or modify the most appropriate units of organization to represent their interests and to mediate their participation in agroforestry, social forestry and land tenure reform activities. It is here that the research frontier beckons loudest, and where women's future access to land, trees and their products will be determined.

REFERENCES

Afonja, S. 1981. Changing Modes of Production and the Sexual Division of labor among the Yoruba. *Signs*. 7 (2): 299-313.

Ahooja-Patel, K. 1982. Another Development with Women. *Development Dialogue* . (1-2): 17-28.

Arizpe, L. 1982. Women and Development in Latin America and the Caribbean: Lessons from the Seventies and Hopes for the Future. *Development Dialogue*. 1982. (1-2): 74-84.

Ayensu, E.S. 1983. The Healing Plants. *Unasylva*. 35 (140): 2-6.

Barnes, C. 1984. The Historical Context of the Fuelwood Situation in Kisii District, in C. Barnes, J. Ensminger and P. O'Keefe. (eds.) *Wood Energy and Households: Perspectives on Rural Kenya* . (Stockholm and Uppsala): The Beijer Institute and The Scandinavian Institute of African Studies: 61-78.

Berreman, G. 1984. From Gandhi to Chipko: The Movement to Save the Himalayas. *The Global Reporter* 1(4):16-18. Anthropology Resource Center.

Bhatt, G.S. 1980. Woman's Relation with Her Habitat in the Polyandrous Tracts of Uttar Pradesh Himalayas. *Proceedings of the Seminar on the Role of Women in Community Forestry* 4-9 Dec. 1980. Dehra Dun (India): Forest Research Institute and Colleges.

Black, N. and A.B. Cottrell (eds.) 1981. *Women and World Change: Equity Uses in Development.* Beverly Hills: Sage Publications.

Brain, J. L. 1976. Less than second class: Women in rural settlement schemes in Tanzania, in N.J. Hafkin and E.G. Bay (eds.) *Women in Africa* Stanford: Stanford University Press,

Buch, N. 1980. Role of Women in Nutrition Gardens in Social Forestry. *Proceedings of the Seminar on the Role of Women in Community Forestry* 4-9 Dec. 1980. Dehra Dun. (India): Forest Research Institute and Colleges.

Cernea, M.M. 1982. Tribal Peoples and Economic Development: Human Ecologic Considerations. Washington, D.C.: World Bank.

Cernea, Michael. 1985. Units of Social Organization Sustaining Alternative Forestry Development Strategies. Agriculture and Rural Development Department. Washington, D.C.: The World Bank.

Chakin, M. 1985. Nutrition surveillance and intervention programme, Mbita Division, South Nyanza, Kenya. Final Project Report UNICEF. Nairobi.

Chakravorty, S. 1980. Nutrition Gardens, Plantations of Quick Growing Fuel Trees - Role of Women. *Proceedings of the Seminar on the Role of Women in Community Forestry* 4-9 Dec. 1980. Dehra Dun. (India): Forest Research Institute and Colleges.

Chambers, Robert. 1983. *Rural Development: Putting the Last First.* London: Longmans.

Chaney, E. and M. Lewis. 1980. Planning a family food production program, some alternatives and suggestions for Plan Sierra. Unpublished report, San Jose de las Matas, Plan Sierra.

Christophersen, K. A. and F. Weber. 1981. Energy Potential from Native Brushland in Niger: The Economic Perspective. Report to USAID Office of Energy. (AID/USDA Bioenergy Team; PASA AG/STB - 4709-6-79).

Colfer, C.J.P. 1981. Women, men and time in the forests of East Kalimantan. *Borneo Research Bulletin* (September): 75-85.

Cultural Survival Quarterly. 1982. Deforestation, the Human Costs 6:2.

Cultural Survival Quarterly (Editorial) 1984a. Introduction 8:2.

Cultural Survival Quarterly (Editorial) 1984.b The Disinherited 8:2.

Dahlberg, E.M. ed. 1981. *Woman the Gatherer.* New Haven: Yale University Press.

Das Gupta, M. 1984. Microperspectives on the Slow Rate of Urbanization in India-Informal Security Systems and Population Retention in Rural India. Paper presented at the IUSSP Seminar on the Micro-Approaches to Demographic Research. Sept., 1984. Canberra.

Deere, Carmen Diana 1981. Changing social relations of production and Peruvian peasant women's work. *Latin America Perspectives* IV.

Deere, C.D. 1986. Guest lecture to the Conference of Gender Issues in Farming Systems Research and Extension. Feb. 26-March 1, 1986. University of Florida. Gainesville. Women in Agriculture Program.

Deere, Carmen Diana and Magdalena Leon de Leal. 1981. Peasant Production, Proletarianization and the Sexual Division of labor in the Andes. *Signs* 7 (2): 338-60.

Endicott, K.L. 1984. The Batek De of Malaysia. *Cultural Survival Quarterly* 8:2.

Etienne, M. and E. Leacock. 1980. "Introduction" in *Women and Colonization: Anthropological Perspectives.* New York: Prager Publishers.

FAO. 1979. The legal status of rural women: limitations on the economic participation of women in rural development. Home economics and social programmes service. Human resources, institutions and agrarian reform division. FAO Economic and Social Development Paper 9. FAO Rome.

Fleuret, A. 1979. Methods for Evaluation of the Role of Fruits and Wild Greens in Shambaa Diet: A Case Study. *Medical Anthropology.* (Spring).

Flores Paitan, S. 1985. *Informe Sobre el Papel de Umari en los sistemas de produccion agroforestal en fincas de la poblacion indigena y los mestizos en la zona de Iquitos* Manuscript. University of Iquitos.

Fortmann, L. 1981. "The Plight of the Invisible Farmer: The Effect of National Agricultural Policy on Women in Africa." In Roslyn Dauber and Melinda Cain (eds.). *Women and Technological*

Change in Developing Countries. AAAS Selected Symposium 53. Washington D.C.: AAAS.

Fortmann, L. 1985. Tree Tenure: An Analytical Framework for Agroforestry Projects. Background Paper for the International Consultative Workshop on Tenure Issues in Agroforestry. ICRAF and LTC/Ford Foundation. May.

Fortmann, L. and D. Rocheleau. 1985. Women and Agroforestry: four myths and three case studies. *Agroforestry Systems* 2:4.

Hardin, G. 1968. The Tragedy of the Commons. *Science* . 162: 1243-1248.

Haugerud, A. 1983. The Consequences of Land Tenure Reform Among Smallholders in the Kenya Highlands. *Rural Africana*. 15/16: 65-90.

Hoskins, M. 1979. Women in Forestry for Local Community Development: A Programming Guide. Office of Women in Development AID/Otr-147-79-83. Washington D.C, 58.

Hoskins, M. 1983. Rural Women, Forest Outputs and Forestry Projects. FAO. Rome.

Huxley, P.A., D. Rocheleau and P.J. Wood. 1985. Farming Systems and Agroforestry Research in Northern Zambia. Phase I report - Diagnosis of Land Use Problems and Research Indications. Unpublished Report. ICRAF. Nairobi.

ICES. (International Centre for Ethnic Studies). 1985. Beyond cultural diversity, women face some problems. IFDA Dossier 46.pp. 27-29.

Jain, Devaki. 1984. In Poor Families Women's Income is the Lifeline. *Ceres* 17(4): 35-38.

Jain, Shobita 1984. Standing up for the trees: Women's role in the Chipko Movement. *Unasylva*. Vol. 36. No. 146.

Lee, R.B. 1979. *The Kung! San: Men, Women, and Work in a Foraging Society*. New York: Cambridge University Press.

Livingstone, R. and R. Zamora. 1983. Medicine trees of the tropics. *Unasylva* 35 (140): 7-10.

Lowdermilk, M. and W.R. Laitos. 1981. Towards a participatory strategy for integrated rural development. *Rural Sociology* 46 (4): 688-702.

March, K. and R. Taqqu. 1982. Women's informal associations and the organizational capacity for development. Ithaca: Cornell University Rural Development Committee.

Max-Neef, A. Manfred 1982. From the Outside Looking In: Experiences in 'Barefoot Economics'. Dag Hammarskjold Foundation. Uppsala.

Mayer, A.E. 1984. Law and Women in the Middle East. *Cultural Survival Quarterly*. 8:2.

Mazumdar, Vina. 1982. Another Development with Women: A View from Asia. *Development Dialogue* 1982. (1-2): 65-73.

Mazumdar, Vina. 1984. With Progress for Some: Women and Development in India. The IDRC Reports 13(2): 4-6.

Messerschmidt, A. Donald. 1983. "Gaun Sallah: The Village Dialogue Method for Local Planning in Nepal." Min. Forest and Soil Conservation, RCUP. Kathmandu, Nepal.

Mickelwait, D.R., M.A. Riegelman, and C.F. Sweet. 1976. *Women in Rural Development: A Survey of the Roles of Women in Ghana, Lesotho, Kenya, Nigeria, Bolivia, Paraguay and Peru.* Boulder: Westview Press.

Mishra, A. and S. Tripathi. 1978. *Chipko Movement, Uttarakhand Women's Bid to Save Forest Wealth.* New Delhi: People's Action.

Muntemba, Shimwaayi. 1982. Women as Food Producers and Suppliers in the Twentieth Century. The Case of Zambia. *Development Dialogue* 1982. (1-3): 29-50. Uppsala: Dag HammarsKjold Foundation.

Niñez, A. 1985. Introduction: household gardens and small-scale food production. *Food and Nutrition Bulletin* 7 (3): 1-5.

Nowak, B.S. 1984. Can the Partnership Last? *Cultural Survival Quarterly* 8:2.

Obi, S.N.C. 1983. *The Ibo law of property.* London: Butterworths.

Okoth-Ogendo, 1985. Commentary and discussion. International Consultation Workshop on Tenure and Agroforestry. ICRAF, Nairobi and LTC, Madison.

Onger-Hosgor, Tulin. 1983. The Effects on Women of Land Tenure Changes and Agrarian Reform. Expert Consultation on Women in Food Production. Rome, Italy 7-14 Dec. 1983. Rome: FAO, (ESH:WIFGP/83/12).

Pala-Okeyo, A. 1980. Daughters of the lakes and rivers: colonization and the land rights of Luo women. In: M. Etienne and E. Leacock (eds.) *Women and Colonization: Anthropological Perspectives:* N.Y.: Prager Publishers 186-213

Palmer, Ingrid. 1978. Integration of Women in Agrarian Reform and Rural Development: An Analysis of the Situation in Asia and the Far East Region. Unpublished internal document. FAO, Rome.

Raintree, J.B. and K. Warner. 1985. Agroforestry Pathways for the Integral Development of Shifting Cultivation. IX World Forestry Congress. Mexico City. July 1-10, 1985.

Rocheleau, D. 1984. An ecological analysis of soil and water conservation in hillslope farming systems: Plan Sierra, Dominican Republic. Unpublished Ph.D. dissertation. University of Florida, Dept. of Geography, Gainesville.

Rocheleau, D. 1985. Criteria for re-appraisal and re-design: intra-household and between-household aspects of FSRE in three Kenyan agroforestry projects. In C. Flora and Tomacek (eds.) *Selected Proceedings;* Annual Symposium on Farming Systems Research and Extension, Oct. 7-18, 1984. Kansas State University, Manhattan, Kansas.

Rocheleau, D., M. Mutiso, B. Muchiri Wanjohi, I. Opala, E. Achola, P. Khasiala, P. Mandu and G.A. Wajuang'a. 1986. Mid-Term Report on women's use of off-farm lands: agroforestry potetnials. Project report to the Ford Foundation. ICRAF. Nairobi.

Roy, S. 1980. Case Study on Fuelwood Collection and Problems of Rural Women. Proceedings of the Seminar on the Role of Women in Community Forestry 4-9 Dec. 1980. Forest Research Institute and Colleges. Dehra Dun. (India).

Surin, V. and T. Bhaduri. 1980. Forest Produce and Forest Dwellers. Proceedings of the Seminar on the Role of Women in Community Forestry, 4-9 Dec. 1980. Dehra Dun. (India): Forest Research Institute and Colleges. .

Tanner, R. 1960. Land Rights on the Tanganyikan Coast. *African Studies.* XIX:14-25.

Unasylva. 1984. Effects of scarcity upon women. *Unasylva* 36 (146).

Uphoff, Norman T., John M. Cohen, and Arthur A. Goldsmith. 1979. "Feasibility and Application of Rural Development Participation: A State-of-the-Art Paper." Ithaca: Rural Development Committee, Cornell University.

Wachira, K., D. Rocheleau, B. Muciri Wanjohi, I. Opala, E. Achola, P. Khasiala, P. Mandu, G.A. Wajuang'a and M. Mutiso Akatsa. 1987 Use of off-farm and boundary lands by women: agroforestry potentials. Final Report to Ford Foundation. ICRAF. Nairobi.

Weber, F. and M. Hoskins. 1983. *Agroforestry in the Sahel.* Department of Sociology, Virginia Polytechnic Institute and State University. Blacksburg, Virginia. 102 p.

Whalen, Irene. 1984. Land Tenure and Technological Innovations in the Ethiopian Highlands. Paper prepared for the ARPT/CIMMYT Workshop on the Role of Anthropologist and Rural Sociologist in Farming Systems Research and Extension. 27-29 Nov. 1984. Lusaka.

Wiff, Mercedes. 1984. Honduras: Women make a start in agroforestry. *Unasylva* 36, (146).

Wijngaarden, J. van. 1983. Agricultural self help groups and their potential role in agroforestry. Draft Report. Agricultural University, Wageningen.

Williams, Paula. 1984. "La periode de soudure." Report on human use of forest resources in Burkina-Faso. Institute of Current World Affairs. Hanover, N.H.

Williams, P.J. 1985. Women and Forestry. Invited Special Paper. Theme III. 6.1. Ninth World Forestry Congress. Mexico City, 1-10 July 1985. Rome : FAO.

Woods, Bernard. 1983. Altering the Present Paradigm: A Different Path to Sustainable Development in the Rural Sector. Unpublished working paper. Washington D.C.: The World Bank.

8

The State and the Forest

The state is an actor that has appeared frequently in these readings. After all, the state creates and protects tenure in land and trees through its national legal system and, through its various agencies, promotes tree planting and forest protection. Forest protection and management by the state is the focus of this chapter.

A recurrent theme of colonial forestry, especially salient in the British experience in south Asia and Africa, is that forests must be shielded from growing demographic pressure. The major tenurial initiative of this period was the establishment of forest reserves, usually taking forests from under traditional community control and placing them under the protection of the state.

Troup, writing in 1940, presents a classic statement of British forestry practice. He compares the European and developing country experiences with tenure arrangements for the preservation and sound management of forests. He argues that private and communal tenure of forests pose a serious danger to preservation and sound exploitation of forests, and that the state must take over control of the forests and carefully regulate their use. In the colonial context, where forests had usually been the subject of the territorial claims of traditional communities and were often used unintensively for hunting and gathering, this policy usually proved relatively easy for colonial governments to implement. The forests became resources to be protected by the state against their former users.

In India, this process has been chronicled by Kaul (1979) and Gupta (1982). The process of reservation has taken place more recently in some Asian countries, in this generation in Nepal. It has generated insecurity on the part of traditional users and—because the state has not been able to effectively police reserves—led to increasingly abusive exploitation by users who no longer see themselves as having a long-term interest in the resource (Anon., 1982; Fleming, 1983). This process of reservation produced violent peasant reactions in some areas. *Guha* (1985) describes the opposition and incendarism which forest reservation provoked among peasants in Kumaun in the Central Himalaya at the turn of the century, initiating a tradition of protest of exploitation of forests by outside agencies which endures today in the Chipko movement.

Timber was in many colonies an important export, and colonial forest departments became involved in the creation of new, mono-specific forests for harvesting. Under a system developed in Burma and known as *taungya*, limited numbers of traditional cultivators were allocated areas to be reforested, where they could provide labor for tree-planting and at the same time cultivate their subsistence crops among the young trees. Once the canopy closed, they would move on to another area to be reforested. *Goswami* provides a concise history of the development of *taungya* as a tenurial instrument for economical afforestation, cataloging both its positive and negative aspects. Providing cultivators access to land scheduled for afforestation, *taungya* initially provided only the most temporary tenure in a particular piece of land, and access to land for only so long as there was land to be reforested. Goswami notes a recent trend to provide cultivators with more secure tenure within the forests. He suggests that *taungya* is a new name for an older practice of traditional mixed farming systems involving tree crops. This requires scrutiny: traditional agro-forestry provided sustainable and more permanent opportunities.

King examines the legal options for tenure in state forests under *taungya*, which he characterizes as "agro-silviculture." Like Troup, he operates from a premise of state-owned or at least state-managed forests, and sees the best legal basis for *taungya* as essentially contractual, with the state providing access to land in the forest under a precisely delineated set of conditions. Based on a review of such contractual arrangements, he provides a valuable catalogue of the potential rights and duties of cultivators under such arrangements. He does not, however, note what is perhaps the most critical contractual obligation of the cultivator under most *taungya*: the obligation to move on.

As population pressure around forest reserves has increased, there has been a growing interest in ways to provide livelihoods for some citizens in the reserves, consistent with sound management. But several commentators have noted the way in which lack of security undermines the operation of *taungya*. Boonkird (1978 and 1984) urges the need for more stability and security of tenure for *taungya* practitioners in Thailand. Soerianegara (1982) notes that in Indonesia there is a tendency for those employed in the *taungya* system to damage the young trees, in order to prolong their access to the forest land for their crops.

Taungya has spread to Africa, and the remarks of commentators there echo these concerns. In Nigeria its introduction has met with considerable success (Adeyoju, 1975), and Adeyoju (1981) has examined its legal basis. Ball and Umeh (1981) and Enabor *et al.* (1981) review recent developments in *taungya* in Nigeria and note that the planting of perennials such as cocoa and rubber by forest laborers had been proscribed but urge that this must be accepted, and is in fact increasingly accepted. The transfer of the system to Africa has not always been successful. In Togo the system was introduced in 1954 for tea cultivation, but the hostility of traditional users resulted in massive and uncontrolled invasions of the forest by the former custodians. An attempt to reintroduce the system in 1972 had to be abandoned because crop rotation was forbidden and the two-year turnover time did not allow sufficient labor input to maintain the plantation (Nadjombe, 1981).

Exploitation of state forest resources is often arranged through the "concession," a temporary and conditional form of tenure employed by the state to permit exploitation of the forest resource by private timber companies. *Colfer* examines the situation of a community of Kenyah (Dayak) settlers in East Kalimantan, Indonesian Borneo, located within the forest concession of an American-based multinational, and in particular the impact of the advent of the chainsaw on forest use. Contracts between the government and the concessionaire specify that the local people are free to utilize the forests in their "customary manner," but obviously something quite different is happening. *Yauieb* (1979) examines exploitation of forests by concessionaires in Papua New Guinea in a different tenure context, where traditional landholding groups have recognized rights in the forests. In New Zealand, traditional landowning communities have been incorporated to allow them to contract with concessionaires (Williams, 1979).

Relations between concessionaires and traditional users are sometimes highly conflictual. In northern Thailand, large areas are being reforested on contract by concessionaires, irrespective of swidden use. This has already led to armed confrontations between concessionaires from the lowlands seeking to complete their contracts and highland villagers who receive no benefit from the land, which will henceforth be protected forest (Kunstadter, 1980).

In the case of natural forest reserves, which sometimes have limited commercial potential because of their mix of species, policies of exclusion of traditional users have been increasingly questioned. At certain population levels and ecologically sound use levels, these forests provided a livelihood or part of the livelihood for traditional cultivators and herders. Why can they not continue to do so? Often the question is not even asked by foresters. Fortmann and Fairfax (1987:7) have recently argued that American forestry professionals (and presumably those whom they train) bring to their work in the Third World a strong predilection for large-scale comprehensive government resource management, a progressive era tenet that is not necessarily appropriate in very different conditions.

In this vein, *Grandstaff* examines the land tenure and land use practices of Thai and other ethnic swidden cultivators in Northern Thailand, whose incursions into forested areas have been a source of growing concern to government and other observers. He makes an important distinction between "established" and "pioneer" swiddeners in terms of their impact on the environment. He argues for the establishment of systems of sustainable, integral swidden cultivation, and for the granting of tenure over discrete territories including forest to villages as a key element in this process. The proposal represents a new and attractive angle of approach, which argues not for state protection but for providing local communities with secure tenure in forest resources and therefore the incentive to manage them soundly.

The advocates of such an approach sometimes characterize it as "integral" rather than "partial" *taungya*, the former being described as "a more complete and culturally integrated approach to rural development; not merely the temporary use of a piece of land and a poverty level wage of labor, but a chance to participate equitably in a diversified and sustainable agroforestry economy" (Raintree, 1985:28). The distinction was developed by Conklin (1957). Nations and Nigh (1978) have argued for a Lacandon Maya alternative to current patterns of over-exploitation in Central America. For Borneo, Weinstock (1983) has stressed the need to maintain the traditional use and tenure patterns and ecological balance in the rain forest, and Dove (1986) has recently produced a searching analysis of the mis-perception by development officials of the interests at stake in traditional use systems in the Riam Kanan valley in South Kalimantan. Fernandez and Sharad (1983) and Commander (1986) have called for a new forestry policy for India based on a more integral approach to forestry planning.

Local control over resources is part of the message of these authors, and it should be noted that such control, in order to be effective, need not be traditional. Protection restrictions have been successful in the case of the Maria Tecum Forest in Guatemala because it is the property of the local municipality, governed by a respected council of elders (Budowski, 1982). In the Ikalahan area of Luzon, the Philippine Bureau of Forest Development in 1974 "released" 14,730 hectares on a 25-year lease to the Kalahan Educational Foundation, to be managed under an agroforestry plan for the watershed by a local board of trustees. An evaluation conducted in the seventh year of the project indicated substantial acceptance of some elements in the land use control plan and a marked decline in tenure insecurity (Aguilar, 1982).

Grasmick proposes a legal strategy for the forest-dwelling South American Indians. The threat to the forests of the Amazon Basin clearly comes not from the traditional users, the Indians, but from land-hungry peasant and commercial ranching enterprises whose assault on the forest the state has failed to control and has frequently actively promoted. For Grasmick, the granting of legal tenure to the Indians is a precondition for their defense of their forests. He reminds us that for many minority groups in developing countries the protection of their forest environment is a matter of cultural survival.

Forestry law is the other legal front in this struggle for control of resources. Schmithü sen (1981) provides a comprehensive review of recent trends in forestry legislation in developing countries, but there are relatively few serious studies of the interaction between this statutory law and customary use rights. An exception is Snyder (1970), a study of *"l'acculturation juridique du droit forestier"* in Senegal and Ivory Coast.

Which is the more promising tool for preservation of forests: forestry laws which state prohibitions whose enforcement depends on weak state machinery, or property rights for users which create incentives to conserve the resource?

REFERENCES

Adeyoju, S. K. 1975. "Where Forest Resources Improve Agriculture." *Unasylva* 27 (110): 27-29.

Adeyoju, S. Kolade. 1981. "Agro-Forestry and Forest Laws, Policies and Customs," In L.H. MacDonald (ed.), *Agro-Forestry in the African Humid Tropics*. Tokyo: United Nations University, pp. 17-21.

Aguilar, F.V. 1982. *The Kalahan Educational Foundation: A Case Study of Social Forestry in the Upland Philippines*. Quezon City: Institute of Philippine Culture, Ateneo de Manila University.

Ball, J.B. and L.T. Umeh. 1981. "Development Trends in Taungya Systems of the Moist Lowland Forest of Nigeria Between 1975 and 1980," In L.H. MacDonald (ed.), *Agro-Forestry in the African Humid Tropics*. Tokyo: United Nations University, pp. 72-78.

Boonkird, Sa-Ard. 1978. "Taungya System: Its Applications, Ways and Means of Improvements in Thailand," in *Proceedings, VII World Forestry Congress*. Jakarta: IUFRO.

Boonkird, S.A., E.C.M. Fernandes and P.K.R. Nair. 1984. "Forest Villages: An Agro-forestry Approach to Rehabilitating Forest Land Degraded by Shifting Cultivation in Thailand." *Agroforestry Systems* 2: 87-102.

Budowski, Gerardo. 1982. "The Socio-Economic Effects of Forest Management on the Lives of People Living in the Area: The Case of Central America and Some Carribean Countries," In E.G. Hallsworth (ed.), *Socio-Economic Effects and Constraints in Tropical Forest Management.* Chinchester: Wiley, pp. 87-102.

Commander, Simon. 1986. "Managing Indian Forests: A Case for the Reform of Property Rights." Network Paper 3b, ODI Social Forestry Network. London: ODI.

"Community Forestry Project in Nepal." 1982. *Agricultural Information Development Bulletin* 4: 2-9, 38.

Conklin, H.C. 1957. *Hanunóo Agriculture.* FAO Forestry Development Paper No. 12. Rome: FAO.

Dove, Michael R. 1986. "Peasant Versus Government Perception and Use of the Environment: A Case Study of Banjarese Ecology and River Basin Development in South Kalimantan." *Journal of Southeast Asian Studies* 17: 113-136.

Enabor, E.E., J.A. Okajie and I. Verinumbe. 1981. "Taungya Systems: Socio-Economic Prospects and Limitations," In L.H.   MacDonald (ed.), *Agro-forestry in the African Humid Tropics.* Tokyo: United Nations University, pp. 59-64.

Fernandez, Walter. 1983. *Towards a New Forest Policy: Peoples' Rights and Environmental Needs.* New Delhi: Indian Social Institute.

Fleming, William A. 1983. "Phewa Tal Catchment Management Program: Benefits and Costs of Forestry and Soil Conservation in Negal," In Lawrence S. Hamilton (ed.), *Forest and Watershed Development and Conservation in Asia and the Pacific.* Boulder, CO: Westview Press, pp. 217-288.

Fortmann, Louise P. and Sally K. Fairfax. 1987. "American Forestry Professionalism in the Third World: Some Preliminary Observations." Berkeley.

Fortmann, Louise and James Riddell. 1985. *Trees and Tenure: An Annotated Bibliography for Agroforesters and Others.* Madison and Nairobi: Land Tenure Center and Interrnational Council for Research in Agroforestry.

Guha, Ramachandra. 1985. "Forestry and Social Protest in British Kumaun, c. 1893-1921," In Ranajit Guha, (ed.), *Subaltern Studies* IV. Delhi: Oxford University Press, pp. 54-100.

Gupta, P.N. 1982. "The Effects of Government Policy on Forest Management in the Himalayan and Siwalik Region of Uttar Pradesh, India." In E.G. Hallsworth (ed.), *Socio-Economic Effects and Constraints in Tropical Forest Management.* Chichester: Wiley, pp 65-73.

Kaul, S.K. 1979. "Human Aspects of Forest Development," at pp. 152-170 of Krishna Murti Gupta and Desh Bandu (eds.), *Man and Forest: A New Dimension in the Himalaya.* New Delhi: Today and Tomorrow Printers and Publishers, pp. 152-170.

Kunstadter, Peter. 1980. "Implications of Socio-Economic, Demographic and Cultural Changes for Regional Development in Northern Thailand," In Jack D. Ives, Somga Sabhasri and Pisit Vorauri (eds.), *Conservation and Development in Northern Thailand.* Tokyo: United Nations University.

Nadjombe, O. 1981. "*Taungya* Practices in Togo," In L.H. MacDonald (ed.), *Agro-Forestry in the African Humid Tropics.* Tokyo: United Nations University, pp. 70-71.

Nations, J.B. and R.B. Nigh. 1978. "Cattle, Cash, Food and Forest: The Destruction of the American Tropics and the Lacandon Maya Alternative." *Culture and Agriculture* 6: 1-5.

Raintree, John. 1985. "Agroforestry, Tropical Land Use and Tenure." Background paper for International Workshop on Tenure Issues in Agroforestry, Nairobi, 27-31 May.

Schmithüsen, Franz. 1981. "Recent Trends in Forest Legislation in Developing Countries," In *Proceedings of XVII International Union of Forest Research Organizations World Congress, Kyoto, 1981.* Kyoto: Japanese IUFRO Congress Committee, pp. 317-328.

Snyder, Francis G. 1970. "L'acculturation juridique du droit forestier au Sénégal et en Côte d 'Ivoire." *African Law Studies* 3 : 53-76.

Soerianegara, Ishemat. 1982. "Socio-Economic Aspects of Forest Resource Management in Indonesia," In E.G. Hallsworth (ed.), *Socio-Economic Effects and Constraints in Tropical Forest Management.* Chinchester: Wiley, pp. 73-86.

Weinstock, Joseph A. 1983. "Rattan: Ecological Balance in the Borneo Rainforest Swidden." *Economic Botany* 37: 58-68.

Williams, E.W. 1979. "Afforestation on Maori Lands in New Zealand." In K.R. Shepard and H.V. Richter (eds.), *Forestry in National Development: Production Systems, Conservation, Foreign Trade and Aid.* Canberra: Development Studies Centre, Australian National University, pp. 13-20.

The Editors

Forest Ownership: State Control and Assistance

R.S. Troup

> *British colonial forestry's basic premise was that forest reserves were national resources to be protected from their former users by the state. Troup provides some reflections o n comparative experience circa 1940 that tend in that direction. Where forests are primarily for local supply of wood, he is more open to management by "native" communities.—The Editors*

I.   Forest Ownership: General Considerations

Classification. So far as ownership is concerned, it is usual to classify forests into three categories; (1) State (or Crown); forests; (2) communal forests (belonging to communes, municipalities, and other corporate bodies); and (3) private forests. Forests belonging to native communities and tribal authorities are classed as communal. . . .

. . . It is interesting to note that in East Africa the forests are predominantly State-owned, whereas in West Africa they are mainly in native ownership. In Kenya and Northern Rhodesia the considerable percentages of communal forest are due to the existence of tracts of forest in the native reserves. In Nyasaland, Tanganyika, and Uganda, where the system of native reserves is not in operation, the formation of forest reserves under Native Authorities should result in an eventual increase in the percentage of forest reserves under Native Authorities classed as communal.

Outside Africa, the only territories possessing any large percentage of non-State forest are British Honduras and Mauritius. In the former this is due to the alienation, in the earlier years of the Colony, of

Excerpted from R.S. Troup, *Colonial Forest Administration* (Oxford: Oxford University Press, 1940). Reprinted with the permission of the publisher.

extensive areas of forest to persons interested in the exploitation of logwood and mahogany. In Mauritius large areas of forest were alienated during the French occupation, though some of these alienated lands have been re-purchased since the middle of last century, chiefly in the interests of water-supplies. Further information on the question of forest ownership in different Dependencies will be found in Part II.

II. Merits of different Forms of Ownership.

If State ownership of forests is considered necessary in European countries where the importance of forestry is well understood, it is even more necessary in the Colonies, where the inhabitants have as yet developed little or no 'forest sense,' and are often antagonistic to forest preservation in any form.

The lesson of British Honduras should be a warning against the ill-considered alienation of State forest land. In the earlier years of the colony nearly half the forests of the country, including all the richer and more accessible mahogany areas, were alienated without any conditions as to conservative working, with the result that extensive areas have been depleted to the extent of exhaustion. To a country where prosperity in the past has been based on its forest wealth, and whose exports to the extent of over 80 percent in value have consisted of forest products, this is a matter for very serious concern, as a recent examination of the finances of the Colony has revealed. Had the proper action been taken at the beginning, namely to retain the forest in State ownership and place them under systematic management, they would by now have become an asset of immense and permanent value, as are the teak forests of Burma, which were saved from a similar fate in the middle of last century through the far-sighted policy of Lord Dalhousie, Viceroy of India.

It may be laid down as a maxim that State ownership should form the basis of forest administration in the Colonies. Where administrative conditions prevent this, as in West Africa then some procedure which will guarantee the forests the same permanency as State-owned forests is essential. In West Africa much has been done, by education and persuasion, to secure the reservation of forest areas. Under the forest laws the reserved forests, although native-owned, are given a status equivalent to that of Government forest reserves. The requirement as to reasonable permanency is thus secured, and provided the trained personnel is maintained at sufficient strength to ensure the proper protection and management of the forests, their future should be safeguarded. It should be noted, however, that the formation of forest reserves in West Africa is a more difficult and complicated matter than it is on Crown or Government lands in East Africa.

Although State ownership should, where possible, form the basis of forest administration in the Colonies, this does not rule out the question of maintaining, under suitable conditions, a certain area of forest of the 'communal' type as a useful supplementary measure. . . .

In Nyasaland, Tanganyika, and Uganda, certain areas have been or are being set aside as Native Authority forests to provide local supplies of fuel, other produce, and to educate the native Authorities in the management of forest. Where natural tree-growth is insufficient, afforestation is undertaken in these areas. In Kenya and Northern Rhodesia the forests in native reserves are being maintained for the benefit of the natives and subjected to special rules for their protection. In one native reserve in Kenya the Forest Department has undertaken to plant a considerable area, Government bearing the cost and receiving all the revenues from the plantations until the cost has been covered.

In Nigeria the Forestry Ordinance, 1937, provides for the formation of Native Administration forest reserves, the protection and management of which is undertaken by the Native Authority constituting them, subject to the supervision and control of the Resident acting on the advice of the Chief Conservator of Forests. Fees received in respect of Native Administration forest reserves are paid into the Native Administration treasury.

In Africa the question of how far forests should be handed over to Native Authorities for management is one requiring very careful consideration. At first sight the idea of applying the principles of indirect rule to forestry has its attractions. But unless this is done with adequate safeguards it must inevitably fail. Experience in civilized countries has amply demonstrated that without State control there is no assurance that private and communal forests will not sooner or later become devastated. If forests are thus endangered in countries where their value is well understood, they are hardly likely to meet with a better fate in countries where forest destruction is an established custom.

So far as it is possible to lay down any general policy in this matter, it may be said that forests required for the benefit of the country as a whole—whether for purposes of protection or of production—should be retained under the direct administration and management of Government, while those maintained solely for the local supply of produce to native communities might be handed over to Native Authorities, but with adequate safeguards. Generally speaking, the latter would be forests of comparatively small area and no great timber value. The mere handing over of such areas, however, is not likely to ensure the preservation and good management of the forests, as the rapid extermination of native forests in Uganda has shown. The success of any scheme of native forest management is likely to depend on a sufficient degree of control, a considerable amount of direct assistance in technical matters, and a staff of good native foresters. If it is true that in Nigeria the large timber-producing forests of Benin have been handed over to the Native Administration forest reserves, and the technical assistance provided by the Forest Department, such an arrangement could not be expected to prove satisfactory.

While the development of native forestry on proper lines in Africa has much to commend it, and has already made a promising start, it is interesting to note that in Asia attempts to create village forests have not always been attended with success. In Ceylon the area of village forest constituted under Forest Ordinance, 1907, is as yet small, amounting to only 0.2 per cent of the total forest area of the country. The Burma Forest Act of 1881 provided for the constitution of village forests, but this was omitted in the revised Forest act of 1902, since it was found to be unnecessary, no village forests having been formed. In Assam the policy of forming village forests under the Indian Forest Act, 1927, has been abandoned, and those created have been cancelled. Large areas of village (*panchayat*) forest have been set aside in the Madras Presidency and the Kumaun Himalaya, but their management is still in an experimental stage: more recently steps have been taken to form village forests in Punjab, and the results may be awaited with interest.

Forestry and Social Protest in British Kumaun, c. 1893-1921

Ramachandra Guha

The reservation of forests as national resources and the exclusion of traditional users has sometimes produced violent reactions. Guha chronicles peasant resistance to the reservation of forests for commercial exploitation in India's Central Himalaya at the turn of the century. The forests have not been returned to local communities, but neither have they abandoned their protest.—The Editors

This essay examines the trajectory of social protest in Kumaun during the early decades of this century. Since 1973, Kumaun has been the epicentre of the Chipko Andolan, possibly the best known contemporary movement against the exploitation of forests by outside agency.[10] Nonetheless, Chipko is only one—though undoubtedly the most organized—in a series of protests against commercial forestry dating from the earliest days of state intervention. While the absence of popular protest in the first century of British rule had given rise to the stereotype of the 'simple and law abiding hillman,'[11] the reservation of the Kumaun forests in 1911-17 'met with violent and sustained opposition,'[12] culminating in 1921 when within the space of a few months the administration was paralyzed, first by a strike against *utar* (statutory labour) and then through a systematic campaign in which the Himalayan pine forests 'were swept by incendiary fires almost from end to end.'[13] . .

Excerpted from Ramachandra Guha, "Forestry and Social Protest in British Kumaun, c. 1893-1921," in Ranajit Guha (ed.), *Subaltern Studies* IX (Delhi: Oxford University Press, 1985). Reprinted with the permission of the publisher.

II. Kumaun: Economy and Society[21] ...

The Central Himalaya is composed of two distinct ecological zones: the monsoon-affected areas at middle and low altitudes, and the high valleys of the north, inhabited until 1962 by the Bhotiya herdsmen who had been engaged in trade with Tibet for centuries. Along the river valleys cultivation was carried out, limited only by the steepness of land and more frequently by the difficulty of irrigation. Two and sometimes three harvests were possible throughout the last century, wheat, rice, and millets being the chief cereals grown. The system of tillage and methods of crop rotation bore the mark of the hillmen's natural environment. With production oriented towards subsistence needs, which were comfortably met, there remained a surplus of grain for export to Tibet and southwards to the plains. Usually having six months stock of grain at hand, and with their diet supplemented by fish, fruit, vegetable, and animal flesh, the hill cultivators were described by Henry Ramsay, commissioner from 1856-84, as 'probably better off than any peasantry in India.'[25]

The absence of sharp inequalities in land ownership among the cultivating proprietors who formed the bulk of the population was the basis of solidarity within the village community. Single-caste villages were not uncommon, and in these the village *panchayat*—an institution quite different from the caste *panchayat* of the plains— dealt with social disputes, arrangements for festivals, etc., with every adult member having a voice in its affairs. The establishment of British rule notwithstanding, *panchayats* frequently continued to deal internally with matters technically under the jurisdiction of civil and criminal courts. [26]

The hill land-tenure system inherited by the British differed no less strikingly from that in the plains. The first commissioner, G.W. Traill, observed that at least three-fourths of the villages were *hissedari*, i.e. wholly cultivated by the actual proprietors of the land; the revenue demand on them was restricted to their respective shares of the village assessment. The remaining villages were divided into (i) those in which the right of cultivation remained with the original occupants (called *khaikhar*), and (ii) a handful of villages owned by a single individual, where again individual tenants (called *khurnee*), were able to wrest easy terms owing to the favourable land-man ratio.[27] As even the most important landowners depended not on any legal right but on the actual influence they exercised over village communities, there was not one estate which could be termed 'pure *zamindari*'. Government revenue and certain customary fees were collected by the *elected* village *padhan* (headman), who reported in turn to a higher revenue official (called the *patwari*, in charge of a *patti* or group of villages) entrusted with police duties and the responsibility of collecting statutory labour for public works.[28] While over time much of the class of *khurnee* merged with that of *khaikhar*, the latter differed from the *hissedar* only in that he could not transfer land and had to pay a fixed sum and *malikhana* to the proprietor—this sum representing the conversion into cash of all previous-levied cesses and perquisites. But by the end of the century, fully nine-tenths of all hillmen were estimated to be *hissedars*, cultivating proprietors with full ownership rights.[29].

III. The Development of Organized Forestry in Kumaun

Stable forest cover on any terrain is established through the process of ecological succession.[39] This succession can generally be divided into three stages: (i) the initial stage, in which certain species of trees, usually with small or light seeds, take possession of newly exposed ground; (ii) the transitional stages, in which changes take place on ground already clothed with some vegetative cover; (iii) the climactic stage, which represents the farthest advance towards a hygrophilous (i.e. adapted to plentiful water supply) type of vegetation which the locality is capable of supporting. While it could be said that in the Himalaya the oaks and other broad-leaved species represent state (iii) and the conifers stage (ii), in the days before forest management mixed forests were the norm. In general, the more favourable the locality is for vegetation the greater the number of species struggling for existence in it.

Two points may be noted. First, while the oaks (and other broad-leaved species) are more valuable for hill agriculture on both ecological and economic grounds, the conifers have had, since the inception of 'scientific' management, a variety of commercial uses. Second, while 'progressive' succession—from stage (i) to (ii) to (iii)—occurs in nature, 'retrogressive' succession—from (iii) to (ii) to (i)—can be caused by man, either accidentally or deliberately. Foresters are cautioned that in many cases 'the natural trend of this succession may be diametrically opposed to what is desirable from an economic point of view'.[40]

The importance of forests in hill life gave rise to a 'natural system of conservancy' that took different forms. Through religion, folklore and tradition the Khasa communities drew a protective ring around the forests. Often, hill tops were dedicated to local deities and the trees around the summit and on the slopes were preserved. Many wooded areas were not of spontaneous growth and bore marks of both plantation and preservation.[41] Particularly in eastern Kumaun, and around temples, deodar plantations had become naturalized. Temple groves of deodar varied in extent from a few trees to woods of several hundred acres.[42] As late as 1953 it was reported that the finest strands of deodar, found near temples, were venerated and protected from injury.[43] An officer newly posted to the hills in the 1920s was struck by the way communal action continued to survive in the considerable areas which served as village grazing ground, and by the fact that fuel and fodder reserves were walled in and well looked after.[44] Traditionally, many villages had fuel reserves even on *gaon sanjait* (common) land measured by the government, which the villagers cut over in regular rotation by common consent. *Chaundkot pargana* in Garhwal was singled out for its forests within village boundaries, called *'banis'*, where branches and trees were only cut at specified times and with the permission of the entire village community.[45] Cooperation of high order was also manifest in the settlement of 1823. Within these boundaries the inhabitants of each village exercised various proprietary and other rights of user. In some areas a group of villages had joint rights of grazing and fuel, secured by long usage and custom.[46]

Since an analagous situation existed in many other forest areas, the inception of commercial forestry disrupted existing patterns of resource utilization.[47] The landmark in the history of Indian forestry is undoubtedly the building of the railway network. The large-scale destruction of accessible forests in the early years of railway expansion led to the hasty creation of a forest department, set up with the help of German experts in 1864. The first task before the new department was to identify the sources of supply of strong and durable timbers—such as sal, teak and deodar—which could be used as railway sleepers. As sal and teak were very heavily worked out,[48] search parties were sent to explore the deodar forests of the Sutlej and Jamuna valleys.[49] Intensive felling in these forests—1.3 million deodar sleepers were exported from the Jamuna valley between 1865 and 1878—forced the government to rely on the import of wood from Europe. But with emphasis placed on substituting indigenous sleepers for imported ones, particularly in the inland districts of North India, the department began to consider the utilization of the Himalayan pines if they responded adequately to antiseptic treatment.[50]

Successful forest administration required checking the deforestation of the past decades,[51] and for this the assertion of state monopoly right was considered essential. A prolonged debate within the colonial bureaucracy on whether to treat the customary use of the forest as based on 'right' or on 'privilege' was settled by the selective use of precedent and the principle that 'the right of conquest is the strongest of all rights—it is a right against which there is no appeal.'[52] Since an initial attempt at asserting state monopoly through the Forest Act of 1865 was found wanting, a comprehensive all-India act was drafted thirteen years later. This act provided for the constitution of 'reserved' (i.e. closed) forests, divested of existing rights of user to enable sustained timber production. The 1878 Act provided for an elaborate procedure of forest settlement to deal with all claims of user, which, if upheld, could be transferred to a second class of forest designated as 'protected.'[53] While the burden of proof to establish 'legally established rights' was on the people, the state could grant both 'non-established rights' and 'terminable concessions' at its discretion.[54]

The systematic management of the Kumaun hill forests commenced with the constitution of small blocks of reserved forests to furnish a permanent supply of fuel and timber to the administrative centres of Naini Tal and Almora and the cantonment town of Ranikhet.[55] A survey was commissioned to report on the detailed composition of the hill forests, particularly those within 'reasonable distance' of land and water, and select sites for roads and saw mills.[56] This was followed in 1893 by the declaration of all unmeasured land in the Kumaun division as 'district protected forest' (DPF). What was thought 'of primary importance was to assert the proprietary right of Government in these forests and lay down certain limits to the hitherto unregulated action of right-holders'.[57] Official interest in these forests—dominated by the long-leaved or chir pine—quickened further when two important scientific developments were reported by Indian forest officials. The tapping of chir pine for oleo-resin had been started on an experimental basis in the 1890s, and by 1912 methods of distillation had been evolved which would enable the products to compete with the American and French varieties that had hitherto ruled the market. At the same time, fifty years of experimentation on a process to prolong the life of certain Indian woods for use as railway sleepers through chemical treatment finally bore fruit. Of the timbers successfully treated, the chir and blue pines were both found suitable and available in substantial quantities, and could be marketed at a sufficiently low price.[58] ...

Within a few years of commercial working the Kumaun forests had become a paying proposition. When one full fifteen-year cycle (1896-

1911) had revealed that resin tapping did not permanently harm trees, attempts were made 'to develop the resin industry as completely and rapidly as possible'.[60] Between 1910 and 1920 the number of resin channels tapped rose from 260,000 to 2,135,000,[61] a rate of increase matched by the production of resin and turpentine (Table 2). When the construction of a new factory at Bareilly was completed in 1920—with a rated capacity of 64,000 cwts of resin and 240,000 gallons of turpentine, a capacity that could be easily expanded fourfold—production was outstripping Indian demand. This put under active consideration proposals for the export of resin and turpentine to the United Kingdom and the Far East.[62] Indeed, the only impediment to increased production was the inadequacy of means of communication. The extensive pine forests in the interior had to remain untapped, with extraction restricted to areas well served by mule tracks and sufficiently close to railheads. . . .

IV. Begar In Kumaun

The system of forced labour in Kumaun, known by various names during the colonial period (*coolie utar, bardaish, begar, godam*) has been the subject of a fine recent study.[66] The British in fact operated the system, a legacy of the petty hill chiefs who preceded them, from Darjeeling to Simla, on grounds of administrative convenience in tracts whose physical situation made both commercial transport and boarding houses economically unattractive. As embodied in their settlement agreements,[67] landholders were required to provide several sets of services for all government officials on tour and for white travellers (e.g. *shikaris* and mountaineers). The most common of these involved carrying loads and building *chappars* (temporary rest huts), and the supply of provisions (*bardaish*) such as milk, food, grass, wood and cooking vessels. . . .

With the advent of the Forest Department, the burden of these services on the Kumaun villager dramatically increased. The reservation of the forest and its future supervision involved extensive touring by forest officials who took utar and bardaish for granted. Coming close on the heels of the demarcation of the forests, the additional burdens created by the new department evoked a predictable response, Forest officers touring in the interior of Garhwal were unable to obtain grain, as villagers, even where they had surplus stock, refused to supply to a department they regarded 'as disagreeable interlopers to be thwarted if possible'.[75] Utar, in the words of the Kumaun Forest Grievances Committee 'one of the greatest grievances

which the residents of Kumaun had against the forest settlement'[76]—
when coupled with the curtailment of community control over forests
represented an imposition unprecedented in its scope and swiftness. . . .

V. Early Resistance To Forest Management

It is important to understand the dislocations in agrarian practice
consequent on the imposition of forest management. The working of a
forest for commercial purposes necessitates its division into blocks or
coupes, which are completely closed after the trees are felled to allow
regeneration to take place. Closure to men and cattle is regarded as
integral to successful reproduction, and grazing and lopping, if allowed,
are regulated in the interests of the reproduction of favoured species of
trees.[87] Further, protection from fire is necessary to ensure the
regeneration and growth to maturity of young saplings. Thus the
practice of firing the forests had to be regulated or stopped in the
interests of sustained production of chir pine. While the exercise of
rights, where allowed, was specified in elaborate detail, rightholders
had the onerous responsibility, under Section 78 of the Act, of
furnishing knowledge of forest offences to the nearest authority and of
extinguishing fires, however caused, in the state forests. In general, as
endorsed by the stringent provisions of the Forest Act, considerations of
control were paramount.

We find evidence of protest at the contravention of traditional
rights well before the introduction of forest management. Charcoal
required for smelting iron in the mines of Kumaun was brought from
neighboring forests, and where these lay within the boundaries of
villages the inhabitants prevented wood being cut without the
payment of malikhana.[88] And in the years following the constitution
of the DPF in 1893, the Deputy Commissioner (DC) of Garhwal
reported that 'forest administration consists for most part in a running
fight with the villagers'.[89]

Even where discontent did not manifest itself in overt protest, the
loss of control over forests was acutely felt. The forest settlement
officer of British Garhwal, at the time of the constitution of the
reserved forests, commented:

(The) notion obstinately persists in the minds of all, from the
highest to the lowest, that Government is taking away their
forests from them and is robbing them of their own property. The
notion seems to have grown up from the complete lack of restriction
or control over the use by the people of waste land and forest during
the first 80 years after the British occupation. The oldest

inhabitant therefore, and he naturally is regarded as the greatest authority, is the most assured of the antiquity of the people's right to uncontrolled use of the forest; and to a rural community there appears no difference between uncontrolled use and proprietary right. Subsequent regulations—and these regulations are all very recent—only appear to them as a gradual encroachment on their rights, culminating now in a final act of confiscation...(My) best efforts however have, I fear, failed to get the people generally to grasp the change in conditions or to believe in the. . . . historical fact of government ownership.[90]

This brings out quite clearly that alternative conceptions of property and ownership lay at the root of the conflict between the state and hill villagers over forest rights. There did not exist a developed notion of private property among these peasant communities, a notion particularly inapplicable to communally—owned and managed woods and pasture land. In contrast, the state's assertion of monopoly over forests was undertaken at the expense of what British officials insisted were individually claimed rights of user. With the 'waste and forest lands never having attracted the attention of former governments'[91] there existed strong historical justification for the popular belief that all forests within village boundaries were 'the property of the villagers.'[92]

The affirmation of state control—and its obverse, the diminution of customary rights—had an unfortunate effect, with the loss of control contributing to a growing alienation of man from forest. The demarcation of reserved forests having given rise to the speculation that the state would take away other wooded areas from their control, villagers were in certain cases deforesting woodland. But where ownership was still vested in the community, forests continued to be well looked after, such as the twenty-mile stretch between Rudraprayag and Karanprayag in the Alakananda valley, where the government had explicitly made over these forests to the neighboring villages.[93] As later developments indicated, the small extent of forests under the control of village *panchayats* was invariable well managed.[94]

Discontent with the new forest regulations manifested itself in various other ways. Desertion was considered by a group of villagers belonging to Tindarpur patti in Garhwal, who approached an English planter for land 'as the new forest regulations and restrictions were pressing on them so severely that they wished to migrate into another district and climate rather than put up with them any longer'.[95]

Another time-honoured form of protest—non-compliance with imposed regulations—was evident when villagers gave misleading information at the time of fixation of rights.[96] As villagers were 'not in a frame of mind to give much voluntary assistance', one DFO predicted accurately their 'active resentment' at the fire protection of large areas and their closure to grazing and other rights.[97]

The year 1916 witnessed a number of 'malicious' fires in the newly constituted reserved forests. In May the forests in the Gaula range of Naini Tal division were set ablaze. The damage reported was exclusively in chir forests, and 28,000 trees which were burnt had to be prematurely felled. For the circle as a whole it was estimated that at least 64 per cent of the 441 fires which burnt 388 square miles (as against 188 fires that had burnt 35 square miles in the preceding year) were 'intentional.'[98]

The 'deliberate and organized incendiarism' of the summer of 1916 brought home to the state the unpopularity of the forest settlement and the virtual impossibility of tracing those who were responsible for the fires. Numerous fires broke out simultaneously over large areas, and often the occurrence of a fire was the signal for general 'firing' in the whole neighborhood. Forty-four fires occurred in North Garhwal division, almost all in order to obtain a fresh crop of grass. In Naini Tal and in the old reserves of Airadeo and Binsar of Almora district—areas which had been fire protected for many years—an established crop of seedlings was wiped out. The areas chosen for attack had been under both felling and resin-tapping operations. In Airadeo the fire continued for three days and two nights, with 'new fires being started time after time directly a counterfiring line was successfully completed'. As a result of such 'incendiarism', several thousand acres of forest were closed to all rights for a period of ten years.[99]. . .

NOTES

10. See A. Mishra and S. Tripathi, *Chipko Andolan* (Delhi, 1978); B. Dogra, *Forests and People* (Rishikesh, 1980).
11. P. Mason, *A Matter of Honour* (London, 1975), p. 451; cf. also T.W. Webber, *The Forests of Upper India and Their Inhabitants* (London, 1902), p. 39.
12. E.P. Stebbing, *The Forests of India* (London, 1922-27), vol. III, p. 258.
13. E.A. Smythies, *India's Forest Wealth* (London, 1925), p. 84.
21. In this article, Kumaun refers to the British civil division comprising the districts of British Garhwal, Almora, and Naini Tal. Historically the latter two districts constituted Kumaun. I

shall however use Kumaun to include Garhwal as did the official sources from which I have largely drawn. The Kumaun Division (hereafter KD) was separated from Nepal in the east by the river Kali; from Tibet in the north by the Himalaya; from the state of Tehri Garhwal in the west by the Alakananda and Mandakini rivers, and from the adjoining division of Rohilkhand in the south by the outer hills.

25. H.G. Walton, *Almora: A Gazetteer* (Allahadad, 1911), pp. 57-9; S.D. Pant, *The Social Economy of the Himalayans* (London, 1935), p. 137 ff; 'Correspondence relating to the scarcity in Kumaun and Garhwal in 1890', in *British Parliamentary Papers*, vol. 59 (1890-92). The quoted excerpt is taken from the last mentioned source (Chief Secy, NWP & O, to Secy. GOI, dated 25-4-1890).

39. This brief description of the nature and composition of the Himalayan forests is taken from R.S. Troup, *Silviculture of Indian Trees* (Oxford, 1921), intro., and passim. Early white travellers were impressed by the density and extent of the Himalayan forests, e.g., Hardwicke ('Narrative', 327) who proclaimed that 'the forests of oak, fir, and boorans are here more extensive, and the trees of greater magnitude, than any I have ever seen'.

40. Troup, 'Silviculture', pp. iv-v. 'Economic' is a euphemism for 'commercially valuable'. Within this division between coniferous and broad-leaved trees, the most important (and common) species, especially in the altitudes inhabited by human population, are the *banj* oak (*Quercus incana*) and the *chir* pine (*Pinus roxburghii (longifolia)*).

41. G.B. Pant, *The Forest Problem of Kumaun* (Allahabad, 1922), pp. 30-1.

42. S.B. Bhatia, *Working Plan (WP) for the East Almora Forest Division, 1924-25 to 1933-34* (Allahabad, 1926), pp. 13, 22.

43. N.L. Bor, *Manual of Indian Forest Botany* (Oxford, 1953), p. 13. Dietrich Brandis, the first Inspector-General of Forests, had reported the existence of numerous sacred groves, the 'traditional method of forest preservation', in almost all the provinces of India. See his *Indian Forestry* (Woking, 1897), p. 12.

44. J.K. Pearson, 'Note on history of proposals for management of village waste lands', dated December 1926, in Forest Department (FD) file 83 of 1909, Uttar Pradesh State Archives (UPSA), Lucknow.

45. Note by V.A. Stowell, D.C., Garhwal, on 'Nayabad grants for reafforestation purposes', n.d., prob. 1907; note dated 13 August 1910, by Dharmanand Joshi, late Depy. Collector, Garhwal, both in ibid.

46. T.D. Gairola, *Selected revenue decisions of Kumaun* (Allahabad, 1938), p. 209 ff; A.E. Osmaston, *W.P. for the North Garhwal For. Div., 1921-22 to 1930-31* (Allahabad, 1921), p. 8; note by D. Joshi, cited in fn. 45.

47. These two paragraphs are a somewhat simplified summary of a complex historical process described in detail in my 'Forestry in British and post-British India.'

48. Thus, by 1869, the sal forests of the outer hills were all 'felled in even to desolation'. See G.F. Pearson, 'Sub Himalayan forests of Kumaun and Garhwal', in *Selections*, 2nd series, vol. 2 (Allahabad, 1869), p. 132.

49. G.P. Paul, *Felling Timber in the Himalayas* (Lahore, 1871); Col. R. Strachey, Secy., GOI to Secy., PWD, NWP, dated 29 March 1864, no. 10, Revenue B. Progs, May, 1864, Foreign Dept., National Archives of India (NAI).

50. D. Brandis, 'Memorandum on the supply of railway sleepers of the Himalayan pines impregnated in India', *Indian Forester* 4:365-85 (April, 1879). While every mile of broad gauge railway required 1,800, sleepers, each sleeper lasted 12 years. The railway network had expanded from 843 to 9,215 miles in 1860-80, levelling off at around 32,300 miles by 1910. See GOI, *History of Indian Railways* (Delhi, 1964), p. 214. Thus, at the time Brandis was writing, well over a million sleepers were required annually.

51. A vivid account of the offical measures that induced this deforestation can be found in Stebbing, I, pp. 36-62, 288-9, 505-9, 523-30. By 'successful' forest administration I mean successful from the viewpoint of strategic imperial needs.

52. C.F. Amery, 'On Forest rights in India', in D. Brandis and A. Smythies, eds., *Report of the proceedings of the forest conference held at Simla, October 1875* (Calcutta, 1876), p. 27.

53. For the 1878 Act, which, apart from minor modifications continues to be in operation, the basic documents are: B.H. Baden-Powell, 'On the defects of the existing Forest Law (Act VII of 1865) and proposals for a new Forest Act', in B.H. Baden-Powell and J.S. Gamble, eds., *Report of the proceedings of the forest conference, 1873-74* (Calcutta, 1874), pp. 3-30; D. Brandis, *Memorandum on the forest legislation proposed for British India (Other than the Presidencies of Madras and Bombay)* (Simla, 1875).

54. 'Instructions for forest settlement officers in the NWP & O', no. 682/XIV, 328-63, dated 29 May 1897, in file no 279, dept. IVA, list no. 2, post-Mutiny Records, RAD. Such flexibility equipped the act to deal with the diverse socio-political situations in which state monopoly was asserted.

55. See D. Brandis, *Suggestions regarding forest administration in the NWP & O* (Calcutta, 1882).
56. Webber, 'Forests of Upper India', esp. pp. 38-43.
57. Note by J.S. Campbell, Comm. K.D., dated 6 August 1910, in FD file 83/1909.
58. Puran Singh, 'Note on the distillation and composition of turpentine oil from the chir resin and the clarification of Indian resin', *Indian Forest Records*, vol. IV, part I (Calcutta, 1912); R.S. Pearson, 'Note on the antiseptic treatment of timber in India, with special reference to railway sleepers', IFR, vol. III, pt. 1 (Calcutta, 1912). Also idem, 'A further note on the antiseptic treatment of timber, with results obtaining from past experiments', IFR, vol. 6, part 9 (Calcutta, 1918). These two sets of findings finally led to the constitution of the Kumaun circle on 2 October 1912 and forest settlements in the three districts. The two chief products of oleo-resin, turpentine and resin, had a wide variety of industrial uses. See Smythies, 'India's forest wealth', p. 80.
60. E.A. Smythies, 'The resin industry in Kumaun', *Forest Bulletin No. 26* (Calcutta, 1914), p. 3.
61. Stebbing, III, p. 660. The work was done by small contractors (practically all from outside Kumaun), under the supervision of the department.
62. Imperial Institute, Indian Trade Enquiry, *Report on lac, turpentine and resin* (London, 1922), esp. pp. 29-51. India was the only source of oleo-resin within the British dominions.
66. Shekhar Pathak, 'Uttarakhand mein coolie begar pratha: 1815-1949', unpublished Ph.D. thesis, Dept. of History, Kumaun University, 1980. Also his 'Kumaun mein begar anmulan andolan', paper presented at Seminar on Peasant Movements in UP, Jawaharlal Nehru University (JNU), 19-20/10/1982 (I am grateful to Shahid Amin for giving me this reference). These are hearafter referred to as Pathak (1) and (2) respectively.
67. As Taradutt Gairola argued,the Allahabad High Court had passed judgments that the practice was in fact illegal. See his speech in the Legislative Council of UP, dtd. 16-12-1918 in file no. 21 of 1918-19, dept. xv, Regional Archives, Naini Tal (RAN).
75. D.O. no. 10x, dt. 6 February 1917 from DFO, North Garhwal to Conservator of Forests (CF) Kumaun Circle, GAD file 398/1913.
76. *Report of the Kumaun Forest Grievances Committee* (hereafter KFGC), in Progs. A, June 1922, nos. 19-24, file no. 522/1922, Dept. of Rev. & Agl. (Forests), p. 2, NAI.
87. See Ramachandra Guha, 'The nature of forestry "Science"', *PPST Bulletin* (Madras), 3(1), May 1983.

88. J.O.B. Beckett, 'Iron and copper mines in the Kumaun division', report dated 31 January 1850, in *Selections* vol. III (Allahabad, 1867), pp. 31-8. 'There is *not a single* malgoozar of any of the villages in the neighbourhood of the iron mines, who has not at one time or other endeavoured to levy a tax on *all* the charcoal burners . . .' (Ibid., p. 36, emphasis added).

89. 'Note on forest administration for my Successor', by McNair, DC Garhwal, dated February 1907, in FD file 11/1908, UPSA.

90. J.C. Nelson, *Forest Settlement report of the Garhwal district* (Lucknow, 1916), pp. 10-11.

91. Pauw, Garhwal SR, p. 52.

92. Gairola, *Selected revenue decisions*, p. 211. Emphasis added. Gairola's account (ibid., pp. 209-13) brings out the changed conditions in which the state deemed it necessary to usurp a previously non-existent 'right' of government to forests and waste land. This dichotomy between colonial and indigenous notions of property right was at the root of much of the discontent in tribal areas over forest regulations. See, for example, G.V.S. de Silva, N. Mehta, M.A. Rahman and P. Wignaraja, 'Bhoomi Sena: a struggle for people's power', *Development dialogue,* no. 2 of 1979, pp. 4-11.

93. T.D. Gairola to Secretary, Govt. UP, dated 8 January 1918; note by D. Joshi cited in fn. 45, both in FD file 83/1909.

94. See C.M. Johri, *WP for the Garhwal For. Div., 1940-41 to 1954-55* (Allahabad, 1940), p. 20; D.N. Lohani, *WP for the North and South Garhwal Divisions, 1958-59 to 1972-73* (Allahabad, 1962), p. 35.

95. District and Sessions Judge, Moradabad, to Pvt. Secretary to L-G, UP, dated 2 Mach 1916, in FD file 163/1916 ('Forest Settlement Grievances in the KD'), UPSA.

96. Nelson, *Forest Settlement Report,* pp. 2-4, 13,25.

97. Osmaston, *North Garhwal WP,* p. 67.

98. APFD, 1916-17, p. 7; *Report on the administration of the United Provinces of Agra and Oudh,* 1915-16 (Allahabad, 1916), p. viii.

99. APFD, 1915-16, p. 7f. H.G. Champion, 'Observations on some effects of fires in the *chir (Pinus longifolia)* forests of the West Almora Division', *Indian Forester* 45 (1919): pp. 353-63. H.G.Chamnpion, *WP for the Central Almora For. Div.* (1922), pp. 13-14.

Agro-Forestry—Practices and Prospects as a Combined Land-Use System

P. C. Goswami

Agro-forestry is an agricultural system which ranges across a broad spectrum of tenure arrangements, from the individual holding to forest plantations. In the plantation context, it is known as the taungya system. The system has important tenurial implications, providing access for taungya farmers to forest reserve land, but usually with little security of tenure.— The Editors

Growing crops and trees together is not a new invention or concept—the practice in different forms is age-old in all the continents, more extensively in the humid tropics. The concept has, however, re-emerged now because of the factors outlined earlier. Agro-forestry has received added impetus with the establishment of the International Council for Research in Agro-forestry (ICRAF) in 1978 under the auspices of the Food and Agriculture Organization of the United Nations, with an institute functioning in Nairobi, with the main objective of accelerating programmes on agro-forestry in the developing countries. The FAO continues to be a leader entity in the aspects of agro-forestry. "Agro-forestry" is a new name for an old practice. It is also called "Agro-silviculture" or "Agri-forestry." Often the practice includes forage crops and raising of livestock when it may be designated as agro-silvo-pastoral land-use. Since the practice dates back to the origin of agriculture itself and varies so much that only a broad definition is now possible, which however may need modifications to incorporate new patterns or improved techniques.

Combe has described agro-forestry as follows: "Under the heading of agro-forestry techniques, is understood the group of land management

Excerpted from P.C. Goswami, "Agro-Forestry—Practices and Prospects as a Combined Land-Use System," *The Indian Forester* (June 1982): Volume 108, Number 6: 385-396.

techniques that imply the combination of forest trees with crops, livestock or a combination of both. The association can be simultaneous or staggered in time and space." . . .

The first systematic application of agro-forestry for raising forest plantations is what is now widely known as the *Taungya* System or *Sistema Taungya*. With the object of raising forest plantations generally of teak, cheaply at the time, and of meeting the shortage of labour for plantation work, the Forest Departments of the then Indian Empire adopted this system in the middle of the last century. The word *"taungya"* is of Burmese origin, referring to a tribe of shifting cultivators in northern Burma, who were first employed in 1862 to raise teak plantations allowing also to grow rice along with the forest species for two or three years. The farmers could not grow their crops any longer on the same site due to closure of the forest canopy. They were, however, given another area for the purpose. The system thus became a solution for several forestry problems, specially:

1.   Meeting the labour shortage in very remote areas for raising forest plantations.

2.   Raising forest plantations cheaply.

3.   Controlling the destructive practice of shifting cultivation to some extent by inducing shifting cultivators to re-convert the cleared land into well stocked forest plantations within a short period of two or three years.

Not only in Burma but in many other parts of India, *taungya* soon became almost the standard method of raising forest plantations in remote areas inhabited sparsely by ethnic tribes. Thousands of acres of forest plantations raised by the *taungya* system are now to be seen in various stages of maturity in many parts of India and Bangladesh.

In retrospect, it is now seen that the *taungya* as practiced then had several drawbacks, specially:

The system was confined to Government Reserved Forests only. Thus no thought was given to where the farmers would cultivate once the available Reserved Forest land were planted up. This actually happened, perhaps sooner than thought of, and the scope for *taungya* plantations became limited after a few decades.

The *taungya* farmers remained semi-nomadic and greatly dependent on the forest authority.

Emphasis was not placed on evolving a proper combination of agricultural and forest crops on the basis of soil potentialities. If, for instance, spacing of forest trees were made wider instead of the traditional, the farmers could have continued cultivation for another two years or so without jeopardizing successful forest plantations.

Happily, the necessity of combining the farmers' interests with the silvicultural requirements is now receiving the attention of the Forest Departments in India and many modifications have now been made. Thousands of acres of poplar plantations have now been raised in Uttar Pradesh, India, in widely spaced lines permitting crops to be grown in between almost throughout the rotation (15 years). Leguminous trees are now being preferred for *taungya* instead of soil exacting large leaf trees. In some areas, farmers are also allowed to grow shade preferring crops like ginger and tumeric, within natural forests or established plantations.

Agro-forestry in Different Countries

To prevent the alarming devastation of the forests, the *taungya* system was first adopted in 1911 in Thailand. The system in effect became the method of reforestation by squatters, and the shifting cultivator tribes. The rate of forest destruction, however, continued and the system was revised in 1968 and oriented towards settling of shifting cultivators. . . .

Taungya as adopted now in many West African countries by the forest authorities is different from the Asian practice in that the farmers are paid by the Government for all the forestry operations such as cutting and clearing the bush and planting. But the farmers are allowed to cultivate the land only for one year, rarely two.

In Uganda, the system appears to have started at the time of raising cocoa plantations when the hard wood species Musisi (*Maesopsis eminii*) was grown as a shade tree for cocoa removing them later for timber. The system is currently applied with adjustments for many other trees, local and exotic and in combination with other crops.

Taungya has been adopted in Latin American countries also where it is know as *Sistema Taungya*. In these countries it is considered a means of gradually converting shifting cultivation into an economy based on fast-growing forest species or as a means of improving degraded forests or converting forests of useless species into commercial timber plantations. . . .

The *taungya* system was introduced in Jamaica during the early stages of large scale forest plantation programme. Farmers were given lands to cultivate in new forest plantations for a period of 3-5 years. The importance of the *taungya* system in Jamaica declined over the years as the younger generation was not attracted to farming and the demand for farm land within forest reserves decreased. However, a trend is now seen in some areas, of increased demand for land, especially for perennial crops. Both for accommodating land requirement of new farmers and for improving and sustaining the existing multiple use hillside farms, agro-forestry in Jamaica has a very important role to play. The rural development projects currently under operation and planning is giving due importance on agro-forestry practices.

Agri-Silviculture (Taungya System): The Law and the System

K.F.S. King

*The essence of the **taungya** system is the provision of land for subsistence agriculture and possibly other remuneration in return for the rearing of young trees. King's 1968 research bulletin remains our only comparative review of the precise terms of the contract between the **taungya** farmer and the forest reserve administration. How could the terms here be altered, consistent with the purpose of the agreement, to provide the farmer with more secure tenure and/or expectations?—The Editors*

One of the means of implementing forest policies is through the enactment of legislation which ensures that the measures necessary for the pursuance of the policies are performed and not thwarted. The law, in such cases, gives effect to a policy already formulated. But the law may also have a constructive function: that is, in addition to being an instrument of policy implementation, it may help to mold and shape it. Therefore, in the absence of declared policies by those agencies which practice the system of agri-silviculture an attempt will be made to analyse the legal conditions which control the system so that not only may these policies and their social philosophy be ascertained, but their efficacy determined. An analysis of the legal conceptions which under-line the practice may also reveal the degree of the incorporation of agri-silviculture into the country's legal structure.

The use and occupation of the land are necessary factors in the system of *agri-silviculture*. In most communities those rights and duties which regulate how the owner for the occupant of land, holds, uses and disposes of it, are controlled by customary law and practice, by enacted law, or by a body of rules, sometimes written and sometimes unwritten.

Excerpted from K.F.S. King, "Agri-Silviculture, The Taungya System," Forestry Bulletin No 1 (Ibadan: University of Ibadan Press, 1968).

A study of the land tenure laws and customs of those countries in which the system is performed ought therefore to reveal the true nature of the *agri-silvicultural* tenure.

It was found, however, that customary law and practice do not contribute very much to the evaluation.[1] Although the system of *agri-silviculture* is in fact a modification of the system of shifting agriculture, the affinities are more physical and biological than legal. For an essential ingredient of the system of agri-silviculture does not exist in shifting agriculture, i.e. the land utilized under shifting cultivation is not owned *and* its development planned and controlled by a second party as it is in *agri-silviculture*. As Gordon (1955) has pointed out, shifting cultivation is generally not practiced under a legal system which recognises *individual* freehold rights. The cultivator establishes exclusive rights, often of a vague and unascertainable nature, through his clearing of tribal and family land, and these rights are either those of a temporary owner, or occupier, or are merely usufructuary. On the other hand, in *agri-silviculture* the land is either owned by the State or a Local Authority and is generally controlled and managed by the Forest Department with a specific object in view. In addition, the rights of the farmer are often clearly defined, and duties, an entirely new concept to the shifting cultivator, now become an important factor in land-use. In short, the rights which the shifting cultivator formerly enjoyed through *status* are now his as a result of *contract*.

This degree of contractual agreement is clearly brought out in an investigation which was made of the terms and conditions under which agriculturists are permitted to plant their crops in the forest reserves. Although about one-third of the countries in which agri-silviculture is practiced do not employ any document to formalize their arrangements there is, even in these countries, some recognition of the two-way flow of rights and duties. In many countries where the terms are reduced to writing the documents are specifically called *agreements* or *contracts*. In a few countries they are called *licences,* in some *permits,* and in one a *lease.* In some countries, there is no necessity to draw up a formal contract or even to make an oral agreement with the cultivator. For example, in Brazil, the Forest Law or *Codigo Forestal Brasileiro,* makes provision for the practice of *agri-silviculture,* and all that is required is that the farmer should follow the conditions specified in that law.

However, although the general term 'contract' appears to cover adequately the arrangements between the farmer and the forester, it would perhaps assist the investigation if the legal nature of the rights which accrue to the cultivator under the contract was considered. It seems that that form of tenancy know to English law as a licence most aptly describes the *agri-silvicultural* agreement. Megarry (1949) has defined a licence as "a permission given by the occupier of land which, without creating any interest in land, allows the licensee to do some act which would otherwise be a trespass." In the *agri-silvicultural* context, the agreements permit the cultivator to enter forest land to fell, burn, and farm. One important result of this interpretation of the nature of the tenure of *agri-silviculture* as a licence, is that in many of the countries which base their law on the English legal system, a licence is regarded not as a separate entity, but merely as part of the contract creating it, so that even if the contract is not specifically enforceable the licensee is probably protected. Thus, to take a hypothetical case, the Courts may recognise the cultivator's right to enter upon forest land after he has moved to another area, so that he may harvest fruit from, say, his orange trees which he had previously legally planted under an *agri-silvicultural* agreement.

The terms of the agreements investigated will now be listed.

The forester permits the cultivator

(a)   To hold forest land free of rent,[2,3]
(b)   To plant farm crops among the forest trees,
(c)   To plant farm crops in an area specially allotted to him in addition to that among the trees,[4]
(d)   To reside on the forest estate,[4]
(e)   To pasture stock,[4]
(f)   To cut, collect, and remove free of charge from the area allotted to him all timber and firewood below a certain size, provided that he uses it himself,[4]
(g)   To make charcoal free of charge,[4]

The cultivator agrees

(a)   To clear all land allocated to him,[5]
(b)   To burn the felled area,
(c)   To cut pegs for the planting of forest species,[6]
(d)   To plant forest trees or sow forest seeds among his agricultural crops,[7]
(e)   To weed and tend the tree crop,
(f)   To extinguish any fire in the forest area or its vicinity,[8]
(g)   To construct and maintain firelines at his own expense,[9]

- (h)   To construct and maintain bridle paths at his own expense,[9]
- (i)   [missing in original (ed.)]
- (j)   To "beat up" the forest plantation at his own expense,[10]
- (k)   To place all weeds after harvesting along contours to prevent erosion,[9]
- (l)   To deposit a certain amount of money against breaches of the agreement,[10]
- (m)   To undertake work in other parts of the forest estate, on other jobs, for a specified period,[10]
- (n)   Not to plant certain specified agricultural crops,[10]
- (o)   Not to plant agricultural crops within specified distances of the tree crops,[10]
- (p)   Not to engage in certain types of weeding practice,[11]
- (q)   To maintain such standards of personal hygiene as reasonably conforms with the standard laid down by the Chief Conservator,[12]
- (r)   To register all members of his family resident in the forest estate with the Forestry Officer,[10]
- (s)   Not to allow any person other than a member of his family to pass the night in his dwelling house without written permission,[12]
- (t)   To pay to the authorized officer such proportion of the proceeds of the sale of crops harvested from his farms not exceeding 10 per cent, for payment into the forest Welfare Fund,[13]
- (u)   To sell surplus, produce only to such syndicates or traders as are approved by the Forest Department,[13]
- (v)   Not to prepare any alcoholic liquor in the forest area without written permission,[13]
- (w)   Not to construct any house or building in the forest reserve without authority.

In addition to the conditions listed above, there are usually provisions:

- (i)   Prohibiting the transfer of rights or the subletting of the land allocated;
- (ii)   Regulating the period of notice needed for termination of the licence;
- (iii)   Taxing the compensation payable by the cultivator in the event of any breach of the terms of the agreement; and

(iv) Allowing for the payment of rewards and bonuses to competent cultivators.

NOTES

[The page-specific system of notes used by Troup required renumbering of the notes for this excerpt. Editor's note]

1. It is interesting to note, however, that exceptionally, in Sierra Leone the influence of customary law and practice is felt in the establishment of *agri-silvicultural* plantations. Thus the land tenure practice gives the original 'land owner' the preference to farm the year's plantation. This right may be exercised by someone else only after 'land owner'has rejected the offer to farm the area and has given his approval for someone else to do so (Sawyer, 1965).

2. Although this condition is common to most countries, the situation in Kerala (India), calls for a special explanation. Here, coupes of an average of 30 acres are sold by auction to lessees who in turn distribute land, varying in area from 1 acre to 5 acres, to farmers.

3. Rent is, of course, paid-through the farmer's labour.

4. These conditions are far from universal.

5. Sometimes the Forest Department pays for the felling of the larger trees.

6. These conditions are far from universal.

7. Sometimes the Forest Department plants the forest seedlings themselves.

8. In those countries in which this condition is not expressly stated in the agreement, the Forest Department may be covered by the Forest law which demands this from all citizens.

9. These appear to apply only to Kerala (India).

10. These conditions are far from universal.

11. For example in Mauritius the farmer is not permitted to scrape soil from the base of young trees.

12. These conditions appear to apply only to Kenya.

13. These conditions appear to apply only to Kenya.

REFERENCES

Megarry, R.E. 1949. *The Law of Real Property*. Stevens and Sons.

Sawyer, J.S. 1965. "The Evolution of Silviculture in Sierra Leone." Paper presented to the Conference of the West African Sci. Ass. Freetown.

Change and Indigenous Agroforestry in East Kalimantan

Carol J. Pierce Colfer

In East Kalimantan in Indonesia, local people have long practiced indigenous agroforestry. But the advent of forest concessions in the area has made the chainsaw a household tool, with major impacts on forest use. Technology alters systems of resource use and exploitation and ultimately affects systems of tenure as well. —The Editors

Most of the research on which this analysis is based was conducted in Long Segar, East Kalimantan, where I lived and worked from October 1979 thru August 1980. . . .

Long Segar had a *de facto* population of 1,052 inhabitants in June 1980, almost all of whom gain their livelihoods by means of shifting cultivation. This is supplemented in some cases by wage labor, sale of agroforestry products, and cottage industry. The village is situated within an American-based, multi-national timber concession, near a German aid-sponsored plantation pilot project, and is accessible by plane (one half hour), speedboat (9 hours), and longboat (36-48 hours) from Samarinda. . . .

A man—and NOT a woman—can hire himself and his chainsaw out to his neighbors and family to clear land for ricefields at Rp. 5,000-7,000 per day (field owner buying fuel and food); during slack periods in the agricultural cycle, he can clear forest at the nearby plantation for Rp. 5,000 per day; or he can go to work as a logger for one of the timber camps that dot the East Kalimantan map. Such companies, in the log Segar area, now hire loggers and their chainsaws, rather than supplying the chainsaw as was previously common practice. There, if

Excerpted from Carol J. Pierce Colfer, "Change and Indigenous Agroforestry in East Kalimantan," in *Interaction Between People and Forests in East Kalimantan: Indonesian-U.S.* (Washington, DC: Man and Biosphere Project, 1980).

he is strong and industrious, he can earn as much as Rp 150,000 per month, though a more usual figure would be Rp 100,000 per month. The local American timber company pays such loggers Rp 150 per cubic meter of timber cut.

A third use to which a chainsaw can be put is to make boards and beams. Beams, for instance are cut in the forest and sold in the forest (Rp 15,000 per cubic), in the village (Rp 25,000 per cubic), or in Samarinda (Rp 45,000 per cubic). Two men with one chainsaw can expect to cut 1-2 cubic meters of lumber per day. From the above discussion, it is clear that from a "standard of living' perspective, acquiring a chainsaw and using it are rational actions which result in clear benefits for the particular family in question.

What then are the impacts of this innovation on the forest? If people can fell ten times as many trees in one day with a chainsaw as they can by traditional means, this is a substantial change in the "balance of power" between people and forests in East Kalimantan. The availability of the chainsaw has meant that one family can potentially clear a much larger ricefield (a factor that is particularly significant taken in conjunction with the increased time available to the people from adoption of the *ces* and rice-huller). . . .

The more thorough clearing of fields that is now possible likewise has adverse impacts on the forest. A large tree which might well have been left standing in the past, and which could have provided seed in the forest regeneration process, is now felled without hesitation.

The impact of the chainsaw on the forest is intimately tied up with the role of timber companies in the area. Adicondro (1979:312) reports that "Due to the increasing anti-logging sentiments in Kalimantan, the provincial parliament of East Kalimantan even asked the government to ban the use of chainsaws." This seems an improbable outcome, but testifies to the widespread awareness of the significant impacts of the chainsaw on the forest. . . .

Lumber is sold to the longboats, or even brought directly by Long Segar residents to Samarinda. There is a welter of conflicting laws, rulings and customs related to the use of timber within timber concessions; but because of 1) the obvious discrepancy in wealth between the people and the companies, 2) the fuzziness of the law, and 3) a shortage of enforcement personnel, the people are essentially free to do as they choose in harvesting timber. The contracts between the Government and the timber companies specify that the people are free to utilize the forests in their "customary manner," including using trees for house building. This right is sometimes used to justify timber harvesting for sale, on the theory that nails and other goods must be brought with money to finish a house. Clearly, the phrase "customary manner" is open to diverse interpretations in the changing circumstances that characterize East Kalimantan.

Men are drawn to this economic activity because of its profitability and the freedom to determine times of work. But only about ten men pursue this option repeatedly (and no one on a daily basis). Constraints that limit involvement in this activity include:

- the strenuousness of the work,
- availability of a chainsaw,
- uncertainty about its legality both on the part of the would-be cutter and the longboat owner who typically buys such products. . .[20]

In determining the appropriate rights and responsibilities of timber companies, current uses of the forests by indigenous populations must be attended to. The fact that Kenyah lives are intimately inter-twined with the forest cannot be denied, nor can their dependence on it. Indeed, the same question must be addressed when we look at the question of Transmigration in the area. Both timber companies and transmigrants represent an influx of potential users who are or will be competing for what are increasingly scarce resources (the forest and the land).

The issue is a complex one, because it is clear that the land and the forest cannot long support the kinds of human activity currently anticipated. Transmigrants in many other parts of East Kalimantan have had to resort to shifting cultivation, following local patterns, because of the infertility of the land (with sometimes disastrous infestations of Imperata cylindrica resulting); there is no reason to suspect otherwise in the Telen River region. Nor is there space for all the expected transmigrant families to support themselves by means of the quite extensive shifting cultivation methods utilized by the Kenyah—particularly located in the midst of timber concessions, bent as they are on one goal: timber removal.

Traditional land use rights of indigenous peoples are expressly protected by the Indonesian Government. Recognition of traditional land use rights must consider the fact that these systems are agroforestry—not simply agricultural—systems. Those "fallow" fields are in actuality areas where products other than rice are harvested. A recent Transmigration planning document (LEAP 1980), for instance, notes that only 5-10% of the land along the major rivers in the Telen River area is cultivated at one time. From this, they conclude that ". . . present land uses are not considered a significant constraint on land planning for transmigrantion settlements." (Ibid:26) Recognition of

Kenyah economic practices as part of an agroforestry system requires alteration of this conclusion. Indeed, if the 10 year regeneration cycle used by the Long Segar Kenyah for their owns fields is adhered to, that land use figure would go up to *50-100 percent* of the land along the major rivers in use at any one time.

NOTES

20. Legality also varies with species. The private sale of *meranti* in any form, without paying a royalty to the concession holder, for instance, is clearly illegal. Ironwood is the species about which the most conflict and confusion exists, as it is *not* owned by the concession holder, it is considered an endangered/protected species, yet it holds a prominent place in traditional human timber use patterns in the area.

REFERENCES

Adicondro, G.Y. 1979. "The Jungles are Awakening," *Impact* (September): 310-14.

LEAP (Land Evaluation and Planning Group). 1980. "Phase II: Outline Planning, Muara Wahau East." Samarinda: TAD Project.

Land Tenure and Forestry in Papua New Guinea: Problems and Solutions

A.M.D. Yauieb

> *In Colfer's East Kalimantan case, there was no provision of village land rights for the settlers by the concessionaire (or government). In Papua New Guinea, however, traditional land holding groups have rights in the forest, and private forestry companies must negotiate concessions with the resource-owning clans. Yauieb describes the system, and provides a case study of the Madang Wood Chip Project.—The Editors*

Customary Land Tenure . . .

The basic nature of customary land tenure is a combination of rights and powers exercised by groups and individuals at different levels depending on the need to assert those rights in particular cases. This must be kept to the forefront of our thinking. Large groupings ('tribes,' for want of a better term) are significant in relation to land in that they protect the group's sovereignty to its territory against threats from outside. Tribes are made up of clans, usually based on descent groups, and have acknowledged powers of allocation of certain land within the tribe's territory. Actual exploitation and occupation of the clan's land is carried out by individuals and families. 'A high degree of flexibility, and scope for individual/clan/village initiative is embodied in the tenure system' (Nagle 1976). . .

Excerpted from A.M.D. Yauieb, "Land Tenure and Forestry in Papua New Guinea: Problems and Solutions," in K.R. Shepard and H.V. Richter (eds.), *Forestry in National Development: Production Systems, Conservation, Foreign Trade and Aid* (Canberra: Development Studies Centre, Australian National University, 1979). Reprinted with the permission of the author.

Land Tenure and Forest Management

"The land tenure systems of Papua New Guinea create many difficulties for the traditional approaches to forest management" according to Nagle (1976). Nagle suggests that such systems are unlikely to encourage 'the correct spacing and timing of production over a large area needed to produce "a predictable output each year for several decades, while retaining basic productive capacity." At the same time, the "attachment of local people to their land, and their affinity for the existing ecosystems, may be positive forces in guiding long-run forest management." Carson (1974) commented that native ownership of land does not, however, mean that there cannot be sound forest management policies covering the forest estate, "but it does mean that management will have to be re-oriented to take account of the existing local circumstances and conditions." . . .

Procedural Alternatives for Forest Operations . . .

The right to operate in timber areas in PNG could previously be carried out in any of four ways, of which the first, in effect lease from government is overwhelmingly the most important. They are:

a. *By Timber Permit Based on Timber Rights Purchase*

Under the current Forest Act 1936 (as amended) the government may purchase the rights to the standing timber, with various exclusions (see below), and then negotiate with a private forestry company on extraction and processing rights. . . .

b. *By Agreement Under the Forestry (Private Dealings) Act 1971*

This Act specifically provides for direct dealings between the timber (i.e., land) owners and the proposed development company. The Act allows foreign or national companies to enter direct negotiations with owners, and to start an industry based on the timber resources. . . .

c. *By Native Timber Authority*

Under the Forestry Act 1936 (as amended) landowners may sell small lots of timber to buyers/sawmillers under the Native Timber Authority (NTA). . . .

d. *By Cutting on Freehold Property*

Such small areas of freehold property as existed in PNG prior to the change to leasehold allowed unrestricted logging operations. The total volume aggregated only .03 percent of the total logs cut in 1976.

The Solutions

The complexity of customary ownership and the alternatives available for forest operations pose problems for forest development in PNG. What are the solutions?

The basic solution appears to be to work with the operative group throughout the transaction. In the case of Timber Rights Purchases we should be dealing with the resource-owning groups, the clans. In essence a clan is a corporate body in that it exists as a recognizable entity and its members are bound by an accepted set of rules, the customs of the clan. There is provision at present for the legal recognition of clans as corporations, the Land Groups Act 1974, an Act which is expected to be used generally for the purpose of Timber Rights Purchases. Once a land group is incorporated, the representative body of the group can dispose of interests in customary land to the extent allowed by custom (this latter qualification would not pose any problem in disposing of timber rights).

It is proposed to introduce new legislation shortly which will clarify the powers of groups to enter into agreements about customary land. This legislation, while providing for checks on the exercise of powers by a body representing a land group, will strengthen the legal effect of agreements validly entered into. As far as Timber Rights Purchases are concerned, its repercussions will be limited to the establishment of group boundaries. If these cannot be settled by agreement, then there is provision for any dispute to be dealt with under the procedures of the Land Dispute Settlement Act 1975. The order of a Land Court under that Act is binding on the parties.

Once groups and areas have been settled, the representative bodies of the incorporated land groups will be able to enter into enforceable Timber Rights Purchases for the timber rights within their areas. . . .

Current Problems

The forestry industry has recently run into two major problems with owner groups arising out of land tenure: logging and reafforestation.

a. *Logging*

Work is sometimes disrupted by landowners (or previous owners in the case of 'waste and vacant' areas) who are aggrieved and interfere with logging, roading, etc., for various reasons. For example, the clan leaders claim that (i) the 'waste and vacant' declarations were improper; (ii) that they were tricked into selling either land or timber at below fair market value; or (iii) that they are not satisfied with the flow of royalty payments.

b. *Reforestation*

The other chief problem concerns reforestation. Policy is that forestry should be on a sustained yield basis. But there is a natural reluctance amongst the landowners to allow customary land to be leased to government for on-leasing to reforestation companies, because this involves long term withdrawal of such land from customary usage. Clans may also feel they will need the land for agriculture before the end of the normal pulp rotation (10-12 years). In view of the customary attachment to the land, it is now obvious that PNG agreements, for example, must be more definite in providing for reforestation. There has been a tendency to gloss over the problem of land acquisition in the hope that it will disappear with the anticipated success of forestry industry development and acceptance by the local people participating in its benefits.

In the event, this hoped-for acceptance has not occurred. Thus it appears necessary to follow Carson's (1974) recommendations:
1. In [the] future, timber rights purchase areas and agreement in principle for leases for reforestation areas should be negotiated at the same time as part of one deal, and there should also be an option for owner participation under the terms of the lease.
2. There should be a reforestation obligation written into the agreement; either for planting up a percentage of the annual coupe area or for payment of a cess (resource tax) to a central fund to finance reforestation operations.

General Conclusion

Forestry in Papua New Guinea encounters a number of problems associated with customary land tenures. The present system of Timber Rights Purchases has a poor reputation among the people. Many claim that it is not fair because first payments and royalties are low, and there is often little provision for participation by the local people. Timber Rights Purchases do not legally alienate the land from the customary owners, but in practice tie it up. Where the Purchase is not quickly followed by timber milling, this is sometimes resented by local people. If timber milling is not likely within a reasonable period and the local people are meanwhile inhibited from commercial farming, some relaxation of the Timber Rights Purchase over part of the area should be considered. Forestry officials should advise legal owners how they can develop their land for agriculture without damage to the trees that the government has bought.

The Timber Rights Purchase system is not an adequate legal basis for reforestation and other long-term follow-up work on the land after timber cutting. The most suitable arrangement seems to be for the customary rightholders to register their land and lease it to government on terms which give them a minor share of royalty payments, guaranteed employment, training in the industry, and shareholding in the whole development on the land.

One method of involving the local population successfully in modern forestry in their area is through Timber Working Groups. This method is outlined in the next section, which describes how such a group is helping to smooth operations for the Madang chip industry.

The Madang Wood Chip Project: A Case Study of a Solution

In the Madang project, the government has been successful in tackling the problems arising for forestry out of customary land tenures, as well as a number of other issues between the project managers and the local people.

The Madang project is Papua New Guinea's one integrated wood chip and reforestation enterprise. It is a joint venture between the government and JANT, a wholly-owned Japanese subsidiary. JANT is responsible for logging and chipping operations. For reforestation, a joint company has been set up, the Gogol Reforestation Company, in which JANT hold 51 percent and the PNG government 49 percent. The company is charged with reforesting a large part of the chipped area with species acceptable for pulp harvest so that viable operations can be carried on in perpetuity.

To avoid problems likely to interfere with the project's success, the government established the Madang Timber Working Group (MTWG) to oversee, coordinate and facilitate the whole operation. The most important problem to be tackled was that of further land acquisition. No specific undertaking had been required of the landowners at the time of the Timber Rights Purchase to commit a defined area to reforestation following logging, to allow the industry to develop. The MTWG's primary function has thus been to acquire land on behalf of Gogol for continued and expanded operations, and it has had to be very active securing land on a year by year basis for each season's planting.

The MTWG comprises representatives of four major government departments (Forestry, Agriculture, Lands, and Provincial Affairs), and seven representatives of the people of the timber areas. The Timber Company is invited to attend meetings and take part in patrols.

The main functions of the MTWG are:

a. Day to day coordination of the various departmental activities.

b. To provide for liaison ('problem solving') between the government, the people, and the JANT Company.

c. The acquisition (leasing) of adequate land for major reforestation purposes. The MTWG was set up in 1972 immediately after the signing of the agreement and the issue of the permits for wood chipping. Its primary task was to patrol all areas to be affected and keep the people informed on developments. In addition it was to seek the people's view on all aspects of the development, including the necessity to provide land for reforestation and to advise the people that they had a body (MTWG) to assist them in their dealings with the company.

In its activities the MTWG has, in fact, been able to soften the apparently catastrophic effect such a project can have on the land and its people. MTWG has operated to smooth out these problems and find solutions. In particular, it has to a large degree been able to overcome the natural reluctance of the land owners to allow adequate land to be withdrawn from customary use and made available, under lease to the government, for on-leasing to the Gogol Reforestation Company for planting or logging.

The Reforestation Company currently leases a total of 1175 hectares for reforestation, acquired in successive lots of 165, 250, 300 and 360 hectares in the four years 1974-75 to 1977-78.

The Working Group has also tackled the problem of allocation of land in logged-over areas between agriculture and forestry. The MTWG liaison enabled satisfactory land use studies to be carried out and acceptable planning of post-logging land use, from many possible alternatives, to be developed as a basic management tool for the area. Broad scale planning was made possible by the fact that chip logging is virtually clear felling of a major proportion of the area.

The survey and MTWG liaison has allowed identification of the area required in the longer term for reforestation, agriculture, etc., and facilitated the immediate leasing of such land to the Reforestation Company.

Broad planning has been made possible for post-logging land use. It is expected that after logging, the area will be further utilized somewhat after the following pattern:

Proposed Use	Percent
Smallholder use for intensive gardening	6
Capital intensive agriculture development (mechanized rice, or large scale cattle development)	2
Bench mark reserves (biosphere reserves)	2
Pulp reforestation	39
Enrichment planting to long rotation timber species for selective logging	44
River, swamp, etc.	7
Total	100 percent

The MTWG has also conducted research on the people of the area; and its work underlines the problems encountered in fostering such a development. The genealogies compiled by the MTWG showed the Gogal and Naru areas of development covered:

1. an area of 63,000 hectares;
2. a population of only 2,300;
3. eight language groups; and
4. 250 distinct land owning groups.

The difficulties involved in drawing up a land use plan to meet the needs of all the owners can be imagined. Nevertheless, the MTWG can report that at present 10,000 hectares has been logged; 1,175 hectares reforested; that smallholders have been assisted in developing 100 hectares of cattle projects and 100 hectares of crops such as cocoa; that reserves have been established; royalties distributed and problems solved.

The Madang Timber Working Group is now used as an example for others to follow. Consequently, a TWG has been set up in the Open Bay Timber Development Area in East New Britain Province, and other Timber Working Groups will follow in each major timber development area.

REFERENCES

Carson, G. 1974. "Report on Forestry and Forest Policy in Papua New Guinea." Unpublished. Port Moresby.
Nagle, G. 1976. *Report on Forest and Environment Management.* Rome: UNDP/FAO.

Shifting Cultivation in Northern Thailand: Possibilities for Development

Terry B. Grandstaff

"Soft" states have often made poor forest guards, and alternatives to simple state protection and exploitation of forests have been sought. In recent years there have been increasing calls for a new look at the viability of traditional forestry use systems. Grandstaff examines swidden cultivation in northern Thailand, distinguishes a more ecologically sound integral swidden from "pioneer " swidden, and argues that tenure is a key need for maintaining the system on a sound basis.—The Editors

The present study is aimed not at Thai part-time swiddeners but at those groups who practice swiddening as a major livelihood and who have well-developed, time-tested "group styles" to do this (Bennett 1976, p. 850), people whose cultures and societies are intimately connected to these practices—in short, people who swidden as a way of life. These are the so-called hill peoples of Northern Thailand. In Conklin's (1957) terminology they are "integral" swiddeners, not only in the sense that the food-production system is integral (Conklin's usage, as opposed to "partial," where some major portion of the agricultural produce is obtained through some other system, such as wet-rice for the Thai partial swiddeners) but also in the sense that the type of society and the method of agriculture are (and have been for centuries) intimately related. In the latter sense, integral swiddeners are attached to their way of life and this attachment is reflected in

Excerpted from Terry B. Grandstaff, *Shifting Cultivation in Northern Thailand: Possibilities for Development,* Resource Systems Theory and Methodology Series No. 3 (Tokyo: The United Nations University, 1980). Reprinted with the permission of the author.

their beliefs and values (see Watters 1960, p. 66). They possess a great deal of highly sophisticated information about swiddening which has been gained through long experience and is carefully taught to each succeeding generation (Ruddle and Chesterfield 1977; 1978). Swiddening is their primary occupation, receives the majority of their labour, and is the basis for countless discussions, legends, and stories, and problem-solving. Such groups do not simply do swiddening, they are swiddeners. As long as they can make a living from swiddening, to give it up would be unthinkable, even assuming viable alternatives existed. Integral swiddeners in Northern Thailand can be conveniently classified according to Conklin's basic distinction of "established" versus "pioneer" (Conklin 1957, p. 3; Walker 1975, pp. 5-6). "Pioneer" swiddeners are those that prefer to swidden in primary forest when they can. In general, they use their swidden plots in a more exhaustive manner than the "established" swiddeners and move their villages to new areas when yields become insufficient. In Northern Thailand, they include Hmong, Yao, Lisu, Lahu, and Akha—all "Sino-Tibetan" groups (LeBar et al., 1964). . . .

The "established" swiddeners in Northern Thailand include the Lawa, Khmu, and T'in (Mon-Khmer groups) as well as the Karen (a Sino-Tibetan group; see LeBar et al., 1964). Established swiddeners live within relatively fixed swiddening village territories where they farm secondary forest on a rotational basis. Many of these groups have farmed the same land for centuries. Many of the villages also have constructed small numbers of wet-rice terraces which they farm in order to supplement the swidden rice regime. Because of this, a classificatory question arises as to whether such groups ought to be referred to as "integral" swiddeners. Probably the term "integral" does apply here, in that (1) these groups have a long history of swiddening; (2) for the vast majority, swiddening is the main occupation and preoccupation; (3) in most villages, even those who own terraces all still swidden regularly; (4) the attachment to an importance of swiddening is reflected in their beliefs, values, educational systems, social organizations, etc. The term "integral," then, although perhaps not fully appropriate, serves well to distinguish them from such partial swiddeners as the lowland Thai who have been recently impelled to adopt swiddening as a necessary supplement to a clearly preferred societal and agricultural style that is very different in orientation. . . .

Before proceeding to examine Northern Thailand pioneer and established swidden systems in more detail, it is advisable at the outset to deal with a few popular hoary generalizations regarding these groups to ensure that the more detailed discussion to follow is not obscured by any unwarranted predispositions.

1. Do hill groups destroy millions of dollars' worth of teak reserve each year (a commonly voiced supposition in Thailand)? Integral swiddeners (the hill peoples) prefer to swidden in Evergreen Forests, where greater biomass, faster regeneration with greater species diversity, and relatively greater moisture can be expected to produce better yields for cropping a field several years in a row or to allow them to return to it after a relatively short regeneration (fallow) period. *Tectona grandis* (teak), however, is found primarily scattered throughout Mixed Deciduous Forests, and also (generally less commercially valuable teak) in the *Dipterocarp* Forests. In terms of altitude, teak does not grow above about 700 m elevation, and relatively few hill-group swidden sites are below this level. But Mixed Deciduous Forests are being increasingly swiddened by lowlanders, as mentioned above. A map study, conducted by the author, of swidden sites in a valley near Chiang Mai revealed that none of the swiddens in Mixed Deciduous Forests could be attributed to the integral swiddeners in the area. All the swidden sites in this type of forest were in the lower portions of the forest, near to the Thai villages. Nevertheless, it is still unlikely that even Thai partial swiddeners themselves are responsible for the massive teak losses attributed to swiddening. In the first place, it seems likely that the figures are questionable, not only because many of these "reserves" are not really economic assets in the foreseeable future but also because of the extreme difficulty in assessing non-plantation teak assets. In its natural state, *Tectona grandis* is individually scattered throughout the Mixed Deciduous Forests in irregular patterns, making swidden loss assessment a most difficult task. There is little doubt, however, that exploitative hit-and-run logging practices by unlicensed commercial enterprises are responsible for much teak loss in Northern Thailand, and for no small degree of environmental degradation as well.

2. Do hill groups destroy other commercial timber reserves? This question is not as simple as it appears and cannot be simply answered. It is certainly true that most primary forest in Northern Thailand has disappeared due to population pressure, commercial logging in the late nineteenth and early twentieth centuries, and swiddening. The really big trees and virgin forests are a thing of the past, not only in Northern Thailand but, increasingly, throughout the world. With the lumber requirements that the modern world imposes, it is unlikely that such pockets that remain would make much of a dent in our needs and there is a far better argument for conserving them as biogenetic reserves (Dasmann *et al.*, 1973, p. 26). It is clear, then, that forest industries will have to adapt themselves to the harvestings of secondary forests if needs are to met (Dasmann *et al.*, 1973, p. 70). Some swiddening

practices have been lavish in forest usage, and areas of *Imperata* and scrub have resulted. Although some timber reserves have thus been destroyed, it should be pointed out that most sites were generally located far back in the mountains and thus would not have been available for commercial use in the foreseeable future. Among the Karen (who form the majority of integral swiddeners in Northern Thailand), however, secondary forest swiddening practices are highly conservational. Secondary forest reserves in Karen areas are not "lost," although commercial harvesting of timber on Karen lands must be carefully considered, since forest regeneration is essential to Karen agricultural practices. This subject will be returned to in more detail below.

3. Could growing population among integral swiddeners result in ecological cataclysm? Archaeological and historical records point in the direction of ecological catastrophe for populations dependent on riverine economies when highlands are deforested, perhaps due to excessive swiddening. Pendleton (1939, pp. 45-48) has made this argument for Angkor and Meso-America, while Gourou (1949, p. 9) has constructed similar arguments concerning areas in China. The basic argument is usually alluded to in most general discussions of swiddening. The scenario envisions a growing population in mountain areas with consequently increased swiddening, causing fallow periods to steadily decrease until virtual deforestation has occurred. Loss of ground cover then results in laterization and massive erosion during heavy rains. Loss of water-retention capability causes flooding and heavy siltation in the lowlands, destroying lowland fisheries, waterways, and agricultural irrigation systems and disrupting cropping patterns, followed by dry-season drought. Resulting famine then causes the total collapse of the lowland civilization. The scenario is a convincing one. Indeed, "before and after" pictures for a valley in China are said to have convinced Teddy Roosevelt and the Congress to establish the U. S. Forest Service (Eckholm 1976, p. 35) . . . .

. . . To my knowledge, we have no evidence that integral swiddeners ever caused such a catastrophe. More than anyone else they are constantly aware of the absolute necessity for forest availability if their agricultural system is to be continued. A rapidly expanding valley population, however, might, in desperation, have turned to the hills, where hyperbolically increasing hit-and-run swiddening, firewood-cutting, charcoal-making, or other subsidiary practices could conceivably have caused such damage before people realized (if they ever did) the effects of their rash actions. Permanent-field agriculturists, unschooled in the complexities of swiddening, could easily cause such damage without realizing the extent to which they were "fouling their own nest."[3] At any rate, since nearby large lowland populations existed in all the cited cases, it makes sense to include their influence on their surroundings in a more interrelated form of explanation, rather than breaking the situation into independent parts and placing the blame on "swiddening" *per se*. Perhaps the evidence could be re-examined with this in mind. . . .

. . . Is swidden agriculture a primitive and unsophisticated form of agriculture, practiced by peoples who don't know how to do a better job of it? Among those who have studied swidden systems in detail the unequivocal answer to this question is no. Even by the early 1950s researchers set about refuting this common allegation (see Judd 1964, p. 5) and, soon after, detailed works such as those of Conklin (1957) had shown that integral swiddeners possess incredible amounts of information concerning their environment and have developed highly skilled and adaptive methods, utilizing complex decision-making processes, for practicing swidden cultivation. . . .

Evolutionists have generally taken the position that swidden agriculture probably preceded permanent-field agriculture and is in this sense more primitive (i.e., older). In many areas of the prehistoric world (but probably not all), environmental conditions (extensive forests) and local population levels would have favoured swidden agriculture over permanent-field agriculture and would probably have involved less work per yield for the practitioners (see Boserup 1965; Brookfield 1972). Whatever the case, swidden societies have evolved through the same lengths of time as other societies and we have no reason to assume that their knowledge and ability to cope with their surroundings have not kept pace in adaptive sophistication. In Southeast Asia it is probable that swidden systems and wet-rice systems have existed side by side for thousands of years, and it would therefore be entirely unwarranted to assume that swiddeners have not adopted wet-rice because they were generally unaware of its practice and benefits.[4] Rather, they have continued to swidden because they found this method of agriculture highly suitable to local conditions and were able to make a good living from it. . . .

What has not been covered in the above sections is an appreciation of the ways in which the many different parts of a more productive and viable swidden system are to be successfully integrated, and an appreciation of the complex relationship between society and resources that will undergo changes with the development of swidden agriculture. In the past, development among swiddeners considered itself extremely enlightened in this regard if it proceeded with some sort of overall massive land-classification scheme so that each bit of resource usage was appropriate to some sort of environmental criterion (see, e.g.,

Holdridge 1959, pp. 275-277). As McKinnon (1977) points out, however, this land-survey type of development is virtually doomed to failure if it disregards the most important element in any resource system: the people themselves. Unless development is people-oriented it can easily become a rather nasty as well as unsuccessful enterprise. . .

If development channels are to be established that would convey the results of technological findings to swiddeners and perform educational functions when requested to, such channels should also involve social scientists who could help to assess the (ongoing) relationship of technological changes to social changes and make this information available too. . . .

To begin with, we must attempt to arrive at some sort of (very general) picture of the feasible types of improved (i.e., more productive and viable) resource systems among integral swiddeners. What sorts of systems would be likely to find favour among integral swiddeners? What are the "weak points" in such systems, both from the standpoint of changes in swidden lifestyle that the swiddener might have to make in order to achieve greater benefits from his labour? . . .

Some of the outlines of viable and productive swidden systems are already clear. In areas where there is low population density and fallow periods are long, viability is not an immediate issue. Even in these areas, however, integral swiddeners are being increasingly threatened by encroachment from outside. The best way to protect the interests of these swiddeners and the environment as well is to promote the establishment of village territories, protected by law from outside encroachment. Areas should be sufficiently large (and should contain such good forest) that viability will not be threatened. This can be done in close consultation with the integral swiddeners themselves, and every effort should be made to conform to the rights and requirements which they themselves already recognize. These territories will have to be protected from more influential "land development" interests, such as forest industries, mining companies, large-scale agriculturalists, and ranchers, in order for swiddeners to have the change to develop.

In areas where established swiddeners already manage discrete village territories, the first priority should be to grant legal land tenure. Usually such rights are already well recognized by integral swiddeners themselves, but not by permanent-field farmers or other outsiders who may wish to appropriate swidden lands for their own purposes. Modern aerial survey technology can greatly assist in this task and help to overcome the burdensome survey work often cited as one of the reasons for not establishing legal swidden land rights. The nature of these land rights need not amount to outright ownership in the sense that swiddeners can then do anything they like with the land, any more than the various complex building codes and zoning regulations of modern societies grant their owners unlimited rights. Land tenure codes alone, however, will not be sufficient to protect swidduners from encroachment by others. Broad political implications are involved (discussed below).

Individual land rights within the village territory are a complicated matter. Nye and Greenland (1960, p. 137) feel that the greatest obstacle to the improvement of swiddening is the land tenure system, specifically the lack of individual ownership among integral swidduners. Although some researchers have recommended corporate village ownership for swidden development (the corridor methods— see also Kio 1972), cash-cropping experiences among swidduners have demonstrated that this would probably be unwise for intensively cultivated cash-cropped land and could lead to land degeneration. Opium swiddens among the Hmong, for example, are never corporately owned as long as they are producing. Such plots have been frequently bought and sold. Furthermore, although rice is pooled at the household level, opium is not. Whereas rice plots "belong" to the entire household, opium plots belong to individuals. Fruit trees are planted in worked-out opium swiddens and the orchards thus produced continue to belong to the individual owner. The natural trend of cash-cropping practices, then, may well be in the direction of private individual ownership, not corporate ownership. The lesson here would seem to be that the subsistence sector might be continued with traditional swidden tenure, but that cash-cropped land should be "owned." If permanent plots are maintained this presents no problem, but where cash crops are grown in swiddens the land tenure system will have to be carefully examined. Study at the local level is needed here, but, as long as viability can be successfully maintained, the traditional system should be adhered to as much as possible. If individual ownership of swiddens is deemed necessary or is desired by the swidduners themselves, this is not an impossible task. Procedures could be instituted for marking trees at key points on swidden boundaries, if no similar system already exists. A simple system of public verification could be used rather than the complicated surveying and recording procedures required for land ownership in the lowlands.

Given the technological options involved for a variety of cash crop and subsistence combinations, it seems likely that at least two and perhaps more categories of land tenure would evolve (e.g., individually owned; individual rights but corporately owned; corporately owned). In time certain types of land would be recognized as suitable for certain types of usage, but this is a process that the swidduners themselves will have to work through in order to arrive at the best mix. Developers should recommend matching land type with usage, basing their recommendations on solid research. Where necessary, certain types of land use could be rightfully restricted if viability were clearly threatened, or if such usage caused downstream deterioration for others. But this is a different type of approach from starting out with overly detailed land classification programmes, devised by people who have never swiddened and will never have to bear the burden such planning puts on the swiddeners. . . .

At the village level, it is inevitable that a developing village economy will necessitate some degree of institutional change. With respect to each sector in which such institutional change or development is necessary, the important question will be to what extent the government can help provide the necessary functions and to what extent these will be handled internally. Availability of credit, for example, seems a likely area in which government could easily lend a hand and ensure fair practices as well. Land tenure rules, on the other hand, are an area where the rules of the larger society and the traditional rules of the swiddeners must be carefully articulated. Among many swidden groups, land tenure rules will not in themselves be sufficient to allow the swiddener careful management of his own plot through all phases of the swidden cycle to ensure maximum productivity and viability. But government regulation in this area must not approach the reformulation of land tenure principles that efforts such as taungya and corridor methods attempted—to do so would attack the very basis of swidden society values and bring more harm than benefit. Recommendations in areas such as this will have to be weighed most carefully indeed and will have to be finely tuned to the local swidden group, its existing institutions, and its value.

NOTES

3. Many researchers believe it is partial swiddeners rather than integral swiddeners who do the greatest damage (see Conklin 1961 [This reference in presumably to Conklin 1957 or 1957a (ed.)]; Reed 1965, p. 47; Keen 1972, p. 16; Waters 1971, pp. 9-12).

4. Interestingly, the same argument has been made in Mexico, where swidden systems were quite extensive and apparently even supported elaborate social organizations. Watters (1971, p. 16) comments that there are Indian communities in Mexico "where it is impossible to discern whether stabilized agriculture and shifting cultivation were practised consecutively, or whether they have always existed side by side."

REFERENCES

Bennett, John W. 1976. "Anticipation, Adaptation, and the Concept of Culture in Anthropology." *Science,* 192 (4242): 847-853.

Boserup, Ester. 1965. *The Conditions of Agricultural Growth: The Economics of Agrarian Change under Population Pressure.* Chicago: Aldine.

Brookfield, H.C. 1972. "Intensification and Disintensification in Pacific Agriculture—A Theoretical Approach." *Pacific Viewpoint* 13 (1): 30-48.

Conklin, Harold C. 1957. "A Report on an Integral System of Shifting Cultivation in the Philippines." *Hanunóo Agriculture.* Rome: Food and Agriculture Organization of the United Nations.

———. 1957a. "Shifting Cultivation and Succession to Grassland Climax." *Proceedings of the Ninth Pacific Science Congress* 7: 60-62.

Dasmann, Raymond F., John P. Milton, and Peter H. Freeman. 1973. *Ecological Principles for Economic Development.* London: John Wiley & Sons, Ltd.

Eckholm, E.P. 1976. *Losing Ground.* World Watch Institute and UN Environment Programme. New York: W.W. Norton and Co.

Gourou, Pierre. 1949. "The Development of Upland Areas in China." *In The Development of Upland Areas in the Far East* 1: 1-24. New York: International Secretariat, Institute of Pacific Relations.

Holdridge, Leslie Rensselaer. 1959. "Ecological Indications of the Need for a New Approach to Tropical Land Use." *Economic Botany* 13 (4): 271-280.

Judd, Laurence C. 1964. Dry Rice Agriculture in Northern Thailand. Cornell Southeast Asia Program Data Paper No. 52. Ithaca, New York, USA.

Keen, F.G.B. 1972. *Upland Tenure and Land Use in North Thailand.* Bangkok: SEATO.

Kio, P.R. 1972. "Shifting Cultivation and Multiple Use of Forest Land in Nigeria." *Commonwealth Forestry Review* 52 (2): 144-148.

LeBar, Frank M., et al. 1964. *Ethnic Groups of Mainland Southeast Asia.* New Haven, Conn.: Human Relations Area Files Press.

McKinnon, John. 1977. "Shifting Cultivation: Who's Afraid of the Big Bad Wolf?" Paper delivered at 77th seminar in series Agriculture in Northern Thailand, Chiang Mai University, Chiang Mai, Thailand (mimeographed).

Nye, P.H., and D.J. Greenland. 1960. *The Soil under Shifting Cultivation.* Commonwealth Agricultural Bureau, Farnham Royal, Bucks., United Kingdom.

Pendleton, Robert L. 1939. "Some Interrelations between Agriculture and Forestry Particularly in Thailand." *Journal of the Thailand Research Society, Natural History Supplement* 12(1): 33-52.

Reed, Robert R. 1965. "Swidden in Southeast Asia." *Lipunan* (Institute of Asian Studies, University of the Philippines, Quezon City) 1 (1): 24-52.

Ruddle, Kenneth, and Ray Chesterfield. 1977. *Education for Traditional Food Procurement in the Orinoco Delta. Ibero-Americana* 53. Berkeley: University of California Press.

──────. 1978. "Traditional Skill Training and Labor in Rural Societies." *Journal of Developing Areas* 12 (4) : 389-398.

Walker, Anthony R. (ed.) 1975. *Farmers in the Hills: Upland Peoples in North Thailand*. Universiti Sains Malaysia, Penang, Malaysia.

Watters, R.F. 1960. "The Nature of Shifting Cultivation." *Pacific Viewpoint* 1: 59-99.

──────. 1971. *Shifting Cultivation in Latin America*. FAO Forestry Development Paper No. 17. Rome.

Land and the Forest-Dwelling South American Indian: The Role of National Law

Joseph Grasmick

For many minority peoples in developing countries, protection of their forest environment is a necessary condition for their cultural survival. The American Indians of the Amazon Basin find their forest environment under intense pressure. The state as the regulator of forest use has done little to protect their interests. Grasmick urges property rights for the Indians, but such proposals are opposed by powerful interests, including politicians who represent land-hungry peasant farmers migrating into the upper reaches of the Basin. —The Editors

The "forest-dwellers" referred to here are the indigenous inhabitants of the more isolated areas of South America, and are only a part of the total indigenous population in South America. This article focuses only on forest-dwellers for two reasons. First, the forest-dweller is historically culturally distinct from his more integrated counterparts who are often culturally defined as "peasants" or campesinos[2] —rural cultivators more integrated into the national state society and subject to the demands and sanctions of power-holders outside the native social stratum.[3] The nomadic or semi-nomadic existence of the forest-dwellers, and the fact that their relationship to the land is especially vital for welfare and survival, present a special challenge to the national land tenure system. Second, there is greater need for study of land tenure as it affects the more isolated Amerindians. Data are scarce and incomplete, while there has been substantial research relevant to the land situation of more integrated

Excerpted from Joseph Grasmick, "Land and the Forest-Dwelling South American Indians: The Role of National Law," *Buffalo Law Review* 27 (1979): 759-800. Reprinted with the permission of the publisher.

groups.[4] There is a special urgency in dealing with these land tenure questions. While the population of many Indian groups is increasing, the number of forest-dwellers is decreasing exponentially,[5] due in part to the separation of the Indians from their forest land resources.

Effective land rights are vital for the preservation of the physical and mental well-being of the individual Amerindians and for the maintenance of the groups' cultural stability. This premise has been widely recognized by international and governmental organizations,[6] by other groups and individuals concerned with indigenous welfare,[7] and most importantly, by the Amerindians themselves.[8] Land rights can serve three important functions: prevention of pernicious contact with non-Indians, adequate economic subsistence base in the face of such contact, and preservation of sacred and spiritual connections with the land . . . .

Although restraints on alienation are traditionally discouraged in property law,[139] history has shown that allowing the sale of Indian land is disastrous to the less integrated communities. Simon Bolivar effectively dissolved the indigenous landholding communities in the Andes simply by permitting any member of the community to sell the communal land that he held in usufruct.[140] The land was sold for small amounts of money by the Indians who thus contributed to the formation of the large estates.[141] The Indians' apparent inability to retain landholdings can be explained by the indigenous peoples' lack of familiarity with market economics. In the less complex economic system of the forest-dweller, land simply is not a marketable commodity.[142] Even in more complex systems where markets do exist, land is one of the last items to "get transacted through the price-making mechanism of market exchange."[143] A legal land transaction, whether sale, lease,[144] or mortgage,[145] is therefore meaningless to many forest Indians.

Although prescriptive ownership and liberalized prescriptive-type mechanisms requiring an "occupancy," "exploitation," or "possession" of land for a determined period of time are not workable methods of land acquisition for the forest Indian,[146] they are effective as a means of extinguishing forest-dweller land rights. Prescription was used for the first time in the New World to legalize *de facto* colonist occupation of Indian lands.[147] Any liberalization of the ownership requirements in special legislation benefits the sedentary encroachers, making their encroachment legally protected.

The physical removal of tribal peoples, and their transplantation into an alien area, is another major mechanism for extinguishing

indigenous land rights.[148] In this way, any physical and legal man-
land relationships are immediately terminated.[149] Where conflict
between encroachers and Indians threatens the peace, it is often easier
to solve the problem by the removal of the tribal group. Since the
entities that must implement Indian legislation often represent other
non-Indian interests, the alternative of removal of the Indians is all too
attractive to the governments involved.[150]

. . . The need for special restrictions on the transfers of Indian
property has long been recognized in Latin American law. The Law of
June 11, 1594 outlawed all transfers of Indian property not made before a
judicial officer under conditions designed to ensure an adequate return on
land sold.[151] Nonetheless, there are arguments for allowing these land
transfers. The forest-dweller's only marketable assets are usually his
land and labor. Once the national market economy begins to displace
the indigenous economy, complete reliance on labor can lead to
exploitation and debt peonage; without land to offer as collateral,
credit becomes difficult to obtain. For forest-dwellers in this position,
restraints on alienation can become paternalistic and discriminatory.
This, coupled with the traditional hostility towards restraints on
alienation, causes most law and policy-making entities to strike a
balance between allowing free alienation of native land and protective
laws preventing such alienation.[152]

In practice, the delegation of decision-making responsibility to
government agencies regarding native land alienation has not been
uniformly successful. In fact, it has provided a livelihood for the
grileiro—a Brazilian specialist in shady land deals who obtains
native land by manufacturing evidence of abandonment, by ignoring
evidence of seasonal occupancy, or even by driving Indians away . . . .

Several general premises must be accepted before specific legal
solutions can be attempted: (1) special measures must be taken to
compensate for the inferior and unique status of the frontier natives; (2)
the value and complexity of indigenous resource use patterns must be
respected — land rights should not entail forced culture change; (3) the
magnitude of the Amerindian land problem requires a new balancing of
interests: national policy must be redirected to support native interest,
while interests of other actors must be channeled so as to prevent
encroachment on native land; and (4) there must be a minimum of
substantive and procedural impediments to vindication of native land
rights, and a maximum of such impediments to restriction of such rights.

An immediate presumption of native occupancy of the tierras
baldias is necessary to break the encroachment cycle and to destroy the
legal fiction that forest lands are unoccupied.[198] The burden should be

on the encroacher to prove that the area is not used by Indians and was not used at the time of encroachment. Failure to meet this burden should result in the denial of any rights of occupancy or ownership, and the requisite period of occupancy for prescriptive ownership should not begin running in the encroacher's favor until the presumption is overcome. All land transactions in these areas should be judicially supervised,[199] and all costs should be absorbed by the government, or charged to encroachers who lose a given dispute.

Vigorous steps must also be taken to create an indigenous land regime amenable to more direct national legal protection. Minimal signs of an indigenous presence [200] should trigger an ethnological survey that would assess the tribal land needs based on an analysis of the entire tribal ecosystem. The spatial boundaries of land to be protected would then be determined by this survey irrespective of the traditional real property concepts of the state. Allowance should be made for an adequate buffer zone that would soften inter-ethnic contract, incorporate any land subsequently "abandoned" by the natives, and provide room for migration.[201] Priority should be given to areas when encroachment is beginning to take place and the results should be widely publicized and inscribed in the appropriate land register.

Those who subsequently trespass on native land, including those who survey or mark boundaries with a view to settlement, should be subject to strict criminal penalties [202] and should lose the protection of the state.[203] Knowing violation of tribal areas of sacred significance should be considered an aggravating circumstance.

Encroachers already present at the time of the survey should be removed to areas unused by forest-dwellers. Settlers with good faith color of title or right could be relocated or compensated at the state's expense. In the case of pre-existing legal title, eminent domain expropriation procedures could be invoked. Under no circumstances should the forest-dweller be removed, be required to compensate removed encroachers, or be forced to accept money damages in lieu of actual use of the land.

The actual land rights accorded the forest Indians should be superior to civil code ownership rights, paramount to the rights of the state in the land, and based on the concepts of autonomy and self-determination.

Exploitation of resources on native land should be limited to exploitation by members of the tribal groups. If the group's culture and technology has not changed to the point where a given resource can be exploited, or if such development is not desired by the group, it is likely that alien exploitation would lead to pernicious inter-ethnic contract.

Collective landholding should be the only recognized form of landholding, and areas should be designated as belonging to the maximum native territorial unit.[204] Such a unit, as well as individual Indians, should be given legal status for the limited purpose of directly vindicating rights violated by non-Indians, including policy and law-making violators. Simplified legal procedures should be established for this purpose, with presumptions created favoring the forest Indian. Any individual or intra-group land use should be controlled in the traditional way or by new means developed by the tribal group.[205] None of the restrictions and fragility of civil code communal property regimes should apply.

The rights attached to these native lands should be absolutely inalienable in their entirety. Inheritance or succession should be regulated by tribal tradition, and property should never revert to non-Indians or to the state. Credit facilities should replace any future loss of borrowing power created by these restraints on alienation.[206]

A comprehensive Indian land statute containing the norms set forth above should be promulgated and integrated with other law. The land statute must preempt all conflicting federal or local law, and create a presumption in favor of preservation of native land rights in case of any conflicts within the land statute. Conflicting law should be explicitly repealed or modified.

NOTES

2.   J. Steward and L. Faron, *Native Peoples of South America* 4, 446 (1959).

3.   E. Wolf, *Peasants* 11 (1966).

4.   See, e.g., Land Tenure Center, *Publications List* Number 25 (1976). See also International Labor Office, *Indigenous Peoples* 330—31 (1953) (only two of its 628 pages are devoted to the specific topic of forest-dwellers and the occupation and allotment of land),

5.   J. Steward and L. Faron, supra note 2, at 54. Note, however, that there are a few exceptions. Harner, for example, claims that the forest Jívaro populations "have turned the corner demographically" and are growing. M. Harner, *The Jívaro* 211 (1976). For one anthropologist's hypotheses as to why depopulation may affect some groups more violently than others, see Wagley, "Cultural Influences on Population: A Comparison of Two Tupí Tribes," 5 *Revisto do Museu Paulista* 95-104 (1951).

6. See Reports and Inquiries, "The Second Session of the I.L.O. Committee of Experts on Indigenous Labor," 70 *Int'l Lab. Rev.* 420-21 (1954). See also ECOSOC, Commission on Human Rights, Sub-Commission on Prevention of Discrimination and Protection of Minorities, Studies of the Problem of Discrimination Against Indigenous Populations (1972, 1973, 1974, 1975); Ministério da Agricultura, *A Política Indigenista Brasileira* 106 (1962).

7. See, e.g., J. Bodley, *Tribal Survival in the Amazon* 11 (1972); E. Brooks, E. Fuerst, J. Hemming and F. Huxley, *Tribes of the Amazon Basin In Brazil* 1972, at x-xi, 3, 23 (1972) [hereinafter cited as *Tribes of the Amazon Basin*]; Survival International, *A Philosophy for Survival International* 3.

8. See B. Arcand, *The Urgent Situation of the Cuiva Indians of Colombia* 24 (1972); Brazil-Third Congress of Amazon Indians is Held, 2 *Indigena* 8 (1975-1976).

139. The Bolivian Civil Code defines property as "a juridical power that permits the use, enjoyment and disposal of a thing." Código Civil de Venezuela art. 545.

140. See A. García, *Legislación Indigenista de Colombia* 24-26 (1952).

141. S. Varese, *The Forest Indians in the Present Political Situation of Peru* 8 (1972).

142. See generally R. Firth, *Work and Wealth of Primitive Communities in Human Types* (rev. ed. 1958).

143. Dalton, "Economic Theory and Primitive Society," 63 *Am. Anthropologist* 14 (1961).

144. The Brazilian Congress, realizing the harmful effects of long-term leasing, included a provision in the Indian Statute that would have prohibited such leasing, but the provision was vetoed by the President. Davis, "Indian Statute Passes Into Law," 1 *Indígena* 7 (1974).

145. Mortgage can easily lead to dispossession in jurisdictions like Ecuador where an indigenous landowner is in the same position as any other person with regard to the mortgaging of his property as security for his debts. International Labor Office, supra note 88.

146. See text accompanying notes 47-49 supra.

147. Other sources of prescriptive ownership include the Roman law, French law, Spanish law, and the other modern Civil Codes. G. Torres Porras, "La Prescriptión" 15-24 (doctoral thesis, Pontificia Universidad Javeriana, Facultad de Ciencias Económicas y Jurídicas, Bogotá, Colombia: 1960).

148. In Guyana, the Minister is given statutory authority to "make regulations . . . prescribing the mode of removing Amerindians to a District, Area of Village, or from one District, Area or Village to

another." Laws of Guyana, ch. 20:01, Amerindian Act 40 (2) [Act 22 of 1951, amended by Act 6 of 1961]. This provision, however, does not apply to those groups granted title pursuant to recommendations of the Amerindian Land Commission. See note 182 supra.

Under the Brazilian Indian statute, the federal government can "intervene" and remove a tribal group "when it is quite impossible or inadvisable to allow it to remain." Law No. 6.001 of December 19, 1973, dealing with: The Indian Statute art. 20 (Brazil).

149. The ease of removal does not imply an ease of successful relocation. "Indigenous groups have established a relationship of ecological dependence during the course of a long adjustment process." ILO, supra note 6, at 421. As a result of this forced migration, profound changes are likely to occur in any group's cultural system as it attempts to adapt to its new physical environment. "It may take decades, perhaps even centuries, for a new adaptation to fully develop." Since various indigenous social and political units are often relocated in the same areas, it is highly likely that hostilities will occur: "Migration and warfare go hand in hand." K. Otterbein, *Comparative Cultural Analysis* 34 (1977).

150. See C. de Araujo Moreira Neto, supra note 105, at 325.

151. This law is one of the earliest of the Laws of the Indies. Law of June 11, 1594, Law of the Indies, bk, 6, tit. 1, law 27 (Spain).

152. Peru is at the protectionist end of the spectrum, having instituted prohibition on transfers of land belonging to native communities. Decreto Ley No. 20653 de 24 junio 1974, Ley de Comunidades Nativas y de Promoción Agropecuaria de las Regiones de Silva y Ceja de Selva art. 11 (Peru). Bolivia has a similar law prohibiting alienation of the forest-dweller's land, but is less precise about the degree to which mortgage seizures and other devices are included in the prohibition. Ley No. 3464 de 2 agosto 1953 elevado a categoria de Ley 29 octubre 1956, Ley Fundamental de Reforma Agraria art. 130 (Bolivia). Other jurisdictions regulate rather than prohibit transfers, placing part or all of the decision-making power in the hands of a third party. Colombia and Paraguay vest title in governmental or non-governmental entities such as land reform agencies or religious missions. These entities are then responsible for determining if and when land is to be transfered. In Brazil, "native land cannot be the object of leasing and renting or any juridical act or negotiation that restricts the full exercise of direct possession."

Law No. 6.001 of December 19, 1973, dealing with: The Indian Statute art. 18 (Brazil). On the other hand, tribal groups can be removed from their lands if there is cause for "intervention." See text accompanying notes 148-49 supra. Furthermore, if the executive branch determines that land is "spontaneously and definitely abandoned by a native community or tribal group," it reverts to the federal government, which can then dispose of it. Law No. 6.001 of December 19, 1973, dealing with: The Indian Statute art. 21 (Brazil).

153. See Lewis, Genocide, in Supysáua, supra note 9, at 14.

197. See text accompanying notes 162-66 supra.

198. Similar presumptions favoring the native would be created for all bona fide inter-ethnic land disputes.

199. See G. Bennett, *Aboriginal Rights in International Law* (1968).

200. Such signs would include, but not be limited to, the presence of villages or hunting trails, complaints of encroachment lodged by Indians, and representations by frontier residents, government functionaries or anthropologists as to Indian presence.

201. A similar zone was proposed in 1832 by special commissioners appointed by Secretary of War Lewis Cass to gather information for developing United States Indian policy. A neutral strip of land five miles wide on which all settlement was to be prohibited was to separate whites from Indians in areas west of the Mississippi. Report of Commissioners Feb. 10, 1834, in H.R. Rep. No. 474, 23d Cong., 1st Sess. 102-03. For a discussion of the Commissioner's report, see F. Prucha, *American Indian Policy in the Formative Years: The Indian Trade and Intercourse Acts, 1790-1834*, at 257-59 (1962).

202. There are South American precedents for special criminal legislation designed to apply to violation of Indian rights by non-Indians. In the Ecuadorian penal law, for example, it is considered an aggravating circumstance if the victim of the crime is a non-integrated Indian. International Labor Office, supra note 88, at 28. See also Law No. 6.001 of December 19, 1973 dealing with: The Indian Statute art. 59 (Brazil).

203. See Treaty with the Wyandots, Jan. 21, 1785, 7 Stat. 17 for a similar provision in early United States law: "If any citizen of the United States . . . shall attempt to settle on any of the lands allotted to the Wiandot and Delaware nations . . . such person shall forfeit the protection of the United States, and the Indians may punish him as they please.

204. See note 63 supra. Where the boundaries of two indigenous groups overlap, both groups should be designated as a single

landholding entity. In establishing boundaries, it is better to err on the side of overinclusion, than to risk splitting corporate entities. In addition, such a method simplifies registration by minimizing the number of protected land parcels.

205. Forest-dwellers are adaptable to changes in circumstances where given the chance. In tropical Panama, for example, the Cuna tribal council devised new rules governing property rights after the introduction of cattle and the fencing of land into the indigenous subsistence system. U.S. Dep't of Defense, U.S. Army Area Handbook for Panama 79 (1965).

206. In order to prevent alienation of indigenous land, the policy has been gaining ground in a number of countries that the mortgaging of the land to persons or bodies not belonging to the tribe or group should be prohibited or restricted. While there can be no doubt as to the intrinsic wisdom of such a policy, attention must be drawn, however, to the fact that it is not likely to yield positive results if it is not accompanied by the extension of agricultural credit facilities to indigenous farmers that will enable them to secure the necessary capital for developing their holdings economically. International Labor Organization, Living and Working Conditions of Indigenous Populations in Independent Countries Report VIII (1) 68-69 (1955).

9

The Daily Struggle for Rights

Louise Fortmann and John W.Bruce

Deforestation and environmental degradation are progressing at an alarming rate in many developing countries. While myriad afforestation and conservation programs have sought to reverse this trend, many appear to have failed miserably. Increasingly evident in the analyses of failed projects is an inattention of project organizers to land and tree tenure—ignorance about who controls the resources and their benefits. The record of deforestation and afforestation in the Third World points to resource tenure patterns—the ownership of or traditional rights to use resources—as a major cause of environmental degradation, and in particular, deforestation. Afforestation plans commonly stand or fall based upon the incentives and security provided rural populations by tenure arrangements. Resource tenure, in short, is an important and evolving component of all resource management planning, influencing the daily lives of resource users throughout the world, and of women, the poor, and the disenfranchised in particular.

Tenure rules affect land and tree use in general, and the distribution of benefits in particular. Land and tree tenure are not identical, nor are they immutable: the results of changes in tenure can be seen clearly in United States timber harvesting. Nineteenth century America saw an orgy of clearcutting that denuded millions of acres of forest. Lumber companies moved West in search of new lands to buy and cut, lands where the right to harvest was unrestricted. Today, however, tree tenure for commercial species is regulated by fifteen states. In present day California, for instance, rights to harvest timber do not move unrestrictedly with the purchase or ownership of land. Those who harvest not only must cut within ecologically sound guidelines, approved situation by situation, but they must also replant. Effects are notable.

Choked streams, sliding hillsides, and denuded acreages are largely sights of the past, albeit a recent past.

People who are concerned with the protection, preservation or harvesting of existing trees or the planting of new ones often must deal with questions of land and tree tenure before or at the same time as they approach the more technical questions of silviculture or harvesting. Forestry and agroforestry policies along with programs and projects require a sound tenurial strategy in addition to technical strategies if production targets are to be achieved and intended beneficiaries reached. Tenurial strategies require not only identifying rules about who can use what, when and where but also analyzing the institutions that enforce and mediate those rules. Such strategies must be compatible with the capacity of the institutions responsible for implementing and enforcing them.

A sound tenure strategy will avoid some of the most common pitfalls of forestry and agroforestry planning. But it is by no means a cure-all. Providing secure access to tree and forest products does not, for example, ensure that the value of those products will remain high enough to sustain a household's livelihood. A sound tenurial strategy may become outmoded as the level and variety of demands exceeds the physical capacity of the existing resource to meet them. A sound strategy may also be undermined by changes in government personnel or strong local elites.

The interrelationship between tenure and the fate of the forest, the factors affecting the outcomes of a tenurial strategy and the limitations of tenurial strategies are well illustrated by the case of the Bangladesh village of Betagi.

The area on which Betagi now stands was at one time under the control of the Revenue Department and Forest Department. Gradually over the years through encroachment and timber theft (in some cases involving the collusion of the local officials of the Forest and Revenue Departments), the land had been completely deforested and had come to be used by local elites for grazing and the construction of cattlesheds (by which means they hoped to establish rights to the land.) The statutory right of the state had proved to be ineffective in protecting the forest, since economic considerations and social power overcame legal considerations. That is, the value of the forest produce far outweighed the cost of any fine that might be levied, and some officials of the relevant departments could be bribed to look the other way.

In 1976, a new conservator, Professor A. Alim, was placed in charge of the Eastern Circle which included that land where Betagi now stands. In casting about for a way to reforest this denuded area, he seized upon the idea of, as he put it, "linking the naked man with the naked land" (A. Alim, 1986, personal communication). He sought the cooperation of cooperation with Dr. Mohammad Yunus, a professor at Chittagong University and founder of the Grameen Bank which makes loans to the landless and poor, particularly women, and Mahbub Alam Chashi, a early mobilizer of the self-help movement. Together they set out to settle 101 landless households on the land. If it worked, this would have two effects. The households settled on the land would serve as "social fences", protecting trees they themselves had planted. Second, households who were given access to the means of production would no longer have to steal from the government forest (or work for timber thieves) in order to keep body and soul together.

Professor Alim arranged for the government to give the community an annual lease to the land with the assurance that if they could bring the land completely under production within 5 years, they would get a longer term lease. Credit from the Bangladesh Krishi Bank, which provides agricultural loans was arranged. The tenurial strategy adopted had the following components:

- 1) Homogeneity of title holders—all recipients of land were to be landless laborers. A rigorous and mostly successful screening process was undertaken to eliminate landed opportunists resulting in final population of 72 households.
- 2) Medium term security—the group was initially given a one year lease with the opportunity of a five year extension, a period long enough for fast-growing tree species to become productive.
- 3) Group responsibility—the lease for all the land was given to the group as whole rather than to individuals. This had two effects. First, because it prevented outsiders from pressuring or forcing individual households into selling their land, it increased everyone's security. Second, because the whole group was endangered by any household's failure to repay the loan, the group enforced repayment. Group cohesion was witnessed by mandatory weekly meetings as well as instruction in literary and simple accounting procedures.

Six years after the initial settlement, Betagi had more than justi-fied its founders' vision. The ecological effects were clearly positive—the once-bare land was covered with trees and crops. And the people were running their own community with dignity and pride. But the experience had also demonstrated that establishing secure tenure goes far beyond staking out statutory rights.

Security of tenure involves access to power. In its most naked form, it means, as Zillur Rahman (1987, personal communication) has remarked of Bangladesh, that rights need to be established every day. And so it was for the people of Betagi. Their leasehold right to the land could easily have become as ineffective as had been the statutory right of the Forest Department to the long-departed trees. Security of tenure ultimately depended upon force in the face of force and the power of the village's patrons. Local elites who were evicted from the land with the establishment of the village initially waged a campaign of harassment against the villagers—beatings, house burnings, arrests. The villagers fought back and the elites switched tactics, filing some 20 court suits against the village as a whole and against the three patrons individually. The power and prominence of the patrons protected the villagers from a subversion of the justice system and their legal title was upheld in case after case after much struggle.

But security of tenure has a temporal dimension as well and at the end of five years, this became problematic for the villagers. Although the villagers initially planted fast-bearing fruit trees such as lemon and guava, they also planted (and the Forest Department wanted them to plant) long rotation evergreen and leguminous timber species. For nearly two years, attempts to renew the lease were mired in a bureaucratic morass. Once again the village was saved by prominence and patronage. Over its lifetime, as a quick reading of its guestbook demonstrates, it had become a mandatory stop on the South Asia social forestry pilgrimage. The now-international prominence of its patrons and its own status as a success story would have made it difficult for the government to evict the villagers from the land and in late 1987, the wife of the President presented the villagers with a 25 year lease to the land. Each household received inheritable title to its land, which can not be alienated.

The Betagi case illustrates the themes of this book. It shows that the choice of tenurial arrangements has ecological effects. Under group tenure held by the landless, social fencing served to afforest and protect forest land that had been deforested under the statutory protection of the state. However, the length of secure tenure affected species choice, shorter tenure skewing it towards faster-producing species. The tenurial strategy provided benefits to the landless because it was deliberately and carefully designed to do so and its designers implemented it themselves. The potential for community land management was demonstrated by a plot of land planted to fruit trees which were used to finance building a school and hiring a teacher. Further, making the land inalienable provided a kind of security impossible under individual freehold title.

The tenure strategy could not, of course, solve all the villagers' problems. There was no community-wide plan for controlling supply of or marketing produce, and the price of Betagi guavas and lemons quickly dropped as the local market was flooded. Nor was the strategy without its limitations. Although the new lease was made jointly to husbands and wives, it is not clear how successful women will be in defending their legal right in the case of divorce. And when the 25 year lease expires, what struggles will the village need to undertake before it is renewed?

Betagi, then, stands as an example of what is possible. It also stands to remind us that for much of the world's population establishing the rights to trees and to land is a daily struggle.